Exploring the Senses

Exploring the Senses

Editors
Axel Michaels
Christoph Wulf

LONDON NEW YORK NEW DELHI

First published 2014 in India
by Routledge
912 Tolstoy House, 15–17 Tolstoy Marg, Connaught Place, New Delhi 110 001

Simultaneously published in the UK
by Routledge
2 Park Square, Milton Park, Abingdon, Oxon OX14 4RN

Routledge is an imprint of the Taylor & Francis Group, an informa business

Typeset by

Glyph Graphics Private Limited
23, Khosla Complex
Near Samrat Apartments
Vasundhara Enclave
Delhi 110 096

British Library Cataloguing-in-Publication Data
A catalogue record of this book is available from the British Library

ISBN 978-0-415-71106-7

Contents

Preface vii

Axel Michaels and Christoph Wulf
Exploring the Senses in Rituals and Performances: An Introduction 1

Indian and Western Theories of Senses

1. *Remo Bodei*
The Windows on the World: The Senses and Inner Life 25

2. *Angelika Malinar*
Sensory Perception and Notions of the Senses in Sāṃkhya Philosophy 34

3. *Gérard Colas*
Senses, Human and Divine 52

4. *Anand Mishra*
The Divine Embrace: The Role of the Senses in Puṣṭimārga 64

5. *Monika Horstmann*
Managing the Senses in Sant Devotion 78

The Anthropology of Senses

6. *Christoph Wulf*
The Vision: Control, Desire, Perception 95

7. *William S. Sax*
Seeing Ghosts in India and Europe 110

8. *Annette Wilke*
Sonic Perception and Acoustic Communication in Hindu India 120

9. *Karsten Lichau*
"Noise" or "Silence?" Listening to Sacred Sound in 20th-century Europe 145

10. *Holger Schulze*
The Sonic Persona: An Anthropology of Sound 164

11. *Alain Montandon*
Taste as an Aesthetic Sense 176

12. *Astrid Zotter*
Scent of a Flower: Notes on Olfaction in Hindu Worship 187

13. *Axel Michaels*
Untouchability and Tactility in Hindu Death Rituals 206

14. *Gabriele Brandstetter*
Senses of Movement: Kinesthetics and Synesthetics
in Contemporary Dance Practices 221

15. *Jayachandran Palazhy*
Memory, Experience and Imagination in Performance 234

16. *Jan Weinhold*
Family Constellation Therapy: Body Memory and
the Sense of Space 265

17. *Karin M. Polit*
Performative Ritual as Sensual Experience of Body,
Place and Sociality 280

The Unity of Senses

18. *Sundar Sarukkai*
Unity of the Senses in Indian Thought 297

19. *Theofanis Tasis*
The Politics of the Senses: On Vision and Hearing in
Hannah Arendt's "Vita Activa" 309

20. *Mădălina Diaconu*
The Sky Around Our Bodies: Climate and
Atmospheric Perception 317

About the Editors 338

Notes on Contributors 339

Preface

Most chapters in this volume were originally written for the conference "Exploring the Senses — Emotions, Performativity, and Ritual," held at the Freie Universität Berlin in Berlin from November 8–12, 2011. The conference was a joint event sponsored by the Excellence Clusters "Asia and Europe in a Global Context" (Heidelberg) and "Languages of Emotions" (Berlin), and the Collaborative Research Centers "Ritual Dynamics" (Heidelberg) and "Cultures of the Performative" (Berlin), all financed by the Deutsche Forschungsgemeinschaft (German Research Foundation). This meeting was the third and last of three conferences organized by the editors of the present volume, where scholars on South Asia joined with specialists on European themes to discuss the relationship between performativity and rituals. The first conference was held in 2007 in Berlin on the image of the body in India. The second was held at the International Centre in Dona Paula (Goa), in January 2010. The findings of these three conferences have been edited by us and published by Routledge in the short series "South Asian and European Perspectives on Rituals and Performativity:" Volume 1: *Images of the Body in India* (2011) and Volume 2: *Emotions in Rituals and Performance Emotions in Rituals and Performance* (2012). Challenging the ideas that rituals are static and emotions irrational, the group of scholars assembled in this volume again engaged in exploring the manifold qualities of senses in ritual practices and performances.

The editors wish to thank the Deutsche Forschungsgemeinschaft (DFG, German Research Foundation), Silke Bechler (SFB 619, Heidelberg) and Gabriele Di Vincenzo (Anthropology and Education, FU Berlin) for helping get the conference organized; the team at Routledge, New Delhi for the editorial support; Eva Kahlmann and Michael Sonntag for editorial assistance; Matt Hayworth (Berlin) for translating and revising the English of several papers; and last but not least, Quoc-Bao Do for the layout. The conference and the present volume would not have been possible without the generous grants of the aforementioned organizations, especially the German Research Foundation, to which we also extend our gratitude. It goes without mentioning that we alone are responsible for all shortcomings and mistakes.

Axel Michaels and Christoph Wulf

Exploring the Senses in Rituals and Performances: An Introduction

This book presents contributions to Indian and Western theories, histories and anthropologies of the senses, as well as essays on the individual senses of seeing and hearing, tasting and smelling, and movement and touching in various contexts, and finally on the question of the unity of the senses. All contributions to this volume demonstrate the close relation of the senses with each other, and with notions of the body, emotion and cultural memory. The starting point chosen here is to research various historical and cultural perspectives on the senses in order to highlight the significance of the senses and the body in philosophical, religious and anthropological theories. This approach is even more important because, in the era of globalization, far-reaching changes are occurring to sensuousness and to the understanding of the senses, changes in which the new media, for example, plays an important role. In spite of these changes, the essays in this volume clarify the extent to which the senses are embedded in cultural traditions. This embeddedness of the senses in a particular cultural tradition and their experiences of the otherness of these traditions contribute not just to a better understanding of the historical-cultural significance of the senses in various regions of the world, but also to that of the senses in one's own diversely differentiated culture. The classical Aristotelian pentarchy of the (five) senses, for example, which has long been accepted in Europe and partly in India, is by no means accepted everywhere. In two Indian traditions of thought, the school of Vasubandhu and Sāṃkhya, six and even 11 senses are presumed (see MALINAR, in this volume). Similarly, various sense-perceptions discussed later question the Cartesian dichotomy and its dictum of the senses as the "windows to the world."

A better understanding of the culture-specific sensory codes may also contribute to the avoidance of cultural conflicts. According to Michael HERZFELD,

> [t]o stare at someone may signify rudeness, curiosity, flattery, or domination, depending on the circumstances and the culture. Downcast eyes, in contrast, may suggest modesty, fear, contemplation, or inattention. And these are simply the possibilities for cultural coding, within which personal idiosyncrasies may produce further variation (2001, p. 244).

Indeed, the senses cannot be considered in isolation, culturally and individually. The notion of the senses is, for instance, closely associated with notions of the body (KAMPER/WULF 1992, 1984; MICHAELS/WULF 2011) and emotions (MICHAELS/WULF 2012). They also have to be viewed in close association with cosmology or religion. If these contexts are ignored, the cultural and historical particulars cannot be adequately understood. The essays in this volume make it clear that, in the history of India and Europe, complex historical-cultural concepts were developed that differed fundamentally from the ideas that are considered valid today under the influence of the neurosciences and behavioral sciences. These modern ideas have emerged on the basis of an empirical revolution in the sciences that considers, first and foremost, empirically generated and tested knowledge in order for it to be scientific in its framework. But this knowledge also has been developed in certain historical and cultural environments, and it is this dynamic and transcultural perspective that is the focus of the present volume.

The study of senses and emotions mostly suffers from a logocentric, ocularcentric or scopophilic approach to culture that neglects the specific aspects that come through feelings and sensations. The picture of cultures is, therefore, often dominated by somehow desensualized perceptions describing "the language-bound body as a desensualized robot, moving SHIFTILY, unable to taste or smell, preferring to dine on a printed menu than eat an actual meal" (HOWES 2004, p. 2, referring to Michel Serres' *The Five Senses*). Indeed, something remains unexpressed in words — "A perfume is not the same as a sentence" (ibid., p. 3) — and language itself expresses the importance of the senses in understanding the world: why is philosophy often called "viewing" (*darśana*) in India? Why is the Veda called "the listened" (*śruti*)? Why are outcastes called "untouchables?" Why is there "the claim that 'vision' is central to *Wissen* and wisdom" (HSU 2008, p. 434)?

There are thousands of publications by psychologists, physiologists or biologists on the senses, but these mostly regard sensual perception as private, internal, ahistorical, and apolitical. Despite the fact that a "sensory turn" has already been introduced (VAN EDE 2009, p. 61), the anthropology of the senses, with some exceptions,[1] still remains widely unexplored—especially in a cross-cultural and transcultural approach. This has certainly to do with the fact that philosophical and religious ideas have mostly been regarded as a sphere that lies beyond the senses. However, as many case studies in this book and others (e.g., HOWES 2011) show, sensory experiences are intrinsic to the social and

[1] For example, the phenomenology of PLESSNER (1980) and MERLEAU-PONTY (1994), and more recent studies of, *inter alia*, CLASSEN (1993, 1997); GEURTS (2002); HOWES (2003, 2004 and 2009); MEYER (2006, 2009); SEREMETAKIS (1994); STOLLER (1989); and TAUSSIG (1993). Also, see the overview of RICKE (n.d.); SMITH (2007); and HSU (2008) (as well as other essays in this volume of *Ethnos*).

constitutive for cultural variations of perception. This was repeatedly stressed by David HOWES, one of the pioneers in the anthropology of the senses:

> Perception begins at the edge of the man-made environment and is conditioned by the "social preformation" of the senses (HOWES 2009). This conditioning is what makes it so important for the anthropologist to study and emulate in his or her own person the local "ways of sensing." In the absence of such an attempt, the best the researcher can pick up is the sensation without the signification, the feeling without the meaning . . . The anthropologist must [therefore] strive to uncover and interiorize the local "ways of sensing" if she or he is to succeed at understanding how people in the culture under study "sense the world." To speak of "sensing the world" is to play up the double meaning of the word "sense": it can refer to sensation and/or signification, to feeling and/or meaning (2011, p. 93).

Given this approach, the sensory experiences discussed in the chapters in this volume are manifold: there is the hierarchy of the senses, the dominance of the visual and sound among the senses, the peculiarities of regional and local variations, the cultural relativity or culture-specific sensorium versus the universality of sensations, the relation between individual and group or inter-group sensations, the gender aspect, the reflexivity and role of the observer, the representation of sensory data, or the unity and synesthesia of the senses. It is also noteworthy that a number of essays in this volume refer to rituals since they more often than not rouse the senses in an intense form.

Senses and bodies: Western perspectives

Among the peculiarities of the Western notions of senses is that they are directed at the external world, that is, at people and objects, of which we become aware with the aid of senses without perceiving how the senses themselves are related to the object. The senses themselves are constantly directed outwardly, away from the body and towards the world. This directedness corresponds to their intentional character. POLIYANYI describes this peculiarity of the senses as follows:

> Our body is the only assembly of things known as most exclusively by relying on our awareness of them for attending to something else . . . we make sense of the world, we rely on our tacit knowledge of impact made by the world on our body and the complex of our body to these impacts (1969, pp. 147–48).

We perceive something, but not our perception in the process. Each perception is an activity of the entire body, not just the senses. That is why we need to place our body in a certain relation to the environment in order to give it the ability to perceive something. The outwardly directed intentionality of our perception causes our consciousness to become unaware of many of the activities of the body required for perception, leading to a background disappearance of these bodily activities, such as many sensorimotor activities that are only possible through perception. These processes occurring behind the scenes, so to speak, include breathing, digestion, the cardiopulmonary function, and the endocrine system. They show how sensory perceptions are interwoven with, and contribute to, all bodily processes. Our sensory perception of the world is also closely related to an *implicit knowledge* which is not consciously available to us in the process of perception.

Moreover, three aspects can be differentiated in the constitution of this sensory perception and implicit knowledge. The first aspect is physiological and requires that humans use and develop their senses from early childhood, which otherwise atrophy. This physiological side of sensory perception is universal. The second aspect is bound to the cultural and social shaping of our senses, which begins before birth and is effective during our entire lives. The third aspect is biographical; it emphasizes the individuality of each person's sensory perceptions and his or her body in terms of life-historical aspects. All our sensory perceptions are constituted through the working together of these three aspects, which are merged into an inextricable nexus in which the individual aspects can no longer be differentiated from each other.

The senses form interfaces between our body and the environment. The first or the physiological aspect, for instance, shows how the senses "incorporate" the environment in the form of images, sounds, odors, flavors, and tactile experiences, and transform the "outside world" into an "inner world." We experience these processes of sensory perception as meaningful. Thus, it is not just our (lingual) propositions that are meaningful, but also our prelingual sensory experiences. These experiences are bound to physiological processes and the sensorimotor capacity of our body. According to SHEETS-JOHNSTONE, movement is the starting point of all life processes:

> This primal animateness, this original kinetic spontaneity that infuses our being and defines our aliveness is our point of departure for living in the world and making sense of it . . . *We literally discover ourselves in movement.* We grow kinetically into our bodies. In particular, we grow into those distinctive ways of moving that come with our being the bodies we are. In our spontaneity of movement, we discover arms that extend, spines that bend, knees that flex, mouths that shut, and so on. We make sense of ourselves in the course of moving (1999, p. 136).

Movement keeps us in contact with the world and sensory perceptions are the result of these movements. Through the movement of the body and its senses towards people and things, we deduce their meaning. The options for the direction of motion and perception schemata can be further specified; Georg LAKOFF and Mark JOHNSON (1999) suggest a differentiation between several perception movements: *source–path–goal, up–down, into–out of, toward–away from, and straight–curves*. Insofar as our perceptions are bound to the movements of our body, four qualitative dimensions of body movements also play a role in the type and manner of sensory perceptions (SHEETS-JOHNSTONE 1999, pp. 140–51). The tension of musculature and the intensity of effort in a body movement also determine the quality of our sensory perceptions. Thus, the direction of body movement, that is, its *linearity* in relation to the object of perception, for example, plays an important role in perception, which will change with another orientation of the body to the object. In addition, the *amplitude* of a body movement influences the quality of the sensory perceptions. Lastly, our sensory perceptions are influenced by *projection*, that is, through sudden changes in our body movement, such as standing up or sitting down quickly. By and large, movements of the body substantially determine the type and manner of sensory perception.

The second aspect is related to the fact that all sensory perceptions take place in space and time, and are determined through their historicity and culturality (WULF 2013). Changes in our sensory space and time perceptions cause corresponding transformations in our understanding of the world and of ourselves. Parts of our understanding of time and space are changing as a consequence of our exposure to the new media. The acceleration of time in the new media, for example, leads to an acceleration of perception and a growing spatial distribution of its contents. Many sensory perceptions of local and regional spaces are globally distributed, and thus largely ubiquitous. For instance, a German television viewer is familiar with images of Indian cities and landscapes and an Indian viewer with those of Europe and America. Globalization creates new forms of perception and thus influences people's ability to perceive. The new media promotes the hypertrophy of the visual and an increase in the importance of acoustically conveyed products. Only the "nearby" senses appear to resist the media-based acceleration and ubiquity, continuing to convey location-bound experiences. All senses interact with each other and have an intermodal or cross-modal character. Even if one sense dominates in perception, other senses are also usually involved. Experiences perceived with one sense can even be "answered" with other senses. This can result in new, aesthetically interesting forms of presentation and expression.

The third aspect concerns the fact that we individually learn the meaning of our environment through our sensory perceptions, for example, by watching objects, handling them and seeing how they are used. With the aid of senses and the plasticity of body, the quality of objects and the environment in which we live, we, as individuals, experience the world. In mimetic processes, we assimilate and socialize ourselves, take an "impression" of the world and make it a part of our imagination. The senses help in shaping and expressing visual, acoustic, smelling, tasting, and tactile experiences, that is, multimodal "representations" of objects, people and social actions, to be integrated into the mimetic processes that connect with the engrams that have already been incorporated. In his autobiographical work, Walter BENJAMIN (2006) showed how as a child he "assimilated" the spaces, steps, nooks, and the objects in his parents' house, and how they became part of his imagination with their multifaceted and contradictory meanings. Objects in the house were also associated with memories of the atmosphere of individual spaces, with feelings of emotional security, trepidation and erotic lust. The sensory perception of the social actions of other people and the practical knowledge that emerges in the mimetic incorporation are no less important for the development and training of the ability to take action. As implicit knowledge, the practical knowledge that emerges in mimetic actions is the starting point and influencing factor for social actions. Mimetic actions are not mere reproductions that precisely follow a role model. In mimetically accomplished practices, it is rather about the generation of the individual ability to take action (GEBAUER/WULF 1995, 1998). Through the mimetic reconstruction of the lives and practices of other people, new options for action and experience emerge.

In the sensory interaction between individuals and the environment, emotions are created which, like the human senses in today's understanding, have a bio-social character that can be explained as follows:

> Emotions are complex neural, chemical, and behavioral responses to various types of stimuli that typically have positive or negative value for us. They are part of the process, by which our bodies assess their state and make adjustments to maintain a homeostasis within our internal milieu. They include background emotions (e.g., energy or malaise, edginess or calmness), primary emotions (e.g., fear, joy, anger, sadness) and social emotions (e.g., shame, honor, pride, jealousy) (JOHNSON 2007, p. 56).

Emotions find their manifestations in social and cultural relations in which one learns how to handle them. Using their senses, people relate to the emotions of others in mimetic processes, and sensuously perceive how they feel some emotions in particular situations, how they physically experience, stage and perform emotions, and how they present, linguistically conceive and reflect them (cf. MICHAELS/WULF 2012). In these everyday practices, different feelings that are even contradictory sometimes overlap so that it is often the case that no clear but "mixed" emotions emerge. In the genesis and manifestation of emotions, collective and individual elements act together. Many emotions associated with the practical knowledge of people do not enter consciousness, but instead remain "semi-conscious" or even unconscious. Emotions arise not just in sensory relation to other people and their actions, but also in the face of events not caused by people. They are reactions to sensory perceptions and let us know what actions are required and contribute to understanding and reflecting on situations. Emotions often arise before we are conscious of them; for example, they warn us of dangerous situations and let us know what we need to do before we can develop thoughts and make decisions. Sensuously conveyed emotions have a central importance in our lives, since they help us to evaluate the events of our lives and structure our lives. They convey pre-reflexive sensory experiences and let us know what is good for us.

Bodies and senses: Indian perspectives

The three aspects of sensory perceptions mentioned earlier basically also hold true for Indian contexts. However, there are cultural differences that are elaborated in many chapters of this book and that call for a revision of the conceptual approach to the senses. We will limit ourselves in this introduction to only three examples,[2] which, however, have been extremely influential in Indian intellectual history (and beyond). Besides dealing with the agency of the senses and the sense of sight as an intense form of physical contact, we will also briefly elaborate on the question of materiality of the senses and their burden for those who seek liberation.

In Hindu and other Indian religious worldviews, not only humans, deities, spirits, demons, or animals, but also entities such as sky, planets, mountains, rivers, plants, and even stones are alive and thus capable of sensory perception. This idea has to do with a peculiar concept of individuality. Everything that has a sphere of existence (*loka*) has individuality, and through this a feeling and sensuous soul migrates through the worlds unless it is liberated and loses its individuality. In ancient India, one concluded from the observation of germination, in which seemingly inanimate seeds suddenly sprouted shoots, that even immovable or "dead" objects must have an inner power to change themselves. Plants, therefore, could not be without consciousness and senses. How could plants draw water from the ground if they did not have consciousness (*cetanā*), asked, for instance, the *Bhāskara* in the 18th century (Slaje 1989). In the epic *Mahābhārata*, it is mentioned that even trees have five sense faculties and sense organs. As a consequence, it was believed that thunder could destroy the fruits of trees because trees could hear, and also taste because they drink water with their roots. And since trees feel pain and shoot up after their branches have been cut off, they must also have a soul.

These ideas can be compared with the teaching of Paracelsus that each thing has its *scientia* ("knowledge"), its innate plan of living, by which plants know when to grow, for instance. In the *Yogavāsiṣṭha*, an important philosophical text that dates back to approximately 9th–12th centuries, human beings, animals, plants, and even stones are regarded as conscious. In this text, brilliantly analyzed by Slaje (1989), even plants have the capacity of perception with the result that they can suffer, perceive, dream, and remember. But due to their previous births, the consciousness of plants is dull so that they can communicate but not speak. Since plants cannot be seen breathing, they are regarded as inactive. They are reacting to the outer world but are not aware of it. They remain in a state of deep sleep. However, like animals, plants are regarded as

[2] Parts of the following are based on or partly taken from Michaels (2003, 2004) (with more examples and references).

individuals of the Absolute, who have consciousness, and thus can be liberated. Even stones are regarded as individuals on the ground that each one is different from the other (unlike atoms and elements that fully resemble each other). The consciousness of stones is identified with the sleep of death in the *Yogavāsiṣtha*, in which not even the inner world can be perceived. Atoms and elements are classified as not just incapable of perception and consciousness but completely dead. It goes without saying that such a sophisticated and elaborate categorization is not shared by all traditional Hindu philosophical customs. Yet, the *Yogavāsiṣtha* expresses an idea commonly found in Hinduism that animals and plants are also to be considered as sensuous living beings.

Due to the subtle materiality of feelings and psychological perceptions, contact does not only mean touching but also includes senses such as seeing, hearing and smelling, or emotions. The "contact" even with the shadow of a distiller could, for instance, make a traditional Brahmin immediately take a ritual bath. Seeing, therefore, is strongly believed to be a sensuous physical contact. "Seeing is a kind of touching," says Diana Eck (1985, p. 9; cf. Gonda 1969). The mutual sight (*darśana*) of believer and god is considered the central part of Hindu religious service (*pūjā*), through which the devotee and the god come into contact. Often, the statue of the god in the temple is veiled. But when, during the *pūjā*, it is allowed to be viewed while bells are tolled, the crucial and beneficial moment of sensuous encounter happens with the god.

As long as a priest does not bring the statue of a god to life through a special rite (*prānṇapratiṣṭhā*) of painting the pupils of the eyes, it is inanimate. This is probably due to the general experience that the look in the eyes is the evidence of truth. If something malevolent happens, the cause is often seen as a lack of *darśana* ("[proper] seeing") shown to gods, ancestors or spirits. Modern Indian languages have a saying that the look is given and taken (Hindī *darśan denā, darśan lenā*), and that this alone is sufficient to earn religious merit. Thus, *darśana* is basically an exchange of looks, as the look in the eyes can be the most intense experience in the encounter with another person. One "takes" *darśana* from high-ranking people and "gives" it to low-ranking people.

The dangerous side of this sensuous visual contact is the fear of the evil eye, deeply rooted in India (Maloney 1976). All living creatures, as also plants and food, can be affected by evil eye. Small children are especially in peril, and to protect them a black or red thread is often wound around the ankle at the naming ritual (*nāmakaraṇa*) or during the *rakṣābandhana* ceremony in the fifth month of pregnancy. Protective paintings are another favorite means of defense: bodies, houses (especially kitchens and thresholds), cars, machines, and even cattle are often painted with eye motifs to avert all dangers from outside and to prevent malevolent forces from finding a sensuous contact with them.

Due to the physical and sensuous contact caused by seeing, women should avoid the looks of others and pull the sari over their faces when they go in public. Sight is contact, in both good and bad senses; on the other hand, anyone who looks away avoids contact. When women shyly avert their faces, it is considered a sign of courtesy and propriety and cannot be interpreted as coquetry.

Although the eye as evidence of truth is held in high regard[3] — the most reliable witness is the eyewitness (*sākṣin*) — the eye is also suspicious. Someone who knows everything like the gods no longer needs to be able to see: blindness can thus be a higher insight. What is simply seen can be appearance, mirage, illusion (*māyā*), blindness, or deception. True insight does not need sight but rather knowledge and internal vision.

The most prominent idea regarding the senses in Indian religious and intellectual history, therefore, concerns the question: if and how beings, bound by their senses to the world of un-liberated souls and reincarnation, can be liberated. This idea was most prominently articulated in the widespread *Sāṃkhya* system (LARSON 1979, LARSON/BHATTACHARYA 1987) and is presented in a more nuanced way by Angelika MALINAR in this volume. What is important in this cyclical concept of regeneration is that the only constant and repeated change between manifested and un-manifested state of the world is of duration. Only *prakṛti* and *puruṣa* are eternal — two terms central to the influential *Sāṃkhya* system. Both are essential principles; nothing exists apart from them and both oppose each other to a certain extent, for *prakṛti* is female and *puruṣa* is male. *Prakṛti* is materiality, the primordial matter or nature in its totality. It is active but without spirit, senses and consciousness. It is eternal, as well as extremely smooth and subtle (*sūkṣma*), but is regarded as a substance. *Prakṛti* thus comprises both psychic and physical objects. Its three basic constituents or characteristics (*guṇa*) — *sattva* (truth), *rajas* (passion) and *tamas* (darkness) — are, first, in a balanced state of absorption or equilibrium. They are thus un-manifested (*avyakta*) and dormant. In the process of evolution, the *prakṛti* and its *guṇas* move into a state of imbalance. *Puruṣa*, the other basic principle, has a contentless consciousness, pure spirit, light, or the Absolute. However, in the process of evolution, the great *Puruṣa* can have many *puruṣa*s or individual souls (*jīva*). Basically, the single *Puruṣa* and the many *puruṣas* are the same so that the individual souls can be liberated, but due to wrong action or wrong consciousness, for example in the case of illusion (*māyā*), the souls are not aware of their actual state of identity.

In the classical *Sāṃkhya* system, the process of evolution starts with the emergence of the intellect (*buddhi*), which in turn produces the ego (*ahaṃkāra*). The ego produces the mind, the five sense faculties, the five sense organs or action faculties, the five subtle elements, which subsequently produce the five gross elements (see the simplified system in Table 1).

What is important in this context and what has already been demonstrated by the examples of touching and seeing, is the fact that, in this dualistic philosophy, psychic qualities have physical properties by which they can affect other things. Although in truth, the *puruṣas* are also pure spirit, they are differentiated by a

[3] MCHUGH (2007, 2012), however, argues against the superiority of seeing and any fixed sensory order in India.

Table 1: The evolution of materiality according to the *Sāṃkhyakārikā*

(1)	*prakṛti* (original materiality)
(2)	*buddhi* (intellect)
(3)	*ahaṃkāra* (ego)
(4)	*manas* (mind)
(5–9)	*buddhi-indriya* (sense faculties): ear, skin, eye, tongue, nose
(10–14)	*karma-indriya* (sense organs or action faculties): voice, hand, foot, anus, genitals
(15–19)	*tanmātra* (subtle elements): sound, touch, color, taste, smell
(20–24)	*mahābhūta* (gross elements): air, wind, fire, water, earth

subtle body (*sūkṣma śarīra*). But basically, the various *puruṣas* are identical. They are not individuals who migrate through the worlds and world ages, but individuations of the one and only *Puruṣa*, which in itself is eternal, immovable, pure (spiritual) light, and pure or non-attributive consciousness. Therefore, it is only possible for the liberated to know the *Puruṣa*. All others are deluded by their thoughts and senses.

In the *Sāṃkhya* system, we find the idea that the senses are within the world of un-liberated souls, whereas the liberated one is devoid of senses and feelings (as well as without words and consciousness). It happens, if at all, through complete detachment from consciousness and senses. This is expressed, for instance, in the *Mahāvibhāṣāśāstra* wherein the Buddha says:

> When for the Buddha the great detachment is actualized, all sentient beings of all worlds could burn up before his eyes; he would not perceive it. When he actualizes the great compassion, the sight of a single suffering being is enough to cause his inconceivably strong and unshakeable body to tremble like a banana in a storm (cited in SCHMITHAUSEN 1997, pp. 135–36).

The *Sāṃkhya* system is one model of structuring the senses. There are more (discussed later), and not all are as negative regarding the usefulness of the senses for liberation. The examples given earlier, and those by COLAS, HORSTMANN, MISHRA, and WILKE (all in this volume), reveal that the senses are also seen as a means to contact and reach the favored god and thereby receive salvation through him. Often, the idea of two sets of senses, worldly and spiritual, helps to bridge the epistemological gap between the notion of senses as an obstacle to and their requirement as the means of attaining liberation. In Western traditions too, theologians assumed an external (physical) and an internal (spiritual) set of senses:

> Thus, a Christian could practice extreme asceticism in terms of the physical senses, and still lead a rich sensory life with regard to the spiritual senses: seeing divine light, tasting heavenly sweetness, and so on. This double sensory life was

experienced by many mystics, who would seem to have more than made up for their physical deprivations by the intensity of their spiritual delights (CLASSEN 1998, p. 14).

Goal, structure and content of the book

Indian and Western theories of the senses

While the second part of the book focuses on the historical and cultural character of individual senses, the first part examines Indian and Western theories of the senses that go beyond the individual senses. First, Remo BODEI shows that in European anthropology of the senses, there are two ways of dealing with the senses, which also play a role in the Indian reflections about them. The first way aims to overcome the randomness of sensory experiences "through the filter of mind, reason, or soul" in order to search for insight beyond the diversity of the senses. The second way aims to use the five senses in order to bring the "exterior world in biunique communication with the internal one," and develop both of them further. In this way intelligence and the senses are to be molded. Intelligence can be developed into the "pilot of the soul" and lead to insight, and God. In the process, the senses can be further developed into an internal eye and to spiritual hearing. With their possibility of putting people into ecstatic states, they can even lead to mystical experiences of the divine. For AUGUSTINE, the following is certain: God is at the innermost part of human beings; he enables the internal and external life. Something similar is found in NOVALIS' "Hymns to the Night," in which the soul turns away from the exterior world and spreads out itself inside the person without needing the clarity of the light and of the world outside. In contrast to this, DIDEROT and LESSING emphasize the incompleteness of a human and the necessity of molding his reason using the senses.

In Indian philosophical traditions, the senses are seen "as common constituents of being(s) shared by all inhabitants of the cosmos" (MALINAR). Despite a certain ambiguity — the senses are regarded as both instruments for knowledge as well as obstacles — they are understood as the basis for experiencing the world and for the relationships of living things with each other. As already mentioned, the philosophical schools differ greatly in their view of the world and their understanding of the senses. Some philosophers argue that the senses depict the outside world; others emphasize that we only perceive mental constructions of the outside world. Like European philosophy, the *Nyāya* school of philosophy proceeds on the assumption of five senses; Buddhist traditions also add the mind (*manas*) as the sixth "seat." *Sāṃkhya* philosophers add another five "senses of action" to these six senses, making it a total of 11 senses. The senses are understood as "capacities" that have powers to attain knowledge, but can also become obstacles to obtaining higher knowledge. Sensitivity (*vedanā*), desire (*kāma*) and an appropriate attitude toward objects also depend on the senses. The senses convey desire and joy, but also confusion and anger. As in Western philosophy, they can lead to the recognition of the "absolute being" (*brahman*; *nirvāṇa*), that is, of God or of the "immortal self" (*ātman*). In the *Sāṃkhya*, the complexity of the senses is also more closely examined.

The senses play an important role in the relationship between the deity and the devotee in classical Hinduism, especially in later Vaiṣṇava theologies (see Gérard COLAS). Of particular significance are their capability of grasping the divine incarnation and the divine icons. In Indian epistemology, the senses serve as instruments of coming into contact with things, which takes place in space and time. The internal sense organizes the various sensory perceptions and causes them to enter into consciousness. *Yogīs*, i.e., certain practioners of Yoga, can perceive things that are not available in space and time. The perception of God is also space- and time-less. Their worship of icons, however, is based on the belief that "the identification of the icon as a living person that is to say possessing a body and senses, also arises from devotion" (COLAS). Through this the devotee can sensuously perceive the deity and vice versa. The icon, therefore, is not a lifeless image lacking reality; on the contrary, it becomes a sensory living being through devotion.

The material presented by Anand MISHRA confirms the idea that sense-perception is important for epistemic knowledge but with limitations, since the *brahman* or the Absolute is mostly regarded as beyond the senses and cannot be grasped through them. Sense-control is, therefore, important for the attainment of liberation. However, this is to a certain extent different from the *Puṣṭimārga* of Vallabhācārya (1479–1531 CE) who says that a non-sensory spiritual union is possible in order to experience the deity through the senses.[4] He also postulates a special body for the god — with hands, feet, a mouth, and a stomach, and limbs that are pure bliss (*ānanda*) — without a worldly beginning or end.

The case study of Monika HORSTMANN on senses in the *Sant* tradition again starts with the notion that the senses are graded as obstacles for liberation and thus have to be withdrawn from this world. This is somewhat different from related esoteric and tantric *Haṭhayoga* practices of the Nāthyogīs as a special ascetic management of the senses, in which the body represents the microcosm, which is identical with the macrocosm or the "supreme." In these practices, all senses have to be subjected to a reverse discipline. Similar to the evolutionary process of the *Sāṃkhya* described earlier, a multitude of phenomena as perceived through the senses must be reduced to the oneness that is imagined as different, and ultimately results in a sensually experienced wellbeing.

[4] This, to a certain extent, resembles the synesthetic position of the 12th-century Christian mystic and theologian Hildegard of Bingen, who did not consider her sensuous visions to be escapes of her corporeal senses but as something in her soul alone: "I see them much more in my soul alone," she claimed (CLASSEN 1998, p. 15).

Horstmann in her essay demonstrates and illustrates these complex processes by analyzing a Hamhayogic scroll from Rajasthan dated 1869 CE.

The anthropology of the senses

In the second part of the book, central aspects of the various senses in India and Europe are examined under the heading of "Anthropology of the Senses." We do not limit the term "anthropology" to an academic discipline, but instead include a wide range of sense-perceptions and expressions in various present and historical contexts. The subject of the first section, "seeing and hearing," is presently especially affected by the global ubiquitous proliferation accelerated through the new media (television, internet, radio, etc.), which not only influence the perceptions of objects, but also have repercussions on the character of senses themselves. The so-called "nearby senses" — tasting and smelling, touching and sense of motion — are another case. The three senses of "tasting," "smelling," and "touching," in particular, are more "intimate senses" in comparison to the public "far senses" of "vision" and "hearing." In public, they play a rather subordinated role, due to which they are less subjected to the influence of globalization, allowing them to retain and protect traditional culture and knowledge.

Seeing and hearing

This first section opens with an analysis of "The Vision: Control, Desire, Perception" by Christoph Wulf. The history of vision oscillates between the high points of radiant insight and controlling mastery and the low points of being overwhelmed and suffering. In the genealogy of human senses, the sense of sight has become central. The ambivalence and ambiguity of cultural-historical processes are reflected in its history. The sense of sight enables a sort of "intermediate corporeality." The world is "captured by the eye." Vision is directed at an object or another person and makes a selection from the visual environment. It is a movement of attention and focus, and simultaneously one of turning away and exclusion. The affinity of the sense of sight for abstraction lies in its peculiarity of being able to bridge the distance between humans and things while nevertheless maintaining the distance in one's perception, thus creating a "distant proximity." The hypertrophic "transformation" of the world into image contributes to the abstraction of life processes. In the excessiveness of image production, images today often lose their representational character. Images increasingly relate to other images and quote them or excerpt from them. They create reference frames themselves, in regard to which they demand validity. Images, simulacra and simulations generate new image worlds at great speed, and with rigorous editing. These extreme developments, which are induced first and foremost by new media and their virtual image worlds, have an influence on perception; for the time being the extent of their effects can only be assessed gradually.

While conducting research on exorcism rituals in the Western Himalayas of North India, William SAX discovered that nearly all of his informants had "seen ghosts." He, on the other hand, never managed to see one, even though he very much wanted to do so. What does this difference in perception tell us about ghosts? About rituals? About sense-perceptions? In his essay, SAX compares perceptions of ghosts in Europe and South Asia and argues that a great deal depends upon the language in which we frame our questions, and the assumptions that we bring to our research topics.

Do we perceive the world acoustically, and how do we communicate with our acoustic perceptions? These questions refer to the history and culture of sound and hearing that are first discussed by Annette WILKE in her analysis of the relevance of orality and sonality in Indian (Hindu) culture: "Text, sound, and ritual belong together. Both orality and sonality enjoy great cultural significance. This had distinct influence on how people approach texts and left marks on perception, *habitus* forms, and social practice." In everyday life, traditional areas of science, religious literature, and secular Sanskrit literature, language and sound are poetically used and reflected upon philosophically. Sounds are used to stimulate and embody religious feelings. For this, it is necessary to "hear" texts. Texts do not find complete expression of their meanings when they are reduced to their semantics. They are "performative embeddings" that stage and perform their cultural meaning in rituals and gestures. These texts are verbally and acoustically performed and thus express their materiality and corporality, capturing the imagination of readers in this way. Repetitive reciting and hearing of sacred texts, such as mantras, have a purifying function. In Indian culture, phonocentrism not just appears in a religious context, it can also be seen in many other cultural areas. The following becomes clear: no written literature can communicate nuances between the words better than the voice. In contrast to Western traditions, in which there is often a devaluation of the senses and a valorization of the mind, in Hindu tradition there is an "unbroken continuum of the sensory and the mental, and no split between physical sense perception and the non-sensory spirit" (ibid.).

It is also the case, as demonstrated by Karsten LICHAU, that in the European tradition a close relationship exists between sound, hearing and the divine, so that even in the 20th century, one can speak of a "sacred sound" which can be placed between "noise" and "silence," and for which the synesthetic mode plays an important role. Silence is an important prerequisite for finding complete expression of a "sacred noise." The example of the "minute of silence," given by LICHAU, is striking in this regard. With the interest in research into auditive cultures growing, it is also increasing in "filthy noise" and noise abatement as well as in the fundamental question of what sounds, music, and silence are. This question becomes even more important as many traditional demarcations and differentiations can no longer claim to be valid. New oppositions and distinctions emerge between "noise and acoustical nuisance, legal and illegal profane noise, (profane) noise and (sacred) noise, or even between prohibited noise and allowed noise" (ibid.), which require a new assessment of their historical and cultural significance. For the assessment of modern soundscapes and soundmarks, their relationship to historical and cultural significance of silence plays an important role. What do the changing soundscapes mean to people today? Even when reading quietly, we find ourselves in a soundscape in which we are linked with the environment through the sound that we constantly perceive. In every life situation, we are moving in an environment that resonates.

The corporeality of sound cannot be separated from our self-perception. "Being a *body in sound* means you are neither an object nor a subject of individual sound events; but you are *an elastic material*, reacting and acting," notes Holger SCHULZE. If we try to understand our culture from a hearing perspective, this leads to a fundamentally different understanding. "Performing the sonic, sound practices in auditory dispositives" becomes important. The fundamental problem that, then, emerges is: "what is the position of human beings in a specific sonically shaped environment" and what is a "*sonic persona.*" These questions aim at anthropology from a "hearing perspective," in which it must be clarified how the sensory experiences can be linguistically understood and recounted, and what role sensory fictions play in the development of sensorial techniques.

Tasting and smelling

In the second section, there is an examination of tasting and smelling — two senses that show their effect first and foremost in the near and intimate range. Taste is predominantly associated with eating and drinking. We use it to differentiate between good and bad food. Norbert ELIAS (1978) mentions the link between the formation of taste and table manners. The former is among the important tasks of social education or upbringing. Taste is historically and culturally formed through culinary traditions, as Alain MONTANDON demonstrates in his essay. In India, the four fundamental Western savors (sugary, salty, sour, and bitter) are complemented by the pungent and the astringent. In Burma, they distinguish six savors: sweet, sour, pungent, salty, astringent, and bitter, but they are rarely found alone and are often combined. China identifies five savors (sweet, sour, pungent, bitter, and salty). In all cultures, cuisine becomes the origin and point of reference for taste judgments, which also lead to social differentiations and hierarchizations. Taste also plays a central role in aesthetics. It helps us determine the quality of works of art. It is often easier to specify why a work has a lower aesthetic quality than to designate what makes up the higher aesthetic value of another work. The lack of precision and the blurring character of taste are important conditions for taste judgments.

Taste and odor are often intertwined during eating. Odor, nonetheless, has its own sensory quality, whose significance can hardly be overstated. In a study of a *pūjā* in India, the role of the odor of flowers is examined by Astrid ZOTTER in her essay. It is among the favorable odors and is part of the "smellscape" that is characteristic of Indian forms of worship (*pūjā*). The offering of flowers and the odor given off in the process intensify the bodily sensations and contribute to the purification of the people. In many *pūjās*, breathing and breathing control also play a role, which have an immediate effect on what and how something is smelled in a *pūjā*. Flowers also link the smell with the other senses and create synesthetic spiritual experiences.

Touching

The Western dualistic separation between material and spiritual, substance and attribute, is not appropriate for India. Emotional qualities such as sorrow, hatred and love, or the senses are understood as subtle substances, and thus material. The same holds true for other substances that the body excretes through its "windows," the sense organs, that is, the view, the smell, the sound, and so on. All this is part of the essence and nature of the individual, and if somebody sensuously perceives it, it is regarded as touching and potentially polluting. "Untouchables," therefore, had to keep a suitable distance from and live outside villages in some parts of India. Touchability in death rituals, which is the topic of Axel MICHAELS' essay, is normally related to pollution and thus prohibited. This mainly concerns touching the corpse or the chief mourners. However, in the after-death rituals of the Hindu Newar community, objects such as the *piṇḍa* balls represent the deceased person and the forefathers that can and must be touched by the chief mourner. Then death is taken into hands in a way that makes it possible to give emotions a form. Thus, death is not untouchable. On the contrary, only by this form of touching and revitalizing purity is "symbolically" restored for the deceased, even though the situation is quite real for the bereaved.

Moving and performing

In dance, work with the senses plays a central role. The focus here is no longer on visuality but instead, at least since the beginning of the 20th century, on kinesthesia, the sixth sense (see HOWES 2009). What is crucial here is the position of the moving body in space and time. As previously stated and elaborated by Gabriele BRANDSTETTER, the sense of motion is a cross-modal sense that enables aesthetic experiences. In dance, kinesthetics and synesthetics are mutually dependent. One often speaks of "listening to motion" in dance. In the words of Paul VALÉRY: The ear "keeps watch, so to speak, at the frontier beyond which the eye does not see." What is critical for dance is work with the following elements: "momentum," "gravity," "mass"/weight," "chaos," and "inertia." In many body techniques of modern dance, the subject of the dancer is increasingly becoming more important. In this process, work on dance is focusing more and more on the meaning of kinesthetics as an instrument for understanding the body better and as a means for improving aesthetic work. "Attention" predominantly becomes kinesthetic awareness. In dance it is necessary to sense the movement and to feel the flow of movement and feelings.

Jayachandran PALAZHY in his essay is particularly concerned with the conceptualization, creation and the experience of contemporary movement arts in India. He sheds light on some of the thoughts and concerns that have influenced the evolving training methodologies for movement arts. As, in a way, this is closely linked to his own artistic practice, he shares some life experiences and the underlying beliefs that govern them. In an effort to draw on multiple sources that have colored his artistic journey, the essay mentions a few examples, including the workings of some of the physical and performance traditions of India as well as thoughts and practices from other cultures, and contemporary and digital cultures. He gives some insights into the processes that are involved in the making and reception of a performance. The essay is divided into eight sections. In sections 1 through 3 he attempts to establish the context for contemporary performing arts in India by looking at the conceptions of time, space and body. In sections 4 through 6 he looks at the creation and reception of performance and supplements these with ideas on improvisation, structure, abstraction, metaphor, empathy, and synesthesia. The remaining sections include samples of the work and collaborations at the Attakkalari Centre for Movement Arts and elaborate the ideas discussed in the essay.

In the essay that follows, Jan WEINHOLD shows that movement and performance also play a role in Family Constellation, a ritualized form of counseling or psychotherapy conducted in a group setting. Family Constellations were introduced in Germany in the beginning of the 1990s. Compared to conventional forms of psychotherapy, one of its distinguishing features is that the client does not speak much. Instead, after just briefly formulating a problem and with the assistance of a Family Constellation facilitator, the client selects group members who do not have any knowledge about the client's family and sets them up in a shifting spatial constellation. WEINHOLD also demonstrates that, in contrast to verbally-oriented psychotherapy, Family Constellations mainly rely on non-verbal and embodied procedures. He argues that a variety of sensory means (the externalization of clients' corporal sensations into a spatial scenario, kinesthetic sensations of representatives, alterations of positions, and ritualized gestures) enable the gradual explication of the clients' family-related implicit "body memory."

Karin POLIT explores performative rituals as sensual experiences in her essay. Possession and experiences of trance during rituals are described as being connected to collective emotions and are interpreted as part of a locally shaped human existence. The essay discusses how movement, as a kinesthetic sense, in combination with the multi-sensual experiences common in many ritual traditions of South Asia, is strongly connected to the perception of reality and collective emotional responses. These emotions are invoked simultaneously in the moving bodies of the performers and in the people who take part in the ritual as spectating participants. It is argued that ritual performances, during which the divine is called into human bodies, bring about a special kind of collective emotional and sensual experience.

The unity of the senses

Among the difficult problems of an anthropology of the senses is the question: what relationship do the senses have with each other, and to what extent there is a unity of the senses. In Western culture, attention has been paid to this question again and again (STRAUSS 1966), and this question also plays a role in the concluding part of our study. Thus, Sundar SARUKKAI, in his essay, focuses on the unity of the senses, and starts with the widely shared assumption that there are five senses — corresponding to touch, sight, taste, smell, and sound — which are the windows to all our experiences. These senses are associated with specific sense organs, although the sense of touch, associated with the skin, is of a different "kind" as compared to sight, smell and sound. These senses are seen as independent of each other, even though there have also been arguments that taste is akin to the sense of touch. In fact, the independence of these senses is itself a matter of debate and has been used by philosophers to argue for a variety of conclusions, such as the proof of existence of the self and even of the world. But there seems to be little disagreement on the view that the nature of these sensory experiences is exclusive, that is, one cannot experience the nature of sound through eyes; what the ear contributes to that experience is special to that organ. Given this independence, it is natural that throughout history people have associated different "strengths" to these senses, the eye being the most dominant in a number of ways. Sight has been the most dominant metaphor for knowledge and truth; terms, such as insight, enlightenment and so on, illustrate a universal privilege for its "positive" virtues. But the sense of touch is also essential. As Aristotle suggests, while the sense of sight is important, without the sense of touch existence is not possible. Thus, touch is the most essential sense for human beings since we can live even if we are blind, but if we lose the capacity to touch we will die. Senses, thus, have different functions. Given all this, what does it mean to say that there could be a unity of the senses?

It is again made clear by Theofanis TASIS in his essay how little attention has been paid to the "politics of the senses" that has developed in all cultures. This issue has been investigated in a case study on the relationship between vision and hearing in Hannah ARENDT's *Vita activa*, which shows the insignificance of the role played by "touch," "smell" and "taste." TASIS also makes clear the problems ARENDT's differentiation between "public" and "private" and her assignment of light to "public" and darkness to "private" entail. Due to this one-dimensional differentiation, the creative dimension of both areas is only insufficiently understood. The public sphere is associated with light, vision and immortality; the private sphere with the body and darkness. The devaluation of the private and its assignment to darkness corresponds to the devaluation of the body and to the disparagement of the near senses of "touch," "smell," and "taste."

In contrast to this rather traditional assessment, the example of weather, the atmosphere and the starry sky is used to clarify the extent to which experiences of the environment are multi-sensorial or synesthetic experiences of the embodied subject. "Three examples are used to clarify" the broad range of approaches to atmospheric phenomena: "while Aristotle focuses on their scientific explanation, the artist–scientist GOETHE is interested in the morphology of their appearances, and CIORAN regards the weather as the cause of subjective emotional disorders and as a symbol for the human's contingency" (Mădălina DIACONU). The aesthetic experience of the weather, which for long was primarily seen as a visual one, connects and incorporates all senses. It is synesthetic. In the cultural history of climate, humans have resorted to various strategies in order to cope with weather change, ranging from biological adaptation to cultural-symbolic interpretation and from weather-making rituals to geoengineering. More recently, contingency and vulnerability have been extended from the body to the atmosphere; this has converted the tragic from an anthropological to an environmental category and the biological weather sensitivity to the "sensitivity" of the environment itself.

References

BENJAMIN, W. (2006): Berlin Childhood around 1900. – Cambridge, MA.

CLASSEN, C. (Ed.) (1993): Worlds of Sense: Exploring the Senses in History and Across Cultures. – London.

CLASSEN, C. (1997): Foundations for an Anthropology of the Senses. In: International Social Science Journal, Vol. 153, pp. 401–12.

CLASSEN, C. (1998): The Color of Angels: Cosmology, Gender and the Aesthetic Imagination. – London.

ECK, D. (1985): Darśan. Seeing the Divine Image in India. – 2nd edition. – Chambersburg, PA.

EDE, Y. VAN (2009): Sensuous Anthropology: Sense and Sensibility and the Rehabilitation of Skill. In: Anthropological Notebooks 15.2, pp. 61–75.

ELIAS, N. (1978): The Civilizing Process. – New York.

GEBAUER, G./WULF, C. (1995): Mimesis: Culture, Art, Society. – Berkeley & Los Angeles.

GEBAUER, G./WULF, C. (1998): Spiel, Ritual, Geste: Mimetisches Handeln in der sozialen Welt. – Reinbek.

GEURTS, K. (2002): Culture and Senses: Bodily Ways of Knowing in an African Community. – Berkeley.

GONDA, J. (1969): Eye and Gaze in the Veda. – Amsterdam.

HERZFELD, M. (2001): Anthropology: Theoretical Practice in Culture and Society. – Oxford.

HOWES, D. (2003): Sensual Relations: Engaging the Senses in Culture and Social Theory. – Ann Arbor.

HOWES, D. (2004): Empire of the Senses: the Sensual Culture Reader. – Oxford.
HOWES, D. (Ed.) (2009): The Sixth Sense Reader. – Oxford.
HOWES, D. (2011): Sensation. In: Material Religion, Vol. 7.1, pp. 92–99.
HSU, E. (2008): The Senses and the Social: An Introduction. In: Ethnos 73.4, pp. 433–43.
JOHNSON, M. (2005): The Meaning of the Body: Aesthetics of Human Understanding. – Chicago.
KAMPER, D./WULF, C. (Eds.) (1984): Das Schwinden der Sinne. – Frankfurt.
KAMPER, D./WULF, C. (Eds.) (1992): Die Wiederkehr des Körpers. – 4th edition. – Frankfurt.
KAMPER, D./WULF, C. (Eds.) (1994): Anthropologie nach dem Tode des Menschen: Vervollkommung und Unverbesserlichkeit. – Frankfurt.
LAKOFF, G./JOHNSON, M. (1999): Philosophy in the Flesh. – New York.
LARSON, G. J. (1979): Classical Sāṃkhya: An Interpretation of Its History and Meaning. – 2nd revised edition. – Santa Barbara.
LARSON, G. J./BHATTACHARYA, R. S. (1987): Sāṃkhya: A Dualist Tradition of Indian Philosophy. – Delhi.
MALONEY, C. (1976): Don't say 'Pretty Baby' let you zap it with your Eye: The Evil Eye in South Asia. In: MALONEY, C. (Ed.): The Evil Eye. – New York, pp. 102–48.
MCHUGH, J. (2007): The Classification of Smells and the Order of the Senses in Indian Religious Traditions. In: Numen, Vol. 54, pp. 374–419.
MCHUGH, J. (2012): Sandalwood and Carrion: Smell in Indian Religion and Culture. – New York.
MERLEAU-PONTY, M. (1968): The Visible and the Invisible. – Evanston.
MEYER, B. (2006): Religious Sensations: Why Media, Aesthetics and Power Matter in the Study of Contemporary Religion. – Amsterdam.
MEYER, B. (Ed.) (2009): Aesthetic Formations. – New York.
MICHAELS, A. (2003): Notions of Nature in Traditional Hinduism. In: EHLERS, E./ GETHMANN, C.F. (Eds.): *Environment Across Cultures*. – Berlin, pp. 111–22.
MICHAELS, A. (2004): Hinduism Past and Present. – Princeton.
MICHAELS, A./WULF, C. (Eds.) (2011): Images of the Body in India: South Asian and European Perspectives on Rituals and Performativity. – New Delhi.
MICHAELS, A./WULF, C. (Eds.) (2012): Emotions in Rituals and Performances. – New Delhi.
PLESSNER, H. (1923): Die Einheit der Sinne. Grundlinien einer Ästhesiologie des Geistes. – Frankfurt/M.
PLESSNER, H. (1970): Anthropologie der Sinne. – Frankfurt/M.
POLANYI, M. (1969): Knowing and Being. GRENE, M. (Ed.). – Chicago.
RICKE, A. (n.d.): Anthropology of Senses. http://www.indiana.edu/~wanthro/theory_pages/senses. htm#bib (accessed August 31, 2012).
SCHMITHAUSEN, L. (1997): Gleichmut und Mitgefühl. Zu Spiritualität und Heilsziel des älteren Buddhismus. In: A. BSTEH (Ed.), Der Buddhismus als Anfrage an christliche Theologie und Philosophie. – Mödling, pp. 119–36.
SEREMETAKIS, C. N. (1994): The Senses Still: Memory and Perception as Material Culture in Modernity. – Boulder.
SERRES, M. (2009): The Five Senses: A Philosophy of Mingled Bodies. – London.
SHEETS-JOHNSTONE, M. (1999): The Primacy of Movement. – Amsterdam.

SLAJE, W. (1989): Bewußtsein und Wahrnehmungsvermögen von Pflanzen aus hinduistischer Sicht. In: SCHOLZ, B. (Ed.): Der Orientalische Mensch und seine Beziehungen zur Umwelt. – Graz, pp. 149–69.

SMITH, M. M. (2007): Producing Sense, Consuming Sense, Making Sense: Perils and Prospects for Sensory History. In: Journal of Social History, Vol. 40, pp. 841–58.

STOLLER, P. (1989): The Taste of Ethnographic Things: The Senses in Anthropology. – Philadelphia.

STRAUSS, E. (1966): Phenomenological Psychology. – New York.

TAUSSIG, M. (1993): Mimesis and Alterity: A Particular History of the Senses. – London.

WULF, C. (2013): Anthropology: A Continental Perspective. – Chicago.

Indian and Western Theories of Senses

Remo Bodei

The Windows on the World: The Senses and Inner Life

In Shakespeare's *Sonnets*, a striking simile appears that has smell as its protagonist, but masks two other characters: time and eternity.

The flowers of summer soon lose their fragrance and beauty. And yet, if we subject them to a process of distillation, the perfume that is obtained, once enclosed in a flask and sealed, preserves its scent forever. We read in the fifth sonnet:

> Then were not summer's distillation left,
> A liquid prisoner pent in walls of glass,
> Beauty's effect with beauty were bereft,
> Nor it, nor no remembrance what it was:
> But flowers distill'd, though they with winter meet,
> Leese but their show: their substance still lives sweet
> (W. Shakespeare, *Sonnet 5*, vv. 9–14).

And in the next sonnet:

> Then let not winter's ragged hand deface,
> In thee thy summer, ere thou be distill'd:
> Make sweet some vial; treasure thou some place
> With beauty's treasure ere it be self-kill'd
> (W. Shakespeare, *Sonnet 6*, vv. 1–2).

Even time, like the fragrance of flowers, is destined to self-destruct and die. There remains only eternity that, extracting its essence, arrests the time of human life in the vial of ideas, intensifying and rendering immortal fleeting sensations. Thus, according to the recurrent Neoplatonist canon, the firm reality of forms challenges becoming. It renders enduring the transience of beauty, saved and preserved by poetry in a casket of words. The sensations of the senses preserved in ideas save their substance in like manner.

Beautiful images, one might say, but incapable of explaining how the world of the senses might really be understood. Are there ideas that are immutable, indifferent to the variations of time and space, saved from generation and corruption, or are they merely pale and empty abstractions, colored and filled by the senses, but not autonomous from them? Rather than Plato, is it not better to trust Locke, for whom there is nothing in the intellect that has not been previously in the senses; or Condillac, whose statue gradually assumes human faculties starting with smell; or the behaviorists, followers of the principle: "give me a nerve and a muscle and I will make you a mind?"

This is not the place to reopen a dispute that has lasted for millennia and that has seen Epicurus and Lucretius aligned against Plato; Leibniz against Locke; all the way up to Chomsky (who earned some esteem even following the discovery of DNA) against those who support the empirical and tangible genesis of all of our knowledge. It is more interesting to try and understand how and why philosophy, since its Greek origins, has tried to "save the phenomena" by following two paths that run counter to each other, yet intersect.

The first path consists of removing the senses from external life and from the randomness of their appearance, passing them through the filter of the mind, reason, or the soul, which "distills" them and reduces them to appearances, forcing the philosopher into a long and frequent sojourn in the "kingdom of shadows," from which he then returns to a reinterpreted external world.

The second is by identifying in the senses, in the manner of EMPEDOCLES, those openings (Greek *poroi*) that place the exterior world in biunique communication with the internal one, and allow both to develop together — or rather, allow intelligence to grow and the senses feed, in response, on its elaborations:

> But come, consider, by every organ, how each thing is clear
> not holding any vision as more reliable than what you hear,
> nor the echoes of hearing than the clarities of the tongue,
> and do not in any way curb the reliability of the other limbs by which there is a passage (*poros*) for understanding
> but understand each thing in the way that it is clear
> (EMPEDOCLES 2001, pp. 217–18)

Even if the skeptic Sextus Empiricus — forcing the thought of EMPEDOCLES — observes that immediately afterwards, the philosopher from Agrigento underscores the weakness of the senses ("because the organs extending from the limbs are restricted, and they are struck by many base impressions that weaken the mind"), this does not at all imply their devaluation. Certainly, a multitude of impressions of little value dissipates their energies. And yet, the suggested antidote is reinforcing their perspicuity and wakefulness, opening the ears and eyes, observing things "carefully, through clear tests."

However, it is equally important to first understand how and why philosophy may have foreseen the splitting of the corporeal senses, often crossing into mysticism. This splitting places, beside the external eye, an internal one (that becomes more perspicacious as the acumen of the first one declines with age). It places a spiritual hearing beside the ear (capable of also hearing demonic or divine voices) and adds to material touch a *tactus intimus* (capable of making me know myself first and better than any reflection) (See Aristippus in CICERO 1927, p. 24). In AUGUSTINE, even smell and taste find their corollary in the soul:

> [A]nd yet I love a kind of light, and melody, and fragrance, and meat, and embracement when I love my God: the light, melody, fragrance, meat, embracement of my inner man, where there shines upon my soul what space cannot contain, and there smells what breathing does not disperse, and there tastes what eating does not diminish, and there clings what satiety does not divorce (1909, p. 171).

The reference to embracement, to spiritual contact with God that mimics physical contact, might strike us as bold and even vaguely blasphemous. And yet, it is common for those visiting the church of Santa Maria della Vittoria in Rome to be struck, for analogous reasons, by the splendor of a mass of pale marble, suspended in midair in the shadow of a chapel. We are speaking of Bernini's famous statue, *The Ecstasy of Saint Teresa*: an angel upright on his feet, in his hand a lily whose stem is pointed downward, stands over the saint, languidly stretched out with her head reclined towards the viewer and with her lost eyes turned upward. Her face, in particular, shows a deep rapture, a sweet exhaustion of extreme sensuality. Her body, abandoning all her limbs, unleashes an irresistible erotic charge. Those who look at it are often disturbed beyond the intensity of the aesthetic emotion — by a doubt: is the eroticism contained in such forms just the fruit of our irreverent evil, or is it the willful effect of the baroque imagination of the sculptor or, in fact, of his customers?

But none of these hypotheses seems adequate. Our feeling is not irreverent; nor does Bernini's art strengthen the intentions of Christian mysticism (also based on the *Song of the Songs* in the Bible). The latter is found at the confluence of different traditions, both of which insist not so much on the deprivations and mortification of the flesh in and of themselves as much as — and more tenaciously — on the *unio mystica*, understood as spiritual intercourse, pleasure, and orgasm, modelled on the carnal versions, between the Bride (the Soul) and the Groom (God). In these moments, Teresa is seized by a *celestial locura*, a divine madness. She no longer knows who she is; her body loses its weight and "remains as if dead, and unable of itself to do anything: it continues all the time as it was when the rapture came upon it" (SAINT TERESA OF AVILA 1979, p. 125).

Returning to philosophy, even in Plato, the journey of the soul passes through the inner life and the initial renunciation of the physical senses, and it ends in the satisfaction of finding what it was searching for, more or less consciously. Plato urges the philosopher to concentrate first on himself, and not let himself be distracted by the multitude of impressions on the senses, to let the soul go "all alone by itself" (see Plato, *Fedone*, 78 D–79 E) along the path that leads to the "plain of truth," where it will be able to meet the "reality that really is: without color, without figure, intangible" (Plato, *Fedro*, 247 C). Plotinus, in turn, suggests that the philosopher behave like someone waiting "to hear the dearest voice" (Plotinus, *Enneads*, V, 1, 12, 15–21) and not pay attention to noises in the background of the world of the senses. And even DESCARTES, at the beginning of the third of his *Meditations*, follows an analogous path, in his own way: "I will now shut my eyes, stop up my ears, and withdraw all my senses. I will also blot out from my thoughts all images of corporeal things" (2006, p. 19). Taking it to extremes, CICERO had previously held some consolation for possible blindness, noting that

> the thought of the wise man scarcely ever calls in the support of the eyes to aid his researches (*sapientis autem cogitatio non ferme ad investigandum adhibet oculus advocatos*). For if night does not put a stop to happy life, why should a day that resembles night stop it (1927, p. 537)?

But does it end there for excavating a cave of inner life (that mirror opposite that, nonetheless, is complementary to the life of the senses to which men are chained from birth), that consecrated place where the immaterial essences of ideas are solemnly deposited or the non-extensive substance of the *res cogitans* is preserved? And, in order to explain the reality in which we effectively find ourselves, is there not a parallel reality that is manufactured from it—a remote, invisible, intangible, and undepictable duplicate of the world?

There is no doubt that this might be the case. And yet, we may ask ourselves if this is really a case of constructing a cosmos of the inner life that is symmetrical to the external one, or whether it is a case of constructing a place where sensation is settled, that intermediate stage along the path that leads to a reinterpreted external life — to an objectivity that is neither external nor internal. The choice to abandon the senses constitutes, in effect, only half the journey that leads to the turning point from which we begin climbing towards the successful translation of the mute and ineffable world of perceptible signs into the rich and differentiated articulations of intelligence. If this is how things are, the problem does not consist of the devaluation of sensation as much as of the trusting of intelligence, "pilot of the soul." It will lead us either to the constellation of ideas to which the mind limits its contemplation (in order to orient itself in the world of the senses), or to a God of truth to which we can turn, one that cannot deceive us.

In this latter case, where does the truth reside? AUGUSTINE's expression, *in interiore homine habitat veritas*, is often cited; but we forget that there are three steps for him on the staircase that leads to truth. The first is represented by the external life (of the *foris*); the second, by the internal life (of the *homo interior*); and the last by an intimacy within me that goes beyond me, because God is *interior intimo meo* ("within me more than my most internal part": AUGUSTINE 1909, pp. 6, 11). It follows from this that the truth coincides with the *interior intimo meo* in the most radical way, but it is not missing in the exterior life of the *foris*, which can become the path of sensation, the totality of the signals with which creatures display the glory of the Creator. AUGUSTINE shatters the traditional binary opposition between internal and external life, such that the inner life, into which the Stoics retreated to get stronger, reaches an even deeper level with him. Thus, MARCUS AURELIUS ANTONINUS could remind himself that "nowhere is there a more idyllic spot, a villa more private and peaceful, than in one's own mind" (2002, p. 41). Augustine believes that at this place there is a buried treasure, the interior of inner life. Thus, the villa is not truth itself, but the truth "lives" there. It resides and takes refuge there only to meet God, the master of the house.

Leaping far forward in time, we can say that it is with NOVALIS, in the first Romantic age, that reflection on the senses and internal life deepens, and that the Neoplatonist tradition is brought to its ultimate consequences. It seems then that if someone walled himself within his interior world, his inner life would swell beyond measure, ignoring or scorning the external, because he was a victim—HEGEL said—of a sort of "consumption of the spirit," typical of those who fear "dirtying their hands" through contact with reality (1995, p. 211).

The first of NOVALIS' *Hymns to the Night* describes the conversion of the soul from its absorption in the external life of the senses to the inner life. The well-known daylight, because it is so clear, does not speak, while the unknown of the night, after having learned to listen, expresses itself in a voice more persuasive and melodious than the perceptible and solar language of the day. NOVALIS writes of daylight (in words whose beauty no translation can fully render) that

> the giant world [...] floats dancing in its azure flood; the sparkling, ever-tranquil stone, the thoughtful imbibing plant, and the wild, burning multiform beast-world inhales it; but more than all, the lordly stranger with the meaning eyes, the swaying walk, and the sweetly closed, melodious lips (1992, p. 9).

But its brightness blinds and stuns, and does not content the soul which, searching for itself, loves to get lost in its depths:

> Aside I turn to the holy, unspeakable, mysterious Night. Afar lies the world, sunk in a deep grave; waste and lonely is its place. In the chords of the bosom blows a deep sadness. I am ready to sink away in drops of dew, and mingle with the ashes. The distances of memory, the wishes of youth, the dreams of childhood, the brief joys and vain hopes of a whole long life, arise in gray garments, like an evening vapour after the sunset (ibid.).

At this point, the soul notices how the inner world might be more our own, and closer than the external world in that it contains the key for introducing us again to the whole of reality, the perceptible and the extra-perceptible: "We will understand the world when we understand ourselves, because it and we are integrated halves" (NOVALIS 1915, no. 1700). Within us, with the initial nocturnal darkness of the soul dissipated, the entire universe opens up:

> We dream of journeys through the universe; but is the Universe then not within us? We do not know the depths of our own souls–*the secret path leads inwards*. Within us or nowhere lies Eternity and its worlds, the Past and Future. The external world is the world of shadows; it projects its shadows into the kingdom of light (NOVALIS 1903, pp. 147–48).

Every katabasis in the darkness of our selves is, however, an anabasis toward the light of the world: "Every descent into ourselves, every glance toward the internal, is at the same time an ascent, an assumption, a glance toward the *true external reality*" (ibid., p. 162).

The autoscopy, the contemplation of one's *I*, is only the inaugural step of knowledge. Those who are satisfied with it are halfway down the path. The second step consists of the careful re-examination of the external world, with a glance that is educated and rendered penetrating precisely because it had dwelt in the darkness of the inner life, which has taught one to not take the presumed irrefutable evidence of things seriously, and to seek new, invisible correspondences between them.

Novalis' fantasies reach their peak when he imagines that, "if we were blind, deaf and deprived of touch," and "instead, our soul were perfectly open, our spirit were the exterior world of today," then

> who knows if, little by little, with multiple struggles, we would not be capable of producing eyes, ears, etc. Because in that case, our body would be so much under our own power, it would constitute part of our inner life, just as our soul does now (NOVALIS 1915, No. 460)!

Does turning our backs on the world of sensation and turning toward the invisible and intangible Logos, or toward an omnipotent God — in order to avoid infection by what is protean, confused, random, and ineffable in experience — come from a secret fear that transforms reason into an interior eye, one that scrutinizes and listens to us incessantly and threateningly? Is NIETZSCHE right when, in *Twilight of the Idols*, he thinks that one seeks, in reason, a tyrant to avoid the more serious risk of chaos?

> The fanaticism with which the whole of Greek thought throws itself upon rationality betrays a desperate condition; they were in danger, they had only one choice: either go to ruin or — be *absurdly rational* [...]. We must be rational, clear, and distinct at any price: every yielding to the instincts, to the unconscious, leads downwards (NIETZSCHE 1967, p. 6; 2009, p. 13).

Considering the second position, the one laid out by EMPEDOCLES, we can assert that the senses constitute, in effect, avenues to reality, channels of communication between the internal and the external that are often underutilized and insufficiently educated. We are dealing with five narrow windows on the world,[1] literally cut to the size of a man, within which reality manifests itself in his presence, through perception.

Without taking into account "hidden senses" (like verticality, temperature, duration, or pressure), our traditional five senses are generally not as acute or extensive as those of other animals. We do not have the hearing of dogs for ultrasounds nor the sense of smell — thousands of times more sensitive than ours — of fish (to say nothing of the male butterfly, significantly called *Satyr satyr*, which can detect the female's scent from kilometers away). We do not possess the proverbial eagle eye or the visual capacity of picking out only certain movements, like frogs do. We do not perceive ultraviolet like bees or infrared like chickens (a simple and ingenious experiment showed how, when hungry roosters were introduced into a dark room where some grains of corn were illuminated by colors of the spectrum, plus ultraviolet and infrared light, they pecked only at the feed situated in the area of warm colors and infrared).

There is, however, at least one of the five traditional senses in which the human species boasts a primacy, and that is touch, because of our delicate skin, which lacks fur and biological armor like pachyderms or animals equipped with scales, cartilage, or carapaces. Touch involves the entire body, and is sensitive to heat and cold, to smoothness and roughness, to soft and hard, to the punch and to the caress. A history of the flesh would include an art of touch, erotica, and a series of tactile metaphors like "touch the heart." Moreover, touch also provides the sense of certainty, for example, touching with one's hand to ascertain the truth, like Saint Thomas the Apostle who checked the wound in Christ's side.

Touch is a sense that functions without intermittence, like hearing and unlike sight, whose functionality is interrupted by the eyelids. *Auditus sempre patet*, says Cicero: the ears are always open; they do not have eyelids that might close them (or that might open them to the blind sight of dreams). This is why, even at night, they notice either real dangers or those created for them by means of the imagination. Even the Bible, from the very beginning, shows that hearing is the organ of fear. Adam's first words after having eaten the fruit of the prohibited tree are: "I heard the sound of you in the garden, and I was afraid ... and I hid myself" (*Genesis* 3:10).

Touch also functions as an alternative sense for those who have had to close some "windows" — that is, for those who have lost their vision, or who never had it. And paradoxically, touch can be preferred over it. A blind woman, asked if she would like to have sight, responded to DIDEROT that "If it were not for curiosity [...] I would just as soon have long arms: it seems to me my hands would tell me more of what goes on in the moon than your eyes or your telescopes; and besides, eyes cease to see sooner than hands [cease] to touch"

[1] I am alluding to the title of the work, on a completely different subject, by LAZORTHES (1986) and SERRES (1985).

(DIDEROT 1978, p. 33; 1999, p. 153). He adds that with sensory defects, even the metaphysics of individuals change. If a philosopher, blind and deaf since birth, were to construct an image of a man, "he would put the seat of the soul at the fingers' ends, for it is from these that the greater part of the sensations and all his knowledge are derived" (ibid., p. 159; French ed., p. 31, also see p. 28).

If the senses can be modified by education (as anyone who has studied music or painting or who practices seeing and hearing will know), they can also be changed with technology. Not only through prostheses (from eyeglasses to hearing aids to recent systems of biological engineering that, through things like microchips, create artificial senses) but through virtual reality, which changes their constitution. For example, until now, touch has remained a private sense (unlike vision and hearing, which are public senses of distance, and imply the reciprocity of seeing and being seen, hearing and being heard): I touch an object, but no one else can share the same position with me at the same moment. However, if I now put on a helmet and gloves with sensors in the fingertips, together with others connected by the same virtual reality program, we can simultaneously have the same sensation of touching the corners of a cube in cyberspace.

After all, DIDEROT held that man was an incomplete being, endowed with faculties in an embryonic state that had yet to manifest themselves, and LESSING actually composed a work (published posthumously by his son Karl) demonstrating that more than five senses could be developed in man (see LESSING) — an idea shared by the Neapolitan Jacobin Vincenzio RUSSO who believed that, once having put an end to political oppression, new faculties could sprout that had theretofore remained contained in the wrapping of the old, even promoting "*the humanity of the fair sex*," which had been neglected up until that point (see RUSSO 1956, pp. 436–38).

All sensory deprivations and all possible presences in living things with senses different from our own (even those that that lead to perceiving things differently), presume the support of intelligence at some level. This is so not only because, as Wittgenstein said, "a thought echoes in every perception" or because, as is commonly said, we do not see with our eyes, but with our brains; rather, it is because, as Kant hypothesized, the senses can be different. But the rules of thought are equal among all the "rational beings" of the universe. (This is a model unknowingly taken up by NASA when it etches, on spacecraft and probes launched into deep space, Leonardo's image of the Vitruvian man, Einstein's formula $E=mc^2$, and the representation of the solar system — all under the assumption that these signs might be understood by anyone.) After all, according to a Chinese saying, two-thirds of what we see lies behind our eyes.

What lesson is to be drawn in the end from these considerations? It is that, despite all the possible errors, there is no insurmountable opposition between, on the one hand, the road that leads away from the senses (in the manner of

Plato or Novalis) to reach the essence of ideas, and then returns, enriched, to the senses and the world of perception; and, on the other hand, the path that invites us (in the manner of Empedocles or others) to develop and educate both the senses and inner life at the same time. It is a matter of opening the windows of the senses to aerate and oxygenate a musty inner life, to open oneself to the wonders and discoveries of the world and, at the same time, not let ourselves be completely absorbed by sensitivity, living minute to minute, forgetting ourselves and not preserving and increasing the resources that each person can "distill' within himself.

References

AUGUSTINE (1909): Confessions, X, 6, 8. Engl. trans. by PUSEY, E. B.: The Confessions of St. Augustine. – New York.
CICERO (1927): Tusculanae disputations, V, 38. Engl. trans. by KING, J. E.: Tusculan Disputations. – London.
DESCARTES (2006): Méditations métaphysiques. In: Oeuvres, ADAM, C./TANNERY, P. (Eds.) (Paris, 1897–1913), Vol. X, 1. Engl. ed. and trans. by ARIEW, R./CRESS, D.: Meditations objections, and replies. – Indianapolis.
DIDEROT, D. (1999): Lettre sur les aveugles [1749]. In: Œuvres completes, t. IV, Paris, 1978. Engl. trans.: Letter on the Blind. In Thoughts on the Interpretation of Nature and Other Philosophical Works. – Manchester.
EMPEDOCLES (2001): Physics. Engl. trans. by INWOOD, Brad: The Poem of Empedocles. – Rev. ed. Toronto.
HEGEL, G. F. W. (1995): Vorlesungen über Aesthetik, in Werke in zwanzig Bänden, (Frankfurt, 1970). Engl. trans. by KNOX, T.M.: Aesthetics: Lectures on Fine Art. – Oxford.
LAZORTHES, G. (1986): L'ouvrage des sens. Fênetres étroites sur le reel. – Paris.
LESSING, G. E. *Daß mehr als fünf Sinnen für den Mensch sein können.*
MARCUS AURELIUS ANTONINUS (2002): Memoirs, IV, 3. Engl. trans. by HICKS, C. Scot/ HICKS, D.V.: The Emperor's Handbook: A New Transation of The Meditations. – New York.
NIETZSCHE, F. (2009): Götzendämmerung. In: GESAMTAUSGABLE, Kritische/COLLI, Werke V. G./MONTANAR, M. (Eds.) (Berlin 1967). Engl. trans. by COMMON, T.: The Twilight of the Idols and the Antichrist.
NOVALIS (1992): Hymnen an die Nacht. Engl. trans. by MACDONALD, G.: Hymns to the Night, Spiritual Songs. – London.
NOVALIS (1915): Fragmente. In Werke, FRIEDMANN, H. (Ed.) – Berlin.
NOVALIS (1903): Blütenstaub. In Schriften, KLUCKHORN, P. (Ed.) in collaboration with SAMUEL, R., 1960–1975, Vol. II, p. 419. Engl. trans.: The Disciples at Saïs and Other Fragments. – London.
RUSSO, V. (1956): Pensieri politici [1798]. In: Giacobini Italiani, CANTIMORI, D. (Ed.), Vol. I. – Bari.
SAINT TERESA OF AVIL (1979): Libro de la Vida (1565). Engl. trans. by ALLISON, E. Peers: The Life — Life of the Holy Mother Teresa of Jesus/Saint Teresa of Avila. – London.
SERRES, M. (1985): Les cinque senses. – Paris.

Angelika Malinar

Sensory Perception and Notions of the Senses in Sāṃkhya Philosophy

In Indian philosophical traditions, the senses are regularly listed among the common constituents of being(s) shared by all inhabitants of the cosmos. It is generally accepted that the senses are the basis for any experience of the world and for the relationships living beings entertain with each other. The philosophical schools differ in their views on the structure and reality of the world and in their answers to the question of what is actually perceived by the senses. Some argue, for instance, that the senses are in contact with "outer" objects, while others are convinced that all we perceive are only "inner" mental constructions of the world.[1] Another issue is the number of the senses and of the cognitive faculties which process sense objects. While the Nyāya school of philosophy accepts the group of five senses also common in European philosophy,[2] Buddhist traditions add the mind (*manas*)[3] and speak of the "six seats" (*ṣaḍāyatana*).[4] Sāṃkhya philosophers postulate 11 senses by enlarging the group of six senses with five "senses of action" (*karmendriya*). Philosophical texts often concentrate on the former group of five or six senses since they are vital in interpretations of perception as a means of knowledge (*pramāṇa*). Yet, the variety of views on what is regarded as a "sense-faculty" should be kept in mind, in order not to take the "five senses" for granted as the common ground of all traditions. The senses are usually called *indriya,*[5] literally "capacity" or "power." This implies that they are endowed with a specific agency of their own which puts them in charge of their realms. The Sanskrit word "*indriya*," thus, makes "power" an important connotation of senses.

A certain ambiguity pervades the evaluation of the senses in most philosophical traditions, and the larger normative discourses connected to them. The senses are seen as being both instruments for obtaining knowledge as well as obstacles

---

[1] These positions are discussed, for instance, by MATILAL (1986).

[2] See, for instance, SERRES (1985).

[3] In Nyāya, the mind (*manas*) is classified as a separate substance (*dravya*).

[4] This group of the six senses belongs to the 22 *indriya*s, capacities of living beings, taught in Abhidharma Buddhism; see, for instance, Vasubandhu's discussion in *Abhidharmakośa* (2.1–21).

[5] It is not by chance that *indriya* is in Vedic literature often connected to Indra, the name of the king of the Vedic gods. It is also used for any special power of a god. Another word for the senses is *karaṇa*, instrument.

to it. Specific modes of engagement with the world are connected with the senses, such as sensitivity (*vedanā*), desire (*kāma*) or an appropriative attitude towards the objects. The senses are sometimes praised for allowing pleasure and enjoyment, while they are in other contexts depicted as troublemakers, as they follow inclinations which may lead a person astray and must, therefore, be controlled. The senses also play a prominent role in discourses about obtaining "higher" forms of cognition, states of "absolute being" (*brahman*, *nirvāṇa*), or transcendent entities such as God or "the immortal self" (*ātman*). In many instances, these attainments are depicted as an extraordinary mode of sensory perception, such as the visions of divinities, being touched by "absolute being," etc. All of this points to the overall importance of the senses and perception in philosophical discourse. In the following, this shall be put into more concrete terms with respect to Sāṃkhya philosophy, a school that has been particularly influential in the cosmology of Hindu religious traditions.

Senses as "constituents of being(s)"

The earliest evidence for the existence of a philosophical doctrine called Sāṃkhya can be dated around 3rd century BCE. The oldest available systematic treatise is the *Sāṃkhyakārikā* (SK) of Īśvarakṛṣṇa (ca. 4th century CE), which has been widely commented upon. The most important commentaries are the *Yuktidīpikā* (YD) from the seventh to eighth centuries, written by an unidentified author (7th–8th century CE), and the *Sāṃkhyatattvakaumudī* (STK) by Vācaspatimiśra (9th–10th century CE).[6] In systematized accounts of Sāṃkhya, the senses are included in the set of the 25 *tattva*s, "constitutents of being(s)," which are regarded as the common elements of which the world is made. The relationship between the *tattva*s is explained by means of a cosmological model which provides also the referential framework for the Sāṃkhya interpretation of perception (*pratyakṣa*) as a "means of knowledge" (*pramāṇa*).[7] The creation of the cosmos is explained as a gradual manifestation of the *tattvas*.[8] This process starts when the two "highest" *tattva*s, which are regarded as eternal and uncaused, get in contact with each

[6] An older, apparently extensive exposition of Sāṃkhya called *Ṣaṣṭitantra* is lost; see OBERHAMMER (1960). For a survey of Sāṃkhya texts, see LARSON/BHATTACHARYA (1987).

[7] The discourse on the "means of knowledge" (*pramāṇa*) is a characteristic feature of Indian philosophy. The number and definition of the *pramāṇas* vary in the philosophical schools, although the majority accepts "perception" (*pratyakṣa*) and "syllogism" or "inference" (*anumāna*).

[8] This model stands in contrast, for instance, with Vaiśeṣika philosophy, which explains the cosmos as being structured by a set of basic elements (*padārtha*) which are co-present, and entertain relationships such as inherence, causal relationships, etc. HALBFASS (1999) has called this "horizontal cosmology," in contrast to Sāṃkhya's "vertical cosmology." This is a helpful juxtaposition if one bears in mind that Sāṃkhya cosmology also includes "horizontal" features; see MALINAR (2003).

other: the conscious entity (*puruṣa*), which is devoid of any agency or creative power, and the single creative power or eternal "nature" (*prakṛti*), which is devoid of consciousness, but susceptible to the presence of the conscious entity. The causal agency of *prakṛti* is activated when a connection (*saṃyoga*) with the *puruṣa* is established.[9] Then, the causal potential of *prakṛti* unfolds by means of its three creative powers (*guṇa*)[10] which bring about the gradual, hierarchic manifestation of the remaining 23 *tattva*s. The latter are finite, but share as being products of *prakṛti* some of its characteristic features, such as agency and purposefulness.[11] When these 23 *tattva*s aggregate, individual bodies are produced, allowing the *puruṣa* to experience the world. What kind of body is produced depends on the cognitive status of the *puruṣa*, that is, the degree of "discriminative knowledge" already obtained.[12] Each body, and in fact the whole corporeal world, are only produced in order to fulfil the two purposes ascribed to the conscious entity: experience (*darśana*; lit.: "viewing") of the world, and liberation (*kaivalya*; lit.: "isolation") from it. The ultimate goal of liberation is brought about by obtaining "discriminative knowledge" (*vijñāna* or *jñāna*), and this happens when the conscious entity (*puruṣa*) understands its separateness and freedom from the world created by *prakṛti*.

The cosmology implies a hierarchy of "higher" and "lower" principles of being(s) based on a decrease of causal power and size at each stage. This decrease is implied in the gradual transformation (*pariṇāma*) of the creative powers of *prakṛti*, in which "higher," that is, the larger, more powerful and subtle constituents morph into the "lower," that is, the smaller, less powerful and less subtle ones. This process ends in the manifestation of the five "gross elements:" water, earth, and so on. The *tattva*s which emerge first, such as the *buddhi* (faculty of discrimination), are thus larger, more subtle, and more powerful than the *tattva*s that follow them. The conceptualization of the senses is embedded in this cosmological model because the 11 *indriya*s belong to the 23 finite *tattva*s produced by *prakṛti*. As already mentioned, the group of the 11 senses comprises five "senses of cognition" (*buddhīndriya*), i.e., ear,

---

[9] Different answers are given to the question why this connection happens at all. According to Vācaspatimiśra, it results from a wrongful identification of the *puruṣa* with the agency of *prakṛti* (see ARUGA 1993), while the author of the YD stresses the teleological aspect of the connection between *puruṣa* and *prakṛti* (see MALINAR 2010a).

[10] More often than not, the *guṇa*s are rendered as "qualities;" the author of the YD interprets them as "subtle powers" (*sūkcmāḥ śāktayaū*; YD on SK 9, p. 109, 15–17; on SK 16, p. 164, 27–28. The three *guṇas* are *sattva* (luminosity, purity, clarity), *rajas* (dustiness, agility, passion), and *tamas* (darkness, inertia, dullness); see also Malinar (2010b).

[11] See SK (10–11) for the similarities and differences between *prakṛti* and its products.

[12] The range of bodies that can be produced is limited to a set of 14 species (cf. SK 53). On the delimitation of species and *tattva*s, see MALINAR (2003).

skin, eyes, tongue, and nose, five "senses of action" (*karmendriya*), i.e. speech, hands, feet, anus, genitals, and the mind (*manas*) as the 11th. Each sense is accorded a specific function or agency (*vṛtti*), such as listening, touching, seeing, and so on.[13]

The senses are said to be modifications of the preceding *tattva*, ego-consciousness (*ahaṃkāra*), which is, in turn, a product of *buddhi*, the faculty of judgement and discrimination. Cosmologically and ontologically speaking, the senses are modifications of a cognitive capacity; they are not products of the gross material elements as is maintained, for instance, in Nyāya and Vaiśeṣika philosophy. Rather, the senses are regarded as being made up of subtle matter, and take residence in the material sense-organs made of the gross elements.[14] The author of the *Yuktidīpikā* explains that the material sense-organs are the *adhiṣṭhāna*, the "seats" or "operational bases" from which the sense-faculties operate (*vṛtti*).[15] The function of the *indriya*s is not confined to their bases because they own a "special power" (*śaktiviśeṣa*) which allows them to go out and grasp the objects not within the reach of the gross sense-organ. Their contact with sense-objects does not require any direct physical contact between, for instance, the eye and the color blue. In the YD, this "pervasiveness" (*vyāpakatva*) of the senses is taken as an argument supporting the Sāṃkhya view of their being produced by "ego-consciousness" and not by the elements, as argued in Nyāya-Vaiśeṣika:

> How can the senses [when they are thought to be] made up of the elements, deal with a distant object since they are only functioning in [direct] contact [with the object]? But they (the senses) are made of ego-consciousness [and indeed deal with a distant object] because of their pervasiveness.[16]

The group of eleven senses is not the only product of the principle of ego-consciousness (*ahaṃkāra*). It produces the group of five subtle sense-realms (*tanmātra*) as well. "Subtle" means that they are "unspecified" (*aviśeṣa*); they are sound (*śabda*), touch (*sparśa*), form/color (*rūpa*), taste (*rasa*) and smell (*gandha*) "as such," In this way, the senses and the unspecified sense-realms

[13] Cf. SK (26–27) and the commentaries on it. On the order of the senses, see below. The functions (*vṛtti*) of the senses are: desiring (mind), listening (ear), touching (skin), seeing (eye), tasting (tongue), smelling (nose), speaking (speech), grasping (hands), walking (feet), excreting (anus), and sexual delight (genitals).

[14] The production of an individual gross (*prabhūta*) body starts at the moment of conception, and provides the "vessel" which the "subtle, transmigrating body" (*liṅgaśarīra*) inhabits; see SK (39–42).

[15] Cf. YD on SK (26, 197, 31–32). This distinction between the gross sense-organs and the more subtle sense-faculties is also drawn in other traditions, for instance in Abhidharma Buddhism.

[16] *Bhautikāni cendriyāṇi kathaṃ prāpyakārīṇi dūravartini viṣaye bhaveyuḥ/ āhaṃkārikāṇāṃ tu teṣāṃ vyāpakatvād* […] (YD on SK 28, 203, 27–28).

are placed at the same level since they are both produced by the same "higher" *tattva*, ego-consciousness (*ahaṃkāra*), which implies that they have a share in its appropriative, "egotistic" tendencies. In contrast to the senses, the subtle sense-realms are cosmologically productive,[17] which means that they transform themselves into the next group of *tattva*s, the five gross elements (*mahābhūta*). The five elements are said to be produced through a gradual transformation-*cum*-aggregation of the subtle sense-realms.[18] Thus, the first evolving element is the product of one subtle sense-realm, the second of two, and so on. Sound (*śabda*), the first subtle sense-realm, turns into the element ether (*ākāśa*). Next, touch (*sparśa*) in combination with sound becomes manifest in the element wind (*vāyu*). When sound and touch undergo a transformation when joined with color/form (*rūpa*), fire (*tejas*) emerges. Sound, touch and color, in combination with taste (*rasa*), turn into the element water. The set of all five sense-realms is completely manifest in earth (*pṛthivī*), which is produced when smell (*gandha*) joins the aggregated group of the preceding four sense-realms. In a next step, the elements can now aggregate in various combinations and form specific sense-objects (*viṣaya*). This structure also explains why the list of the senses starts with the ear, the list of the subtle sense-realms with sound, and the group of the five material elements with ether. Sound is the "highest," that is, the most subtle and pervasive of all the sense-realms, which is true of the corresponding element ether as well. Therefore, the group of the senses starts with the ear (SK 26). This cosmological correspondence between sound, ether, and ear applies to the other sense-realms, elements and senses as well (color, fire, eye, etc.).

The correspondence between the subtle sense-realms, the material elements, and the senses is a characteristic feature of the cosmological framework in which the interpretation of the senses and of sensory perception is embedded.[19]

---

[17] See SK (24–25). There are two significant differences between the senses and the subtle sense-realms with regard to their cosmological position. First, the senses are produced by the "pure" or "luminous" (*sattva*) causal power of ego-consciousness, while the subtle sense-realms are products of its "dark" or "dense" (*tamas*) causal agency. This mirrors the status of the senses as belonging to the "brighter" cognitive apparatus of the individual, which contrasts with the sense-realms as belonging to the "denser" materiality of the body. Second, the senses have no productive potential, that is, they do not produce another *tattva*. They are therefore classified as being *vikāra*, mere products. The subtle sense-realms, in contrast, are endowed with causal potential, and produce the next group of *tattva*s. They are, therefore, classified as being "products that are productive" (*prakṛtivikṛti*); on this important distinction, see MALINAR (2003).

[18] See the discussion of the different positions on this issue in the commentaries on SK by CHAKRAVARTI (1975, pp. 242*ff*).

[19] As is explained by the author of the *Yuktidīpikā* on SK 3: "when the [elements] earth etc. are produced by the subtle sense objects, different recipients in the form of corresponding sense organs are produced by the ego-consciousness" (*tanmātrair ārabdheṣu pṛthivyādiṣv ahaṃkārāt tadyogyaṃ gṛhakāntaram indriyalakṣaṇam utpadyate*; YD on SK 3, p. 65, 16–19). This suggests that the senses are produced when the subtle

The cosmological position of the subtle sense-realms explains why everything in the manifest world consists of a combination of sounds, tastes, colors, etc., which coagulate in different corporeal, elemental objects. Sensuousness is not an attribute or quality of elemental matter or of individual bodies, but rather its constitutive feature. A concrete visible or tangible object is a specification, an individualized form of the "higher" and more subtle sense-realms. Concrete objects manifest taste, smell, etc., as the qualities of their materiality and are in this way noticed by the senses, for instance, as taste in rain water or smell in flowers. They incite the activity of the senses as the latter are "naturally" (as products of *prakṛti* and via cosmological relatedness) attentive to sound, touch, color, taste, and smell.

Interpretation of sensory perception

This cosmology provides the referential framework for interpreting the role of the senses in the different modes of perception (*pratyakṣa*). From early times, perception has been discussed as implying different stages and modes of perception. This also applies to the exposition of Sāṃkhya in the SK and its commentaries. In the first, initial stage of perception, the senses are said to just engage in their natural mode of activity (*vṛtti*), which in SK 28 is defined as *ālocana*, "taking notice" or "attentiveness:" "The activity of the five senses [of knowledge] is defined as mere attentiveness in regard to color etc."[20] According to the YD, "mere noticing" means that the senses "grasp" (*grahaṇa*)[21] the object through assimilation: "'Grasping' means the functioning of the senses that consists in taking on the same form [as the object] due to the contact with the object."[22] The senses are able to change their form according to the object (*viṣayākārapariṇāmātmikā vṛttir*; YD on SK 28, 293, 28f.). This operation does not imply any identification or conceptualization of the object; it is "pure" content. This interpretation aims to exclude claims made by other philosophical schools which argue that the senses grasp an object at first in its general form, and afterwards the cognitive faculties ascertain the object in

sense-realms morph into the five elements. The specification can be connected to the fact that the *indriyas* have both the subtle sense-realms as well as the five elements as their objects (see also below). The correspondence between the sense-realms and the five material elements is the same as in Nyāya, although the latter postulates that the sense-realms are products of the elements.

[20] *Rūpādiṣu pañcānām ālocanamātram iṣyate vṛttiḥ* (SK 28).

[21] This "consumptive" activity of the senses is also indicated by another word which is sometimes used for the sense objects: *gocara*, (literally, "pasture for cattle"), which hints at the activity of the senses as being seen as "grassing," "grasping," "taking hold of" (for instance *Mahābhārata* 12.46.10; 12.240.14; 12.242.5 etc.).

[22] *Viṣayasamparkāt tādrūpyāpattir indriyavṛttir grahaṇam* (YD on SK 28, 203, 4–5).

its particular form.[23] In this connection, the senses are defined in the YD as being without "cognition" or "idea" (*apratyayam indriyam*; YD on SK 28). Rather, they bring the object to awareness before any identification based on discursive forms of knowledge is made. The author of the YD uses the terms *pratyaya* (conceptualization) and *apratyaya* (non-conceptualization) in order to distinguish the "mere" noticing of the senses from the cognitive classification of sense content.[24]

In the YD, still another qualification of the activity of the senses is adduced when it is pointed out that although the senses are devoid of cognition, they do not lack sensitivity towards each other. The attention given to an object by one of the senses does not leave the other senses unaffected, since they all function for the same purpose, namely, to get hold of the object. This interpretation is based on SK 31, which states: "Each (sense) functions in its own realm as functioning is caused by mutual intention."[25] This is explained in the YD as follows:

> When the form of a mango or a pomegranate fruit is observed by the eye, then the tongue, sensing (*saṃvedya*)[26] the activity of the eye which has come into contact with the object, is affected and eagerly intends to seize its object [i.e., taste]. When sensing the activity of the tongue, the feet start walking and the hands start grasping. This happens as long as the object is not brought within reach of the tongue. Then, the tongue proceeds to its object.[27]

---

[23] This is the case, for instance, in explanations of perception in the Nyāya school of philosophy, which postulates a non-verbal apprehension of a sense-object as a universal (*sāmānya*). At the beginning of his commentary on SK 5, the author of the YD mentions definitions of perception in the other philosophical schools and, in his comment on SK 28, rejects the idea that a sense-organ "grasps" a "universal." See also HARZER-CLEAR (1990, 334, note 9, and 306*ff*). For the Nyāya-Vaiśeṣika theory of perception, see PREISENDANZ (1989).

[24] While the distinction between two stages of perception is well established in the Nyāya and Buddhist schools, it is explicitly in place in Sāṃkhya only in Vācaspatimiśra's *Sāṃkhyatattvakaumudī*, who distinguishes between *nirvikalpa pratyakṣa*, "perception without conceptualization [of the object]," and *savikalpa pratyakṣa*, "perception with conceptualization." HARZER-CLEAR (1990) argues that this distinction is already implicated in the SK.

[25] *Svāṃ svāṃ pratipadyante parasparākūtahetukīṃ vṛttim* (SK 31).

[26] The author of the YD points out that this "sensitivity" does not imply any form of consciousness, and has to be understood "metaphorically" (YD on SK 31, 214, 13*ff*).

[27] *Yadā cakṣusā 'mradādimādirūpam upalabdhaṃ bhavati tadā rasanendriyam upāttaviṣayasya cakṣuṣo vṛttiṃ saṃvedya svaviṣayajighṛkṣayautsukyavad vikāram āpadyate, rasanasya vṛttiṃ saṃvedya pādau viharaṇam ārabhete hastāv ādānaṃ tāvad yāvad asau viṣayo rasanendriyayogayatāṃ <ā>nītaḥ/tato rasanaṃ svaviṣaye pravartate* (YD on SK 31, 213, 35–214, 4). In his commentary on SK 31, Vācaspatimiśra is more concerned with the situation that the functions of the senses do not intermingle

This passage qualifies the activity (*vṛtti*) of the senses as being characterized by eagerness (*autsukya*). The senses are prone to turn to their objects because they are eager to serve the purpose of the conscience entity (*puruṣa*), which is entangled in the corporeal world, and which will only through experiencing the world, find final release in the knowledge of its true being.[28] The activity of the senses is, thus, indispensable for obtaining the highest form of knowledge. This is one of the reasons why in Sāṃkhya philosophy as well as in the many theological-philosophical traditions influenced by it, we do not find any condemnation or negation of the senses. They are regarded as performing indispensable services to all cognitive processes and, thus, have their share in obtaining even the highest forms of knowledge. Such cognitive processes set in when the initial stage of perception as "mere awareness" turns into its second stage, and the object noticed by the senses is identified and conceptualized (*pratyaya* according to the YD; *savikalpa-pratyakṣa* according to Vācaspatimiśra). Here, the content of the senses is presented to the cognitive faculties for determination (*adhyavasāya*). At this stage, perception can become a means of knowledge (*pramāṇa*) as is stated in the definition of perception in SK 5: "Perception is the discernment of the sense-object of each [sense]."[29]

How does this work? Incited by the outside activity of the senses, the inner (*antar*) cognitive process starts with the activation of the mind, *manas*, which is the one and only sense which functions only inside the body. In contrast to the other senses, it has no fixed seat, but is viewed as a mobile entity. The mind is, thus, the "sense-in-between," mediating between the outwardly directed senses and the inner cognitive faculties, namely, ego-consciousness and the faculty of judgement.[30] This explains why the *manas* is also classified as belonging to the *antaḥkaraṇa*, the "inner instrument" or "cognitive apparatus," which consists of the mind, ego-consciousness and the faculty of discrimination (SK 33). The defining feature of the mind is *saṃkalpa*, imagination and volition, that is, wishful involvement with its objects.[31] Being an internal sense, without a seat connecting it to the outside world, the mind has access to the realms of all other senses. The necessity of regarding the mind as a separate sense is justified in the YD *vis-à-vis* an opponent. It is pointed out that the other senses are not capable of developing any desire towards their objects.

(*vṛttisaṅkara*). He compares the operation of the senses with a group of men, each taking his own weapon in order to overwhelm the other.

[28] This is explained in SK 31: "Only [to fulfill] the purpose of the conscious entity is the reason [for this functioning of the senses]. Nobody causes the instrument [the sensual apparatus] to be active" (*puruṣārtha eva hetur na kenacit kāryate karaṇam*).

[29] *Prativiṣādhyavasāyo dṛṣṭam*, SK 5.

[30] Cf. SK 27 on *manas* as a sense functioning in two different directions.

[31] The connotation "desire" is emphasized in a list of synonyms for *saṃkalpa* given in the YD (*abhilāṣa*, desire, *icchā*, wish, *tṛṣṇā*, thirst).

Furthermore, it is argued that the mind is the only sense whose objects are not fixed, while they are fixed in the case of the other senses. This implies that the mind has access to all the objects of the "seated" senses and, therefore, receives all the data which form the bases of its wishful intentions. While the "seated" senses are only eagerly turning to an object, the mind usually develops wishful intentions when it is drawn to the activity of the outward directed senses. Conversely, only when the mind is sensitive to the activity of a sense-faculty can a sense-object be noticed by the "cognitive apparatus." When the mind is elsewhere, the sense-content is not processed, and phenomena like "seeing without seeing" occur. Another characteristic feature of the mind is that it has access to "objects in all three times" (*trikālaviṣayatva*). The activities of the mind are not restricted to actually present objects, as is the case with the other senses, but can also turn to past and future objects. The relationship between the mind and the other senses works both ways. The mind may follow the senses when they attend to an object, and the senses may become active when the mind wishfully imagines an object of the past.[32]

The author of the YD emphasizes that such activation of the senses by the mind should not be understood as if the senses were made an instrument of the mind. The mind has no power to use the senses as a craftsman may use his tools. Rather, when the senses are in touch with the mind imagining a particular object, they by themselves eagerly set out to get it.[33] This self-activation of the senses is based on the referential framework of Sāṃkhya cosmology. One of its most important implications is that all constituents of being(s) (*tattva*) produced by the causal power and materiality of nature (*prakṛti*) are considered to resemble their cause in certain respects.[34] One of the similarities is that they all are endowed with an agency of their own; another is that they are all driven by the general purpose to serve the conscious entity in its experience as well as liberation from the world. Therefore, all products of *prakṛti* have a natural inclination and eagerness (*autsukya*) to be active, thereby fulfilling this purpose. This explains why the cognitive as well as the sensual faculties can become active independently from each other: the mind does not need the senses for its wishful imaginations; the other senses do not need the mind in order to be active and "grasp" their objects. The power of the senses consists also in their being self-active; they do not need to be employed or activated as they are neither passive recipients of data nor mere tools employed by cognitive faculties.

---

[32] "When the mind imagines an object of this or that sense with the purpose of obtaining it, that very sense will eagerly turn [to that object]" (*yasya yasyendriyasya viṣayaṃ mano dhāyaty abhisampattyarthena tasya tasyautsukyaṃ pravṛttiś ca bhavatīti*/ YD on SK 31, 214, 28–29).

[33] YD on SK 31, 214, 33–35 (*svaviṣayasaṃkalpānugṛhītasya manasaḥ saṃśparsāt svayam evendriyaṃ svaviṣayaṃ pratipadyate*).

[34] See SK (10–11) on the similarities and differences between *prakṛti* and its products, and MALINAR (1999).

In the context of interpretations of "perception" (*pratyakṣa*), the outgoing senses are said to function for the inner cognitive apparatus (*antaḥkaraṇa*) as gates (*dvāra*) through which the outside objects are passed on. Only the senses, being the doors to the world, are in direct contact with outer objects; the cognitive faculties are not.[35] However, which objects are actually passed on depends on the cognitive apparatus as well and, therefore, it is called the "gatekeeper" (*dvārin*). While the senses are needed in order to notice anything at all, the cognitive apparatus is needed in order to produce an "idea" (*pratyaya*) about the sense-content. The author of the YD says:

> Conceptualization is a determination [of an object made] by relying on the activity of the sense-organ with regard to the object [i.e. the sense having assumed the form of the object] such as 'This is a cow; it is white; it is running.'[36]

Only when the "inner cognitive apparatus" (*antaḥkaraṇa*) is taking up the sense-content a "cognition" can be produced which can serve as a valid form of knowledge (*pramāṇa*).[37] It is due to *buddhi* that an object can be determined as being "this" or "that." Furthermore, decisions are made whether to obtain, avoid or simply ignore it.[38] In the case of the perception of the cow just quoted, it would be the task of the *buddhi* to decide whether "I" should catch the cow, watch it or leave it alone.[39] The appropriation of the sense-content with the word "I" is the contribution of "ego-consciousness" (*ahaṃkāra*) to the process of perception: it marks the transition from "This is a cow" to "I see the cow." It is up to the *buddhi* to decide what "I" should do with the sense–content; if there is no evaluation in place, "I" usually tends to follow its own fancies (*abhimāna*).[40]

---

[35] Cf. YD on SK (26, 197, 16).

[36] *Tathā viṣayendriyavṛttyanukāreṇa niścayo gaur ayaṃ śuklo dhāvatīty evamādiḥ pratyayaḥ* (YD on SK 28, 203, 6).

[37] This structure also provides the referential framework for discussing error, illusion and delusion when the identification of the perceived object is proven wrong. In this connection, the malfunctioning of sense-organs (*indriyaghāta*; SK 7), which prevents the correct "grasping" of an object, is also discussed. A favorite example in commentaries is the *timira*, a type of eye disease, which results in the erroneous representations of the objects. SK 7 deals with different reasons which prevent sensory perception. On the different theories of error in Indian philosophy, see Potter (1963).

[38] See YD on SK 23. Here, the function of the *buddhi* is defined as "determination" (*adhyavasāya*), which is made the defining feature of perception as a means of knowledge in SK 5.

[39] This situation is explained by Vācaspatimiśra with the example of the reactions to the gradual recognition of a man about to shoot a deadly arrow (STK on SK 30).

[40] See YD on SK (24, 195, 6–7), and STK on SK 36 comparing the processing of the content of the senses with the way in which taxes are collected in individual households and are passed on to the king.

The capacity of the *buddhi* to decide on the sense-content, and to control the senses and the lower cognitive faculties allows sensory perception to be described from two perspectives: firstly, as a "bottom-up" process that starts with an object noticed by the senses, and ends with its conceptualization and evaluation;[41] secondly, as a "top-down" process in which the controlling power of the *buddhi* determines which object should be perceived, and how it should be dealt with. While the other cognitive faculties either indulge in wishful involvement (mind) or egotistic fancies (ego-consciousness), the faculty of discrimination (*buddhi*) allows evaluating the object according to certain criteria, such as an earlier decision to fast or its knowledge about the detrimental effects of certain types of food, etc. The *buddhi* then either overpowers or supports the activity of ego-consciousness, mind and senses. How the faculty of discrimination (*buddhi*) tends to decide and exercise control depends on its disposition. In SK 23, eight basic types of such cognitive dispositions (*buddhibhāva*) are listed which influence the general attitude of an individual towards the activities of the senses. At the one end of the spectrum, these dispositions include individuals indulging in all kinds of sensual appropriations and showing no interest in, say, intellectual endeavors, or not caring very much about the consequences of their indulgence. At the other end of the spectrum are those who tend to relinquish sensual gratification for the sake of obtaining knowledge and true insight: Yogins for instance, or even better, followers of Sāṃkhya philosophy.

Depending on the disposition of the *buddhi* and the capacity of the individual to determine sense-objects and control the agency of the senses, perception can also take the form of a controlled, deliberate activity incited by the *buddhi*. This "top-down" view on the senses and perception is further elaborated in teachings on the methods of controlling the agency of the senses. The ability to control the senses is part of any cultivation of knowledge, which is made a primary goal not only in Sāṃkhya texts, but also in normative discourses supporting ascetic values. Here, the necessity to control, restrain, and even "conquer" the senses is stressed.[42] Only then, it is argued, can the senses be used for other purposes, be they social functionality or liberating insight. The cosmology of Sāṃkhya explains not only the power of the senses but also why they can be

[41] Compare also the description in YD on SK (33, 217, 19–23). Another aspect of the process is taken up in SK 30 when it is pointed out that the senses and the cognitive apparatus operate both sequentially as well as simultaneously when perceiving an object.

[42] The whole complex of concepts and practices can be conveniently summarized with a term used in ascetic as well as normative texts: *indriyajaya*, the conquest of the senses. As an example of an ascetic text, see *Yogasūtra* (2.41, 55, 3.47), and for the employment of this notion in political contexts see, for instance, *Mahābhārata* 5.127.21–29, stressing that a king needs be one who has "conquered the senses" (*jītīndriya*), and *Arthaśāstra* 1.16; see also MALINAR (2007, pp. 45, 264*ff*).

overpowered by the *buddhi*, being the "higher" and, thus, more powerful constituent of being(s) (*tattva*). If the *buddhi* is perfectly in charge of the cognitive processes, the functioning of the senses is turned into a "top-down" process which allows directing the agency of the senses at selected objects. This allows the perception of not only gross objects, but also of the activity of the senses themselves as well as of more subtle objects, such as higher spheres of the cosmos. The control of the senses by the *buddhi* results in what can be called "ascetic" modes of perception that have either such "higher" realms as their object, or make the senses the object of contemplation or detached observation, which ultimately results in relinquishing all desires. Another form of perception, also based on controlling egotistic appropriations of the sense-objects, is the aesthetic mode, which differs from the ascetic in that it does not aim at overcoming, but refining the involvement with the world of sense-objects.[43]

Ascetic and aesthetic modes of perception

In the context of the SK and its commentaries, methods of sense-control are often discussed in connection with Yogins, followers of traditions of meditation and ascetic practices that result in "dispassion" (*vairāgya*) towards the world and its objects. This indifference eventually brings the Yogin in a position of power (*aiśvarya*) over the principles of being(s) (*tattva*) and the cosmic realms (*bhūvana*) they perceive. Such powers regularly include extraordinary forms of perception, such as being able to listen to all sounds anywhere in the world.[44] Yoga practices allow perceiving not only the gross material world in a certain way, but to make the senses perceive the subtle sense-realms (*tanmātra*) and other abstract *tattva*s such as *prakṛti*.[45] In SK 34, it is stated that both specified (*viśeṣa*) as well as non-specified (*aviśeṣa*) entities are the objects of the senses. The author of the YD explains that the range of objects which can be perceived by the senses depends on the "perceiver" (*pratipattṛ*), that is, on the "purity" of his or her senses. The gods (*deva*) have "pure" (*viśuddha*) senses, and perceive the subtle objects even before the gross ones; the Yogins are able to do the same, but only after they have managed the gross objects — "however," says the author of the YD — "our senses perceive only the gross objects because

[43] See also YD on SK (5, p. 82, 24–26), on different modes of perception.

[44] The perception of Yogins (*yogipratyakṣa*) plays an important role in the delineation of the methods for obtaining liberating knowledge not only in Sāṃkhya, but also in several other philosophical and theological traditions; see the essays in FRANCO (2009). For an analysis of the role of Sāṃkhya cosmology in explaining the extraordinary powers of Yogins, see MALINAR (2012).

[45] For an analysis of the description of a (misunderstood) perception of *prakṛti* by a Yogin in the YD, see MALINAR (2010a).

they are covered with darkness."[46] "Purity" here signifies the absence of desire and, thus, a high degree of knowledge; "darkness" is the opposite. It comes as no surprise that "passion" (*rāga*) is mentioned as the representative of the "abstract" realms "dispassioned" Yogins are said to perceive. The structure of control which allows such perception is not extensively dealt with in the commentaries to the SK,[47] but is a recurrent topic in texts on sense-control connected to Sāṃkhya, as for instance in the *Upaniṣads*, the *Mahābhārata* epic (including the *Bhagavadgītā*) and Purāṇa literature. Almost emblematic is the comparison of the senses with the horses of a chariot (i.e. the body) which need to be harnessed by a skilful chariot-driver (*buddhi*) who uses the mind as reins. As is explained in the *Kaṭha-Upaniṣad*:

> Know the self[48] as a rider in a chariot, and the body, as simply the chariot. Know the intellect (*buddhi*) as the charioteer, and the mind (*manas*), as simply the reins. The senses (*indriya*), they say, are the horses, and the sense objects are the paths around them. [...] When a man lacks understanding, and his mind is never controlled; his senses do not obey him, as bad horses, a charioteer. But when a man has understanding, and his mind is ever controlled; his senses do obey him, as good horses, a charioteer.[49]

As a result, one is able to actually obtain one's goal without getting diverted by the senses let loose. Moreover, one is able to stop the self-active senses and turn them to objects of Yogic meditation as described in another passage from the *Kaṭha-Upaniṣad* (6.10–11): "When the five senses of cognition are stilled, together with the mind, and not even the faculty of discrimination (*buddhi*) moves — this they call 'highest state.' When the senses are firmly fixed [on one object] they call this 'Yoga'" (6.10–11).

Another result is that it becomes possible to observe the mere functioning of the senses without getting involved in them. In this situation, the sense-activities again become the mere impersonal and physical activities which they actually are. This is described in the following passage of the *Bhagavadgītā* (5.8–9) dealing with the detachment of an accomplished ascetic:

> 'I do nothing at all' — this is what the accomplished one, the knower of reality shall think when he sees, hears, feels, smells, eats, walks, dreams, breathes, talks,

---

[46] YD on SK (24, 218, 3–5).

[47] There is a brief discussion of practices of detachment in YD on SK 23, and a critical account of the Yogin's perception of *prakṛti*(s) in YD on SK 45 and 50; see MALINAR (2010a). These perceptions are usually described visually, that is, as "seeing." For a tactile "perception" of the highest level of being (here called *brahman*), see *Bhagavadgītā* 6.28 and MALINAR (2007, pp. 120–28).

[48] The embodied, immortal self (*ātman*) is equivalent to *puruṣa*, the conscious entity of the SK.

[49] Cf. *Kaṭha-Upaniṣad* 3.3.–6, translation by OLIVELLE (1996, pp. 238–39).

excretes, grasps, opens the eyes and shuts them, because he bears in mind that 'the senses are occupied with the sense-objects.'[50]

This state of being "detached while active," or more precisely, being engaged in impersonal activities,[51] is a characteristic feature of the behavior of an ascetic or Yogin when he is not engaged in other forms of meditation in which the senses are withdrawn from their outer objects and directed at "higher" objects. The latter is described as follows: "When he entirely withdraws his senses from their objects like a tortoise withdraws its limbs, his insight is firmly established" (*Bhagavadgītā* 2.58). The image of the tortoise is frequently used in order to illustrate Yogic withdrawal and concentration on higher, more subtle realms as described in the same passage: "The sense-objects vanish for a person, who no longer takes them, with the exception of drink; but also drink disappears for him who has seen the highest."[52] What is perceived at such stages of meditation is interpreted differently in Indian philosophical and theological traditions. In Sāṃkhya texts, stress is placed on the stability (*sthiti*) and transparency (*prasāda*) of the *buddhi*, which are the prerequisites for understanding the fundamental difference between the material world and the conscious entity and thus for obtaining "liberating" knowledge.

When dealing with the attainment of this liberating knowledge, the SK draws on the image of a theatre performance.[53] The recognition that the conscious entity is actually free from the corporal world is compared with the moment a spectator watching a theatre performance realizes that the play he was engrossed in has nothing to do with him at all. Previously, the spectator had appropriated the play by identifying with this or that actor, suffering and rejoicing with him or her. Now, he or she has become an insightful spectator, watching the play without such identification. The embodiments which the conscious entity has taken on during the involvement with the world are, thus, nothing but the roles and costumes of an actor (SK 42). This is understood when liberating insight sets in, and this stops the theatre

[50] *Naiva kiṃcit karomi iti yukto manyeta tattvavit / paśyañ śṛṇvan spṛśañ jighrann aśnan gacchan svapañ śvasan//5.8/ pralapan iva sṛjan gṛhṇann unmiṣan nimiṣann api / indriyāṇi indriyārtheṣu vartanta iti dhārayan//5.9*; see also MALINAR (2007, pp. 108–20).

[51] The ability to stay detached while being active in the world is made a criterion which distinguishes "true" Yoga practice (also called *karmayoga*) from the wrong one. The latter is a form of meditation in which an inactive "Yogin" constantly thinks of the sense-objects he seemingly has relinquished; see BhG 3.6–7 and MALINAR (2007, p. 80*ff*).

[52] *Bhagavadgītā* 2.59; see MALINAR (2007, pp. 75–79).

[53] The theatre image is also used in the description of Yogic insight in texts belonging to the philosophical-theological school of Kashmir Śaivism; see *Śivasūtra* 3.9–11 (8th–9th century) and Kṣemarājā's commentary *Vimarśinī* (11th century); for an analysis, see MALINAR (2004).

performance for the one spectator "who has seen." This is described in SK 59 as follows: "Like an actress who has shown herself to the audience stops acting, *prakṛti* withdraws when she has shown herself to the conscious entity (*puruṣa*)."[54] When the conscious entity stops identifying with the play, its involvement has stopped, it has seen that the play has nothing to do with it — even if the performance continues for others still lost in identification. This is described in SK 65–66 as follows:

> *Prakṛti* [is what] the conscious entity sees, who like a spectator remains seated being himself [or: being unharmed/in good spirits]. The one (the spectator/*puruṣa*) (thinks): 'I have seen her'; the other (the actress/*prakṛti*) withdraws (and thinks): 'I have been seen.'[55]

This metaphorical description of obtaining liberating knowledge draws on what can be called the aesthetic mode of perception. While the aesthetic mode is also based on controlling the usual process of appropriating sense-objects, it does not aim at abandoning the involvement with the agency of the senses. Rather it aims at the refinement and intensification of sensory perception. The earliest Indian source for the idea that there is something like an "aesthetic" mode of perception is the "Treatise on Theatre" (*Nāṭyaśāstra*; 2nd–3rd century CE) ascribed to Bharatamuni.[56] This form of perception does not result in a clear discernment of an object, but culminates in experiencing a peculiar form of "relish" or "delight", which is called *rasa* — "tasting the taste" of the theatre performance. It is described as a form of "relish" which differs from the usual consumptive attitude in which the sense-objects are simply "swallowed." In the *Nāṭyaśāstra* (6.36*ff*), it is pointed out that the experience of *rasa* is possible because there is something to be tasted (*āsvādyatva*). This is illustrated by comparing the production of *rasa* in theatre with the preparation of a refined dish containing an exquisite combination of spices. This is similar to the aesthetic perception of art which is also about being able — intellectually as well as sensually — to "taste the taste" of the art of theatre. This is only possible if one is a "connoisseur" (*suhṛdaya*) who is able to understand the art of theatre and, therefore, does not indulge in identifications with the characters of the play. The discourse of "I" and "mine" is stopped for once. This "tasting the taste"

---

[54] *Raṅgasya darśayitvā nivartate nartakī yathā nṛtyāt / puruṣasya tathātmānaṃ prakāśya vinivartate prakṛtiḥ //* SK 59 /.

[55] *Prakṛtiṃ paśyati puruṣaḥ prekṣakavad avasthitaḥ svasthaḥ// SK 65 / dṛṣṭā mayety upekṣaka ekaḥ / dṛṣṭāham ity uparamaty anyā / sati saṃyoge 'pi tayoḥ prayojanaṃ nāsti sargasya//* SK 66 /.

[56] Although it seems highly probable, it cannot be taken for granted that Īśvarakṛṣṇa knew the *Nāṭyaśāstra*. In any case, the theatre image is sufficiently complex to suggest his familiarity with an aesthetic discourse on theatre.

(*rasa*) is a peculiar form of perception in which not only all appropriations, but also all discursive and intellectual classifications are suspended.[57]

Thus, not only ascetic modes of perception imply advanced skills in the removal of consuming, ego-oriented appropriations, but also aesthetic ones. Both result, each in their own way, in an attitude of a highly concentrated detachment from the sense-objects which allows either to view them differently or to direct them at objects of a different kind (such as a theatre-play or "sound as such"). The theatre image, as used in the SK, brings both aspects together. On the one hand, it draws on the distance and the knowledge a spectator must have in order to watch and "relish" a theatre performance as theatre (art). On the other hand, the image is used in order to point to a moment of a not unpleasant[58] disenchantment when it is recognized that all the suffering and the fun was nothing but theatre. At this moment, actor and spectator part company, with no intention of ever resuming the play. This is a situation a Sāṃkhya philosopher would cherish, but a true "connoisseur" (*suhṛdaya*) would certainly find not only undesirable, but perhaps also unbearable. In any case, all this is possible because of the eagerness and the agency of the senses which are controlled by extraordinary forms of concentration. This situation is not infrequently described as pleasant and gratifying in both ascetic as well as aesthetic discourses. While a connoisseur tastes an exquisite dish, but does not devor it, an ascetic will know "it's delicious, so better not taste it." The pleasures that may accompany ascetic and aesthetic modes of perception differ from more ordinary ones as they are based on distancing oneself from egotistic appropriations of the senses which are eagerly active in order to accomplish a goal they have the power to accomplish. In any case — it is the senses which make it happen.

References

ABHIDHARMAKOŚA (1923): L' Abhidharmakośa de Vasubandhu, traduit et annoté par Louis de la Vallée Poussin. – Louvain.

ARUGA, K. (1993): On Vācapatimiśra's explanation of the cause of samyoga. In: Journal of Indian and Buddhist Studies, Vol. 41, No. 2, pp. 32–36.

CHAKRAVARTI, P. (1975): Origin and Development of the Samkhya System of Thought. – New Delhi.

FRANCO, E. (Ed.) (2009): Yogic Perception, Meditation and Altered States of Consciousness. – Vienna.

---

[57] This interpretation is elaborated less in *Nāṭyaśāstra* than in later poetological literature; see GNOLI (1968).

[58] This is implied in the word "*svastha,*" used in SK 65 for describing the spectator who "has seen." It can mean either "being himself," or "being unharmed," or "in good spirits," that is, not truly affected by the performance.

GARBE, R. (1891): Der Mondschein der Sāṃkhya-Wahrheit, Vācaspatimiśras Sāṃkhya-tattva-kaumudī. In: deutscher Übersetzung, nebst einer Einleitung über das Alter und die Herkunft der Sāṃkhya Philosophie von R. GARBE. – Munich.

GAUḌAPĀDABHĀṢYA (1964): Les Strophes de Sāṃkhya (Sāṃkhyakārikā) avec le commentaire de Gauḍapāda: Texte Sanskrit et traduction annotée, ed. and tr. by ESNOUL, A.-M. – Paris.

GNOLI, R. (1968): The Aesthetic Experience according to Abhinavagupta. – Varanasi.

HALBFASS, W. (1999): Ākāśa: The elusive element. In BURGER, M. and SCHREINER, P. (Eds.) The perception of elements in the Hindu traditions. – Bern, pp. 159–180.

HARZER CLEAR, E. (1990): Īśvarakṛṣṇa's two-level perception: Propositional and non-propositional. In: Journal of Indian Philosophy Vol. 18, No. 4, pp. 305–340.

LARSON, G. J. (1979): Classical Sāṃkhya. – Delhi (2nd rev. ed.).

LARSON, G. J./BHATTACHARYA, R. S. (1987): Encyclopaedia of Indian Philosophies. Vol. 4, Sāṃkhya: A dualist tradition in Indian philosophy. – Princeton.

MAHĀBHĀRATA (1933–59): The Mahābhārata for the first time critically edited by a board of scholars. 18 Vols. – Poona.

MALINAR, A. (1999): Prakṛti as sāmānya (Nature as a common cause). In: Asiatische Studien, Etudes Asiatiques, Vol. 53, No. 3, pp. 619–643.

MALINAR, A. (2003): Completeness through Limitation: On the Classification of tattvas in Sāṃkhya Philosophy. In: Berliner Indologische Studien, Vol. 16–18, pp. 304–321.

MALINAR, A. (2004): Körper-Theater und Selbst-Erkenntnis. Konzepte von Erfahrung in der indischen Philosophie. In: MATTENKLOT, G. (Ed.): Ästhetische Erfahrung im Zeichen der Entgrenzung der Künste. Epistemische, ästhetische und religiöse Formen von Erfahrung vom Vergleich. – Hamburg, pp. 211–231.

MALINAR, A. (2007): The Bhagavadgītā: doctrines and contexts. – Cambridge.

MALINAR, A. (2010a): Something like liberation: Prakrtilaya (absorption in the cause(s) of creation) in Yoga and Sāṃkhya. In: BIGGER, A. et al. (Eds.), Release in Life: Indian Perspectives on Individual Liberation. – Bern, pp. 129–156.

MALINAR, A. (2010b:) Guna. In: JACOBSEN, K.A. et al. (Eds.): Brill's Encyclopedia of Hinduism. Vol. II: Sacred Texts and Languages, Ritual Traditions, Arts, Concepts. – Leiden, pp. 758–762.

MALINAR, A. (2011): Yoga Powers in the Mahābhārata. In: JACOBSEN, K.A. (Ed.), Yoga Powers: Extraordinary Capacities Attained through Meditation and Concentration. – Leiden, pp. 33–60.

MATILAL, B.K. (1986): Perception: An Essay on Classical Indian Theories of Knowledge. – Oxford.

MOTEGI, S. (1986): On tanmātra. In: Journal of Indian and Buddhist Studies, Vol. 34, pp. 958–953.

NĀṬYAŚĀSTRA (1998): The Nāṭyaśāstra: Text with introduction, English translation and indices in four volumes by UNNI, P.N. – Delhi.

OBERHAMMER, G. (1960): The Authorship of the *Ṣaṣṭitantram.* In: Wiener Zeitschrift für die Kunde Süd- und Südostasiens, Vol. 4, pp. 71–91

OLIVELLE, P. (1996): Upaniṣads. A new transation by OLIVELLE, P. – London.

POTTER, K. H. (1963): Presuppositions of India's Philosophies. – Englewood-Cliff.

PREISENDANZ, K. (1989): On ātmendriyamanorthasannikarṣa and the Nyāya-Vaiśeṣika theory of vision. In: Berliner Indologische Studien, Vol. 4–5, pp. 141–214.

SĀṂKHYATATTVAKAUMUDĪ (STK): Vācaspatimiśra's Tattvakaumudī: ein Beitrag zur Textkritik bei kontaminierter Überlieferung, SRINIVASAN, S. A. (Ed.). – Hamburg 1967.

SERRES, M. (1986): Philosophie des corps mêlés (1): Les cinq sens. Paris (Trans.: SERRES, M. 2008): The Five Senses: A Philosophy of Mingled Bodies I. – London and New York.

UPANIṢADS (1958): Aṣṭadaśa-Upaniṣad/Eighteen Principle Upaniṣads, LIMAYE, V.P. VADEKAR, R.D. (Eds.). – Poona.

YUKTIDĪPIKĀ (YD): Yuktidīpikā: the most significant commentary on the Sāṃkhyakārikā: critically edited, WEZLER, A./MOTEGI, S. (Eds.). – Stuttgart 1998.

Gérard Colas

Senses, Human and Divine

Senses have an important place in the relationship between the deity and the devotee in classical Hinduism. This chapter will briefly comment on sense-perception, including that of God, as discussed in classical epistemology. It will then examine several aspects of sense-perception in a religious context, especially with regard to divine incarnation and divine icons.

Human and divine senses and sense-perception according to epistemic systems

In Indian epistemic literature, perception is a fundamental instrument or means of knowing. It is defined as the contact of the senses with an object. Since it has a beginning and an end, it is temporary, limited in time and space. On the contrary, the perception in God, when it is mentioned in these texts, is believed to be eternal. The term *indriya,* which refers to the senses in epistemic systems, often signifies sense-faculties, not physical sense-organs. Senses are the five faculties of hearing, seeing, tasting, touching, and smelling. Some traditions add the internal sense (*manas* or *antaḥkaraṇa*)[1] as the sixth sense, through which pleasure and pain are known. The thesis of a unique sense, that of touch, is also mentioned. Logicians reject it because, if this were the case, the sense of touch would enable a blind person to see and, also, each sense-faculty would not have its specific objects.[2] The notion of the co-functioning of the senses is generally not admitted. According to Indian logic, the contacts of senses with their respective objects could be simultaneous,[3] but the perceptions (or cognitions) derived from them are successive. The internal sense puts the different sense-perceptions in order, and brings them one by one to the awareness of the perceiver.[4] In the absence of this function, sense-perceptions would be

[1] For instance, later texts of logic like the *Bhāṣāpariccheda* (57). The Vivaraṇa school of Advaita considers the internal sense as a sense-faculty, while the Bhāmatī school does not (SUNDARAM 1968, p. 19). It appears that early Buddhism (not taken into account in this paper) considered the internal sense as a sense-faculty (ROBINSON 1970, p. 163).

[2] See *Nyāyasūtra* (3, 1, 52–60); *Nyāyamañjarī*, Vol. 2, p. 53.

[3] See MATILAL (1986, pp. 207 [n. 21], 251, 253).

[4] *Nyāyasūtra* 1, 1, 16. For a discussion on the internal sense in Mīmāṃsā, see BHATT (1962, pp. 168–73, 169–70) on the succession of sense cognitions despite the

simultaneous, leading to confusion between different objects perceived and the sensations to which they give rise.

Although the contact of the senses with objects is essential for perception to take place, some Indian epistemic systems also recognize perceptions where this contact is absent. In yogic perception,[5] for example, objects that are not present to the senses are perceived by the yogis. These also include objects not perceptible to ordinary persons (like atoms, divine sounds), past and future events, etc.[6] Another extraordinary perception (*jñānalakṣaṇa*), which is accepted by logicians, is when a past perceptual knowledge is associated with a present perception.[7] For instance, one is said to perceive the fragrance of sandalwood seen from a distance, far beyond the range of the sense of smell.

What do the ancient Indian epistemic systems have to say about sense-perception by the gods? The question did not arise before the notion of gods' bodies became a topic of discussion in these systems, that is, clearly not before the 5th century. A main issue was how could an omniscient and eternal God be bound by a finite body, and attributed sensorial perceptions limited by time and space. The pre-12th century epistemic systems were reluctant to accept that God possesses a body and senses; and when they did accept this idea, it was under certain conditions. The school of Mīmāṃsā, for example, did not accept that gods possess a body. The non-dualistic (Advaita) school accepted from the point of view of ordinary life (*vyāvahārika*) that gods can take a body, but that question does not arise from the highest metaphysical point of view (*pāramārthika*), the non-dual Brahman being the only reality.[8] The logician Udayana (11th century) stated that God need not have a body, but can take one for a specific purpose: to teach Veda, for instance. But this body, unlike the human body, is free from the senses, and does not undergo pleasure and pain. Udayana stated that God's cognition too may be considered as direct perception, but does not depend on the senses and does not follow temporal succession.[9] A later logician, Viśvanātha (17th century) briefly mentioned

---

simultaneous contacts of sense-organs). According to Laugākṣibhāskara, Vedāntins consider that the simultaneity of sense cognitions or its absence depends respectively on the extension or contraction of the internal sense (see JHALAKĪKAR BHĪMĀCĀRYA 1978, p. 642).

[5] Variously called *yogaja-pratyakṣa*, *yogi-pratyakṣa*, etc. The Cārvāka school and the Bhāṭṭa subschool of Mīmāṃsā do not accept it: see *Mānameyodaya*, p. 26; BHATT (1962, pp. 160–163, 185).

[6] See *Bhāṣāpariccheda* 65–66 with *Siddhāntamuktāvalī*; *Mānameyodaya*, p. 26; *Yogasūtra* 3, 35 and its commentaries.

[7] See *Bhāṣāpariccheda* 65 with *Siddhāntamuktāvalī*. Advaita disagrees with this conception: for a discussion, see CHATTERJEE (1965, pp. 218–227). On *jñānalakṣaṇa* and *yogaja* perceptions, see also DATTA (1972, pp. 121–131).

[8] See COLAS (2004b, pp. 55–156, 2011; 2012 [chapter 7]); PARRINDER (1997, pp. 50–53).

[9] See CHEMPARATHY (1972, pp. 152, 173–174).

God's perception. According to him, God's way of perceiving does not correspond to ordinary human perception, for it is not produced (being eternal, it is without a beginning or end). It is also not divided according to the senses.[10] As it does not correspond to common human perception, we may compare it to yogic extraordinary perception that includes the faculty of seeing the past and the future.[11]

Though the Vedānta school of Viśiṣṭādvaita supported the notion of divine incarnation (*avatāra*) and body of God (SRINIVASACHARI 1970, pp. 157–160), it demarcated God's senses and their perception. It described the world as a body and God as the possessor of this body.[12] According to Rāmānuja's commentary on the *Brahmasūtras*, God has a form (*rūpa*), but it is divine, supranatural (*aprākṛta*), unique to Himself, and supremely auspicious. He enjoys odors, savors, etc. that are supranatural and unique to Himself.[13] Rāmānuja's presentation of the notion of divine incarnations (*avatāra*) is concessive, for although God takes birth at will in a great variety of forms, conditions, qualities and actions, he does not relinquish his own nature.[14]

Divine senses and sensuality in religious texts

The religious Hindu attitude, contrary to the views expressed in the epistemic systems, unreservedly attributes to gods a body, senses and sensibility as in human beings. The human aspects of gods' incarnations are insisted upon; but, at the same time, they are given a transcendental dimension surpassing time and space. The humanized form hides a divine essence which can manifest itself as a fierce force or an extraordinary appearance in certain circumstances and conditions. For instance, when Kṛṣṇa's foster-mother, Yaśodā, asks him to open his mouth to verify that he has not swallowed mud, she sees in it the entire universe (*Bhāgavatapurāṇa* 10, 8, 36–39). The human appearance of the god is characterized by an equivocality (between absence and presence, revelation and concealment) that devotional and Purāṇic works do not highlight.[15]

---

[10] *Siddhāntamuktāvalī* on *Bhāṣāpariccheda* (52), pp. 64, 65.

[11] See *Yogasūtra* 3, 36.

[12] See *Śrībhāṣya*, Vol. 1 (on sūtra 1, 1, 1): *passim*, for instance, pp. 234, 238, 239; *Vedāntasāra* (1, 1, 1): pp. 10, 19; SRINIVASACHARI (1970, pp. 221–250).

[13] See *Śrībhāṣya*, Vol. 1 (1, 2, 2), pp. 292–293.

[14] *Śrībhāṣya*, Vol. 2 (1, 3, 1), p. 3. In his introduction to his commentary on *Bhagavadgītā* (p. 11), Rāmānuja says that the Lord descends repeatedly into the worlds for incarnation (*avatīryāvatīrya*) without losing his own nature (*svasvabhāvam ajad eva*); see also his commentary on 4, 6. Rāmānuja adopts the common religious view that ritual propitiations of God please him, and that he rewards devotional actions (CLOONEY 1988, pp. 293–294). God can feel displeasure. However, according to DASGUPTA's analysis of Viśiṣṭādvaita (1975, pp. 296, 304), he does not feel such negative feelings as pain, and his anger does not relate to any disappointment.

[15] See MALINAR's discussion (2007, pp. 149–151).

Anthropomorphic forms of a god are of two kinds: incarnations and icons. The notion of incarnation has its roots in the Vedic conception of divine manifestation. Vedic texts called *Brāhmaṇas* state that the gods made themselves invisible but that specific ritual actions, helped by the utterance of Vedic formulas, can make them appear. The verb *āviṣ kṛ* and the word *āvirbhāva* describe such induced manifestations.[16] The *Kena-Upaniṣad* (3, 1–2) employs the verb *prādur bhū* to describe the apparition of the highest reality (*brahman*) to other gods. In the post-Vedic religion, the notion of incarnation becomes a central topic in mythological texts, especially of the followers of the god Viṣṇu. The most popular term to designate divine incarnations is *avatāra*; but *āvirbhāva* and *prādurbhāva*, both of Vedic origin, are also commonly used.[17] These mythological texts mention the physical form of the incarnations, but do not discuss their senses at any length.

The case of Kṛṣṇa, an incarnation of Viṣṇu, is particular. He not only possesses senses, but is also described as inclined to extreme sensuality. He is depicted as a lover or a charming cowherd who attracts the love of cowherdesses. Texts such as the *Bhāgavatapurāṇa*, Jayadeva's *Gītagovinda* and the poems of the Tamil *Divyaprabandham* describe this figure. Kṛṣṇa's frolics with cowherdesses are often depicted in erotic vocabulary, especially in the *Gītagovinda*. While textual descriptions are the main source for building the devotional representation of a sensual deity, they are not the only means; others include theatre, opera, songs, and music, like the Araiyar cēvai in South Indian temples[18] or the representations of scenes of the *Bhāgavatapurāṇa* in North India. Such repeated evocations of the divine lead the devotee to a sort of mystical obsession, where he is constantly aware of the god, his acts and his sensuality.

But this sensuality needs to be interpreted theologically to be accepted socially. For, in the absence of such a guide, the description of the deity's sensuality could be taken as a legitimation of sexual indulgence. Examples are not lacking of religious leaders misbehaving with women disciples under the pretext of enacting Kṛṣṇa's sensuality (Maharaj Libel Case, 1862). The interpretation of an amorous or erotic text as depicting an ideal mystical relationship with God is backed by deeply rooted literary and cultural traditions.[19] Two notions of Indian poetics may be mentioned in this context: those of *śleṣa* and *dhvani*. *Śleṣa* is a poetic figure that consists in creating a verbal double meaning.[20] It helps

[16] See (Krick 1975, pp. 25, 34–35, 51–72).

[17] See Colas (2012, chapters 1 and 4).

[18] For which, see Colas (2002, pp. 291–299).

[19] Hermeneutical commentary is not the only way of justifying divine behavior when it contradicts ordinary public morals. The *Bhāgavatapurāṇa*, for instance, legitimizes the socially reprehensible philandering of Kṛṣṇa by describing it as behavior prompted by divine *dharma*, distinct from mundane *dharma*: see Davis (2007, pp. 250–251).

[20] See De (1923, pp. 19–26); Colas (2004a, *passim*).

to encode and decode a spiritual meaning in profane expressions and descriptions. It is also a convenient device for seeing a supposedly hidden spiritual meaning in a profane text. The rise and development of the notion of *dhvani* in poetics (from the 9th century onwards) formed an important step in expanding the space of the interpretation of literary and religious works. The supporters of this notion clearly drew the distinction between the explicit meaning and the suggested meaning, and between mundane and supramundane aesthetic experience.[21] They promoted the notion of aesthetic bliss (*rasāsvāda*) as a supramundane experience brought forth by suggested meaning. Depiction of sensuality, made acceptable through theological hermeneutics, is also common to other religions. Catholicism accepts the mystical interpretation of Salomon's Song of Songs by Saint Bernard, and mystical marriages of various female saints with their Lord. Certain Sufi poems of an apparent erotic nature are said to convey mystical emotions and relations between God and the believer.

Icons and senses

The notion that a god also incarnates in an icon to receive worship from devotees is ancient; but the specific term *arcāvatāra*, "incarnation for (receiving) worship," was coined comparatively later in Vaiṣṇavism.[22] The conception of the icon as a person stems from two perspectives: legal and devotional. It is difficult to determine how these two combined. Perhaps donations of lands and buildings made to an icon (often in stone) were considered long-lasting and reliable in comparison to donations to human beings who represented the Buddha or the deity. *Stūpas* (monuments generally containing Buddhist relics) have also been considered as legal owners (Schopen 1997, pp. 128–131). The identification of *stūpas* as owners strengthens the hypothesis that the attribution of legal personality to an icon is distinct from the attribution of life to it.[23] The oldest testimonies of icons as owners are Buddhist and may date back to the 2nd century of our era. The icon-Buddha is considered a permanent resident in Buddhist monasteries. It (he) lives in the so-called Perfume Chamber (*gandhakuṭī*) of the monastery, where it is worshipped. As shown also by inscriptions from the 4th or 5th century onwards, this chamber is held as a cell or room reserved for the Buddha, where he can receive gifts (Schopen 1997, pp. 260, 263–278, esp. 271). Epigraphy from the 5th century onwards also testifies to the Hindu icon-deities residing in temples as legal owners.[24]

The identification of the icon as a living person — that is to say, possessing a body and senses — arises from devotion. The belief and perception by the

[21] See Colas (2004a, pp. 20, 22, 24).

[22] An early appearance of the word *arcāvatāra* dates from the 13th century (Colas 2012, chapter 4).

[23] See Colas (2012, chapter 4).

[24] Colas (2009, pp. 110–117); and Colas (2012, chapter 4).

devotee that the temple icon is a body possessing senses pervades the poems of the Ālvārs, the Vaiṣṇava Tamil saints of the 6th to 9th centuries.[25] This perception is described as a special kind of perception in religious texts. For example, the *Vaikhānasasmārtasūtra* (composed between the 4th and probably the 8th century) describes the practices of a class of yogi named *asaṃbhakta*. He has the deity as the unique object of his spirit and senses (COLAS 1996, p. 37). He practices meditation: he sees the divine form — that is to say, the icon — with his eyes, enjoys its perfume with his nose, and salutes it with his hands, etc. The earlier Ālvārs also refer to a yoga closely associated with devotion, as part of their spiritual practices (HARDY 1983, pp. 296–300). The devotional yoga of the Ālvārs and the *Vaikhānasasmārtasūtra* cannot be identified with the yogic perception that arises without contact with external objects as described by the philosophers. In yogic devotion, the senses are diverted from ordinary objects and directed to the icon-deity; they obtain mental and at the same time physical perception of the deity through their senses. The external icon and the image of the god are unified in the heart of the devotee (ibid., pp. 296, 300 [n. 146]).

The identification of the icon with a living person is realized through two simultaneous processes. In the first process, the ordinary perception is parenthesized and replaced by an ideal perception. Piḷḷai Lokācārya (13th century), for example, in his *Śrīvacanabhūṣaṇa* (195–196), states that the devotee should not pay attention to the material of which the icon is made — stone, metal or mud — but perceive it as a living being. The visual perception is, thus, transcended. A free-standing sculpture of the deity is a visual *trompe l'œil* that gives the impression of God's immediate presence in a tangible body. Perhaps, the representations of the deity in painting or bas-relief need more effort of the imagination from the devotee.

The other process facilitating the identification of the icon with a living person is the attribution of consciousness to it. This arises from two different operations: devotional and ritual. The devotee spontaneously attributes consciousness to the icon out of devotion. His relation with the god is direct and immediate: he goes to a temple to visit a living conscious god. As for ritual, it brings consciousness into the icon through the mediacy of elaborate rites during its solemn installation. Ritual manuals mention the introduction of consciousness (*cit*) into the icon, though they speak of power (*śakti*) introduced into the icon more often. The notions of divine consciousness and power are mutually inclusive; they are not clearly defined, these texts being ritual, not epistemological.[26]

Once it is accepted that the icon possesses consciousness, it is also assumed that it perceives through senses. Worship (*pūjā*) of the icon is meant to satisfy its senses. The functioning of the senses of the icon agrees with the definition

[25] See HARDY (1983, p. 269).

[26] See COLAS (2012, chapters 4 and 6).

of human perception. The icon possesses five senses. It sees, hears; enjoys perfume, incense, flowers, food (Hardy 1983, p. 290). Its senses grasp objects appropriate to them. Ritual manuals classify and organize offerings to the icon-deity into visible, tangible, consumable, audible, and fragrant (Colas 1996, pp. 303–304, 318–320). The capacity of the icon to enjoy through its various senses justifies the temple arts: music, singing, dancing, jewellery, painting, architecture, sculpture, gastronomy, all of which focus towards a single aim, namely, to satisfy the senses of God out of mere devotion, or to obtain in return material or spiritual benefits. These also create around the icon an atmosphere that stimulates the sentiment of devotion in the devotee.

The icon–deity is also believed to react negatively when its body is ill-fashioned or impaired in one way or another. The ritual manuals insist on the necessarily perfect condition of sense-organs in man-made icons. For instance, it is said that damage or imperfection in the eyes of the icon would result in blindness of the patron, and damage or imperfection in the ears would result in his deafness.[27] The discovery of such defects in the sense-organs of icons requires their material restoration accompanied by a rite of atonement.[28] The ritual manuals do not seem to distinguish in this context between physical sense-organ and sense-faculty as can be deduced from epistemic texts. It may be pointed out that a devotee perceives damages in the icon sentimentally, not with the severity of the prescriptive ritualism. There are instances where the devotee's affection towards the icon makes him perceive a living being beyond the sculptural representation, and consequently accepts any defect.[29]

The manuals of Hindu temple rituals often refer to four senses in the icon: vision, audition, taste, and touch. The gaze of an icon affects human beings as well as the deity. It emits a power that is intense and can be dangerous. It is said that Śiva (the deity and not only the icon) does not fix his gaze anywhere, so as not to destroy the objects he sees.[30] Probably for similar reasons, the gaze of

[27] See Colas (1986, p. 189).

[28] See, for instance, *Vimānārcanakalpa* (74, pp. 440–441; the restoration of defective limbs of the *pratyaṅga* category, i.e. ears, nose, etc., and ritual reinstallation of the icon; if the restoration is not possible, ritual disposal of the icon, making of a new icon similar to the previous one, and reinstallation).

[29] Anand Mishra (Heidelberg University) reports the following incident, which he heard in 2009 from Goswami Shyam Manohar (Kishangarh-Mumbai), a scholar of the Puṣṭimārga. The house of a Vaiṣṇava family in Mumbai caught fire and a burning wooden slab fell on the metal icon of Kṛṣṇa (Ṭhakurjī), deforming it. A son of the old lady wanted his mother to replace it with a new one. But the lady wished to continue worshipping the damaged icon. They asked Goswami Shyam Manohar to settle the issue. The lady argued that she was not worshipping an icon, but "her Ṭhakurjī," and that just as a mother would not replace a son who lost his feet or arms, she could not replace "her Ṭhakurjī" simply because he was deformed. Her argument was accepted by all, and she continued to worship the damaged icon.

[30] See, for instance, *Mudrārākṣasa* (1, verse 2, p. 8).

the icons of certain deities is said to be beneficial for a village, while the gaze of certain other deities, being fierce, is directed away from the village (COLAS 1996, pp. 301–302). The direction of the gaze of the icon-deity is of utmost importance according to ritual texts: it should be straight, not directed upwards, downwards or sideways (COLAS 1986, p. 172). This gaze is also receptive. The icon-deity should see pleasant or auspicious objects. The decoration of the temple, architectural beauty, etc. may be interpreted as part of this strategy of pleasing the deity.

This combination of receptivity and power of the divine gaze is well-illustrated by the ritual opening of the eyes of the icon which the Hindu ritual manuals customized and recorded from the 9th century onwards. This rite seems to have originally been a craft rite which priestly communities integrated into the ritual installation of icons. It consists in tracing the various parts of the eyes of the icon accompanied by mantras. In some manuals, the parts of the eyes are respectively identified with the five elements and the supreme god (COLAS 1986, p. 77). This act, perhaps, signifies the connection of the icon to the universe.[31] The opening of the eyes of the icon is immediately followed by the presentation of auspicious objects in front of the eyes, like a cow with her calf, clarified butter, honey, yogurt, milk, and various sorts of grains.[32] Manuals do not explain the meaning of this presentation; it could be a desire to please the deity or direct its gaze towards objects that are auspicious, but also perhaps to produce a peaceful state in the divine mind.

Darśana is a key notion in the relation between the icon-deity and the devotee. It may have different meanings in the ritual and devotional context. Referring to the devotee, it signifies his vision of the icon. This meaning seems to have been well-anchored in religious practice from the beginning of our era, as is shown by several Buddhist sources. Early Buddhist texts state that the aim of making icons of Buddha was to enable men to gain merits by contemplating it; seeing a holy Buddhist place was also comparable to a contact with a living presence of the Buddha residing there.[33] *Darśana* also refers to an action of the icon-deity: it designates the ostensible presentation of itself to favor the devotee with grace or proximity. In *belles-lettres*, *darśana* refers to the manner in which a person wishes to appear to the public.[34]

Another divine sense that is important in Hindu rituals is audition. The performance of rites is constantly accompanied by sounds of auspicious value, agreeable to the icon-deity: recitation of texts in Sanskrit and vernacular, music,

---

[31] However, the opening of the eyes should be distinguished from the introduction of power or consciousness into the icon, which takes place at a later stage in the rite of installation of the icon. For more details, see COLAS (1986, p. 77; 2010, pp. 327–333).

[32] See for instance COLAS (1986, p. 205).

[33] HUNTINGTON (1985, pp. 46–47); SCHOPEN (1997, pp. 117, 137).

[34] COLAS (2012, chapter 4).

devotional songs and shouts of victory. The production of *brahmaghoṣa*, literally, "murmur from sacred texts," during rites is prescribed, as it creates the auspicious atmosphere of Vedic sounds dear to the deity (COLAS 1996, pp. 245–249).

The sense of taste of the deity is often referred to, especially in temples dedicated to Viṣṇu. The icon-deity is offered a large variety of delicious food. The leftovers are offered or sold to the devotees. Food, thus, serves as a means of exchange between the god and his devotees. Elaborate recipes are sometimes found in Vaiṣṇava manuals of temple rituals.[35] In contemporary India, we find typical cuisines specific to religious groups and geographic areas. Certain temples are famous for a particular food preparation offered to the deity and which is sold to devotees after worship, for example, the *laḍḍu* of Tirupati Śrīveṅkaṭeśvara temple in Andhra Pradesh or the deep-fried doughnut (*goṭa*) of Ḍākor Ranchodrai temple in Gujarat.

Pleasing the sense of touch of the icon-deity can also be mentioned in this context. Manuals identify and list tangible homages to deities, like offering a seat to sit on, pouring water on the feet, applying perfumed paste, decorating with flowers, etc.[36] The sense of touch is also crucial in a socio-religious perspective. It is the object of strict social regulation in daily Hinduism. Hindus often avoid physical contact with those who are not socially on a par with them. As is well-known, touch is identified as a major source of social "pollution" in traditional treatises governing daily behavior. This concern is reflected in temple ritual manuals. According to some of them, the icon is purified from the touch of the craftsman during the rite of installation (COLAS 2010, p. 39). Once the icon is ritually installed, the icon can only be touched by the priests of that temple. The touch of non-priests requires atonement, especially when it comes from a person of lower caste.[37] However, in rare temples in contemporary India, the icon can be touched by all devotees, as in the case of the liṅga of the Kāśī Viśvanāth temple of Varanasi.

Conclusion

According to Indian epistemic systems, succession in perception and the finiteness of resulting knowledge are characteristics of human perception. This, in part, explains why philosophers, at least up to the advent of later Vaiṣṇava theologies, were reluctant to attribute senses and perceptive faculties (similar to the ordinary ones of human beings) to omniscient and omnipresent God. It would have involved logical contradictions that only dogmatic assertions could

[35] For recipes of Vaikhānasa Vaiṣṇava temple cuisine, see the 10th century *Vimānārcanakalpa* (43, pp. 265–268); for recipes of another Vaiṣṇava group, *Pāñcarātrika*, see a later manual, the *Viṣṇutilaka* (3: 36–40).

[36] See, for instance, COLAS (1996, p. 303, n. 8).

[37] See, for instance, *Vimānārcanakalpa* (69, p. 417).

have overcome. However, the epistemic schools admit the existence of supra-sensory perception. For example, yogic perception that transcends time and succession and is unconnected with the mediacy of objects. Another example is the combination of past perception of one sense and present perception by another sense. This reminds us of the *madeleine* of Marcel Proust, that is, about the experience of a past impression in a present perception.

In contrast with the views expressed in epistemic works, the devotee believes in the existence and activity of senses in the deity he worships, be it in the form of an incarnation or an icon. These divine forms combine the characteristics of an omniscient God and a sensory living being. In certain cases, for example, Kṛṣṇa's amorous acts, the deity's sensory perception is decoded and interpreted mystically as a metaphor, and accepted by the society.

The perception of the devotee with regard to the icon is transformed by his devotion. For him, the icon is not a lifeless image. Conceding his devotional perception to be imaginary would amount to admitting that its object, namely the icon-deity, lacks reality, at least to some extent. He also recreates, with various devices, a world that nourishes his sentiment of devotion. Temple art and rituals amount to a total art where all senses, both of the deity and the devotee, are stimulated.

References

Sanskrit and Tamil texts

BHAGAVADGĪTĀ with Rāmānuja's commentary (1972): VIRARAGHAVACHARYA, U. T. (Ed.), Śrīmadbhagavadgītā, with Rāmānuja's Bhāṣya, Vedāntadeśika's Tātparyacandrikā sub-commentary and editor's Rasāsvādākhyaṭippaṇa. – Madras.

BHĀṢĀPARICCHEDA [= Kārikāvalī] with Siddhāntamuktāvalī commentary (1981): ḌHUNḌHIRĀJA (Ed.), Kārikāvalī with Viśvanātha's Siddhāntamuktāvalī commentary and Nārāyaṇatīrtha's Nyāyacandrikā commentary. 2nd edition. – Vārāṇasī.

KENA-UPANIṢAD (1943): RENOU, L. (Ed. and trans.), Kena-upaniṣad, Publiée et Traduite. – Paris.

MĀNAMEYODAYA: KUNHAN Raja, C. & SURYANARAYANA Sastri, S. S. (Ed. and Trans.) (1975): Mānameyodaya of Nārāyaṇa (An Elementary Treatise on the Mīmāṃsā). – 2nd edition. – Madras.

MUDRĀRĀKṢASA (1976): KALE, M. R. (Ed. and Trans.), Mudrārākṣasa of Viśākhadatta with the Commentary of Ḍhunḍirāja, Edited with an English Translation, Critical and Explanatory Notes, Introduction and Various Readings. 6th edition. – Delhi.

NYĀYAMAÑJARĪ (1936): Sūryanārāyaṇaśukla (Ed.), The Nyāyamañjarī of Jayanta Bhaṭṭa, Edited with Notes etc. – Benares.

NYĀYASŪTRA (2003): TARANATHA and AMARENDRAMOHAN (Ed.), Nyāyadarśanam with Vātsyāyana's Bhāṣya, Uddyot[a]kara's Vārttika, Vācaspati Miśra's Tātparyaṭīkā and Viśvanātha's Vṛtti. Reprint of the 1936–1944 edition. – Delhi.

ŚRĪBHĀṢYA: VĪRARĀGHAVĀCĀRYA, U.T. and ŚRĪVATSĀṄKĀCĀRYA, V. (Ed.) (1989): Rāmānuja's Śrībhāṣya with Sudarśanasūri's Śrutaprakāśikā commentary. Reproduction of the 1967 edition. – Madras.

ŚRĪVACANABHŪṢAṆA (1979): LESTER, R. C. (Ed. and Trans.), Śrīvacanabhūṣaṇa of Piḷḷai Lokācārya. Edited with English Translation. – Madras.
VEDĀNTASĀRA (1979): KRISHNAMACHARYA, V. (Ed.) and NARASIMHA Ayyangar, M. B. (Trans.): Vedāntasāra of Bhagavad Rāmānuja. 2nd edition. – Madras.
VIMĀNĀRCANAKALPA (1927): RAṂGĀCĀRYA, Ḍi. et al. (Eds.), Vimānārcanakalpaḥ. – Īgāvāripāḷeṃ.
VIṢṆUTILAKA (1896): RĀGHAVĀCĀRYA, K.I. (Ed.), Śrīviṣṇutilaka. – Bangalore.
YOGASŪTRA (1982): ḌHUNḌHIRĀJ Śāstrī (Ed.), Yogasūtram by Maharṣipatañjali with Six Commentaries [...]. 2nd edition. – Varanasi.

Secondary sources

BERENSON, B. (2004): Les Valeurs Tactiles (French trans. GILLET, L.). In: FMR (Nouvelle série) 2, pp. 124–130.
BHATT, G.P. (1962): Epistemology of the Bhāṭṭa School of Pūrva Mīmāṃsā. – Varanasi.
BHĪMĀCĀRYA, Jh. (1978): Nyāyakośa or Dictionary of Technical Terms of Indian Philosophy [...], revised and re-edited by [...] V. Shāstrī ABHYAṄKAR. – Poona.
CHATTERJEE, S. (1965): The Nyāya Theory of Knowledge: A Critical Study of Some Problems of Logic and Metaphysics. – Calcutta.
CHEMPARATHY, G. (1972): An Indian Rational Theology: Introduction to Udayana's Nyāyakusumāñjali. – Vienna.
CLOONEY, F. X. (1988): Devatādhikaraṇa: A Theological Debate in the Mīmāṃsā-Vedānta Tradition. In: Journal of Indian Philosophy, Vol. 16, pp. 277–298.
COLAS, G. (1986): Le Temple selon Marīci: Extraits de la Marīci-saṃhitā, Étudiés et Traduits. – Pondichery.
COLAS, G. (1996) Viṣṇu, ses Images et ses Feux: Les Métamorphoses du Dieu chez les Vaikhānasa. – Paris.
COLAS, G. (2002): Variations sur la Pâmoison Dévote: À propos d'un Poème de Vedāntadeśika et du Théâtre des *araiyar*. In: BOUILLIER, V. and TARABOUT, G. (Eds.), Images du Corps dans le Monde Hindou. – Paris, pp. 275–314.
COLAS, G. (2004a): Emotion and Aesthetic Experience According to Sanskrit Poetics. In: SANTANGELO, P. (Ed.), Expressions of States of Mind in Asia. – Naples, pp. 15–27.
COLAS, G. (2004b): The Competing Hermeneutics of Image Worship in Hinduism (Fifth to Eleventh Century AD). In: GRANOFF, P. and SHINOHARA, K. (Eds.), Images in Asian Religions: Texts and Contexts. – Vancouver and Toronto, pp. 149–179.
COLAS, G. (2009): Images and Territory of Gods: From Precepts to Epigraphs. In: BERTI, D. and TARABOUT, G. (Eds.), Territory, Soil and Society in South Asia. – New Delhi, pp. 99–139.
COLAS, G. (2010): Pratiṣṭhā: Ritual, Reproduction, Accretion. In: ZOTTER, A. and ZOTTER, C. (Eds.), Hindu and Buddhist Initiations in India and Nepal. – Wiesbaden, pp. 319–339.
COLAS, G. (2011): God's Body: Epistemic and Ritual Conceptions from Sanskrit Texts of Logic. In: MICHAELS, A. and WULF, C. (Eds.), Images of the Body in India. – Delhi, pp. 45–55.
COLAS, G. (2012): Penser l'Icône en Inde Ancienne. – Paris.

DASGUPTA, S. (1975): A History of Indian Philosophy, Volume 3, 1st Indian edition. – Delhi.

DATTA, D.M. (1972): The Six Ways of Knowing: A Critical Study of the Advaita Theory of Knowledge. – Reprint of 2nd revised edition. – Calcutta.

DAVIS, D.R. (2007): Hinduism as a Legal Tradition. In: Journal of the American Academy of Religion, Vol. 75, No. 2, pp. 241–267.

DE, S.K. (1923–1925): Studies in the History of Sanskrit Poetics. 2 Vols. – London.

ECK, D. (1985): Darśan: Seeing the Divine Image in India. Revised edition. – Chambersburg.

JHAḶAKĪKAR BHĪMĀCĀRYA (1978): Nyāyakośa or Dictionary of Technical Terms of Indian Philosophy [...], Revised and Re-edited by [...] Vāsudev Shāstrī ABHYAṄKAR. – Poona.

HUNTINGTON, J.C. (1985): The Origin of the Buddha Image: Early Image Traditions and the Concept of Buddhadarśanapuṇyā. In: NARAIN, A.K. (Ed.), Studies in Buddhist Art of South Asia. – New Delhi, pp. 23–58.

KRICK, H. (1975): Der Vaniṣṭhusava und Indras Offenbarung. In: Wiener Zeitschrift für die Kunde Südasiens, Vol. 19, pp. 25–74.

MALINAR, A. (2007): The Bhagavadgītā Doctrines and Contexts. – Cambridge.

MATILAL, B.K. (1986): Perception: An Essay on Classical Indian Theories of Knowledge. – Oxford.

MADHAVANANDA, S. (Trans.) (1977): Bhāṣā-pariccheda with Siddhānta-muktāvalī by Viśvanātha Nyāyapañcānana. – 3rd edition. – Calcutta.

PARRINDER, G. (1997): Avatar and Incarnation: The Divine in Human Form in the World's Religions. – Oxford.

ROBINSON, R.H. (1970): Chapter IV: Classical Indian Philosophy. In: ELDER, J.W. (Ed.), Chapters in Indian Civilization, Vol. I: Classical and Medieval India. Revised edition. – Dubuque, pp. 127–227.

SCHOPEN, G. (1997): Bones, Stones, and Buddhist Monks: Collected Papers on the Archaeology, Epigraphy, and Texts of Monastic Buddhism in India. – Honolulu.

SRINIVASACHARI, P. N. (1970): The Philosophy of Viśiṣṭādvaita. Reprint of the 1943 edition. – Madras.

SUNDARAM, P.K. (1968): Advaita Epistemology with Special Reference to Iṣṭasiddhi. – Madras.

Anand Mishra

The Divine Embrace: The Role of the Senses in Puṣṭimārga*

Sense-perception is accepted by all Indian philosophical systems as a valid means of epistemic knowledge. Most of them also acknowledge categories or entities which are beyond the senses and, therefore, cannot be known through direct sense-perception. Accordingly, other means of veridical knowledge, like inference (*anumāna*), verbal testimony (*śabda*), comparison (*upamāna*), inference from circumstances (*arthāpatti*), non-recognition (*anupalabdhi*), equivalence (*sambhava*), and traditional instruction (*aitihya*) are accepted by different philosophical schools.[1]

Theoretical postulations regarding the existence (or non-existence) of absolute reality is attempted to be established by taking recourse to one or more of the above mentioned instruments of epistemic knowledge. Sense-perception is central to all of them. Even if it is not directly instrumental in providing knowledge about entities which are beyond the senses, it is still indispensable for receiving, processing and passing on the information about this knowledge.[2] For example, the statements of authoritative persons (*āpta-vacana*) are heard and learned. This is possible through the faculties of speaking and hearing which rest on the senses. Any tradition evolves and continues on the basis of the knowledge carried over generations with the help of the physical senses. Indian tradition, therefore, lays special emphasis on keeping them healthy and strong so that this responsibility is carried out effectively. For example, prayers before beginning the teachings of Upanishads (*śānti-pāṭha*) indicate the desire to have healthy and capable senses as in the beginning of *Kenopaniṣad*: "May my limbs, speech, vital force, eyes, ears, as also strength and all the organs become well developed" (Trans. Gambhirananda 1957, p. 32)[3] as also the following invocations in *Taittirīyopaniṣad*: "My body, may it be untrammelled! My tongue, may it say the sweetest things! My ears, may they hear the wealth of sacred lore!" (Trans. Olivelle 1996, p. 180).[4]

---

* I am thankful to Gérard Colas and the editors of this volume for their comments and suggestions.

[1] For a detailed discussion, see Tripathi (1997, p. 9).

[2] See, for example, Franco (1987, p. 17).

[3] *Āpyāyantu mamāṅgāni vākprāṇaścakṣuḥ śrotramatho balamindriyāṇi ca sarvāṇi/* (*Śānti-pāṭha* to *Kenopaniṣad*).

[4] *Śarīraṃ me vicarṣaṇam/jihvā me madhumattamā/karṇābhyāṃ bhūri viśruvam/* (*Taittirīyopaniṣad* 1.4.2).

The senses are not only instruments of epistemic knowledge but are essential in experiencing pleasure and pain. According to Vātsyāyana, pleasure is gained when the five senses, together with mind and soul, get associated with their respective sense-objects. He defines this pleasure as *kāma* in his *Kāmasūtra*.[5]

In Indian philosophical writings, however, there is a clear division between "that which can be grasped through senses" and "that which is beyond them." The Upaniṣads abound in such statements. One of the ways in which the Absolute (*brahman*) is typically defined is "that which cannot be grasped through senses."[6] The senses are "directed towards the outer physical world and not the inner self,"[7] and in the order of basic categories (*tattva*), listed at a lower level.[8] For the realization of the Absolute, it is pertinent to restrain the senses and prevent them from connecting with their objects.[9] *Yogasūtra*, for example, defines *pratyāhāra* (restraining of the sense-organs) as a state "when separated from their corresponding objects, the senses follow, as it were, the nature of the mind (*citta*). This brings about the supreme control of the sense-organs"[10] (Trans. MUKERJI 1963, p. 273). The *Vyāsabhāṣya* discusses the different positions in detail:

> Some say that *a-vyasana* or indifference to objects like sights and sounds etc., is under the control of the sense-organs. The word *vyasana* used in this connection means attachment or fondness; in other words, that which moves people away from righteousness. Others say that the enjoyment of objects like sound etc. not forbidden by *śāstras* is right, meaning that this is the subjugation of the senses.

---

[5] *Śrotra-tvak-caksur-jihvā-ghrāṇānām ātma-saṃyuktena manasādhiṣṭhitānāṃ sveṣu sveṣu viṣayeṣv ānukūlyataḥ pravṛttiḥ kāmaḥ/sparśa-viśeṣa-viṣayāt tv asyābhimānika-sukhānuviddhā phalavaty artha-pratītiḥ prādhānyāt kāmaḥ/* (*Kāmasūtra* 1.2.11–12). (Pleasure, in general, consists in engaging the ear, skin, eye, tongue, and nose each in its own appropriate sensation, all under the control of the mind and heart driven by the conscious self. Pleasure in its primary form, however, is a direct experience of an object of the senses, which bears fruit and is permeated by the sensual pleasure of erotic arousal that results from the particular sensation of touch [Trans. DONIGER 2002, p. 8]).

[6] *Yaccakṣuṣā na paśyati* (*Kenopaniṣad* 1.6).

[7] *Parāñcikhāni vyatṛṇatsvayambhūḥ tasmāt parāṅpaśyati nāntarātman/* (*Kaṭhopaniṣad* 2.1.1) (The Self-existent One pierced the apertures outward, therefore, one looks out, and not into oneself [Trans. OLIVELLE 1996, p. 240]).

[8] *Indriyebhyaḥ parā hyarthā arthebhyaśca paraṃ manaḥ/* (*Kaṭhopaniṣad* 1.3.10). (Higher than the senses are their object; higher than sense objects is the mind [Trans. OLIVELLE 199, p. 239]). See also, *Sāṃkhyakārikā* 26.

[9] *Tasmādyasya mahābāho nigṛhītāni sarvaśaḥ/indriyāṇīndriyārthebhyaḥ tasya prajñā pratiṣṭhitā //* (*Bhagavadgītā* 2.68). (Therefore, O hero! his wisdom is stable whose senses have been withdrawn on all sides from their (respective) objects [Trans. KRISHNA WARRIER 1983, p. 86]).

[10] *Svaviṣayāsamprayoge cittasya svarūpānukāra ivendriyāṇāṃ pratyāhāraḥ // tataḥ paramā vaśyatendriyāṇām/* (*Yogasūtra* 2.54–55).

Figure 1: Śrīnāthjī and Vallabhācārya embracing each other

Source: http://www.vallabhaseva.com (accessed November 18, 2011).

There are still others who say: out of one's own free will, the application of the senses to objects like sound etc. without being a slave to them means the control of the senses. Again, there are others who say: the experience of sound etc. without feelings of happiness or misery on account of the absence of attachment or aversion, is subjugation of the senses. Jaigīṣavya says: when the mind becomes one-pointed, the disinclination to objects of the senses or the detachment from objects that arises, is control of the senses. Hence, what is stated by Jaigīṣavya constitutes the supreme form of sense-control of the Yogins in which, when the mind ceases its activities, the senses also stop theirs. Moreover, when this is attained, the Yogins have not to depend on other forms of effort for the subjugation of the senses (trans. MUKERJI 1963, pp. 274–276).[11]

Despite the veridical nature of sense-perception,[12] philosophically speaking an important shortcoming is associated with it. Sense-perception is "limited in time and space" (see COLAS 2013, this volume). Pleasure or pain, gained through the instrumentality of the senses are, therefore, also limited and transitory. Thus, although the senses are important in experiencing (worldly) happiness, and ample examples of strengthening the senses and making them fit for relishing objects are present in Indian literature, yet most Indian philosophical systems suggest sense-control for the attainment of liberation (*mokṣa*). To those seeking eternal bliss, sensory experiences appear futile — and even obstacles — in the way of advancing further towards their goal. Their area of application is this material world and can fetch only limited and fleeting happiness. The senses have little role to play in the realization of the Absolute or in its direct experience. This is primarily because the nature of the Absolute is such that it cannot be grasped by the senses; and also, the nature of the senses is such that the Absolute cannot be an object of their perception.

The instrumentality of the physical senses, therefore, is limited to the secondary role of carrying and transmitting primary knowledge. To gain primary knowledge about the Absolute, a special kind of perception which is beyond the senses (*atīndriya*), or the perception of the yogis (*yogaja-pratyakṣa*) is required, which leads to an immediate and direct experiential realization of the Absolute (*aparokṣa-jñāna*).[13]

A different approach is evident in the theistic philosophical systems where there is an emphasis on serving God out of affection. Physical senses are not just a hindrance in realizing the Absolute, nor are they only capable of executing the secondary function of carrying and conveying worldly experiences, but

---

[11] *Śabdādiṣvavyasanam indriyajaya iti kecit/saktirvyasanaṃ vyasyatyenaṃ śreyasa iti/aviruddhāpratipattirnyāyyā/śabdādisamprayogaḥ svecchayetyanye/rāgadveṣābhāve sukhaduḥkhaśūnyaṃ śabdādijñānamindriyajaya iti kecit/cittakāgryādapratipattireveti jaigīṣavyaḥ/tataśca paramā tviyaṃ vaśyatā yaścittanirodhe niruddhānīndriyāṇi/ netarendriyajayavat prayatnakṛtam upāyāntaramapekṣante yogina iti //* (*Yogasūtra Vyāsabhāṣya* 2.55).

[12] *Tattvopaplavasiṃha* of Jayarāśi Bhaṭṭa points towards the deficiencies of the definitions of sense-perception in different philosophical schools. See FRANCO (1987).

[13] Śaṅkarācārya distinguishes between "knowledge" (*jñāna*) and "experiential knowledge" (*vijñāna*): *jñānaṃ śāstroktapadārthānāṃ parijñānaṃ, vijñānaṃ tu śāstrataḥ jñātānāṃ tathaiva svānubhavakaraṇam* (*Bhagavadgītābhāṣya* 6.8) ("Knowledge" means conversance with the principles enunciated in the *śāstras*; on the other hand, "experience" means the exact realization of whatever has been learned from the *śāstras* [Trans. KRISHNA WARRIER 1983, p. 225]).

through them a direct communion with God is possible. The senses become central in ensuring a firm relationship between God and his devotee.

This special and important role of the senses is a significant feature of the philosophical system of *Brahmavāda* and the religious tradition of *Puṣṭimārga*, propounded by Vallabhācārya (1479–1531 CE). It is extensively visible in their religious practices as well as abundantly recorded in the accompanying literary and other artistic works.[14] One such narration is about the manifestation of Śrīnāthjī[15] where his meeting with Vallabhācārya is recounted: "Next morning, Śrī Ācāryajī Mahāprabhu, in great joy, went to meet Śrīnāthjī, accompanied by all his disciples. Śrīnāthjī received him with great happiness" (Śrīnāthjī Prākaṭya kī Vārtā. Trans. VAUDEVILLE 1980, p. 25).

This episode is frequently represented in paintings where Śrīnāthjī and Vallabhācārya embrace each other (as in Figure 1). It conveys the essence of the philosophy of Puṣṭimārga: the absolute reality, of its own desire, manifests itself in the form of Śrīnāthjī. God puts his hand of *līlā* (divine play) upon the shoulder of the devotee, and the devotee puts his hand of service (*sevā*) upon the shoulder of God. Traveling together in this manner, while embracing each other joyfully, is the "path of grace" (*Puṣṭimārga*).[16] The writings of Vallabhācārya and his successors are an attempt to establish the above idea as the teaching of the Vedic corpus.

In this context, certain issues of theological and philosophical importance can be raised. Is the above representation as well as similar instances of interaction of God with the devotee in the literature and practices of *Puṣṭimārga* just a figurative representation of the non-sensory spiritual union? Or, is it possible to experience God through senses? If this is indeed possible, then the question that arises is: what is the nature of God, the senses, and sense-perception?

---

[14] See, for example, the narrations (*vārtā*s) recorded in the *Caurāsī Vaiṣṇavan kī Vārtā* (Accounts of 84 Vaishnavas) or *Dosau-bāvan Vaiṣṇavan kī Vārtā* (Accounts of 252 Vaishnavas). See: *Gosvāmī Śrī Harirāya praṇīta Caurāsī Vaiṣṇavan kī Vārtā* (2027 VS) Śrī Govardhana Granthamālā Kāryālaya — Mathurā; *Gosvāmī Śrī Harirāya praṇīta Dosau-bāvan Vaiṣṇavan kī Vārtā* (2008 VS), 3 Vols. the Śuddhādvaita Academy. — Kānkarolī.

[15] According to Vallabhācārya, there are three kinds of manifestations of God, namely, *prākaṭya*, (*aṃśa-*) *avatāra* and *prādurbhāva*. *Prākaṭya* is when God manifests himself for the sake of one or few devotees (usually in the form of an idol); *avatāra* is when he incarnates himself for protection of *dharma*; and *prādurbhāva* is when he appears in his own form, i.e., as Kṛṣṇa, in order to liberate everyone. See here TDN Pr 1.1 and Mishra 1971, pp. 1–4. The manifestation of Śrīnāthjī is *prākaṭya*. Śrīnāthjī is worshipped as one of the main deities of Puṣṭimārga. See VAUDEVILLE (1980).

[16] The actions of Kṛṣṇa are his *līlā* (divine play), and the actions of the devotee for the sake of Kṛṣṇa are the devotee's *sevā* (service). God puts his hand of *līlā* on the shoulders of devotee, and a devotee puts his hand of *sevā* on the shoulder of God. *Puṣṭimārga* is traveling together, joyfully embracing each other. I take this imagery from Goswami Shyam Manohar (GOSWAMI 2060 VS, p. 3).

The following discussion is mainly based on *Tattvārthadīpa-Nibandha* (TDN), which is an important text composed by Vallabhācārya in which the central aspects related to his philosophy are stated in a concise form. Vallabhācārya considers the *Bhāgavata-Purāṇa* (BhP) to be the most authoritative source of knowledge,[17] and contends that:

> The meaning of BhP should be understood at seven different levels, namely (i) the meaning of the text as a whole (*śāstra*), (ii) its different cantos (*skandha*), (iii) main topics or thematic groups (*prakaraṇa*), (iv) chapters (*adhyāya*), (v) sentences (*vākya*), (vi) words (*pada*) and (vii) each syllables or constituents of the word (*akṣara*). Only a coherent and non-contradictory resulting conclusion, after taking into consideration, meanings at each levels leads to liberation.[18]

TDN is written to explain the meaning of BhP at the first four levels, the last three being explained in the *Subodhinī* commentary of BhP.[19] It is composed in a carefully planned manner and is divided in three parts: The first part deals with the fundamental tenets of his philosophy; the second with the refutation of other philosophical positions; and finally, the third part provides a detailed analysis of the meaning and purpose behind the macro level structure of BhP.[20] Vallabhācārya himself wrote a commentary on TDN, which he calls *Prakāśa*.[21] His son Viṭṭhalanātha (1516–1588 CE) added upto the 20th chapter of the fifth canto (III.5.20). Gosvāmī Puruṣottama (1667–1753 CE) has composed a commentary named *Āvaraṇabhaṅga* on *Prakāśa* upto III.5.20, as also *Yojanā-Ṭīkā*, a gloss on the rest of the TDN.

Vallabhācārya distinguishes between the world (*prapañca* or *jagat*), which is real and a creation of God;[22] and an illusory construction (*saṃsāra*), which does

---

[17] *Vedāḥ śrīkṛṣṇavākyāni vyāsasūtrāṇi caiva hi | samādhibhāṣā vyāsasya pramāṇaṃ taccatuṣṭayam || Uttaraṃ pūrvasandehavārakaṃ parikīrtitam ||* (*Śāstrārtha-Prakaraṇa* of TDN 1.7–8). The Vedas (together with the Upaniṣads), *Bhagavadgītā*, *Brahmasūtra* and *Bhāgavata-Purāṇa* are the four authoritative sources. The later ones explain the doubts arising in the previous ones.

[18] *Śāstre skandhe prakaraṇe'dhyāye vākye pade'kṣare | ekārthaṃ saptadhā jānan navirodhena mucyate ||* (*Bhāgavatārtha-Prakaraṇa* of TDN 1.2).

[19] *Arthatrayaṃ tu vakṣyāmi nibandhe'sti catuṣṭayam |* (*Subodhinī* on BhP 1.1.9). The *Subodhinī* commentary by Vallabhācārya is available only on the first, second, third and tenth canto (*skandha*) of BhP, and up till the first five chapters (*adhyāya*) of the eleventh canto.

[20] The first part, *Śāstrārtha-Prakaraṇa* (I) has 104 verses (*kārikās*), the second *Sarvanirṇaya-prakaraṇa* (II) has 329 verses, and the third *Bhāgavatārtha-Prakaraṇa* (III) contains 1922 verses.

[21] This is available on the *Śāstrārtha* (I) and *Sarvanirṇaya-Prakaraṇa* (II) and only up till the first chapter of the fourth canto of *Bhāgavatārtha-Prakaraṇa* (III.4.1).

[22] *Prapañco bhagavatkāryaḥ |* (TDN 1.23). *Prapañca* or the world is creation of God. According to Vallabhācārya, *brahman*, *paramātman* and *bhagavān* are ascriptions

not have any real existence and is caused by the ignorance of the individual soul. The real world can be considered *the world as it is* and the illusory construction to be *the world as we think it to be*. The world and the illusory construction differ in terms of their material and instrumental cause, their essential nature as well as the manner of their origin and termination.

Brahman is the material as well as the instrumental cause of the world,[23] whereas the illusory construction does not have any material cause. *Brahman* transforms itself into the world, and this transformation is such that the essential nature remains intact in the transformed state as well. This principle of "unmodified transformation" (*avikṛta-pariṇāmavāda*) explains Vallabhācārya's position of considering the world not only a creation of God but his form as well. It suggests that the transformation is such that the material cause remains unmodified. He cites the example of forming a jewel out of gold. Here, although a new form is acquired, yet the gold remains unmodified.[24]

Further, creation does not bring forth something utterly new, or which did not exist before. In other words, the effect is ontologically not different from the cause. The relation between the material cause (*upādāna-kāraṇa*) and its effect (*kārya*) is guided by the principle that the cause inherently exists in the effect (*satkārya-vāda*). Both, the cause as well as the effect, are real. So, the world is real (*sat*) because it is caused by God (who is real). Moreover, the world is not only a creation of God but is also a form of God (*tadrūpa*). Otherwise, the unacceptable situation of the un-real (*asat*) coming into existence out of the real (*sat*) will follow.[25]

Creation brings to surface certain results or effects, which are latent in the cause. It is the manifestation of the effect (*āvirbhāva*); destruction is the retracing of the effects back to the cause, and continuing in a state of dormancy (*tirobhāva*). Vallabhācārya follows the principle of manifestation and dormancy (*āvirbhāva-tirobhāva-vāda*) to explain the process of creation. The creation of world, therefore, manifests certain characteristics to the surface, and dissolution retraces them back to the core, or the non-manifest state. Brahman or God creates the world in this manner.

---

of the Absolute in the *Upaniṣads*, *smṛti*s and *Bhāgavata-Purāṇa* respectively. In his theistic tradition, there is no fundamental difference between *brahman* and *bhagavān*, and the two words are used interchangeably. See here TDN 8 as well as Subodhinī on BhP 1.2.11 and BhP 2.10.7.

[23] *Jagataḥ samavāyi syāt tadeva ca nimittakam* | (TDN 1.68). In Vallabhācārya's philosophical system, *samavāyi-kāraṇa* (or the concomittantly inherent cause) is not an independent cause, but is included within the *upādāna-kāraṇa* (or material cause). Confer (*Āvaraṇabhaṅga*, p. 116): *samavāyaśca tādātmyameva, na tu padārthāntaram.* The concomitant inherency (*samavāya*) is, in fact, mutual identity (*tādātmya*) and not an independent entity. See also, MISHRA (1971, p. 214).

[24] See: *Aṇubhāṣya* 1.4.26. *Śrī Brahmasūtrāṇubhāṣyam.* Part I (2038 VS). Śrīnāthadvārā Temple Board. — Nathdwara.

[25] *Tādṛṣo 'pi bhagavadrūpaḥ* | *anyathā asataḥ sattā syāt* | (TDN Pr 1.23).

In the authoritative texts,[26] *brahman* is stated as existence–consciousness–bliss (*sat-cit-ānanda*), and the world is nothing but the manifestation of these three characteristics. The manifestation of *sat* is existence i.e. the physical as well as the mental world, including the senses. This conglomeration is called *jaḍa* or the material world.[27] The manifestation of *cit* is termed as *jīva* (conscious soul). There are beings which abide in the inner core of the Absolute: the *antaryāmins* in whom bliss (*ānanda*) is in a state of manifestation. They originate in a manner similar to sparks emanating from fire (*visphuliṅgavat udbhava*). Here, the emanation is not an illusory superimposition (*upādhi*) but is real. The material cause (*upādāna*) of this emanation is *brahman* as well as its locus (*adhikaraṇa*), and also its agent (*kartṛ*). Therefore, the parts which get emanated, the place where they exist, and the source of their existence — all is *brahman*.[28] It is not that material world is inherently without consciousness or bliss, but they are dormant in it. Similarly, in a conscious being, bliss is dormant. A conscious being, when it gets associated with the material world, attains a physical body. This happens because of ignorance, and when knowledge dispels this ignorance, it attains its own state of pure consciousness. Although *brahman* is immanent in physical bodies (*jaḍa*), conscious souls (*jīva*), and blissful *antaryāmins*, it still does not have the divisions characterized by them.[29]

Brahman, which is without differentiation and all pervasive like the sky,[30] becomes limited through the creative power of God. This creative power resides in God and is called *māyā*. It is the instrumental cause of the creation of the world. Through creation, God sports delightfully in the created world (*līlā*). Destruction is when he takes back the world into himself, and delights in his unextended own form.

The illusory construction, on the other hand, has ignorance (*avidyā*) as the instrumental cause. Ignorance is the deluding power of God which affects conscious beings. Its nature is to impose wrong perceptions (*adhyāsa*). In this case, it constructs an illusory world which takes away the perception of the world as it really is, and imposes a deluding vision of the world which belongs to one's self or to which one is much attached. This deluding super-imposition

---

[26] What is meant here is perhaps the Purāṇas related to the Vaiṣṇava tradition. (See Mishra 1971, p. 77).

[27] This may be compared to *prakṛti* (main cause) and its modifications in the Sāṃkhya philosophical system. See: *Sāṃkhyakārikā* 3 and 22 (Bhattacarya 1976, pp. 27, 167).

[28] See Mishra (1971, p. 92).

[29] *Sajātīya-vijātīya-svagata-dvaita-varjitam* | (TDN 1.66). According to *Prakāśa* (TDN Pr 1.66), by *sajātīya* (homogeneous categories) are physical bodies (*jaḍa*) meant, by *vijātīya* (non-homogeneous categories), conscious souls (*jīva*) and by *svagata* (belonging to one's self), those residing in God (*antaryāmin*).

[30] *Ākāśavad vyāpakaṃ hi brahma* (TDN 1.25).

can happen corresponding to the body (*deha*), senses (*indriya*), life-breath (*prāṇa*), and inner sense-organs (*antaḥkaraṇa*). As a result of it, the conscious soul becomes unaware of its real nature (*svarūpājñāna*). There are thus five stages of ignorance corresponding to the body, senses, life-breath, inner sense-organs and unawareness of the real nature of the conscious soul.

Knowledge (*vidyā*), which is also a power of God, destroys ignorance and liberates the souls. It is important to note that only the illusory super-imposition regarding body, senses etc. is destroyed, and not the body or senses themselves. Thus, the destruction is that of the illusory construction only and not of the world as such; and since the body, the senses etc. fall within the sphere of world, they are not destroyed. This also explains liberation while still alive (*jīvana-mukti*).

A central tenet of the philosophy of Vallabhācārya is his advocacy of *brahman* as "blissful form." This is called *sākāra-brahmavāda*. On the one hand, it negates *brahman* having worldly form or body and, on the other hand, it does not accept it to be completely without form. *Brahman*, he posits, is essentially of the nature of "blissful form."

In the philosophy of Vallabhācārya, *ānanda*[31] or bliss yields a special form, which is called *ākāra*.[32] This is special because it has no trace of worldliness or physicality associated with it (*alaukika*, *aprākṛtika*); it is pure bliss (*ānanda*) without any trace of worldly existence or consciousness. Therefore, worldly entities are termed as without blissful form (*nirākāra*, *nirānanda*). That it is beyond normal worldly creations is expressed through the "four-armed blissful form" of Viṣṇu. Here, it should be noted, that it is not only that *brahman* takes up a form — for example as world, or incarnation, or other manifestations — but it is essentially of the nature of the blissful form. The world, or incarnation, or other manifestations are considered as the *brahman* taking up some form. This however does not imply that an essentially formless (*nirākāra*) *brahman* has form only in its physical manifestations. On the other hand, the essential nature of the *brahman* is "the blissful form" which is an expression of the *ānanda* or bliss. The blissful form is described through the following verse (TDN 1, 44):

> The essential form of God (*vigraha*) is without blemish and with all and every good characteristics. He is independent or dependent on himself only (*ātmatantra*) and without unconscious body and its qualities. His hands, feet, mouth, stomach and other body parts are of the nature of pure bliss (*ānanda-mātra*).[33]

---

[31] For a semantic history of the word *ānanda*, see OLIVELLE (1997).

[32] *Ānando brahmavāde ākārasamarpakaḥ* | (TDN Pr 1.44). Instead of translating *ākāra* as simply form, I prefer "blissful form" to specify the difference between "physical form" or simply "form" which is manifestation of the *jaḍa-aṃśa*, and "blissful form" or *ākāra* which is manifestation of *ānanda*.

[33] *Nirdoṣa-pūrṇa-guṇa-vigraha ātmatantro niścetanātmaka-śarīra-guṇaiśca hīnaḥ/ ānanda-mātra-kara-pāda-mukhodarādiḥ sarvatra ca trividha-bheda-vivarjitātmā //.*

Vallabhācārya explains further:

> The blissful form, is the own form of God and is also called *vigraha*. It is without blemish (*nirdoṣa*) and with all and every good characteristics (*pūrṇa-guṇa*) like peace or knowledge etc. Normally in the world, these good qualities are found in a person together with bad ones. This happens even in the case of the exalted ones. For example, a person with knowledge is not without attachment. Similarly, ascetic penance is accompanied with anger. In the same way, ritual action (*dharma*) is without compassion. In the case of God, it is not like this, but his own form is, on the one hand, without any fault and, on the other hand, with all the good qualities. The reason for using the expression *vigraha* is to indicate that worldly speaking contradictory qualities reside in God.[34]

Although, God has all these good qualities, yet he is not dependent on them. "To remove any doubts regarding dependence of God on these qualities, he is termed as dependent on himself only, i.e. independent (*ātmatantra*)."[35] If we consider God having a form with all the good qualities, then, as in the case of physical bodies or senses in the world (*laukika*) which are considered as an effect (and therefore with beginning and an end), we will have to accept the body and senses of God as an effect, and hence with a beginning and an end. To placate this doubt, He is termed as being without (*hīna*) unconscious (*niścetanātmaka*) body (*śarīra*) and its qualities (*guṇa*), like having a beginning or an end.[36] Thus, the blissful form is without a worldly beginning or end, and is completely different from physical bodies. Further, his hands (*kara*), feet (*pāda*), mouth (*mukha*), and stomach (*udara*), etc., are pure bliss (*ānanda-mātra*).Thus, *brahman* has hands and feet everywhere (*sarvataḥ pāṇi-pāda*), but these are not worldly limbs (*aprākṛta*).

Since worldly sense perception can perceive only physical worldly objects, *brahman* (as also this blissful form) cannot be perceived by them. It is because of this reason that this blissful form is of dark complexion, like that of Kṛṣṇa. It is like the *sphaṭika* (crystal) in which the pure *sattva* of God, which is of dark color,[37] gets reflected, and the absolute bliss (*ānanda*) appears as dark complexioned (Kṛṣṇa). Here, it should be noticed that it is not *brahman* that has a dark complexion as its attribute; it appears dark complexioned because of

[34] *Guṇāḥ śānti-jñānādayāḥ/te loke doṣasahitā dṛṣṭā mahato'pi/yathā jñānaṃ kvacit, tanna saṅga-varjitam iti/tathā tapaḥ krodha-sahitam/tathā dharmo dayā-rahitaḥ/tathā na bhagavati, kintu nirdoṣāḥ pūrṇā guṇā vigraharūpā yasya/vigraha-padena paraspara-viruddhā api loka-dṛṣṭyā bhāsanta iti jñātavyam/* (TDN Pr 1,44).

[35] *Guṇādhīnatvamāśaṅkya āha — ātmatantra iti/* (TDN Pr 1,44).

[36] *Dehendriyādīnāṃ kāryatvapratīteḥ lokavaddehendriyāṇi bhaviṣyanti ityāśaṅkya āha — niścetanātmaka iti/cakārāt taddharmairapi hīnaḥ/* (TDN Pr 1,44).

[37] Vallabhācārya mentions a different association of colors with the three qualities: *Sattva* = dark/black color, *rajas* = red, and *tamas* = white. Sāṃkhya philosophy connects white color with *sattva*, red with *rajas,* and black with *tamas*.

its own nature. This is explained through the example of a cloudless blue sky. Eyes capture a substance with some form and, in its absence, see the absence as dark blue, or black. This, however, does not imply that the sky or darkness has some attribute of any form. That is, the blue color or the dark color is not the quality or attribute of the sky; but because the sky cannot be perceived, therefore, it appears blue. Thus, the blue color is because of the inherent form of the sky. Similarly, it is with *brahman*. Since *brahman* cannot be perceived through the senses, it therefore appears to be dark complexioned. If anything can be grasped through the senses, it will cease to be "beyond the senses" (*para*).

As in an empty room, because of the lack of objects, nothing is seen; similarly, in *brahman*, because of the absence of physical form, sense-perception of *brahman* is not possible.

To fulfil the aspirations of his devotees, God manifests or incarnates Himself. It can be for one person or for everyone. In the first case, it is appearance at any time, and is related to the circumstances or wishes of a particular individual. This is called *prākaṭya*. The other kind is for some general purpose, at a specific time, when the God incarnates Himself to protect his devotees. In this case, it is called *avatāra*.

Many attributes of *brahman* seem to contradict each other. For example, *Īśopaniṣad* describes *brahman* as: "It moves — yet it does not move. It is far away — yet it is near at hand! It is within this whole world — yet it is also outside this whole world" (Trans. OLIVELLE 1996, p. 249).[38] These contradictions, according to Vallabhācārya, indicate the essential nature of *brahman* which is the simultaneous abode of contradictory characteristics. This theory is called *viruddha-dharmāśrayatā-vāda*. It allows him to accept *brahman* simultaneously as blissful form and without any form.

In the context of Vallabhācārya's philosophy, the senses and sense — perception can now be examined in connection with the world (*jaḍa*), conscious souls (*jīva*), and God (*brahman*). First of all, the senses belong to the real world, are therefore real, and capable of perceiving the material world (*jaḍa*). The senses, in their normal functioning within the material world, cannot perceive conscious souls. This is because the souls do not have any physical form, characteristics or matter, and lack any contact with the sense organs.[39] Therefore, souls cannot be an object of sense-perception. There are, however, three ways of perceiving them: through the meditative practice of yoga; through vision, which is capable of perceiving God; and through divine vision. The mind, which is perfected and trained by yogic practices, can perceive the soul.[40] However, such a vision, according to Puruṣottama, enables one to see the conscious soul

[38] *Tadejati tannaijati taddūre tadvantike/tadantarasya sarvasya tadu sarvasyāsya bāhyataḥ/* (*Īśopaniṣad* 5).

[39] *Rūpādyabhāvāt sannikarṣābhāvācca* | (TDN Pr 1,56).

[40] *Tredhā darśanam/yogena sādhitaṃ manaḥ paśyati* | (TDN Pr 1,56).

only within oneself.[41] The vision capable of perceiving God is like the vision of those present at the time of the slaying of Śiśupāla (BhP 10.74.45), and divine vision like those of the gods at the time of the killing of Vṛtra (BhP 6.12.35). In the case of the latter two visions, it is possible to see the souls outside one's own self as well.[42] There are no other ways to perceive conscious souls.[43]

Brahman is different from the threefold division which constitutes the world. Not being the worldly reality, it cannot be known through worldly logical reasoning.[44] With the help of logic, only that which is within the sphere of the logical world can be known. *Brahman* can be known only through Vedic expressions. However, it is not possible to understand the meaning of the statements propounded in the Vedas through the simple knowledge of words and their meaning (using knowledge about grammar etc.).[45] Other means are required: ascetic penance is the preparatory means, Vedic reasoning is the concomitant means, and the grace of God is the main instrument. These three together, along with the appropriate place and time (*satya-yuga*), can yield the correct understanding of the meaning of Vedic expressions.[46]

Vallabhācārya, therefore, clearly distinguishes between worldly logical reasoning (*laukika-yukti*) and Vedic authority. *Brahman* cannot be an object of worldly epistemic means (*laukika-pramāṇa-viṣayatva*). Here, an objection may be raised. The authoritative texts (like BhG or BhP) speak about the incarnations of God, and they are objects of worldly epistemic means. So, it could be accepted that God is also an object of the epistemic means of knowledge.[47]

However, the incarnations of God are due to the fact that *brahman* can manifest itself (*āvirbhāva*) and also brings itself back to dormancy (*tirobhāva*). These incarnations are of various kinds. Their deeds are beyond any explanation through worldly epistemic means (*laukika-yukti-laṅghana*). For example, neither can the fish (as fish incarnation) can grow as long as one mile in a day (*yojana*), nor the boar (as boar incarnation) grow as big as a mountain in a few seconds. This indicates that it is wrong to accept the incarnations as objects of epistemic means.[48]

---

[41] *Tacca yogena sādhitameva paśyati antareva ca paśyati* | (PR p.2).

[42] *Dṛṣṭistu yābhagavantaṃ paśyati, divyā jñānadṛṣṭiśca yā tayā* | (TDN Pr 1,56).

[43] *Nānyathā taddarśanamityarthaḥ //* (TDN Pr 1,56).

[44] *Alaukikaṃ tatprameyaṃ na yuktyā pratipadyate //* (TDN 1,62).

[45] *Laukikaṃ hi lokayuktyāvagamyate, brahma tu vaidikam/vedapratipāditārthabodho na śabdasādhāraṇavidyayā bhavati /* (TDN Pr 1,62).

[46] *Tapaḥ pūrvāṅgam, vedayuktiḥ sahakāriṇī, bhagavadprasādo mukhyaṃ kāraṇam/ kvacid deśaviśeṣe/satyayuge kāle/pañcāṅgasampattau vākyārthabodho bhavati/* (TDN Pr 1,62).

[47] *Nanu, avatāreṣu bhagavattvaśruteḥ laukikapramāṇaviṣayatvavat laukikaviṣayatvamapi kuto na?* (TDN Pr 1,72).

[48] *Na hi matsyo'hnā yojanaśataṃ vardhate, nāpi kṣaṇena parvatākāro bhavati varāhaḥ* | ... *svato na laukikayuktigocaratvamityarthaḥ* | (TDN Pr 1.72).

But still, Kṛṣṇa and other incarnations were seen by all at that time, and one cannot say that those who saw him at that time had some kind of illusion. So, how can one say, that Kṛṣṇa or God cannot be an object of worldly perception? To this, the answer is that the eyes cannot see God on the basis of their own capacity; but when God wishes that "let him see me," then a person can see Him.[49] In other words, when God, through His own wish, removes the obstacles, then He can be the object of direct perception.

Two factors work in the perception of God: first, the wish of God to make Himself visible so that He can be an object of the senses; and second, His grace upon the devotees to make their senses capable of perceiving Him.

The effective agency in the case of perception of God is not epistemic, but God himself. In the hierarchy of Vallabhācārya's categorization, it functions not on the basis of *pramāṇa* (valid means of knowledge) but due to *prameya* (that which is to be known, the Absolute).

Abbreviations

BṛU	Bṛhadāraṇyaka-Upaniṣad
BhG	Bhagavadgītā
BhP	Bhāgavata-Purāṇa
KS	Kāmasūtra
KenaU	Kena-Upaniṣad
KaṭhaU	Kaṭha-Upaniṣad
PR	Prasthāna-Ratnākara
TDN	Tattvārthadīpa-Nibandha
TDN Pr	Prakāśa commentary on Tattvārthadīpa-Nibandha
VS	Vikrama Saṃvat
YS	Yogasūtra
YSVB	Yogasūtra: Vyāsa Bhāṣya

References

Sanskrit texts

KĀMASŪTRA (2009): DONIGER, W./KAKAR, S. (Trans.), Vatsyayana Kamasutra. – Oxford.

KENOPANIṢAD (1957): SWAMI GAMBHIRANANDA (Trans.), Eight Upaniṣads. Vol. 1 (with Śaṅkarācārya's commentary). – Calcutta.

ĪŚOPANIṢAD, KAṬHOPANIṢAD, TAITTIRĪYOPANIṢAD (1996): OLIVELLE, P. (Trans.), Upaniṣads: A new translation by Patrick Olivelle. – Oxford.

[49] *Tathāpi kṛṣṇādayaḥ sarvairdṛṣṭā api teṣu kathaṃ laukikapramāṇāviṣayatvam* | *tatrāha ... cakṣuḥ na svasāmarthyena bhagavantaṃ viṣayīkaroti, kintu bhagavadicchayaiva māṃ sarve paśyantu ityetadrūpayā tad dṛśyam* | (TDN Pr 1.72).

TATTVĀRTHADĪPA-NIBANDHA (Śāstrārtha-prakaraṇa) (1971): MISHRA, K.N. (Trans. and Ed.), Tattvārtha-dīpa-nibandha (Śāstrārtha-prakaraṇa). – Varanasi.
TATTVĀRTHADĪPA-NIBANDHA (Saprakāśaḥ) (2039 VS): 3 Vols. ŚRĪ VALLABHAVIDYĀPĪṬHA. – Kolhapur.
NYĀYASŪTRA (1913): Mahāmahopādhyāya Satīśa Chandra VIDYĀBHŪṢAṆA (Trans.), The Nyāya Sūtras of Gotama. – Allahabad.
PRASTHĀNARATNĀKARA (Gosvāmi Śrī Puruṣottama praṇīta) (2056 VS): Śrī Vallabhavidyāpīṭha. – Kolhapur.
BHAGAVADGĪTĀ (1983): KRISHNA WARRIER, A.G. (Trans.), Śrīmad Bhagavadgītā Bhāṣya of Śaṅkarācārya. – Madras.
SĀṂKHYATATTVAKAUMUDĪ (1976): BHATTACARYA, R.S. (Trans. and Ed.), Sāṃkhya-tattva-kaumudī. – Delhi.

Secondary sources

COLAS, G. (2013): Senses, human and divine. In: This volume.
FRANCO, E. (1987): Perception, Knowledge and Disbelief: A Study of Jayarāśi's Scepticism. – Stuttgart.
GOSWAMI, Sh.M. (2060 VS): Sevā aur Vrajalīlā. – Mandavi.
MATILAL, B.K. (1986): Perception: An Essay on Classical Indian Theories of Knowledge. – Oxford.
MUKERJI, P.N. (1963): Yoga Philosophy of Patañjali with Commentary of Vyāsa by Swāmī Hariharānanda Āraṇya. Trans. P.N. MUKERJI. – Calcutta.
OLIVELLE, P. (1997): Orgasmic rapture and divine ecstasy: The semantic history of *ānanda*. In: Journal of Indian Philosophy, Vol. 25, pp. 153–180.
TRIPATHI, R. P. (1997): Pāṇinīyavyākaraṇe Pramāṇasamīkṣā. – Varanasi.
VAUDEVILLE, C. (1980): The Govardhan myth in Northern India. In: Indo-Iranian Journal, Vol. 22, No. 1, pp. 1–45.

Monika Horstmann

Managing the Senses in Sant Devotion

Sense-perceptions and the faculty of perception we ascribe to the senses are culturally and historically conditioned. How both are conceived forms a part of complex processes: this is the thrust of this essay. To provide examples, I will use just one particular object: an inscribed scroll depicting the esoteric body. It was produced in the 19th century in the milieu of the Dādūpanth, a widely spread and once influential sect within the Sant religion as it flourished in Rajasthan (Northwest India).[1]

The Sant religion forms a fairly broad spectrum within the religious history of northern India. It started flourishing towards the end of the first half of the second millennium, and proliferated into many sects and innumerable lineages within these. The great names in the Sant religion are Nāmdev, Raidās, Kabīr, Nānak, Dādū, and many others. Once a hard core monastic constituency; it now survives in extremely reduced form. However, over those several centuries, it produced a stupendous wealth of literature and developed specific forms of religious practice. The Sant religion spread over northern India with immensely mobile preachers and singers of Sant compositions. The monastic constituency was in the past complemented by a large lay following of many stripes, not necessarily aligned to any sect, but consisting of sympathizers who might otherwise have followed ordinary Hindu social and religious customs. Today, Sant monastic constituencies have dwindled away and lay patronage is rather diffuse. Regardless of this, the fact remains that the difference between lay and monastic religious practice touches upon the religious management of the senses.

Especially from the late colonial period, the Sant religion was affected by new paradigms which were fueled by colonial discourse. The Sant religion practices non-iconic worship, with an emphasis on the interior realization of the Supreme, though this principle operates in a more complex reality. The Sants deny that orthodox ritual and caste are relevant for salvation. To sensibilities inspired by colonial discourse, such principles commended the Sants as an example of reformist enlightenment.[2] In the 20th century, when the image of modern man and the future of India formed a dominant topic of cultural reflection, this was not just an issue of debates in what one usually imagines to have constituted

[1] The sect is named after Dādū (1554–1603).

[2] The character of this discourse is well captured by Bandyopadhyay (2002).

the colonial public sphere. Rather, it had a direct impact on the various Sant groups themselves, whom to perceive as marginal actors in that sphere would be erroneous. They, in fact, responded to and were actively involved in the issues debated in that sphere. The role the body and the senses of both the *homo religiosus* and *politicus* was a vital aspect of that discourse.

In their compositions, the Sants tirelessly tell us about their perception and the management of the senses, a topic crucial for salvation. Sant sects, and adjoining institutions and groups related to these have endured into our time. The forms of their organization, however, have changed. In consequnece of the erosion of the monastic constituency, paradigms and forms of practice sustained by the religious virtuosi have almost vanished. Also, from within the monastic constituency, adjustment to modern requirements was sought, mainly motivated by the erroneous hope that this would stay the erosion of the monastic branches. Finally, patronage was a key factor in the creation of new religious sensibilities. Over some two centuries, the patrons of the Sants — among these were merchant caste elites, with a continuous record of patronage of particular religious institutions — developed a novel understanding of religion which, accordingly, informed and shaped the groups they patronized.

The Sant religion is governed by the belief that the world — in the sense of the worldly phenomena that we grasp mentally or physically — is transient, and thereby ultimately false. Nothing amidst phenomena can pilot you away from the cycle of existence to an eternal abode of liberation. The senses reveal something to you that is ontologically false. Yoked to the senses, you go astray. By religious practice, and assisted by a guru — human or divine — and the company of fellow devotees, you have to penetrate the erroneous notions created by the world to arrive at the insight that the soul and the Supreme abide in primeval union. This primeval union is, however, disturbed by the false consciousness with which we engage with the finite world. Accordingly, the primeval unity, which is the blissful infinite being-as-such (*sthiti*), needs to be restored. This can only be achieved by withdrawing the senses from the world. According to the Sants, and in consonance with commonly held Indian views, the senses roam the world where they encounter many sense objects. Their realm is characteristically called the "cattle pasture" (*gocara*), the word for "sense" and "cow" being the same. What the restlessly roaming senses perceive is digested by the sense organ called *man*. This is the mind or, in the sense of the seat of emotions, the heart. *Man* is the organ of volition, emotion, and conceptualizing. The sense perceptions of a manifold, fragmented, and unstable world confuse the mind. The person is besotted with ego-fantasies which suggest to him that he is discrete from all else. In fact, he is ultimately integral to the one Supreme if only he can let go of his ego. The deluded mind is pathetically fickle, ever craving for the world, stubbornly averse to turning away from the misery of worldly confusion. The mind is subordinate to *buddhi*, the sense which is able to discern and judge. Like the other senses, both *man* and *buddhi* are part of the transient nature of things. The *buddhi*, however, forms a relay between the transient world and the transcendent, that is, the imperturbable eternal soul, the Supreme embodied in humans. As long as the mind is unsteady, *buddhi* cannot make out the path to salvation.

The mind and the senses — the mind's harmful companions — have to be stopped from roaming. Sant compositions express this profusely in violent tropes: "The cow needs to be starved to produce milk." "The creeper will only grow if you deny it water." "The mind needs to be tortured and threatened to be slain." These are common messages of Sant literature; they are expressed in popular tropes inherited from traditions of yore. They are communicated through devotional singing and religious discourse. These two practices are the main expressions of communal worship, which bring together the lay and the monastic Sant constituency. Sant worship is, therefore, an experience with several facets: it deploys the sense faculties to create artistic, mainly musical, performances. The senses are depicted as imbibing the nectar stream of words and music in the course of a performance, and symbolize the devotee's travel from the finite to the infinite. Characteristic of Sant practice are night-long sessions of religious singing, interspersed with religious discourse. They take place at religious feasts, often featuring those vigils over consecutive days, as well as in private homes. The arena of worship, particular during mass festivals is, at the same time, also the mundane arena for socializing and politicking. It is no less part of the world than any other locale wherein attention is roaming continuously. Outside this arena, when worship is concluded and the vision has shifted from the framed religious to the ordinary perspective, the world prevails as usual. The experiences of the devotees are individual: they may either deepen or wear off the devotional groove in which their minds are running anyway, and their experiences are fleeting.

The message of Sant compositions (as they are performed in communal worship) points to a universe of ideas about the person and the senses which is related to another regimen. This is the universe of the ascetic practice of Haṭhayoga as it was particularly spread by the Nāthyogīs (Mallinson 2012). They trace their genealogy to Gorakhnāth (Gorakṣanātha; referred to from the 13th century) and other *yogīs*. They have been influential — and also symbiotically related to political power — over the length and breadth of the Indian subcontinent. In northwestern India, these *yogīs* are akin to the Sants, with regard to both their religious practice and tenets. Sant devotion and yoga blend: both are predicated on *bhakti* to God and guru (Bouillier 2008, Horstmann 2006). Sant literary culture, especially of the once dominant Dādūpanth, has appropriated and transmitted the works of Nāths in impressive richness. Whereas the concepts of yoga inform what is articulated in communal worship, the actual practice of yoga is rather removed from the venue of communal worship, for it has its locus in the *yogī*'s own body. Symbols derived from Haṭhayoga are profusely mentioned in the devotional songs and couplets recited in communal worship, but they rather appear as frozen tropes with the audience hardly relating them to the concepts they are derived from, let alone to living practice.

For yogic concepts suggesting a practice derived from these, we need to turn to the ascetic management of the senses as it formed part of the Sant tradition. The Hathayogic practice is predicated on the tantric body.[3] The body represents the microcosm, which is identical with the Supreme, the macrocosm. This is, therefore, inscribed in the microcosm. The yogic practice aims at straddling the opposites of finite existence and infinite being as well as female and male, with the female representing finite creation, and the male, the infinite immovable soul. The finite world is the manifestation of a female power, Śakti, who is not different from the one soul, but was extrapolated from the Supreme by himself so that he might be able to reflect himself. This lies at the beginning of diversification, the proto-stage of the phenomena as they appear to the mind and can be named and, therefore, grasped as discrete. Evolution from oneness to the multitude of phenomena is thought of as a gradual descent from subtle to gross manifestation. The point where union prevails is the space above the fontanel of the skull. Here all — such as speech sounds — merges into proto-speech sound, and thence into the idea of sound, and finally into the "unstruck," that is, the physically unmanifest, sound as symbol of union. Conversely, the point of full-fledged fragmentation into discrete phenomena is the bottom of the trunk. All physical processes take a downward direction. The quintessence of vital energy, semen, is shed and wasted in the procreation of diversity. It needs to be prevented from this through a practice by which all vital processes are reversed so that they move upward, progressively transformed on their way to the ever increasingly subtle until they merge into the shapeless. As for the semen, this is transformed into the one effulgent drop which is perceived by the *yogī* as it merges with the "unstruck sound" in supreme reality, but is also tasted as the nectar of immortality, dropping from the summit of perfection back on to the practitioner's palate. All senses have to be subjected to that reverse discipline. Withdrawn from their fleeting objects, they are transformed — but not annihilated — and merged into the state of "*so'ham*," "This is I." The traveler on the yogic path has this in his mind, and needs to memorize this and the regimen required at the various stations of his arduous travel by constant contact with a guru. The mind as traveler to the Supreme is identified with the goose (Anser indicus), *haṃsa*, on its way to the abode of Śiva, the lord of Mount Kailās in the Himalayas which is, in macrocosmical proportion, the summit of the universe. Exhaling is *haṃ*, inhaling *sa* (*so*), whereby the devotee himself in the rhythm of his breath becomes *haṃsa-so'ham*. The practice consists mainly in first cleansing the bodily conduits, and upon this regulating breathing over long periods, this being accompanied by visions, sound perceptions, and other physical sensations, and by meditation in which the objects inhabiting the stations are visualized by their gendered or ungendered characteristics, their number, colors, and so forth. Most of these stations are conceived of as diagrams which have their

[3] For the quite recent history of the medical reification of the tantrically imagined body, see ZIMMERMANN 2002.

counterpart in the ritualistic sphere. They are the seat of various deities and their retinue and symbols. By breath discipline, the energy, Śakti — perceived as a snake named Kuṇḍalinī and coiled up in the practitioner's abdomen above the anus — ascends. It is goaded up along the spine, while the breath circulating through thousands of conduits, drives it up further and further across the various stations. The spine is identical with the mythical Mount Meru on which the Supreme, Śiva according to the Nāthyogīs, resides.

The tantric traditions, including Haṭhayoga, are not openly accessible, but esoteric. They are cultivated in the relationship between guru and disciple, transmitted by personal instruction as much as by texts and charts of the esoteric body as they are used by the *yogī* on his itinerary. Gavin FLOOD (2006), making a strong point against the dislocation of Tantra from its cultural and especially textual sources into the realm of sensual well-being, has called this an "entexted" cultural practice. The yogic progress is a matter of "experience" (*anubhava*); but experience is prefigured by the tradition. "Experience" drawn from exoteric communal worship or, for that matter, from exercises alien to the original context, arises from the collective mood, but, against the esoteric practice handed down from master to disciple, it may be purely arbitrary, or idiosyncratic.

How the yogic ascent is to be achieved is depicted graphically, and in written explanation on the scroll which serves me as an example. It was made in 1869 in Bagaṛ, a place in the Jhunjhunu district of Rajasthan. I will say a few words towards the end of this essay about its role as an indicator in the history of sense perceptions.

The yogic esoteric body is not imagined uniformly, and the scroll exemplifies only one of the various concepts. Outside the live context of a religious lineage, where they form aids for practitioners, depictions of the yogic body rather represent objects of art. During the colonial period, the combined interest in exotic practices and art was among the many motives with which the numerous charts and paintings of the tantric body were commissioned. The esoteric body is often depicted with six or nine stations (*cakra*s) along the spine. This scroll

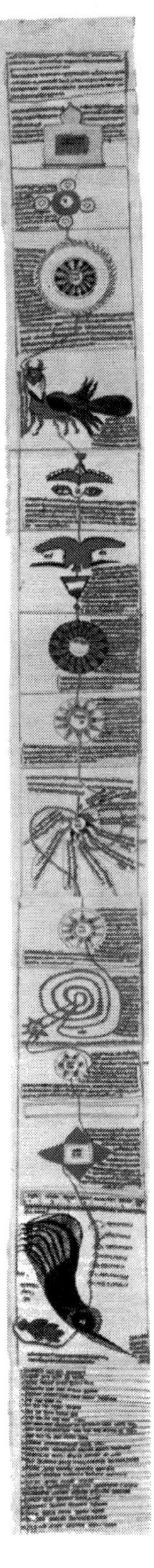

Figure 1: Hathayogic scroll by Bābā Rāmprasād, Bagaṛ (Jhunjhunu district, Rajasthan) in 1869. 250 × ca. 21 cm. Pigment colors and ink on paper.
The scroll is to be read from bottom upwards.

comes from a different tradition and is more akin to, though not identical with, a system which was documented by Gopinath KAVIRAJ (1987) almost 90 years ago.[4] Addressing the issue of differences between the number of stations taught by the different tantric schools, he says:

> very often a certain number of *cakras*, considered minor from one's own point of view, is supposed to form a connected whole. There are other reasons also which would explain the difference of the number in different systems. The actual description of a particular *cakra* is more important to a student for purposes of comparative studies. But even here, there are certain fatal limitations. For instance, the same *cakra* may not look exactly alike to different *sādhakas* (practitioners — MH). The personal *saṃkalpa* (resolution to carry out a religious task — MH) of the aspirant, either conscious or sub-conscious, and, that of his *Guru* go a great way towards determining the nature of the Vision. The reality observed is, in a certain sense, only ideal (1987, p. 53).

The transformation of the senses and the restoration of the primeval union of the soul and the Supreme is conceived of as a ritual performed as interior worship (*mānasī pūjā*). At every station of his interior travel, the practitioner makes over his ordinary senses to the transforming process, which implies both physical practice and esoteric sense perceptions as they take place at the respective stations. In the course of their progressive transformation, the senses operate synaesthetically. This is what the *yogī* is taught to visualize in his body: he sees the snakelike energy rising from his abdomen. On the scroll it is graphically extrapolated from the body; but this is only a pictorial strategy. The text has it properly coiled up where it belongs. A green creature, a tortoise, resides below it. This is related to the spine identical with Mount Meru. The gods and demons used this mountain as a churning stick to churn out of the cosmic ocean the nectar of immortality, along with various beneficial and destructive potencies. The support of their churning stick was the tortoise. The breath moves through the thousands of body channels, out of which the main ones are three. In the world, these are represented by three rivers, one of them spurious and whose confluence is at the pilgrimage site of Prayāg. In the body, these conduits also represent the moon and the sun merging at one of the upper stations, with the central one that runs along the spine. The ascent of the energy is brought about by yogic breath discipline. In the process, the practitioner meditates on what he is taught to encounter at the various stations on that upward travel. Perceived as mostly wheel-like and lotus-shaped and representing a cult diagram (*maṇḍalas*), they are realized as presided over by gods and goddesses, their vehicles escorted by mythic seers. The petals have such and such colors, and are inscribed with such and such syllables of the alphabet, or supra-phonemic sounds. At the

[4] I owe the reference to this article to James Mallinson. Kaviraj's seminal article regrettably offers neither an illustration nor the text of the two specimens he used.

lowest station — the four-petalled wheel where the world is thought to have unfolded to its fullest phenomenal shape, that is, the world as the ordinary senses would perceive it — all the speech sounds are manifest. By speech things are named, and thus come into cognitive, and thence physical existence by being named. Therefore, the perception of the world as consisting of discrete entities is established by language. Accordingly, language itself has to be brought back into its primeval unmanifest state, into the "unstruck sound." The yogic practice is accompanied by murmured prayer which is supposed to be continued over a long period, at the lowest station for a little over 24 minutes filled with 6000 of these prayers. At the topmost station, these prayers lose all physical reality. The soul (*jīva*), less and less encumbered by worldly grossness, is the goose flying to the summit of the mountain of its merging with the supreme. While at the consecutive stations of the yogic process, various kinds of sounds are prescribed as to be heard; at the highest station, the physical qualities of sound fade, and sound dissolves in the "unstruck sound" (*nāda*). The sound perceptions assigned to the various stations of the interior ascent take their raw material from ordinary sound perceptions. The sound of the kettledrum and the conch that resound at climactic points of temple worship are the auditory perceptions you take along with you on your interior pilgrimage. Just as the vigil passes the dark night, and just as the devotees have to be admonished by particular songs not to falter in their pursuit and succumb to the sleep of worldliness, and just as nocturnal community worship is concluded by the ritual of waving lights accompanied by a triumphant sound of just those instruments, the interior journey follows the model of what the senses perceive in the exterior world. Exterior and interior are identical.

The practitioner is asked to meticulously produce the prescribed sense perceptions, as may be illustrated by just one of the stations depicted. At the *man-cakra*, shown in Figure 2, he visualizes an eight-petalled lotus. It is presided over by the god Man, the *Śakti Buddhi*, the seer *Ātmā*, and is located in the middle of the navel, from which it springs, sitting on a ten-finger-long soft, tender stalk, with its blossom like that of a plantain turned downwards. Here, the disorder of the three bodily humors — wind, bile, and phlegm (*vāta, pita, śleṣman*) — is stopped. With reference to the center of the lotus-wheel, it is explained: "In the centre [of it] the soul attains steadiness." The petals represent the geographical main and intermediate directions as they are also indicated in the diagrams used as spaces for worship. To these are assigned the following sense perceptions: (1) East — white; if the mind halts there, it attains a disposition for praising the cosmic order (*dharma*). (2) Southeast — if the mind halts at the red fire (that is, southeast) petal, it attains a disposition for falling asleep. (3) South — if the mind halts at this black southern petal, it is full of wrath and ego. (4) Southwest — if the mind halts at this dark-blue petal, it is full of darkness and wishes: "I want to have a wife and son." (5) West—if the mind halts at this reddish western petal, it feels: "There are joy and feasts." (6) Northwest — if the mind halts at this black wheel, the consciousness is

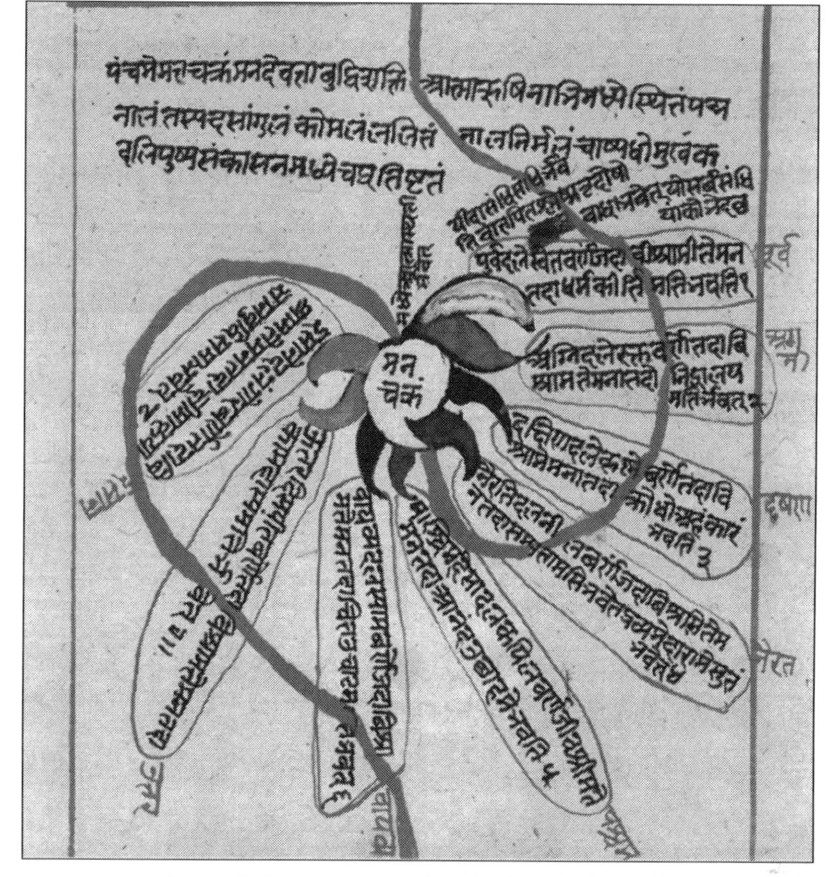

Figure 2: The *man-cakra* (partial view of Figure 1)

inclined to dislocate [adversaries] from their place.[5] (7) North — if the mind halts at this yellow petal, it is disposed for lust and fun. (8) Northeast — if the mind halts at this white petal, it becomes identical with a *buddhi* that is disposed for charitable acts and wisdom.

The example shows the complexity of sense perceptions of form, color, direction, and emotions that need to be learned by the aspiring *yogī* to enable him to proceed on his travel through the esoteric cosmos of his body.

For the sound perceptions, the *Haṭhayogapradīpikā* by Svātmarāma, a classical text of Haṭhayoga, describes, for example, the esoteric transformation of these:

> In the beginning, various sounds are heard within the body resembling those of the ocean, the cloud, the kettledrum and the jarjara drum. In the middle, [the sounds] resemble those of the drum (*mardala*), the conch, the bell and the

[5] One out of six tantric feats.

horn. Finally, the sounds resemble those of tinkling bells, the flute, the *vīṇā*, and bees. Thus are heard the various sounds from the middle of the body.

Even when the loud sounds resembling those of the clouds and the kettledrum are heard, attention should be turned to the subtler and still subtler sounds alone.

Even though the attention may shift from the gross to the subtle [sounds], or from the subtle to the gross [among the inner sounds], it should not be allowed to wander elsewhere, being [by nature] unsteady.

In whatever inner sound the mind first focuses itself, in that it reaches steadiness, and along with it [the sound, the mind] gets dissolved.

As a bee drinking honey cares not for the odor, so the mind absorbed in Nāda, does not crave for the objects [of enjoyment].

The sharp iron goad of Nāda effectively curbs the mind which is like an elephant in rut [difficult to control] wandering in the garden of sense-objects.

When the mind, having discarded its restlessness [caused by its constant identification with sense-objects], is held [steadfast] by Nāda, it becomes totally immobile, like a bird that has lost its wings.[6]

As has been mentioned, a number of stations do not have the form of diagrams or lotus-formed wheels. Among these, is the mythical composite animal (Figure 3) which is on the scroll, and also otherwise depicted as occupying a spot above the eyebrows. In charts of the esoteric body, it is represented in various ways, but is rarely commented on.[7] It is a beast with disturbing looks, and one wonders what obstacles the aspirant may have to overcome to face it. In the material studied by Kaviraj (1987), it is called *kāmadhenu*, "wish-fulfilling cow," and has an udder with four teats from which the nectar of immortality is streaming down continuously.[8] On the scroll, it has the face of a crow, human eyes (in Kavirjaj's material "intoxicant eyes"[9]), the horns of a cow, *līlā* and *brahma* as its wings, the neck of a horse, a peacock tail, and the gait of a goose (*haṃsa*, Anser indicus). The strange nature of the beast may not only have been inspired by the Indic mythical wish-fulfilling cow, but also by the mystic bird *Sīmorgh* which, as the symbol of the Supreme, figures prominently

[6] *Haṭhayogapradīpikā* 4.85–92, (Svātmarāma 1972, pp. 78–79). Similar descriptions occur in numerous other Sanskrit and vernacular texts. This passage of the *Haṭhayogapradīpikā* (ca. 14th century) has not been quoted with the assumption that it is more authoritative than other texts; but it represents one of numerous doxographic ways of establishing the esoteric perceptions.

[7] See White (2002) and cover illustration of the volume in which that essay appeared (British Library MS Add. 24099, f.118), no comment; Flood (2006), frontispiece: Cakra man (Wellcome Ms ā511), no comment.

[8] On the scroll, the udder is not shown. I infer this constituent of the animal from the corrupt text on which I have conjectured taking Kaviraj's lead.

[9] Kaviraj (1987, p. 50).

Figure 3: Station depicted as a mythical animal (partial view of Figure 1)

in Sufi mystic imagery, and for its peacock tail is beholden to India.[10] KAVIRAJ records: "The Yogin who has obtained access to this cakra and abides here becomes immortal and free of the effects of Time" (1987: 50). At the summit, the reversal intended by the yogic process is achieved. What is it exactly that has happened, according to yogic views? The semen, the quintessence of nature that forms and is doomed to perish, has been transformed into pure luminosity. *Bindu* (semen) merges with cosmic sound (*nāda*). The visualization of this is enjoined in a number of ways, one of which is:

> Or one should visualize a tremulous form of star in the *gollāṭamaṇḍapa* (space) situated a little above the forehead, or visualize the form like that of a red bee in the *bhramaraguhā*, or close the ears with the index fingers and listen to the *dhūṃ-dhūṃ* sound (reverberating) in the centre of the head, or else visualize a tiny doll of bluish tinge (situated) in the eyes.[11]

At this stage — shown on the scroll as a building with a knobbed dome — the practitioner will stay forever in the state of deepest meditation, whereas previous to this, he was expected to sustain his contemplation for 200 hours (1000 *ghaṭikās*).

---

[10] SCHMIDT (1980), SCHIMMEL (1995, pp. 434–436).

[11] *Sarvasiddhāntapaddhati*, ascribed to Gorakṣanātha, 2.27; probably 18th century (GHAROTE/PAI 2005, p. 38).

At the highest point of their interior travel, the accomplished Haṭhayogīs are considered to achieve liberation while alive. All vital functions cease, or seem to cease, and the practitioners drop into yogic "slumber." The Sants usually did not strive for this effect, for while they may have practiced yoga as a means, they denied that perfection could be attained at will and while alive.[12] There was a practice in which, upon the attainment of yogic slumber, *yogīs* were buried alive. Political reactions to such acts have had a role to play in the history of the senses as will be explained presently.

In the concluding part of this essay, I return to the history of the yogically defined senses in the religious practice of the Sants. I believe that some lineages of the early Sants, who hailed from milieus where Haṭhayoga was practiced, were also actively pursuing the practice of this kind of yoga. Sant literature describes the yogic process in detail, both in the original works and in the commentaries. Sants collected and edited Nāthyogic texts, and made drawings of the yogic practice. The architectural program of Sant settlements (monasteries, temples) features meditation caves which are specific to yogic practice. The tradition of locating yogic perfection in a mountain cave is ancient and widely documented.[13] We find meditation caves also in the basements of cenotaphs, and very often in the underground chambers of Sant monasteries. Wealthy patrons built these for their gurus. In numerous places, these are preserved or even restored, and devotees visit them as places to be revered. The caves are usually low and narrow, so that you have to fold yourself up, or even creep in, to become enwrapped in darkness. The use of such caves has not ceased, however various the practitioners populating these. The cave figures also in the esoteric process depicted on the scroll, where it represents the topmost station ("cave of the bee," *bhramarguphā*).

For the sake of historical precision, let us turn to the monastery where the scroll was produced in 1869. It is one of two monasteries which are genealogically connected with Jaimal Cauhān, a *yogī* disciple of the Sant Dādū, hence of the 16th/17th century. The scroll was made by Bābā Rāmprasād in 1869, that is, more than two centuries later. Rāmprasād's guru was Bhaktrām, who

---

[12] In the monastery of the Śivnārāyaṇī Candravār Dhām in the Baliya district of Bihar, the grave of the guru of this Sant order, with a basically Dalit following, is venerated. He is said to have gone into the deepest form of meditation, signifying liberation at lifetime, and was buried in this state, i.e., alive.

[13] "Dans les traditions médiévales des Siddha, une grotte montagneuse était la réplique macrcosmique de la voûte crānienne du yogin en méditation aussi bien que la chambre haute d'un appareil alchimique mésocosmique à l'intérrieur duquel l'alchimiste se transformait lui-même en opus alchimicum. L'univers à la Moebius des Siddha était ainsi construit qu'il permettait à ses praticiens à la fois d'identifier les montagnes cosmiques à leur propre corps subtil et de pénétrer dans ces montagnes pour réaliser le but final de leur pratique, leur propre transformation en habitants semi-divins de ces mêmes montagnes" (WHITE 2002, p. 208).

died around 1857. Bhaktrām enjoyed the patronage of wealthy merchants who invited him to settle in Bagaṛ, where they built him a handsome monastery. Until that point he had lived at the cenotaph of a princess.[14] The regional nobility also stepped forward as his patrons. Bhaktrām was a *Bhāgavatapurāṇa* specialist and said to have known this huge sacred text of Vaishnavism by heart. This corresponds to the common profile of Santism being close to Vaishnavism. Bhaktrām's disciple Rāmprasād, the maker of the scroll, was an ayurvedic practitioner, and into our time, the monastery of Bagaṛ has been a popular well-stocked dispensary of ayurvedic medicine. Rāmprasād greatly developed his place, and was acclaimed for his charity and patronage of buildings and water-reservoirs also elsewhere in Rajasthan. He was a man of means, investing the wealth that had come to him by patronage. As for the scroll Rāmprasād made for himself, it represents an object of religious (self-) instruction rather than an object of art.[15] Rāmprasād's successor was Mayārām who, even now, long after his death, is revered in Bagaṛ for his saintliness. He had a disciple who became an ascetic. For several years, this man dwelt in a cave in the hills above the pilgrimage site of Ṛṣikeś. Mayārām's successor, Svāmī Ātmārām, who passed away in 2007, was a university-educated specialist of grammar and Vedānta. He grafted on the sacred vernacular scripture of his sect a philosophical commentary in Sanskrit, an erudite but hybrid work.

Rāmprasād reached out to his followers with discourses on the *Bhāgavata*; but by the scroll can also be seen as having cultivated his yogic disposition. The one talent was put into use for the satisfaction of his following; the other for himself — or so at least I imagine, perhaps claiming a contrast where an effortless blending of pursuits may have prevailed. During a stay in Bagaṛ in 2006, when I asked Svāmī Ātmārām (then well over 90 years old) for materials in his library that might deserve examination, he had the scroll produced for me by his servant–disciple. Interestingly, he himself showed the least bit of enthusiasm for it; neither did he care to explain the object to his be-riddled disciple, although he was a proven scholar in this discipline.

These sparse historical hints indicate how yoga as a live form of management and esoteric transformation of the senses popular with the Sants was gradually superseded by other activities and interests. In the Nāthyogic institutions of the region, a similar situation prevails.[16] This development can be related to politics and changing cultural perceptions. Rajasthan, then Rajputana, had become a British protectorate in 1818. Among the customs which the colonialists were interpreting as social evils that had to be redressed was one which was

---

[14] Cenotaphs often feature ground-chambers and meditation caves.

[15] This may account for the strange combination of an accomplished handwriting with positively non-standard orthography. The text of the scroll is in Sanskrit interspersed with Hindi. Certain misspellings suggest that Rāmprasād had before him written or inscribed painted material.

[16] Bouillier (2008); Mallinson (2012).

emblematic of the popular yogic stance prevalent in the region. I mentioned the practices and miracles by which *yogīs* given to magical practice variously impressed or intimidated people. Amongst these figured *samādhi* — literally, "absorption in meditation" — which is marked by the symptoms of deep sleep. Endemic in Rajasthan, the live inhumation in an alleged state of *samādhi* "was practiced either out of devotion for one's master or the ruler or the high priest or out of disgust with the world," as has been summarized from the reports of eye witnesses of the practice (VASHISHTHA 1978, p. 239). In 1839, a woman in Kota who had become a follower of the Nāthyogīs, had herself inhumed alive. These incidents triggered a debate between the British and the regional lords of Rajasthan, who were staunch supporters of the custom. The *samādhi* custom, deeply engrained and tenaciously defended at a critical period when society was undergoing landmark changes, was eventually penalized in 1861. It seems that *samādhi* as live inhumation occurred especially in socially vulnerable milieus. The Nāthyogīs formed a powerful segment of society: in Marwar, for instance, they were for some time the factual rulers until they were removed by the British in 1842.[17] Concurrent with this was the rampant malpractice of fake *yogīs*. For people desperately looking for patronage, to impersonate *yogīs* must have formed a way of finding recognition and support. In consequence of the bad reputation heaped on *yogīs*, Nāthyoga claiming to be leading to a meditation bordering on death (*jīvanmukti*), surely met with increasing disaffection.

Around the same time, the very ideals of yoga also underwent a change. The ideas of Svāmī Vivekānanda (1863–1902) who, since 1893, had sweeping success in spreading his version of a modern form of Hinduism in the United States, propagated a yoga of social action as the only one actually suitable for modern man. His ideas were enthusiastically received in India. The reformist teachings of Dayānand Sarasvatī (1824–1883), and the educational reforms initiated by his reform movement Ārya Samāj, had also started making a deep impact on Rajasthan. This reflected on the Sant monkhood, especially of the Dādūpanth, whose leaders started reforming and academically institutionalizing ayurvedic training, and also founded a Sanskrit college for the education of their monks. In this new educational system, a new ideal of the body was also launched. This can be admired on the photographic mementos of college functions which featured competitions for manly sports. It was no longer the yogic body and esoteric perfection that was sought; now it was the virile body, as it were, of the social activist that was regarded as ideal. This ideal, generated by a debate conducted in Britain and taken to India, became a preoccupation, thus occupying the colonial public space. The male, manly body signified political superiority. The manly body was that of the British colonizer; the allegedly

[17] The king of Jodhpur, Man Singh (1818–1843), was totally given to the influence of his Nāth guru. Eventually, Nāth dominance caused serious maladministration, which prompted the intervention of the British (VASHISHTHA 1978, pp. 120–138).

effeminate body was that of the colonized Indian. This Indian morosity needed to be redressed so that political liberation could be attained. Moreover, once colonial discourse sanitized the Sants by portraying them out of the context of their traditional milieus as enlightened representatives of an interior religion — and thereby akin to Protestant Christians — what had in the past been yogic elements of the Sant practice shrunk to equivocal "yogic metaphors." A number of outstanding scholars, both British and Indian, were among the makers of this image. The famous Sant Kabīr was hailed by the British scholar W.W. Hunter as the Indian Luther (See BANDYOPADHYAY 2002 for this and similar assessments). Of the Sants, P.D. BARTHWAL said: "The religion that they represent is simple, unostentatious and of universal application. By tearing off the superficialities of conventional religions they have brought into bold relief the essential nature of the real religion" (1978, p. xi).

Not a few of the Indian scholars in the period of India's struggle for independence saw their own work as a contribution to the project of Indian modernity. In their view, the Sants typified a religion consonant with the contemporary ideal of liberated, modern man. As a representative of this group of intellectuals one can name Hazārī Prasād Dvivedī.[18]

The patrons of both the Sants and the Nāthyogīs, were now the wealthy urbanized merchants who had made their fortune in the metropolis as well as in inter-regional and world trade, but invested in the places in Rajasthan from which they hailed. They were no less part of that modern discourse. Their patronage carried with it the seeds of change in sensibilities. This is exemplified by the lineage of the yogically minded Sants as well as the Sant-minded Nāthyogīs of the region. The new paradigm of social service (education, health service, charitable institutions) made pursuits such as those depicted on the scroll obsolete, and caused this and related written testimonies to collect dust in the archives.

References

BANDYOPADHYAYA, P. (2002): The Uses of Kabīr: Missionary Writings and Civilisational Differences. In: HORSTMANN, M. (Ed.), Images of Kabīr. – New Delhi.

BARTHWAL, P. D. (1978): Traditions of Indian Mysticism Based upon Nirguna School of Hindi Poetry. – New Delhi.

BOUILLIER, V. (2008): Itinérances et vie monastique. Les ascètes Nāth Yogīs en Inde contemporaine. – Paris.

BOUILLIER, V./TARABOUT, G. (Eds.) (2002): Images du corps dans le monde hindou. – Paris.

FLOOD, G. (2006): The Tantric Body. The Secret Tradition of Hindu Religion. – London.

[18] For a pioneering study, see SIMH (1982). See also HORSTMANN (2002, pp. 115–26).

GHAROTE, M.L. and PAI, G.K. (Ed., Trans.) (2005): Siddhasiddhāntapaddhatiḥ. A Treatise on the Nātha Philosophy by Gorakṣanātha. – Lonavla.

HORSTMANN, M. (Ed.) (2002): Images of Kabīr. – New Delhi.

KAVIRAJ, G. (1987): The System of Cakras According to Gorakṣanātha. In: SHASTRI, G. (Ed.): Id., Notes on Religion and Philosophy (The Princess of Wales Sarasvati Bhavana Studies, Repr. Ser. No. 3). 1st edition – Varanasi, 1923.

MALLINSON, J. (2012). Nāth Sampradāya. In: Brill's Encyclopedia of Hinduism, Vol. 3: 409–428.

SCHIMMEL, A. (1995). Mystische Dimensionen des Islam. Die Geschichte des Sufismus. – Frankfurt/M. and Leipzig.

SCHMIDT, H.P. (1980): The Sēmurw. Of Birds and Dogs and Bats. In: Persica 9, pp. 1–85.

SIMH, N. (1982): Dūsrī paramparā kī khoj. – Delhi.

SVĀTMĀRĀMA (1972): Haṭhayogapradīpikā, with the commentary Jyotsnā of Brahmānanda and English translation. – Madras.

VASHISHTHA, V.K. (1978): Rajputana Agency 1858/1932. – Jaipur.

WHITE, D.G. (2002): Le monde dans le corps du Siddha. Microcosmologie dans les traditions médiévales indiennes. In: Bouillier and Tarabout, pp. 189–212.

ZIMMERMANN, F. (2002): Ce qu'un hindou dit à son corps. La réécriture des représentations traditionelles. In: Bouillier and Tarabout, pp. 49–69.

The Anthropology of Senses

Christoph Wulf

The Vision: Control, Desire, Perception

The history of vision oscillates between the high points of radiant insight and controlling mastery and the low points of being overwhelmed and suffering. In the genealogy of the human senses, the sense of sight has become the central sense. The ambivalence and ambiguity of cultural-historical processes are reflected in its history. The sense of sight allows the expansion of the human body; according to a formulation by Herder, it flings us "great distances far beyond ourselves" (1891, p. 64). Objects and people outside the body can be captured by the eye and brought into the interior of the body. In vision, the foreign is experienced "on the sensing areas of one's own body" (Plessner). The sense of sight enables a sort of "intermediate corporeality." The world is "captured by the eye." Vision is directed at an object or another person, and makes a selection from the visual environment. Vision is a movement of attention and focus and simultaneously one of turning away and exclusion. The affinity of the sense of sight for abstraction lies in this peculiarity of the sense of sight bridging the distance between humans and things while nevertheless maintaining the distance in one's perception, thus creating a "distant proximity." The hypertrophic "transformation" of the world into image contributes to the abstraction of life processes. In the excessiveness of image production, images today often lose the relationship to that which is outside of the image; their representational character disappears. Images increasingly relate to other images, and quote them or excerpts from them. They create reference frames themselves, in regard to which they demand validity. Images, simulacra, and simulations generate new image worlds at great speed and with rigorous editing. These extreme developments, which have been induced first and foremost by the new media and their virtual image worlds, have an influence on perception; for the time being, the extent of their effects can only be gradually assessed (Baudrillard 1983, McLuhan 2001, Virilio 1994, Wulf 2013).

In contrast to the senses of touch, smell, and taste, which are relegated to the sphere of the private, the sense of sight lays claim to the sphere of the *public*. Through its public character, it takes on *control* and *self-control* functions, and contributes to the restriction of the variety of vision and to the endangerment of the diversity of sensuous experiences. Each individual sense conveys genuine experiences and results in the enablement for the individual of a sensuous certainty of the world and himself. The interweaving of various sensuous experiences helps to create *sense*. Erwin STRAUS expresses these issues and their significance for human experience and self-experience as follows:

> The present nature of sensuous feeling — and thus sensuous feeling in general — is the experience of co-being, which develops into the subject and the object. He who is sensing does not have sensations, but instead has himself because he is sensing (1956, p. 272).

The sensing of one's own presence in the sensuous reaction to the world conveys body and subject with the world and the objects. In this sensing, one experiences transformations and continuities. This is a prerequisite for human consciousness of the self.

> It is not until it senses that the subject attains itself. As such, it first has a Here and a Now ... The sensuous certainty of the outside world would not be able to be derived from *individual* sensations: we would have to lack this certainty if individual sensations were something other than a differentiation and delimitation of the original 'I-world relationship' of sensation (ibid.).

The senses are *reflexive*. When seeing, man experiences not just the visible, but also himself as the one who is seeing. In the words of MERLEAU-PONTY:

> The puzzle lies in the fact that my body is simultaneously seeing and visible. He who can observe all things can likewise observe himself, and in that which he sees at the moment, he can recognize the 'other side' of his ability to see (1967, p. 16).

Vision, thus, involves an interweaving of the perception of objects — which can also include one's own body — and one's own subjectivity. This is the peculiarity of vision, of the relationship of man to himself and of his relationship to the world in general. In the face of another person, one seeks with the eye the eye of the Other and is reflected in it. Seeing the Other, one is also seen and perceives oneself as seeing. The crossing of views is the *chiasma of vision*. The eye becomes the "window of the soul" into which one looks. But, at the same time, it is also the "window" through which one looks, through which one crosses the border between the interior and the exterior of one's own body. The notion of "mere" vision which just pictures objects or people is a short circuit of superficial insight. Memories, ideals, and fantasies of the seeing person influence the vision; they generate an individual, perspective-laden image of the Other and the world.

SARTRE has already pointed out that viewing another person differs greatly from viewing an object. One views another person as an object and as a person at the same time. As a person, he as well as I can see objects, and he can turn his gaze to me. This refers to a "state of being coupled to the Other." If the object–Other is defined in conjunction with the world as the object that sees what I see, my basic relationship to the subject–Other must be able to be traced back to my constant possibility of being able *to be seen* by the Other (SARTRE 1952, p. 342). The option of being able to be seen by the Other differentiates the Other from "mere" objects. If I catch the glance of the Other, I no longer see his eyes as objects. His glance is reference to myself. MERLEAU-PONTY's posthumously published book *The Visible and the Invisible* (1994) takes an additional step in the same direction.

These reflections on vision, which arise with more of a claim to universality, also need to be historically and culturally relativized. On the basis of the release of the eye–hand field in association with walking upright, vision develops in a variety of ways in accordance with the respective historical and societal conditions (LEROI-GOURHAN 1993). Each historical epoch develops a special relationship to the sense of sight and a special *politics of vision*. The transition from orality to literality in the time of Plato represents such a caesura in the history of vision. With *literacy*, vision comes under the influence of written language. As "theoria," it becomes a knowledge movement that gradually results in a logocentric transformation of the sense of sight. Similarly, profound caesuras in the history of vision came about due to the invention of book printing, which led to the proliferation and establishment of logocentrism. The medialization of the sense of sight through the telescope, microscope, and new media led to further far-reaching changes to vision: vision is a physiological and historical–culturally shaped process with strong social and individual differences. In the course of European history, it has developed a variety of manifestations, several of which will be presented below.

Antiquity and the Middle Ages

It was already at an early point in its development that Greek philosophy concerned itself with the question of how visual perception occurs. Democritus and Epicurus start from the assumption that the images entering individuals from the outside, images which are referred to as *eidola*, generate perception and thought. Vision is understood as a process in which images emanate from objects and encounter the eye. A material substance is attributed to these images; they are thought to be physical. As EPICURUS writes:

> For the outward flow from the surface of the body proceeds in steady succession ahead of itself without announcing itself through diminution, because replacement for it arrives; in the process, the image that is flowing outward preserves the position and order of the atoms on the fixed body for a very long time, even if it becomes confused at times (1921, p. 245).

Lucretius continues these thoughts, and speaks of *simulacra*, of "little films" that are sent outward from visible objects. In these "reception theories," vision seems to be a special case of the sense of touch. Diderot, Herder, and Gehlen seized on these ideas, and modified them within the scope of their theories of vision. In contrast, according to Plato's understanding, vision is created through a beam of fire coming out of the eye and merging with sunlight. This "ray theory of vision," which can be traced back to Empedocles, among others, finds expression in *Timaios* and *Theaetetus*. He states the following in this regard:

> If the light flowing out from the face is now absorbed by daylight, like meets like and merges into a single body of the same type in the straight direction from the eye, where the fire flowing outward from within always meets up with something that steps in its way from the outside. Since this substance universally experiences the same effects as a result of its homogeneity, it shares with the entire body all movements that it receives — in part through its touching of another, in part through triggering on the part of another — and allows them to penetrate through to the soul. The perception that we call 'vision' arises in this way *(Timaios* 45b-d).

ARISTOTLE (1961, 418b pp. 5–9) opposes the "receiver" and "sender theories" of his predecessors, but he cannot do without a materially understood intermediary between the given object and the viewing soul. In his understanding, the medium of vision is the transparentness that can be found with all bodies, especially in the case of air and water. The transparent is determined to be that "which is visible, to be sure; not from itself however, but instead, due to the color of another thing. Water, air, and many solid bodies are of this type." Light is the color of the transparent; it is the disembodied state of a medium that bridges the space between the visible object and the interior of the eye. It is moved by the color of the object; it itself then arouses the sensing organ of the soul located in the interior of the individual. Aristotle admittedly challenges Plato's understanding of the sending and merging of rays, but he accepts his understanding of the existence of a common visual medium that creates the connection between the object and the observer (LINDBERG 1987, pp. 30*ff*). Euclid's seven theorems of optics, Heron of Alexandria's science of vision with his theory of optics, refraction, and reflection, as well as Ptolemy's theory of perception lead to further differentiations in the classical theory of vision.

In the Islamic world, Euclid's mathematical sending theory of vision developed by Ptolemy and al-Kindi met with a rival but very similar Galenic sending theory that was further developed by Hunain ibn Ishaq and others. But even in the Islamic world, opponents of these theories can be found. Al-Razi, Abu Nasr al-Farabi, Avicenna, and Averroes are among the most well-known. Avicenna and Averroes take up the Aristotelian ideas on the theory of vision and develop them further. The following can be found in the commentary on the Aristotelian *Parva Naturalia* in the critique of Euclid, Ptolemy, Galen, and al-Kindi in this regard:

> We assert that air, by means of light, first receives the forms of the objects and then passes them onto the outermost sclera. This membrane then passes these

> onto the other skins until the movement reaches the innermost membrane, behind which the general sense is located. The latter perceives the form of the object (AVERROES 1961, p. 18).

In the Middle Ages, the conflict in regard to the correct understanding of vision continues. In the late Middles Ages, three different positions regarding the theory of vision can be discriminated:

- Albertus Magnus advocates the Aristotelian theory.
- Roger Bacon draws on Plato's and Alhazen's theory of vision and tries to integrate the various theories of the time.
- Theological notions regarding the theory of vision are derived from the Bible.

The classical theories of vision continue to be influential in the Renaissance as well. The extent to which they make a contribution to the development of perspective is controversial in research. In Leon Battista Alberti's treatise *Della Pittura*, which was dedicated to Brunelleschi, a short description of the cone of vision or the pyramid of vision appears. In this work, Alberti avoids taking a position in the controversy regarding the conditions of vision. What interests him more are the practical techniques of the production of images with perspective. These include Brunelleschi's peephole for the illustration of perspective, a "velo" device consisting of a curtain, and the mirror. Ghiberti's writings show basic knowledge of vision theories from antiquity and the Middle Ages. They use the cone of vision to explain the "geometric process through which the three-dimensional field of vision is projected onto the two-dimensional board" (LINDBERG 1987, p. 273). Leonardo da Vinci's theory of vision is based on a "reception theory" of vision, according to which the forms go from the objects to the observers.

Astronomers from this time, such as Kepler, were also aware that the validity of their observations depended on the adequacy of their theories of vision. Accordingly, Kepler's research produced lasting results. His theory of the retinal image is one of his most important results.

Power and control

The struggle with the central perspective in the painting of the Renaissance led to the establishment of a mathematically logical vision that orders the world of the visible with regard to the position of the seeing person who forms the focal point of the visual order. This led to the dominance of a perspective-distancing view in painting (HELLER 1982, BELTING 2008). Over the course of the next three centuries, a monitoring and controlling view is established in the emerging sciences, one that again instrumentalizes and functionalizes vision. Objects and social conditions are perceived from this perspective. Ambitions that already exist guide the view; elements that confound them are excluded from perception. In this view, man's aspiration to have dominion over nature and other people prevails. The world of the visible is reified and objectified. Excerpts are selected and regarded with a "cold" view; they are shrunk or enlarged, and the results of the study are inserted into a system of interpretation in which the phenomena are only expressed to the extent that they have been queried. In the Preface to the second edition of *Critique of Pure Reason* (1787), Kant defines this process as follows:

> Reason, holding in one hand its principles, according to which alone concordant appearances can be admitted as equivalent to laws, and in the other hand the experiment which it has devised in conformity with these principles, must approach nature in order to be taught by it. It must not, however, do so in the character of a pupil who listens to everything that the teacher chooses to say, but of an appointed judge who compels the witnesses to answer questions which he has himself formulated (Norman KEMP-SMITH's translation of *Critique of Pure Reason*, 1929, p. 20; http://www.hkbu.edu.hk /~ppp/cpr/toc.html).

Kant, thus, formulates the program of modern science which, in its search for general laws, makes itself into the judge over nature, which is surveyed and experimented upon. It is necessary to regard nature with the "independence" and "objectivity" of a judge, and to make it into the object of knowledge. "Thinking now means conducting experiments, operating and transforming with the sole reservation of an experimental control in which only heavily processed phenomena arise, which are more generated by our instruments than merely registered" (MERLEAU-PONTY 1967, p. 13).

The world responds in the reference system of operations to which mankind subjects it. The consequence: in the end, man confronts only his logos, his theories and concepts — the results of his action. The eye is armed: with eyeglasses, telescopes, microscopes — with instruments that only provide an excerpt from the world, on which the investigating eye of the "appointed judge" concentrates. A "one-eyed" view emerges (FOUCAULT 1976), which becomes a means of distancing and power, which controls, subjects, and asserts dominance. The great diversity of the world and the sensuousness of the eye are sacrificed. The ideal now becomes "pure" vision, which attempts to rid itself of the individual observer. Man plays a role only as the bearer of the controlling view, which makes the world uniform on an indiscriminate and inter-subjective basis. The eye is functionalized; it serves previously determined objectives to which it is directed. Irritations and digressions must be avoided; they weaken the claim on dominance, and must be referred to spaces and times outside of science. Vision is subject to the constraint of instrumental reason: it is directed at that which is unambiguous, at that which is already given in the order of the visible.

Using the example of the "Archaeology of Medical Perception," FOUCAULT (1976) showed how new scientific understanding usurped vision in the last decades of the 18th century. It is bound to a changed understanding of illness, an altered relation to language, vision, and knowledge in medicine and to the activity of the doctor. Along with this came the development of a national medical supply system, which led to a developed medical monitoring and control of the population. In the creation of this new medical knowledge, the clinics play a major role; they become the preferred location of medical experience. At the center of this experience is the medical view which is, at the same time, knowledge. Medical science takes its bearings from the "decisions of the view."

> The view of the doctor reorganizes itself. It is one day no longer the view of some observer, but instead the view of a doctor, supported and legitimized by an institution, a doctor who can make decisions and intervene. This view is, thus, no longer bound to the tight grid of structure (of form, disposition, number, size), but instead can and must register the colors, variations, the smallest anomalies, by constantly lying in wait for deviations. In the end, it is a view that does not satisfy itself with the determination of that which is immediately visible; it needs to help comprehend opportunities and risk; it is a calculating view (FOUCAULT 1976, p. 103).

The disease symptoms are the signs that make it possible for the recognizing view to identify the disease behind them. The doctor decodes them, and integrates them into the order of truth that is one with the order of language. It is not until then that he becomes therapeutically active. His view has two directions. On the one hand, he observes, faithfully assimilates the immediate, exercises restraint with theoretical interpretations, leaves everything in its place; on the other hand, he allows himself to be led by his knowledge by integrating that which is seen into a general order. It comes to an interplay between the "spoken and perceived moments in observation," and the attempt to "create a fixed correlation between the view and language" as well as to the ideal of an "exhaustive description." Medical experience is constituted through the fact that the medical view is infused with knowledge, and every symptom has its own meaning — or is given meaning — in conjunction with other symptoms. The more precise the observation, the greater the chance of gaining an adequate knowledge of the disease. What is of interest is the totality of the visible; that is what constitutes the overall structure of the statements. "Over all efforts that clinical thought makes in order to define its scientific methods and standards, the myth of a pure view sublimely floats, one that is pure language: the myth of the speaking eye" (ibid., p. 128). This idea applies to modern scientific observation: here the pure view reigns — which is pure language, strengthened by instruments and apparatuses, and which is completely delivered up to the order of the visible and its description.

The development and spread of the monitoring and disciplining view is reinforced through societal institutions that increasingly develop in these decades, especially through the *military, the police, the prison, the school system* (FOUCAULT 1977). Precise drill regulations emerge, and these assist in the continuation of the discipline that occurs under the watchful eye of the supervisor down to the coordination of individual body parts. The police presence continues to grow. While the convict led an existence in the darkness of the dungeon away from view during the era of absolutism, ideas for reforming the penal system now emerge. In Jeremy Bentham's prison, the crucial element is that the prisoner is subjected to absolute visibility, and thus to much more effective control. Sitting in a central tower, withdrawn from the views of the prisoners, the guard can observe the prisoners in their cells arranged in a circle around the tower. The consequence: the prisoners believe that they are under constant surveillance. In the field of education, general compulsory school education is gradually achieved; it leads to continuous monitoring through the "pedagogical view" within the scope of lessons. This view compares and classifies pupils, and is geared towards the adherence to rules (WIMMER 2006, GEBAUER/WULF 1993). The development of a "speaking eye" in the sciences, and the development of a monitoring view in social institutions, go hand-in-hand. With the aid of technology and administration, a tight network of controls is created, one in which the world of the visible is captured along with the seeing individual.

The many locations in which surveillance cameras are installed represent important indications that many technical and medial developments are targeted at the advancement of monitoring and control. Traffic monitoring, security services, and identification cameras are just a few examples of the growing number of options for camera-driven registration and monitoring. In this context, more and more "seeing machines" replace the human view (VIRILIO 1994). They are based on computer-controlled programs and identification images that these machines use to carry out material checks, in the scope of which qualitative deficiencies can be identified.

Wish and desire

This vision, which is aimed at control and objectivity, is pitted against vision driven by desire. What are repressed here are demands for enlightened and sovereign vision. The eyes no longer obey the will; they take on a life of their own and force one to cede their wanderings. This view is disturbing; it defies decency and social order. It is aggressive, attacks its victims, and swallows them. In contrast to the mouth, whose gluttony destroys, the cannibalistic view injures; it does not destroy the victim. The desire of the view leads "the subject back to his significant dependence" (LACAN 1975). It takes its basis from the separation that occurs due to birth. The deprivation that results from this is painful. The desire suggests satisfiability in vain. Experience is needed to show the unsatisfiability of the desire. FREUD also saw the erotic character of the eye and view, and wrote about it in multiple instances. In his essay "The Uncanny," FREUD interpreted E.T.A. Hoffmann's *Sandman* psychoanalytically in this way. At the center of his interpretation is the eye motif. In reference to the self-blinding of Oedipus, FREUD sees a symbol for the phallus in the "eye." According to his interpretation, the fear of the loss of the eye, which grips the young Nathanael due to a threat from the sandman the attorney Coppelius as the embodiment of the "mean father" is a literary handling of the fear of castration. A parallel to this childhood scene at which Nathanael risks a look is the fight of the professor Spalanzani with the optician Coppola. The victim, the doll Olympia, loses its sight; the resistance of the good father is in vain. Insanity grips Nathanael; the consequence of the castration of the doll is expressed in the ripping out of its eyes. Nathanael confronts the doll as a liberated complex of his own person, and that finds expression in Nathanael's compulsive love. In FREUD's words: "We have the right to call this love narcissistic and understand that the one overcome by it is estranged from the real love act" (1970, p. 256).

The erotic and sexual character of the eye becomes even clearer in Georges BATAILLE's *Story of the Eye*. The eye appears here as a symbol for the vagina, the anus, and the mouth. It becomes an indication of the desire for incorporation with which the discontinuity of life is to be overcome. The eye registers the erotic as "agreement to life unto death" and creates an inexhaustible desire that is targeted at merging with the desire of the Other. The eye appears again and again in this history as an indication of the arousal of the body, as allure to surrender and commitment of the body to the lover. In Simone's "break an eye, gouge out an egg," the phallic symbolism and the destructive violence of the erotic find expression. For BATAILLE, the eye is also the image of inner experience. "It is a mirror and lamp." Its fire presses outwards and makes the world visible; at the same time, it collects the "light of the world" in the iris and transforms it into the "clear night of images." It is the image of being that is nothing other than the overstepping of one's own limits. Accordingly, it is a peculiarity of the eye that it oversteps its limits in its view.

> It wears itself out in the day in a movement that only reveals its white, [...] and the eye turns the nightly circularity of the iris toward the darkness in the middle, illuminates it like a flash, and reveals it as night. The broken eye is simultaneously that which is most securely closed, and that which is most widely open (BATAILLE 1979, p. 83).

The broken eye is an expression of erotic ecstasy and of death, which limits its possibilities, pushes it into speechlessness, and extinguishes it. The broken eye refers to the realm of language, in which language and death converge.

Perception and thought

With all their differences, the controlling view which is oriented toward objectivity, and the one driven by desire, are not completely different from each other. Building on the latter works of MERLEAU-PONTY, Jacques LACAN made it clear how strongly desire influences vision. As a consequence of the original division associated with birth, a desire to reverse this separation emerges. This is necessarily directed outward, from where a satisfaction of the want on which the desire is based is expected. The subject, subjugated to the desire, hopes to overcome the division through which the desire is constituted by overcoming the divide from the object located in front of him in the field of the visible. Even though the hope is illusory, the subject must hold on to it so that the subject and object are connected to each other through the structure of the desire. Like the mimicry of many animals, in the course of which the world of objects "falls into" them, and makes them into a part of the "tableau" of the object world in color and form, there is a view on the part of the objects that demands the assimilation of the seeing persons through the structures of mimesis. The seeing person feels looked at and prompted to assimilate. He no longer confronts the object world, but is instead part of the object world, which is in him before it lies before him, and by which he hopes to be desired. LACAN formulates it as follows:

> The subject is not completely there; it is remotely controlled. In amendment of my formula for desire as unconscious — *the desire of man is the desire of the Other* — I would like to say that it is a sort of desire for the Other/desir à l'Autre, at the end of which is the giving-to-see/le donner-voir. The desiring view seeks the desire of that which is looked at. This applies to other people, but also to the perception of nature and other objects. Against this backdrop, control and objectification of vision is perceived as an attempt to escape integration into the desire structure of vision. The will to power reduces the perception of the world. The attempt to create objectivity reduces the desire. The power gained over things and the Other serves as compensation for the insufficient desire of the world (1975, p. 85).

A form of vision in which the power-and-control aspiration of people has not asserted itself in regard to objects, but in which the visible is also not sacrificed to individual passions, is the *visual thinking* that GOETHE developed within the scope of his natural science studies. One of GOETHE's maxims formulates the basis of this kind of access to the world: the educated person was immediately re-educated, and, if we want to arrive to some extent at a living perception of nature, we need to keep ourselves in such a nimble and ductile state according to the example with which it precedes us. The objective of beholding thought is not the gaining of a standpoint from which the natural phenomena are to be described and measured at an objective distance. It is rather about behaving in a "lively and ductile manner" like nature, using one's eyes to follow its growth and formation, and practicing "recreating malleability." GOETHE is not targeting the development of the logical correlations between things; for him it is about the creative re-creation of the development process — of plants, for example. The past development stages are to be connected with the present and future ones in the reproducing perception, that is, the visible is to be conceptually fused with that which is no longer visible (FLÜGGE 1963). *An Attempt to Explain the Metamorphoses of Plants* (published in 1790) contains the development of this "delicate empiricism, which makes itself most intimately identical with the object and, thus, into the actual theory" (GOETHE 1952, p. 639), in which beholding, observing, thinking, and questioning are carefully connected with each other. The task is the development of a genetic imagination, with the help of which the development of nature can be figuratively understood. "Wanting to capture the whole in perception" is the objective of GOETHE's knowledge theory, which is not involved in the explanation of the causal connection between the regulative ideas inherent in individual phenomena.

> According to this understanding, the sum of phenomena does not result in the whole; it is not possible to use these to put it back together and revive it. It is rather the case that science needs to find in each individual the index to the whole as that which is living. The metaphor of this living thing is the form — not just in natural science (MATTENKLOTT 1987, pp. 22*ff*).

It is only possible to assure oneself of this form when beholding it by recreating it with the eyes, thus incorporating it into oneself in its living whole (IMDAHL 1994, GEBAUER/WULF 1995, SEEL 2005). In this process, one needs to abstain from a fast linguistic interpretation so that the richness of the viewed form is developed in the inner perception. A hurried conceptual formulation would detract from the vitality of the viewed form. The eye would be "relieved" of perception, linguistic torpor would hardly be able to be avoided as a consequence of the conceptual designation, and a slackening of visual thought would be the inevitable result. This insight on the irresolvable existence of phenomena is found in exaggerated form in one of GOETHE's "sayings in prose:"

> The highest good would be to comprehend that everything factual is theory. The basic law of chromatics is revealed to us by the blue hues of the sky. One does not search for what is behind the phenomena; they themselves are the lesson (1952, p. 640).

The objective of beholding thought cannot be more clearly formulated than that it opposes the distancing, controlling, and classifying view of the emerging sciences. GOETHE attempts to study nature without subjugating it. Man should "seek to enter nature and its sacred life with all loving, honoring, pious powers" (ibid.) and record the correspondence between nature and man. Here, the eye is understood neither as a vision ray that is expelled and illuminates the objects (as asserted by Empedocles), nor as a passive camera into which the objects simply penetrate. Rather, GOETHE sees a similarity between nature and man, between light and the eye, into which ideas about vision from antiquity enter: "If the eye were not 'sunnish,'/How would we be able to view light?/ If God's own power did not live within us,/How could divinity delight us" (GOETHE 1952)?

Aisthesis and the hypertrophy of vision

The mimetic thought of GOETHE objected to the reification and objectification of the world in the name of perception and living experience. With a demand for a "poetization of the world," similar perspectives are developed and similar aesthetic experiences are sought in early Romanticism. Again and again it involves the relationship of *aisthesis* and *thought*. This became a defining topic in the human sciences at the beginning of the 21st century as well. An aestheticization of the living environment can now be perceived. It includes individual "styling," consumption behavior, and urban design. The new media fosters the transformation of the world into image. This also affects the social relationships of people to each other. Aestheticization increases particularly in the erotic and in sexuality, but also in politics and in the organization of recreational activities. In the viewing of images, all wishes seem to be fulfillable. Telecommunication, in particular, promises immediate fulfillment. Scenes are staged in which the fulfillment of wishes is simulated. Their "overfulfillment" through the simulation of desires and their ostensible satisfaction lead to a proliferation of desired worlds, and to a "hyperaesthetic" (see also, BAUDRILLARD 1996, 2005). The manipulation of the sense of sight through image worlds that serves commercial purposes is widespread and lasting. In view of these developments, the hopes tied to aesthetics that there would be a reconciliation of the divisions of human life, as were aspired to in the context of "visual thinking" (GOETHE) and "aesthetic education" (SCHILLER), are largely obsolete. The aestheticization of the world disappoints the expectations placed on it. It is not able to ensure the intensification of life and the expansion of "living experience" (ADORNO). It often has the opposite effect of the hopes placed on it, and changes into its opposite. This causes it to suffer the same fate foretold for reason by HORKHEIMER and ADORNO (1971). Thus, W. WELSCH (1989) emphasized the necessity of protecting the sense of sight through anesthesia or anesthetics. This can occur through lack of sensitivity toward stimulation through images and through decisive dissociation from the inundation through images. Aesthetic perception is not possible without exclusion and concentration. Complex vision requires limitation and focus (EISNER 2002).

Vision takes place today between *mimicry* and *mimesis*. In the case of mimicry, images "drop" into the eye of the seeing person, and cause immediate assimilation and reification in a reflex. The observer metaphorically becomes the image, in a manner comparable to the adaptation of a chameleon that takes on the color and form of the environment. Such situations result when images immediately "fit" with the desire structure of the beholders or viewers, thus overwhelming them and holding them "captive." On the other side of the spectrum, there are the possibilities of *mimetic vision* (WULF 2013) and aesthetic education (IMAI/WULF 2007, MOLLENHAUER/WULF 1996, SCHÄFER/WULF 1999, SUZUKI/WULF 2007; ZIRFAS et al. 2009). Within the scope of mimetic vision, an assimilation of the beholder or viewer with the seen is involved. In this process, which is at the center of aesthetic experience, the observer exposes himself to the object. He tries to conform to its forms and colors through imitation. In this movement, the image of the object is captured as an image, processed, integrated into the inner image world of the observer, and remembered. The mimetic movement permits a tight perception that does not restrict the freedom of the beholder; it is instead more of an expanding perception whose specificity can be replaced neither through language nor through the other senses. In mimetic vision, an individual act of re-creation by the beholder occurs, whose unique character depends on his personal qualifications and expertise, and on the general historical-cultural conditions of the reception. In close reference to the viewed object, mimetic vision leads to many heterogeneous means of perception, and enables plurality in the processing of aesthetic experiences. With the aid of mimesis, the assimilation of foreign objects, images, and circumstances can occur. This makes it necessary for the beholder to step away from the context that is familiar to him and to experience the Other. Along with this comes a sensitization for *similarities* and *differences,* and for the irreducibility and incommensurability of life forms.

The aesthetization of living environments also has an influence on the human sciences, in which these developments can elicit a great variety of effects that are not individually addressed here (BELTING 1994, 2011, BOEHM 1994, ZUR LIPPE 1987). In this context, new questions and methods, new topics and perspectives have arisen — ones that have led to seminal changes in scientific development. The definitive elements of these developments include, among others:

- the abandonment of logocentrism with its centric and hierarchical understanding of reason,
- the suspension of monosemy and the development of deconstructive thought,
- the increased consideration of aisthesis in science and philosophy,
- and the treatment of anthropological questions after the end of normative anthropology (PARAGRANA 1993, 1995, WELSCH 1989, WULF/KAMPER 2002, WULF 2010, 2013).

In the context of these perspectives, plurality and the treatment of dissent, reflexivity, and deconstruction in particular, increase in significance. New forms of heterogeneity, lack of clarity, and complexity are permitted as well. The ambivalencies of perception are seen clearly and addressed. The relationship of aisthesis and ethics plays a crucial role here. That is because normative differences appear already on the level of perception (HÜPPAUF/WULF 2006, WULF/KAMPER/GUMBRECHT 1994). Criticism is directed at the dominance of the eye, of vision, and of images. A new dispute looms between image veneration and image destruction, between iconodulists and iconoclasts (LATOUR/WEIBEL 2002).

References

ARISTOTLE: Die Lehrschriften: Über die Seele, pub. P. Gohlke. – Paderborn 1961.
AVERROES: Epitome of Parva Naturalia. – Cambridge 1961.
BATAILLE, G. (1977): Story of the Eye. Joachim NEUGROSCHEL (Trans.) – New York.
BATAILLE, G. (1979): Das obszöne Werk. – Reinbek.
BAUDRILLARD, J. (1983): Simulations. – New York.
BAUDRILLARD, J. (1996): The perfect crime. – London.
BAUDRILLARD, J. (2005): The system of objects. – London.
BELTING, H. (1994): Likeness and Presence: A History of the Image before the Era of Art. – Chicago.
BELTING, H. (2008): Florenz und Bagdad. Eine west-östliche Geschichte des Blicks. – Munich.
BELTING, H. (2011): An Anthropology of the Images: Picture, Medium, Body. – Princeton.
BOEHM, G. (Ed.) (1994): Was ist ein Bild. – Munich.
EISNER, E. (2002): The Arts and the Creation of Mind. – New Haven and London.
EPICURUS: Brief an Herodot. In: Diogenes Laertius: Leben und Meinungen berühmter Philosophen. – Leipzig 1921.
FLÜGGE, J. (1963): Die Entfaltung der Anschauungskraft. – Heidelberg.
FOUCAULT, M. (1976): Die Geburt der Klinik. Eine Archäologie des ärztlichen Blicks. – Frankfurt/M. and Berlin and Vienna. Engl. Trans. (1973): The Birth of the Clinic. An Archaeology of Medical Perception. SHERIDAN SMITH, A.M. (Trans.) – New York.
FOUCAULT, M. (1977): Discipline and Punish: The Birth of the Prison. – New York.
FREUD, S. (1970): Das Unheimliche. In: FREUD, S.: Studienausgabe. Vol. IV: Psy-cho-lo-gi-sche Schriften. – Frankfurt/M.
GEBAUER, G./WULF, C. (Eds.) (1993): Praxis und Ästhetik. – Frankfurt/M.
GEBAUER, G./WULF, C. (1995): Mimesis. Culture, Art, Society. – Berkeley and Los Angeles.
GEBAUER, G./WULF, C. (1998): Spiel, Ritual, Geste. Mimetisches Handeln in der sozialen Welt. – Reinbek.
GOETHE, J.W.: Sprüche in Prosa: Betrachtungen im Sinne der Wanderer, No. 126, 136. In: Goethes Werke in sechs Bänden, Vol. 6. – Frankfurt/M. 1952.
HELLER, A. (1982): Der Mensch der Renaissance. – Cologne and Lövenich.
HERDER, J. G. (1891): Abhandlung über den Ursprung der Sprache. In: Herder und die Anthropologie der Aufklärung, Vol. 2 of Werke. – Munich, pp. 251–399 (On the Origin of Language. MORAN, John H. and GODE, Alexander (Engl. Trans.). – Chicago 1996).
HOFFMANN, E.T.A. (2011): Der Sandmann. – Berlin.
HORKHEIMER, M./ADORNO, T.W. (1971): Dialektik der Aufklärung. – Frankfurt/M.
HÜPPAUF, B./WULF, Ch. (Eds.) (2009): Dynamics and Performativity of Imagination: The Image between the Visible and the Invisible. – New York.
IMAI, Y./WULF, Ch. (Eds.) (2007): Concepts of Aesthetic Education: Japanese and European Perspectives. – Münster and New York.
IMDAHL, M. (1994): Ikonik. Bilder und ihre Anschauung. In: BOEHM, G. (Ed.) Was ist ein Bild? – Munich, pp. 300–324.

LACAN, J. (1975): Das Spiegelstadium als Bildner der Ich-Funktion. In: LACAN, J.: Schriften I. – Frankfurt/M.
LATOUR, B. and WEIBEL, P. (Eds.) (2002): Iconoclash. Beyond the Image. Wars in Science, Religion and Arts. – Karlsruhe and Cambridge.
LEROI-GOURHAN, A. (1993): Gesture and Speech. – Cambridge.
LINDBERG, D.C. (1987): Auge und Licht im Mittelalter. – Frankfurt/M.
ZUR LIPPE, R. (1987): Sinnenbewußtsein. – Reinbek.
MATTENKLOTT, G. (1987): Der übersinnliche Leib. – Reinbek.
MCLUHAN, M. (2001): Understanding Media: The Extensions of Man. – New York.
MERLEAU-PONTY, M. (1967): Das Auge und der Geist. – Reinbek.
MERLEAU-PONTY, M. (1994): Das Sichtbare und das Unsichtbare. – Munich (The Visible and the Invisible, LINGIS, Alphonsa [Engl. Trans.]. – Evanston, 1968).
MOLLENHAUER, K./WULF, Ch. (Eds.) (1996): Aisthesis/Ästhetik. – Weinheim.
PARAGRANA (1993): Internationale Zeitschrift für Historische Anthropologie, Vol. 2, No. 1–2: Das Ohr als Erkenntnisorgan. – Berlin.
PARAGRANA (1995): Internationale Zeitschrift für Historische Anthropologie, Vol. 4, No. 1: Aisthesis. – Berlin.
PLESSNER, H. (1980): Anthropologie der Sinne. Gesammelte Schriften, Vol. 3. – Frankfurt/M.
RÖTZER, F./WEIBEL, E. (Eds.) (1993): Cyberspace. – Munich and Vienna.
SARTRE, J.P. (1952): Das Sein und das Nichts. – Hamburg.
SCHÄFER, G./WULF, C. (Eds.) (1999): Bild — Bilder — Bildung. – Weinheim/Basel.
SEEL, M. (2005): Aesthetics of Appearance. – Stanford.
STRAUS, E. (1956): Vom Sinn der Sinne. Ein Beitrag zur Grundlegung der Psychologie. – Berlin etc.
SUZUKI, S./WULF, Ch. (Eds.) (2007): Mimesis, Poiesis and Performativity in Education. – Münster and New York.
VIRILIO, P. (1994): The Vision Machine. – Bloomington.
WELSCH, W. (1989): Ästhetisches Denken. – Stuttgart.
WIMMER. M. (2006): Dekonstruktion und Erziehung. – Bielefeld.
WULF, C. (Ed. 2010): Der Mensch und seine Kultur. Hundert Beiträge zu Problemen menschlichen Lebens in Vergangenheit, Gegenwart und Zukunft. – Cologne.
WULF, C. (2013): Anthropology. A Continental Perspective. – Chicago.
WULF, C./KAMPER, D. (Ed.) (2002): Logik und Leidenschaft. – Berlin.
WULF, C./KAMPER, D. and GUMBRECHT, H.-U. (Eds.) (1994): Ethik der Ästhetik. – Berlin.
ZIRFAS, J. et al. (2009): Geschichte der ästhetischen Bildung. Antike und Mittelalter. – Paderborn.

William S. Sax

Seeing Ghosts in India and Europe

Ghosts and the "ontological question"

Over more than three decades of conducting anthropological fieldwork in Garhwal in the Western Himalayas of North India, I have had a lot to do with ghosts. Ghosts are, by their nature, rather mysterious beings, but one thing about them especially puzzled me: Why had I never managed to see one, even though nearly all of my village friends and acquaintances said they had done so? I think that this question goes to the heart of what it means to do anthropology, and to think like an anthropologist. It brings into focus what I take to be the central problem of anthropology: explaining the causes and consequences of cultural diversity. Why do people in some cultures see ghosts, while people from others can't? Why and how is it that people experience the world so differently? I have pondered over this question often: you might even say that I have been "haunted" by it.

A typical anthropological answer might go something like this: Members of "traditional" societies — like that of Garhwal — have ideas about the supernatural that are very different from those of "modern" people like myself. Weber would say that they still have not experienced the "disenchantment" that is characteristic of modernity: the progressive elimination from the world of magical places and times, and supernatural beings like ghosts. On the contrary, they live in an "enchanted" world: ghosts and gods and ancestors are parts of their everyday life, and the existence of such beings is constantly affirmed by other people in their culture. The reality of such beings is rarely called into question: indeed, many common practices confirm their existence, and so they are often experienced. But in the "modern," "disenchanted" world, the existence of ghosts is constantly denied. They may be a titillating theme for novels and movies, but in general, the belief in ghosts is dismissed as "superstition." Moreover, the denial of their existence is strongest among the educated classes to which I belong, so that even if I believed in them, I could not admit it without compromising my scientific reputation. In short, I will never see a ghost, because I strongly resist seeing ghosts; and even if I did see a ghost, the conventions of my scientific world would prevent me from admitting it.

This is the kind of answer that an anthropologist might give to my question. But I find it an unsatisfying answer because, like the "bracketing" of religious truth claims in the academic study of religion, it begs the ontological question. By "ontology" I mean a theory about the nature of the world and the kinds of forces, beings, and materials of which it is constituted: time, space, matter, energy, God or gods, ancestors, people and, according to some, ghosts. Ontology is receiving quite a lot of attention by anthropologists these days, from those who (like Phillipe DESCOLA and Eduardo VIVEIROS DE CASTRO) conduct traditional ethnographic fieldwork amongst hunters and gatherers, attempting to specify the ontologies that underlie their "worlds," to cutting-edge ethnographers and historians of science — for example, Bruno LATOUR (1991) and Annemarie MOL (2002) — who analyze the production of scientific ontologies. Anthropologists are fond of saying that people in certain cultures "live in another world;" but they rarely specify what they mean by this. Often, they mean that it is "the same" world, but just perceived differently. Some claim that perception constitutes the world, so that the perceived world varies according to historically and culturally variable forms of perception. A great deal hangs on what precisely one means by words like "same," "different," "perception," and "constitution," for there is a range of possible positions on these questions. Some argue that there is only one external world, to which ontological theories more or less accurately correspond, and that science is currently the ultimate arbiter of the adequacy of our representations. This is so despite the attempts by Thomas Kuhn, Paul Feyerabend and Richard Rorty to historicize or otherwise neutralize this claim. In other words, there is no good scientific evidence for the existence of ghosts; therefore, no matter how cleverly I might elucidate (in classical anthropological fashion) the internal logic of the representations of my ghost-believing interlocutors, as a scientist I can only conclude that, for one reason or another, these representations are false, misguided, or deficient in some way.

A second possibility is much more intriguing to me: this is the possibility that our continual making and unmaking of worlds really does depend on historical and cultural contexts. There is a weak case to be made here, but also a strong one. The weak case is when we speak only of the "world of experience," as anthropologists usually do.[1] Basically, this re-states the position I adumbrated above: that there is only one world, perceived variously. But what about the idea that when we name the world, or perceive it, or interact with it in some other way, we really change it? What if, by "seeing" a ghost, speaking to it, feeding it, or exorcising it, we accomplish real transformations in the world (SAX 2008, ch. 6)?

"Seeing" ghosts in Europe

Why was I unable to see ghosts even when my informants could do so? Perhaps the problem lay in the way I formulated this question. Perhaps my focus on "seeing" ghosts was too narrow, a mere artifact of language. Perhaps my

---

[1] A classical (and still influential) example is HALLOWELL's (1955) notion of "behavioral environment."

interlocutors in India perceived ghosts with other senses. It seemed to me that even though they normally used a Hindi phrase denoting the visual sense — "to see a ghost," *bhut dekhna* — their detailed reports invoked other senses. Most commonly they heard noises at night, sometimes pebbles being thrown on the roof; or they felt cold winds; or sensed the malevolent presence of a spirit. Several of them felt ghosts sitting on their chests, a concept that is widespread in North India and Nepal, where it is called *daboc* (KRAUSKOPF 1999), which has been equated by some psychiatrists with "panic attack."

It is certainly true that when Europeans and North Americans describe their encounters with ghosts, they usually speak of "seeing" them. In his book *The Haunted: A Social History of Ghosts*, Owen DAVIES (2007) begins with many examples of people who have encountered ghosts. He describes only visual manifestations, and in most cases, these are images of human beings. In his sections on the personal characteristics of ghosts, their times of haunting, materialization, dress and specific attributes like "headlessness," Davies also writes overwhelmingly of the visual sense. An exception is his section on "invisible ghosts," where he writes that

> many reported ghosts over the centuries were not visible, their presence and sometimes their identity were revealed through the stimulation of senses other than sight. . . [There are] numerous accounts [from the late 19th and 20th centuries] of people feeling an indefinable sensation of a presence, which is sometimes connected with a perceived drop in temperature (ibid., p. 26).

Sometimes ghosts cannot be sensed by humans, but are indirectly recognized through lights turning blue, or through the behavior of animals who are more sensitive to their presence than living humans (ibid). In addition, people "occasionally claimed to have smelt the spirits of the dead," although "(i)nvisible ghosts were more frequently *heard* than smelt" (ibid., p. 27). One person heard the noises of poltergeists, along with footsteps, occupational sounds, and the rustle of silk (ibid). Finally, some people were touched by ghosts (ibid., p. 29). In short, it seems that in what is sometimes called "the West," ghosts are primarily seen; but are also sometimes heard, smelt, or touched.

"Sensing" ghosts in India

When I turned to Indian material, my hypothesis — that "Westerners" tend to see ghosts while Indians use other senses — received a hard knock. In 1993, Ruth and Stanley FREED, two ethnographers working for the American Museum of Natural History, wrote a wonderful and unique ethnography of all the ghosts in a north Indian village. They collected the life stories of these ghosts — and their death stories as well — along with all the details they could find about who had seen them, and where. They then published a monograph on the topic, *Ghosts: Life and Death in North India* (1993), which is surely one of a kind. The "hard knock" to my hypothesis was that according to the

Freeds, Indians also tend "see" ghosts. Or so it seemed at first. However, a closer reading of the texts suggests that the Freeds' assumptions were unexamined, and this distorted their ethnographic reporting in a way that tends to confirm my hypothesis. To be precise, I suspect that for most Indians, senses other than the visual are predominant in the perception of ghosts. However, because the standard Hindi expression for ghost perception is *bhut dekhna* — "to see a ghost" — and because this phrase reinforced Freed's English-speaking American assumption that ghost perceptions are predominantly visual, they failed to appreciate the predominantly non-visual nature of the ghost perceptions of their Indian informants. The point can be illustrated by a series of quotations from the FREEDS' book.

> My mother-in-law's sister's husband saw a ghost recently. The ghost took hold of him, threw him on the ground so he was hurt. He saw the ghost, who told him: "I'm going to kill you," and then the ghost picked him up again and threw him down three times. The ghost was a Muslim. Because he is a practicing priest, he can recognize a ghost easily. He knows everything about such things, but women and girls do not (1993, p. 135).

> I have seen a ghost. . . . I was sleeping with the baby on my bed . . . An oil lamp was burning in the courtyard. The ghost came from the inner room . . . , blew out the lamp by waving his hand, came into my room and snatched my child from me. I awoke and found my breasts had dried up, no milk was flowing, and the baby's mouth was open gasping for air. He made sounds as though he was having difficulty breathing (ibid., p. 136).

The FREEDS write that "(g)hosts are thought to appear sometimes in the form of an animal, plant or tree" (ibid., p. 131). "They are not always seen, but sometimes felt — for example, "his wife felt that something was pressing her chest and parts of her body at night and believed it was a ghost" (ibid., p. 116). One man didn't even claim to "see" the ghost, but only felt how he had walked over him:

> I do not know the identity of the ghost or ghosts; only God knows. If the ghost was a man, I might have seen his apparition . . . it went over my body like a horse . . . I could not catch it. When I crushed it, I could feel the bones . . . Afterwards some people slept in the same place with me because they wanted to see the ghost or whatever it was and catch it. But it was invisible to them. It would run all over my bed (ibid., p. 285).

Other people equate ghosts with air or breeze, which is a common conception in Indian classical and folk medicine. One of the FREEDS' interlocutors invoked this concept (and at the same time, provided his own answer to my question) when he said, "I have never seen a ghost myself. Ghosts are just air which can be seen by some people but not by everyone" (ibid., p. 122). I conclude that there are sufficient grounds for retaining my hypothesis.

Another example of the non-visual nature of ghost-perception among Indians has an interesting genesis. A Punjabi immigrant living in San Francisco was diagnosed as having psychotic hallucinations, and referred to a psychiatrist of Indian descent, Dr Khenu SINGH, because he spoke Punjabi while none of his colleagues did. SINGH was put in touch with me as an expert on Indian ghosts. We had a fascinating correspondence, and I even appeared in his unpublished clinical case study. Here is an excerpt from it:

> On the drive back from LA, at around 11:30 PM, the patient and wife both stated that their car had slowed down in an unusual manner. At that point, Mr. Kumar described feeling a brush on his arm and the presence of what he felt to be a spirit—he initially was quoted as calling this a "devil," but on my subsequent interview he called it a "bhoot," which translates from Punjabi into "ghost" or "spirit." In the initial consult [*sic*] psychiatry evaluation, the resident mentioned a visual component, a visual "hallucination" of a "devil," but when I clarified the details of that night, during our first outpatient encounter, he denied a visual experience and maintained that it had been a felt presence, as well as the feeling of his arm having been brushed or shoved. He told me that this experience occurred over an interval of a few seconds and he denied any other symptoms at the time. In our initial outpatient discussions, he denied being frightened by the experience, stating that no spirit can be harmful if one has faith in *Bhagwan*.[2] This felt a bit defensive, and when I normalized some degree of fear, he acknowledged that he indeed had been frightened for around 20-30 minutes after the experience (SINGH/FRANCIS n.d.).

Note that the psychiatrist — and perhaps even the patient — initially reports a visual experience; but on closer investigation, the relevant sense turns out to be touch. The patient had been classified as psychotic partly because of his "blunted affect;" but once SINGH spoke with him, he became animated. SINGH managed to mitigate the diagnosis of the patient as psychotic by employing the same vague analytical concept that mainstream anthropologists use to solve my problem: "culture." Although he does not use the phrase "culture-bound disorder" (which has been heavily criticized), still this is pretty much what he means when he writes about "culturally-situated beliefs" in his report. He sympathetically quotes the social psychologist Sudhir KAKAR as follows:

> The bhuta-preta are a tangible, living presence for most people. They seem to populate a mental region that is contiguous and has open borders with the land of ordinary consciousness in which ordinary everyday life takes place. Persons may occasionally have encounters with the spirit world without these encounters necessarily regarded as auditory or visual hallucinations of the pathological kind (1982, p. 57).

---

[2] The Hindi word for "God."

Of course, SINGH has his own answer to the ontological question: ultimately, the ghost was a projection of the patient's guilt, associated with the death of a close acquaintance.

Ghosts in the field

I began this article by asking why it was that I had never managed to see a ghost in India, while so many of my informants claimed to have done so. In fact, things are a bit more complicated than I admitted. As it turns out, during my field research, I had actually been seeing ghosts quite regularly for years, if not for decades. My problem was: *I didn't recognize them.* This requires an explanation.

Traditionally when a Garhwali woman marries, she leaves the home of her parents, and takes up residence with her husband and his parents. Nevertheless, she sometimes visits her parents, especially during the first months and years of marriage. These visits by the out-married daughter, who is called a *dhyani*, are associated with particular practices: gifts and especially foods are exchanged between her natal home and her marital home; she should be accompanied by a male chaperone during her journeys; and she has much more freedom of movement and action at her natal home than at her marital home. But when she returns from her natal home to her marital home, the *dhyani* is expected to weep, and this weeping takes a rather stereotypical form: a kind of loud sobbing, punctuated by deep breaths. I will never forget the first time I heard it, while riding a bus through the mountains. I watched as a young woman was torn from her parents' arms and placed in the bus and, as it pulled away, she sobbed as if her heart would break. But as soon as the bus turned the first corner, and her parents were out of sight, she stopped weeping, got out a compact mirror, adjusted her makeup, and began laughing and chatting with her escort!

Of course, feelings of sorrow and longing on both sides — the parents for their daughter, and she for them — are normally quite sincere, as are the proverbial tears of the *dhyani* when she leaves her parent's home. But self-conscious *performances* of weeping, like that of the young woman I saw on the bus, are not uncommon. Weeping at the time of departure is expected, and a woman who does not do so would be regarded as a "bad" daughter. During my decades of research in Garhwal, I have attended dozens, if not hundreds, of family rituals and other gatherings, and have often seen *dhyanis* weeping on the final day of a ritual, before leaving to return to their husbands' homes.

But was I mistaken? Were these weeping women perhaps not daughters, but rather ghosts expressing their sorrow at departure?

The problem is that I find it difficult to distinguish the weeping of a *dhyani* from the weeping of a ghost. I came to realize this while analyzing a video I had made of a ritual in the family of my fieldwork assistant, a young man named Sacchu. At the very beginning of the ritual, I made a video recording of a brief ritual attended by the family and their low-caste priest. In this video,

Sacchu's mother invokes her own mother, and her ghost possesses Sacchu, who begins to weep. Speaking to the ghost in Sacchu's body, the priest says, "You've become an ancestor, we will worship you in the month of *Jeth*. Give us prosperity! Give us prosperity!" In the background, Sacchu's mother can be heard, saying,

> We brought you in a basket (after you died); we will worship you in the month of *Jeth*. Hey Maharaj, if you had had sons, they would have taken care of you as I did. You were so sick and we took care of you, all that shit and piss, and the daughters-in-law took care of you as well. My daughter-in-law didn't care much for me, but she certainly served you!

In the video, the daughter-in-law turns to me and says, "Brother, wherever she was, and however sick she was, I still went to her!"

As we watched the video later, Sacchu explained to me that the old lady's ghost was always invited to attend family rituals, and that when she appeared, she wept, as ghosts normally do. After the ritual was over, the old woman possessed her *dhyani* — Sacchu's sister — and once again wept as she took her leave. While making the video, I had assumed that Sacchu's sister was fulfilling her role as a *dhyani* by weeping. This was not particularly remarkable; and, in fact, on the video, one can hear me joking with the other girls in the family from behind the camera lens. But, when we looked at the footage, Sacchu laughed, and said that, no, it was his grandmother's ghost, and not his sister, who was weeping as she said goodbye to her living relatives.

Not all ghosts are quite as loving as this. Many ghosts afflict their families, and must be exorcized. I saw many such exorcisms in the field. One case had to do with a large family consisting of four brothers, their wives and children, and their aged mother. One day, the youngest brother's wife was found hanging from a tree, and the police ruled that it was a suicide. But the villagers had their doubts: people said that she had been sexually molested by the eldest brother while her husband was away in the military, and it was even whispered that this brother had murdered her. In any event, her death was so tragic that shortly afterwards, the aged mother died too. I attended a night-long ritual in which both ghosts — that of the old woman as well as the young suicide — were exorcized. The exorcism went on for hours, and the ghosts barely spoke: they only wept in that peculiar way that is also the style of the *dhyani* when she leaves her natal home to return to the home of her husband.

Embodied ghosts

There is no single or predominant sensory modality for perceiving ghosts in Garhwal. Sometimes they are heard or felt, sometimes they climb on your chest, sometimes they throw pebbles on the roof. But by far the most powerful and impressive manifestation of a ghost is when he or she actually appears in the body of a living person. The language used in rituals of exorcism is the language of embodiment. The purpose of the ritual is to transform the body of the deceased person, from a *bhutakaya* or "ghost's body" to a *pitrakaya* or "ancestor's body." Here is how the exorcist expresses it, in his ghost song:

1. Oh Lord, the god of my ancestors
2. This is your home and your temple
3. It is your seat and your protection
4. In the underworld, in the world of men
5. I will set you free from the net of Death
6. From the noose of time

. . .

20. Have mercy on this house, oh ghost, oh storehouse of compassion!
21. Leave your ghostly body, take a godly body, ghost!
22. Empty is a city with no people
23. And empty is a tree without a bird
24. And house and home are empty when the family head is gone
25. Our days and months cannot go on forever, ghost
26. The seasons and the months return, but we do not return
27. Leave your ghostly body, take a godly body, ghost![3]
29. The tree is ageless, ghost, but its branches are not ageless
30. Of all the seasons, ghost, tell me, which one is your favorite?
31. The best of all the seasons is the Springtime, oh my ghost
32. Twenty dozen flowers bloom, and the wild doves coo

It is dangerous if the ghost weeps too much. This indicates that it is angry, and might curse or otherwise harm the family. When this happens, the exorcist sings the following lines:

42. Don't be angry with us, oh ghost!
43. Don't be so disturbed with us, oh ghost!
44. Leave your ghostly body, take a godly body now!
45. And in the coming months, we will send an invitation
46. We will sing your songs, oh ghost, and give to you a dowry
47. We will give a cloth for your head
48. And clothing for your body

Notions of embodiment were prominent in all of the exorcisms I participated in. In one case, a young woman had died in childbirth. Her husband had re-married, but still maintained excellent relations with his deceased first wife's family. But the dead woman's mother was never able to reconcile herself to the death of her daughter. She kept seeing her deceased daughter in her dreams, and finally organized an exorcism ritual in her honor. Of particular interest was when the

---

[3] Sometimes, instead of "ancestor's body," they use the word *devakaya*, a "divine (godly) body."

ghost of the deceased woman, temporarily inhabiting the body of her mother, exchanged food with her living husband — an exchange that mirrored a most affectionate part of the Hindu wedding ritual. This exchange of food was very moving because it expressed the continuing love of the family members for each other, even after death, and it did so in an idiom that was very much centered on embodiment and all its associated senses: here the sense of taste.

Conclusion

In this chapter, I have tried to take a few modest steps toward answering two questions. The first question was ethnographic: Why was I never able to see a ghost, even though nearly all of my informants did? And the answer is that I had been misled by my own visual metaphor. Actually, I had been *hearing* ghosts for years! The second question was ontological: Were these ghosts real? Local people had no doubt that they were. Ghosts caused affliction in the form of disease, family strife, and behavioral disturbances. Their blessings resulted in prosperity and good fortune. Most importantly, people interacted with them in ways that were sometimes tender, sometimes aggressive, sometimes intimate, and sometimes distant. What I learned from my research was that in this region, as well as in much of the world, the ghost is not a shade, flitting through the night; it is not something dimly perceived, not something imagined. Rather, the ghost is embodied in a living, breathing human being sitting next to you. You smell them in the cramped room; you feel their heat; you hear them screaming and wailing — sometimes as if from the depths of hell. Who would be so silly as to doubt their existence, when they are so clearly perceived? When we consider the sensory perception of ghosts by the living, we must bear in mind that in cultures where possession by ghosts is common, the most persuasive means of perception, the most powerful manifestation of the ghost, is often a form of embodiment. And embodiment involves all of the senses.

References

DESCOLA, P. (2007): Beyond Nature and Culture. – Oxford.

FREED, R. and FREED, S. (1993): Ghosts: Life and Death in North India. – New York (Anthropological Paper No. 72 of the American Museum of National History, distributed by the University of Washington Press, Seattle.)

HALLOWELL, A.I. (1955): Culture and Experience. – Philadelphia.

KAKAR, S. (1982): Shamans, Mystics, and Doctors. – New York.

KRAUSKOPFF, G. (1999): Places and Memories: Exorcism and Curing Among the Tharus of Western Nepal. In: CARRIN, M. (Ed.): Managing Distress: Possession and Therapeutic Cults in South Asia. – Delhi, pp. 155–167.

DAVIES, O. (2007): The Haunted: A Social History of Ghosts. – New York.

LATOUR, B. (1991): We Have Never Been Modern. – Cambridge.

MOL, A. (2002): The Body Multiple: Ontology in Medical Practice. – Durham, NC.

SAX, W.S. (2008): God of Justice: Ritual Healing and Social Justice in the Central Himalayas. – New York.

SINGH, K./FRANCIS Lu (n.d.): A Punjabi Man "Attacked" by a Spirit: *Bhoota-Preta* — A Culture-Bound Syndrome for the DSM-V (unpublished).

VIVEIROS DE CASTRO, E. (1998): Cosmological Deixis and Amerindian Perspectivism. In: Journal of the Royal Anthropological Institute 4(3), pp. 469–488.

Annette Wilke

Sonic Perception and Acoustic Communication in Hindu India

Anyone speaking about communication in today's Western cultural area will not necessarily think of sound as an independent medium of expression and communication, and anyone studying texts is interested in their content and will hardly be aware that texts also always have a material quality — their sound — and can be perceived in a sensory and emotional way. When Europeans think of sound, they think of music or noise, and not of textual traditions. If they think of texts, they think of the written word and semantic meaning rather than sounds and rituals. We understand words and texts as message bearers and discursive bodies. This is typical of Western culture, and increased substantially since the Renaissance and the Reformation. In Hinduistic India, things are different. Text, sound, and ritual belong together. Both orality *and* sonality enjoy great cultural significance. This has had a distinct influence on how people approach texts, and the marks left on perception, *habitus* forms, and social practice. It has affected not only a stronger sensory and emotive appropriation of the subject but also generated quite particular symbolic forms. In everyday life as well as in scholarly traditions, we find great focus on the sonic dimension. There are complete sound rites, as also an exceptionally rich religious and secular literature in the Sanskrit idiom that uses language and sound poetically and reflects it philosophically. The importance of sound and its perception has led to rites, models of cosmic order, and abstract formulas. Sound serves to stimulate religious feelings, to give them a sensory form and embody them, to facilitate thinking in structures, and also to train abstract and formalistic thought. It has given rise to world views which differ substantially from those in the occidental world, and from Christian concepts of the Divine.

This essay is based on *Sound and Communication. An Aesthetic Cultural History of Sanskrit Hinduism* (WILKE/MOEBUS 2011),[1] which discusses these fields in greater detail. The large volume charts a profile of Hindu India in which the sounding word retained its relevance over the centuries, and across different bodies of texts, ritual performances and knowledge cultures. The research

[1] My co-author, Oliver Moebus, had to cease working on the project a few years before this book took on its present form. If not otherwise indicated, all translations of Sanskrit sources quoted below were done by MOEBUS and WILKE (2011). For the Sanskrit originals, I will refer to them.

design combines a historical long-term perspective with questions of method and theory, and emphasizes the event character of religious texts. This event character of textual traditions should be understood in a dual sense: on the one hand, relating to their potential ability to produce sense in an unfinished, ever new fashion; and on the other, relating to their aesthetic quality, that is their audible physical nature. A fundamental thesis is that texts in Sanskrit Hinduism — whether they occur in everyday religious culture or in the traditions of scholars, whether they belong to sacred or to profane lore — are always texts to be heard. This aspect should be incorporated into hermeneutics itself — the hermeneutics of texts, and the hermeneutics of culture. These hermeneutics must not only consider the fact that texts cannot be abstracted from their sounds, their sensory embodiment, and their performative embeddings, but also take into consideration the cultural imaginations and interpretations of language, sound, and voice, their cosmological framing, religious coding, and place in the cultural symbol system. The guiding interests of *Sound and Communication* were the following questions: What are a culture's vision(s) and interpretation(s) of the world when that culture is strongly characterized by the spoken language and sound perception? What negotiation processes and transformations have they been subject to and, in view of all the historical changes, how can the persistence of live communication systems be explained?

The thesis of this approach is that sound is one of the key media of cultural representation and reproduction and, thus, a key to Indian culture, and to Sanskrit Hinduism in particular. A "sonic cultural history," therefore, promises to expose ongoing themes and common patterns in a highly diversified culture, and at the same time to record diversity and socio-religious change in a cultural continuum. In this essay, I present a sort of summary. The first section starts with a general outline and discusses salient points and paradigmatic examples; the second section tackles the issue of cultural reproduction and worldview more elaborately. A final section draws conclusions regarding the senses and rationality, and sonic awareness and worldview formation.

A phonocentric life-world

Hinduism — in all the various traditions covered by this generic term — is a very pronounced performance culture in which texts — and holy literature in particular — are "sounded out" and embodied. Texts are to be heard even when they are written down. They are memorized, recited, chanted, danced, and staged. This feature has had amazing consistency since ancient times, and is not restricted to the Sanskrit idiom. The cult of Rām, so widespread in northern India for instance, lives almost exclusively from sound rituals, recitatives and texts performed for the senses — from the uninterrupted repetition of the God's name, "*Rām Rām*," to Rām songs (*bhajans*) in simple rhythms, to public recitations and dramatic performances of the vernacular epic *Rāmcaritmānas* of Tulsīdās. Above all, in the devotional traditions of *bhakti* ("loving participation"), with its emphasis on emotional religiosity, music plays a central role. These traditions have often drawn on the vernaculars and not standard Sanskrit. However, practices and *habitus* coincide in many ways, and it is Sanskrit Hinduism which provides the richest source of material on language and sound in India, and did set the cultural standards. Since ancient times, we find not only a vast array of cultural performances centered on the spoken and sounding word, but also numerous mythopoetic and highly reflexive ways to deal with sound and language. Neither the introduction of writing nor book printing and binding were able to wipe out living communication systems, and the cultural forms connected with them.

The most cherished communication channels remain hearing and memorizing, musical and semi-musical recitations, ritual readings, song and dance, dramatic staging, public debate, and the face-to-face communication from teacher to disciple. A strong sonic paradigm pervades public and private spaces. A book is always a book read aloud, and often an actual book is not even necessary, as it is popular to learn texts by heart. Traditional poetry and sacred literature fall neither quite in the category of literature nor in that of music. Unlike in modern Europe, sacred texts are hardly ever "read" in our sense, that is, received purely mentally; and neither are they read out in a normal, everyday voice. Even if a text is not sung, the "reading" is a semi-musical recitation, a *pāṭha*. Reading a text means reciting it in a musically pleasing way, and with utmost care regarding correct pronunciation. One could even say that the philologists' text does not exist as a text type in Indian traditions. Readings are performances, and texts are aesthetic events. They cannot be stripped of their sounds, their embeddings, and their performativity. Many discourses in the past attached great importance to a careful audible realization, and were often also very sensitive to the emotive contents and the communication of moods.

Thus, texts in India affect the imaginations of the "readers" and listeners not only via their contents but also via voice and performative staging. They affect the body and senses as well as thoughts and emotions in a direct and corporal way. When embodied in public performances, they create strong social effervescence, and establish collectively shared spaces for subjective acquisition, text participation, and imaginative elaboration. Sometimes sound perception can be more important than semantic meaning — particularly in the religious field. Simply listening to the sound of a religious text is already held to be auspicious and purifying. There are not only complete "sound rites," such as constant *mantra* practice, but also striking symbolic forms, such as language/speech/voice (*vāc*) viewed as a divine being or the great lord God Śiva who created the world by the sounds of his hand–drum. I will show that these "mythical" ideas were also plumbed by philosophical reflection. The auditive dimension and the multifunctional aspects of sonic communication form very important ingredients of daily religious life, and yet have been too often neglected in the academic study of religion.

It is important to be aware that Indian phonocentrism pervades not only religion but all cultural areas. The loci of truth and authority are not written documents but persons and utterings. Even today, one does not trust the written word because without the personal contact and atmospheric embedding in the speech situation, the letters remain dead and worthless. In my field work, the Indians I interviewed told me that no written literature is able to communicate nuances in and between the words better than the voice. Whereas in Europe higher education and culture is associated with writing, higher culture in India is the library in the head, and the fitting verse and proverb on the tip of the tongue.

Because, in practice, the audible word is so important, language in India has seldom been removed from its acoustic physical nature and its sonic aura. It is revealing that it is difficult to differentiate between words and sounds even in terminology. The central Sanskrit term *śabda* covers the English terms "sound" and "word" equally. In classical Sanskrit, *śabda* is, first and foremost, the general term for the category of what is audible; but at the same time, *śabda* also means "word." For example, the English expression "the word 'cow'" would be *go-śabda* in classical Sanskrit which, in fact, literally means "the sound 'cow'." Furthermore, in the context of human language, *artha* is almost always mentally added to *śabda*, which in linguistic terms means the message that is imparted by the *śabda*, that is, the meaning of the words. However, in contrast to the English pair word and meaning, here there are only sounds (*śabda*) which a speaker can use to communicate the object of his intention. But since *śabda* is not restricted to human language, it can also refer to sounds that occur in the natural world. For example, the expression *paṭapaṭā-śabda* refers to the noise of something falling to the floor, and could be translated as "crash" or "clatter." In general, it can be said that the word *śabda* is used when an identifiable message can be gathered, regardless of whether the message is "cow" or "something is falling on the floor." This shows how difficult it is to translate the term into a European language. *Śabda* is striking evidence of the acute awareness and great value of sonality in the hierarchy of perception. A word is always both a body of sound and a bearer of meaning, that is, a sound that is linked with meaning.

Since late antiquity, grammar, theatre, and poetry have become largely secular systems, and precisely in those areas which are not explicitly religious, it becomes clear just how decisively important sound as a means of communication and expression is in its effects on India's hierarchy of values. The predominance of sensing the world through sounds pervades even the most complex symbolic representations in the traditional sciences. Sound may function as an organizing principle in such abstract conceptualizations as found in grammar, mathematics, and astronomy. At the core of Pāṇini's grammar (5th–4th century BC) lie certain sound codes which re-arrange the Sanskrit alphabet. The alphabet being structured according to the seats of articulation in a strictly phonetic and highly rational order likewise inspired the numeric code systems used by astronomers and mathematicians. Instead of diagrams and numerical tables, we find memorizing systems and poetic verses full of alliterations. The same predominance of sound is seen in metaphysics: the sophisticated cosmologies of the Tantra are also based on the alphabet, which turns here into mysterious sound codes serving to explain the creation of the world and language.

Thus, the phonocentric life-world generated quite specific cultural practices and symbols. It structured perception, and left traces on the interpretation of the world and that which transcends daily life as well as on the ways of "doing science." We find strong sacralizing tendencies, all the way to a deification of language and cosmologically hypostasized sound. And, we also find sonic scientific codes — audible abstractions! — and an intensive occupation with language from very early times, which resulted in a grammar and linguistics that prefigured some aspects of modern language theories. Grammar was the paradigmatic analytical science for Indian intellectuals, and had a defining influence on methodology and scientific representation. In Pāṇini, the father of science in India, it becomes evident how much sonic awareness trained abstract thought. His grammar was dedicated to the formal analysis of the natural structures of language, and developed concepts that today one would call symbolic logic and linguistics. It is noteworthy that Pāṇini's highly technical algebra-like Sūtra language is far better acoustically than visually memorable. The 14 basic phonetic codes (*pratyāhāra*), which re-order the sounds of the alphabet and are valid for all grammatical operations, are learned by being recited in a similar manner to the Veda, and the 4000 grammatical aphorisms based on them were, of course, also memorized and transmitted orally like all important texts in India (despite the fact that one must also presume written circulation to explain the vast regional reach of the Pāṇini Sūtras, which produced a standard Sanskrit). The difference in scientific style from those produced in Europe shows up even more surprisingly in astronomy and mathematics. Mathematicians and astronomers were at the same time poets, and used not only sonic codes but also metrical forms and the most complicated meters to present their gigantic numbers and ground-breaking discoveries, such as the circular shape of the earth and the law of gravitation. Poetic verses instead of "dried" numerals allowed playing with words and double semantic coding, so that an ephemerid table, for instance, can be read at the same time as a prayer.[2]

Such highly aesthetic devices even in mathematics ensured not only easier memorization, but also allowed a more emotive incorporation of abstract subjects, and had a legitimizing role as well. The aesthetic aura and poetic cryptic diction have the function of convincing. One can demonstrate one's brilliance, the beauty of form, and the virtuosity of expression, attract attention, and call for admiration, and the mere form already communicates the importance of the message. Literati took pains to avoid banality at the cost of becoming incomprehensible. Hearers and readers are required to go to a great deal of effort. This would be frowned upon in the Western tradition; but here it

[2] WILKE/MOEBUS (2011, pp. 231–36; 491–92); see also, for the whole paragraph and the next ibid., pp. 225–50; 477–92.

is a kind of self-legitimacy and repeats a cultural pattern: the more important, the more enigmatic. This is less curious when we consider the predominance of liturgical speech in the cultural system, and the Veda as a paradigm of authoritative speech. Liturgical speech is perceived almost forcibly as the most perfect literary form because the Veda — that is, a liturgical text and not other literature such as economic lists or didactic texts, represents the "original text" of Sanskrit culture. This liturgical model of powerful speech also dominates the teacher–pupil-transmission, in which the aura and authority of the teacher play an equally important role as what is taught. The teacher, who is already in possession of the power of knowledge, speaks; whereas the pupil voluntarily subordinates himself and listens. The "community" model in the temple is similar: the priest recites the *mantra*s and litanies while those attending the service only listen. Archetypal literary speech is less about the efficient transmission of information than about the consistency ("Stimmigkeit") of the situation, the appropriateness of the form, and the efficiency of the performance. The Veda was to leave manifold profound marks on Indian cultural life, far beyond the Vedic–Brahmanic milieu, as will be further detailed below.

This chapter illustrates that the phonocentric life-world created very distinct cultural forms. In various ways, sound and its subtle yet very physical quality has been a powerful medium of communication, chosen to invoke ordered relationships, furnish ritual effectiveness, and generate sources of power and value, and not least construct "the sacred," embody assumptions about people's place in a larger order of things, and bring about emotional participation.

Orality and sonality, and the need of extended hermeneutics

In the Indology of the past decades, attention has repeatedly been drawn to the "unparalleled focus on orality" — in the transmission of the Veda in particular and in Sanskrit scholarship in general, and also in popular religious culture.[3] "Sacred sound" was even seen as the most "central mystery" of the Hindu experience of the Divine (Beck 1993). However, this apparent orality has sometimes also been overemphasized. One may debate the role of writing in the early Veda. But from Pāṇini (5th century BC) onwards, the Brahmanic tradition has probably always used a combination of oral and written transmission systems.[4] While there was a tendency to memorize the sacred texts even to the exclusion of scriptualization in the case of the Veda, there was no restriction on writing down secondary texts and post-vedic sacred lore. With a grain of salt, one could establish the rule that the more sacred a text, the more the necessity was felt to memorize it, and to transmit it orally. However, even regarding the Veda, we cannot speak of an oral culture in a strict sense, since it is a highly

[3] Lipner (1986); Michaels (1996, 2001, 2005); Pollock (2007, p. 306); Singer (1972); Staal (1986).

[4] For arguments, see Wilke/Moebus (2011, p. 11, fn. 27; 195–97).

codified orality. The Veda is an acoustic canon based on rigorous mnemotechniques, that is, a system of acoustic signs which is traditionally combined with hand gestures, that is, a set of corporal signs. Classical Sanskrit Hinduism represents an oral culture to a much lesser degree. We find instead a complex co-existence of written and oral forms of expression, with an exceptionally strong inclination toward oral–aural communication systems.

It is, therefore, better to speak of "audible texts." Here, it is necessary to distinguish between orality and sonality: a) because both the spoken and the sounding word kept predominance after writing was introduced; b) because orality primarily connotes transmission, whereas sonality brings in the aesthetic, experiential, sensory, and emotive connotations, and the expressivity of literary production, and c) because the phonocentric life-world exhibited special forms of practice, habitus, and conception (and still does today), and also stimulated linguistic, poetic, philosophical, and theological reflection. Writing in India was more often than not reinforcing the sonic paradigm.

In studying the textual lore of Hindu India, sound must therefore be given particular consideration. This has been rarely done so far. Even when the dominance of the spoken word was noticed, methodological and methodical consequences were hardly ever drawn for the actual study of texts. Access to texts remained poorly sensitive to sound. To include the sensuous and aesthetic aspects, *Sound and Communication* proposes an extended form of text hermeneutics. The following is an example of the method of working: it is certainly unusual to investigate the sung realization of a hymn to the beautiful goddess Lalitā as a framework for the interpretation of precisely this text.[5] But here the contention is: the medium belongs to the message, and sometimes also adds extra meaning to it. This approach is certainly not an indigenous one; but it is more compatible with the Indians' approach to their own texts than is the standard range of instruments for text critique classically prescribed by the European history of research. As a die-hard philologist, one elects to forego an important source of information about Hindu culture if one insists on reading their literary sources as books in the Western sense, that is, only as discursive bodies of data without any audible form or any aesthetic and emotive effect. Likewise, the Protestant textual paradigm in religious studies missed those media channels that are frequently the most central to the Hindus themselves. Since texts cannot be stripped of their sounds, the audible dimension should be included in the interpretation of the text. Indian texts are there to be heard; and they are also composed that way. It is, therefore, expedient to expand our method for text interpretation by including sensory aesthetic dimensions and self-communicating messages: that is, the texts' own performativity, such as sound patterns and language rhythmicity, and also the intonations, pitches, and colors of the voice, and moreover, to "listen" to the meanings ascribed to language and sound, and their role in the cultural symbol system.

---

[5] WILKE/MOEBUS (2011, pp. 799–804); see also, (WILKE 2008, pp. 35–57).

The language cow and her transformations

To a Western reader it is likely to come as a surprise to find in classical Sanskrit dictionaries used by poets, such as the famous *Amarakośa* (5th century AD), that the word "cow" (*go-śabda*) can also mean "language" or "speech" (*vāc*). But in India, the link between the two terms "cow" and "language" by certain associations is very old and highly informative about Indian views of language. In the *Ṛgveda* (RV), *vāc* is addressed as a goddess, and does not (only) indicate comprehensible language but primarily the expressive capacity of sound. The abundance and depth of language is illustrated with the image of the cow that gives milk unceasingly. The "goddess language/speech/voice" is herself seen as a milk cow, and calls are also addressed to her in this form whenever one wishes to ask for effective (ritual) language:

> The cow, who lifts up her voice in the skillfully speaking person [or: who lifts up the beautifully speaking voice], who is attended by all good thoughts, who, being a goddess [even] for the gods, moves around [with them] — let not the mortal be so silly as to relinquish her (RV 8.101.16; WILKE/MOEBUS 2011, pp. 288, 292, 375).

In early Vedic hymns, the predominant idea is that only poetically expressive invocation has magic power and can reach the gods. The term "cow" covers a dizzying diversity of concrete meanings — besides real cows, the term also refers to "water," "earth," "daylight," and not least "voice," "speech," and "language." Language and cow are metonyms to each other, and stand for abundance and all that is good and resourceful in life. Skillful evocative language in ritual is just as indispensable as the milk-giving cow in a semi-nomadic and pastoral society. It is noteworthy that language is associated not only with structured, semantically meaningful, and metrical speech, but also with unstructured, incomprehensible, pure or non-lexical sound, manifest, for instance, in thunder heralding the rain and the lowing of the cow:

> When the gentle Language, the queen of the gods, alights and expresses something that is incomprehensible, it is milking milk and energy from the four [directions of the heavens] ... The goddess Language is the daughter of the gods. She is that which all the animals speak. May she be gentle to us and provide energy and strength (RV 8.100.10–11, WILKE/MOEBUS 2011, pp. 292, 372–73).

For the later Veda, the non-structural element of sound is actually often the more fundamental aspect. It is praised as a kind of primeval, mysterious sound from which all other sounds flow (RV 1.164.39–42). *Vāg-Devī*, the "Goddess Language" was, in the early Ṛgveda, primarily expressivity and efficacy; in the 10th book, she has established herself as the queen of the universe who has cosmogonic power, and is present in everything and contains everything (RV 10.125.1–8). This universalized idea of language corresponds to the universalistic claim of ritual in the late Veda. All forces of the cosmos must be symbolically present in the sacrifice. It, therefore, contains not only semantically meaningful speech but also music, nonsense sounds, and expressive calls. As sacrifice was regarded as a cosmos-maintaining force, knowing and applying the complicated relations between fire sacrifice and the cosmos became the task of a highly specialized elite priesthood whose most important instrument was, again, language. The late Vedic Brāhmaṇas built up excessive, homologizing classifications by means of numerical speculations (about syllables, verses, and meters) and etymological explanations. The authors concentrate so much on language that it appears almost as if they had no interest in actual things, but only in words and names. They do not speak of things, whose substance is matter, but of words, whose substance consists of phonemes and meters. It remains still vital, however, that language also encompasses a dimension which is immeasurable and not reducible to *logos* and calculation, and surpasses the world of ordinary men. In the secret texts, the prevailing notion is that language arose from a dark, amorphous, mysterious primeval sound which, at the beginning, follows on from the old ideas of *Vāc* as the Language Cow, and later on is interpreted ever more metaphysically and ever less mythically.

The focusing on linguistic aspects also characterizes the first academic studies arising in India. These were auxiliary studies for those who were familiar with the Veda, and apart from the study of liturgy and astronomy, they revealingly tackled the whole of language: grammar, etymology, metrics, and phonetics. Two out of the six classical orthodox philosophical schools in India — the Pūrva-Mīmāṃsā and the Uttara-Mīmāṃsā — are exclusively based on linguistic philosophy and hermeneutics.

The link between cow and language in early usage was very concrete. The cow was clearly a metonym for everything that has to do with food and life's resources, for abundance and good life. And indeed, for the Brahmins, language itself was a cow as they worked with language as their tool in the ancient fire ritual which was primarily a *mantra* ritual, which in turn provided them with real cows as gifts. At the time of the *Amarakośa*, Sanskrit had become a secular lingua franca in educated circles and social elites at the courts. Again, the perfect mastery of polished Sanskrit was an important key to success in all areas of life for practically everybody. The artistic poetry made use of the highly polysemantic range of the word "cow," and this is precisely why we find it listed in the *Amarakośa*. For instance, the poet Daṇḍin (7th or 8th century AD) uses the word "cow" in three quite different meanings to show his virtuosity in language (*Kāvyādarśa* 1.6, see WILKE/MOEBUS 2011, p. 531). He was an exponent of the manneristic school of ornamentation and, like other court poets, utterly profane.

The primary symptom of the de-mythified attitude to language in this epoch is the focusing on the (grammatical) term *śabda* instead of the (mythical) *vāc*. In grammar, the language cow enjoyed an interesting transformation. Since late antiquity, grammarians used the word "cow" as a standard example in connection with linguistic questions like: "What links the sounds 'c-o-w' with the actual animal?" or "Does the word 'cow' denote an individual animal or the class of all cows?" Such questions posed for instance by Śabarasvāmin (see *Śabarabhāṣya* 1.1.6.19), the philosopher of late antiquity who belonged to the Pūrva-Mīmāṃsā school, are not far away from those posed by modern Western linguists: "What is the meaning of *cow*? It is surely not any particular animal" (LYONS 1968, p. 40). The ancient and medieval Indian linguists were doubtless rationalists, and no less so than the modern linguists who found inspiration in them. Grammar was the first analytic science in India, which emancipated itself from the Veda (although it started as a "limb of the Veda"). But, the Pūrva-Mīmāṃsā shows that there is not merely a simple development from *mythos* to *logos*, or mythical thought and sensory perception to scientific abstraction and generalization, as has been discerned for the occidental culture. The Pūrva-Mīmāṃsakas, who sought to keep the original Vedic ritual alive, developed their strikingly modern sounding linguistic theory as a by-product, so to speak. Their actual intention was to prove the eternity of the Veda word.

This outline reveals two interesting things. On the one hand, some developments in Indian culture correspond to the theory of symbolic forms that was forwarded by the cultural philosopher Ernst CASSIRER; on the other hand, they betray it in many ways. In his theory of symbolic forms, CASSIRER referred to the Vedic goddess *Vāc* as an illustration of what he postulated as an irreversible development and transculturally valid law in all history of thought: the transition from the mythical and magical to the terminological, and from the individual to the general and universal. CASSIRER saw in the goddess *Vāc* the first emergence of conceptual thought, the transition from the mythical form of language, that is, from the particular word and magic formula and the individual power contained in it, to language as a universal term and language's power of abstraction (1994, pp. 56–57). The only linguistic field where he found persistence of mythic thought was poetry. At first glance, this seems to correlate with the developments of the Indian language cow from mythic thought to linguistic abstraction and metaphoric poetic diction. In later times, we definitely find greater reflexiveness and abstraction compared with the early Ṛgveda. However, already the mention of the Pūrva Mīmāṃsā's attempt to prove the eternity of the Veda by a highly rational language theory makes clear that CASSIRER's theory is not quite fitting for describing the Indian history of ideas and rationality. His thesis of a linear development from *mythos* to *logos* was clearly a Eurocentric — and even a neo-Kantian — construction, and contained a value judgment that is not found in India. In India, much as elsewhere, mythical and abstract thought must be seen as poles of an oscillating system. However, what characterizes India is that myth (as narrative as well as a form of consciousness and guiding cultural image) was not devalued. Some very eminent thinkers even developed reflexive holisms ("universal myths") which blended *mythos* and *logos* ("participatory" and "emancipatory" orientations towards language and reality).

The primary intuition in the image of the "Language Cow" was that language also includes the pre-terminological, the pre-logical, and the sensory, and this cultural knowledge had great persistence. It pervades different forms of acoustic piety, *mantra* practices, and highly sophisticated linguistic philosophies. These philosophies (discussed in the final section of this chapter) took up the old idea of *Vāc* and bound it into a rational discourse by positing rationality within a mythical framework, and explaining mythical embedding in an analytical fashion. But the Language Goddess also took on more tangible forms. Language as a divine being was popularized in numerous iconic images, starting with Sarasvatī, the gentle goddess of language, music, and wisdom, who is known to everybody, and who has also a more esoteric form in Tantric ritual.

The next section discussing these cultural symbols takes up the thread of a sonic history. It outlines persistence and fluidity in the sonic paradigm. If anything, the manifold and shifting correlations between language and the understanding of the world in Hindu India make clear in ever new variations that language is effective in both its terminological, discursive and logical aspect as well as in its sensory and emotive aspects. The main function of language is the creation of sense, and this takes place on a very great number of levels, both semantic and non-semantic, by making propositions and using symbolic forms. In fact, it will be seen that in many religious traditions of India, non-semantic sounds are also a medium of utmost importance for communication.

Persistence and fluidity: Sound as a medium of cultural reproduction

Hinduism is characterized by a plurality of the most varied approaches to language and sound — a plurality that begins as early as the Veda. The Veda exhibits both the fluidity of texts and the aesthetics of sonic communication particularly well. Whereas the Vedic hymns were still evocative calls to the gods and magic poetry at the time that they were composed, in late Vedic times they became sacred language material in which one no longer tried to find a visionary meaning, but was much rather seeking mysterious numeric combinations. In epic times, the mere recitation of the holy text acquired an importance equal to that of the late Vedic fire sacrifice. The *Rāmāyaṇa* depiction of the "holy noise" (*brahma-ghoṣa*) of the resonant three-tone Veda recitation, as it emanates from the simple straw huts of modest-living Brahmins, already completely suggests the Vedic aura and solemn sacredness which is linked to Veda recitation even today. Already the sound of the Veda imparts a meaning associated with one particular cultural habitus: when a Hindu hears the characteristic three intervals of a Veda performance, this transports him to the peaceful, pure, and strictly vegetarian world of ideal Brahminhood. The Veda has kept its sacred power, although it has altered substantially in its reception over the course of time. The very same text was initially understood as a "normal semantic text," then as an esoteric secret formula, and finally, essentialistically, as sacred sound substance.

As is well known, the Veda remained a mere oral canon until the 19th century. The highest precision in correct pronunciation and sophisticated mnemotechniques guaranteed that the holy text was transmitted without change through the centuries. Sound was, in this case, not only a more precise and more effective medium of storage than writing (FALK 1990, STAAL 1986), but it also reinforced sensuous–aesthetic–emotive incorporation. The books on phonetics use very poetic metaphors to communicate the tonal subtleties of recitation, and thereby communicate implicitly the Brahmins' love for their holy text and an aesthetic-emotional flavor (WILKE/MOEBUS 2011, pp. 500–504). The Veda *svādhyāya* or "self-study" remained the holy duty of orthodox Brahmins even after fire sacrifice was replaced by the *pūjā* ritual of classical Hinduism. But, self-study did not mean exegesis, but memorization and recitation.

It is of interest that the scrupulous care given to the Veda as a canon of sound did not include equal care for meaning (WILKE 2011) — an exception to this were only the Upaniṣads. In cultural memory, the Veda came to be seen as myth in itself, a pre-established and pre-lingustic truth underlying cosmic and social order (HALBFASS 1991), and as the very paradigm of sacred sound. The strict orality allowed maximum openness in interpretation, that is, extreme re-semantization, and "aggiornamento" to cultural change. A still harmless example are "Vedic evergreens" which were, in post-Vedic times, interpreted as prayers to the deities of the new pantheon of classical Hinduism, such as the old Ṛgvedic hymn to the speech goddess *Vāc* who is spread everywhere and exceeds heaven and earth, which is known today as a "hymn to the [Great] Goddess" (*Devī-Sūkta*). More and more new Upanisads were also produced. But most striking is the adoption of the Veda title by most varied post-Vedic literatures which have little to do with the original in content and style. Epics and Purāṇas came to be known as the "5th Veda," teaching the same eternal truth in a new fashion for the present age. Indeed, the Purāṇas and other devotional literature projected a self-image to be the Veda that is the most suitable for the present epoch of Kali Yuga. However, theatre studies also declared theatre to be the fifth Veda; Tamil ecstatic hymnology was labeled the "vernacular Veda;" the Pañcarātra Saṃhitās pretended to be the true original, primordial Veda, etc. In many ways, the Veda was to leave profound marks on Indian culture regarding authority, efficiency, and sacred power, with which other literatures also liked to invest themselves or proudly declared of going beyond. This also happened in terms of sound.

Holy hearing and acoustic piety

Today, one can get audio material of Vedic chanting in any Indian music store and on the Internet; but even in the past, the Veda image of sacred sound and the auspicious aura connected with it surpassed the Brahmins' sphere. The "Veda noise" (*brahma-ghoṣa*) belonged not only to the inventory of indispensable features of the Brahmanic forest-hermit settlements in the epics, but also to all the settings that needed auspicious protection. In the 6th century, the astrologer

Varāhamihira, who otherwise has a more worldly orientation, quotes an older source on the right way to crown a king:

> The heralds should call out loudly [the virtues of the new ruler], the people should praise the day, and the Brahmins should declaim the Veda noisily. In addition, auspicious sounds should resound from drums and conch horns. This stifles future unhappiness in the bud (*Bṛhatsaṃhitā* 47.49, WILKE/MOEBUS 2011, p. 468).

The idea that even the acoustic environment of a Veda recitation has auspicious effects and banishes all harmful influences wherever it is heard was adopted and further developed for the theistic texts. The framing story of the "Thousand Names of Viṣṇu," for instance, has the standard formula typical of theistic and devotional texts, stating that the recitation of the names of Viṣṇu purifies and liberates one from all burdens of sin. The devotional texts take on the auspicious power of the deity, and top the soteriological power of the Veda. Merely hearing a Purāṇa recital brings the gift of deliverance, and even counteracts the *karma* laws (WILKE/MOEBUS 2011, pp. 462–472).

The post-Vedic sacred literature became much more important than the Veda in popular culture and daily life. Similar to the Veda recitals, the Purāṇa readings do not necessarily need to be understood. In fact, often they are not because they are in Sanskrit which, even in the past, was known only to the educated elite. It is enough to know that it is a sacred text. And, this is already heard, since "reading" means "reciting" in a semi-musical or musically pleasing way. Vice versa, simply listening to the sound of a religious text is held to be auspicious and purifying. For many, it is sufficient to know this is praise, a litany, a *mantra*, or a story of the god(s) to believe in the text's efficiency and power, and it's bringing the gods to mind. Thus, acoustic piety is wide spread, comprising religious forms in which the act of recitation itself or the devotional attitude range first, whereas the semantic meaning is not necessarily important or known (ibid., 2011, pp. 58–66, 88–125, 151–157, 468–472). According to the emic view, hearing, reciting, and singing leads directly into the divine sphere. Semantics, thus, need not be the primary thing, because sound alone creates contact and participation. Practitioners can see the religious text itself as an icon of the Divine charged with special power, an animate reality. Reading and hearing alone has sanctifying and soteriological power — regardless of whether the Purāṇa is recited by professional bards or simple "laypersons" in the *pūjā* room.

More than anything else, the inherent validity of sounds, as expressed in phenomena such as the "holy noise" of a Veda recital, has left its mark on the Indian understanding of texts even today. If in a southern Indian temple, against a background of bells and the all-pervading notes from the Nādasvaram (a south Indian reed pipe), the priests declaim whole telephone directories of numinous names from memory by calling on the temple deities using their traditional 108 or 1000 names, or if itinerant monks put themselves into a blissful trance by singing to their God Siva "praise, praise, praise" incessantly to the chirruping sound of their *ektars* (one-stringed drone instruments), it becomes clear just how far the category of "text" is stretched here. The total disappearance of language in music (as we find in many of today's *bhakti* traditions) is merely one of the most radical forms in which the self-subsistent validity of sound is expressed. It is not only semantically comprehensible texts but also non-semantic sounds that make up the textual lore of Hindu traditions — even mere phonemes and the letters of the alphabet do so. In fact, such non-lexical sounds are of great relevance in the cultural symbol system as media of communication and religious practice. They are held to be particularly sacred and powerful.

The language goddess and her alphabet rites

As already seen, the central Sanskrit term *śabda* covers the English terms "sound" and "word" equally. The consistent conclusion was a notion that is very strange to the Western way of thinking: it is not only sentences and words that are seen as communicative but also syllables and even individual phonemes. Although they do not impart meaning in the sense of content, they are still bodies of sound with their own audible expressivity. For many religious Indian thinkers, language is not only a means of communication but is also in a way the subject of the communication process. Language itself is envisaged as a person, and even individual phonemes are understood as independent personalities or speech subjects with their very own statements. This has been implemented in rituals, and also thought through in terms of linguistic philosophy.

One especially striking result of this kind of inherent validity (which exists even in the personality of individual phonemes) is the existence of sacred texts that are not composed of words in our sense at all. A remarkable example is the *mātṛkā-pūjā* in Tantrism, a ritual recitation of the Sanskrit alphabet in the esoteric (Āgamic) temple service and private worship. The *Śāradā-Tilaka-Tantra*, a popular ritual manual compiled by Lakṣmaṇa Deśika (probably 13th century, traditionally ascribed to the 10th century AD), describes the deity associated with this rite as follows:

> And now we speak of [the goddess] with the body made of the alphabet, who makes intelligence in the universe possible. If this [alphabet] did not exist in perceivable form, the whole world would be without life . . . [When one prays to her, one thinks to oneself:] I turn to the white-shining three-eyed goddess of language . . . on whose face, shoulders, breast, belly and feet are distributed the 50 letters [of the alphabet] (*Śāradā-Tilaka-Tantra* 6.1. 4; WILKE/MOEBUS 2011, p. 279).

The divergence from the Western idea of language is already expressed through the choice of metaphors. When we in the West consider the "eternal word" and the world-accessing power of language, we are unlikely to think of a beautiful woman with the letters of the alphabet painted on her body. For, in this context, we do not think of the acoustics, and even less of individual phonemes filled with sense and sound. But this is precisely what Lakṣmaṇa Deśika does. For him language is a goddess called Sarasvatī or Śāradā, and she has cosmogonic relevance. The fact that she is visualized as a beautiful woman indicates that this is not a purely abstract absolute, but also something sensory. This idea runs through the whole chapter of the *Śāradā-Tilaka* in which the "rites of the language deity" are described: the prayers to the goddess of language, and the recitations of her living body, the alphabet. For Lakṣmaṇa Deśika, what is important about the image is not the graphemes, and not the written, semantically transparent text, but the 50 "sounding," spoken, or sung syllables of the Sanskrit alphabet, which are recited in the ritual and projected on the practitioner's body. The practitioner becomes, so to speak, the all-knowing Language Goddess who is the cosmos in subtle form, and pervades it with life and intelligence.

Lakṣmaṇa Deśika is not a "weird bird" pursuing strange ideas. As we already know from the Language Cow and the Vedic goddess *Vāc*, he draws support from a venerable tradition of the sacredness of language. If this sacredness manifests itself in sound, and not in the *logos*, the reason for this is that Lakṣmaṇa Deśika's world is so completely filled by the audible experience of language. It is a world in which the repetition of holy formulas (*mantra*s) makes up an important part of religious practice. Even the letters of the alphabet can, in the ritual context, become *mantra*s and powerful deities, able to grant every wish and ward off every evil. Moreover, it is a world in which the alphabet was not a random assemblage of language sounds, but a structured composition, arranged in strict phonetic order according to the seats of articulation. (This typical feature of the Sanskrit alphabet was copied by the vernacular alphabets). The grammarians' interest was to account for all sounds of language in a systematic way. The Tantrists were interested in the alphabet because it formed the basic material of the *mantra*s. In ritual usage, a nasalized sound (*ṃ*) is added to each of the letters to make them *mantra*-like and thereby become numinous forces. In the Tantras and Āgamas, the alphabet has profound esoteric significance. Their sophisticated cosmologies are based on the letters of the alphabet in written and in sonic form. The syllables of the alphabet — and most importantly the vowels A, Ā, I, Ī, etc. — become mysterious graphic and sonic codes which serve as a model to explain the coming about of the world and physical language. It is typical for Tantric discourse that the alphabet is not only a physical symbol of the Language Goddess but her very embodiment. It has itself cosmogonic significance, and hence it is called *mātṛkā*, "mother." It is the mother of the world and the very blueprint of creation. The alphabet is viewed as the basic material out of which not only the *mantra*s and our ordinary language are made, but also the phenomenal world which consists, in a more subtle form, of pure light and sound energy.

Sound rites and language acts such as those of the *Sāradā-Tilaka-Tantra* and the cosmological frames surrounding them are certainly the most extreme manifestations of the strongly sonic orientation of Indian culture. But such extremes are the best examples, for they are the result of the view that language is not exhausted in semantics and denomination, but that the audible physical element of language, too, and its sonic aura play a central role, and that linguistic signs reach into the pre-terminological.

Mantra power

One of the most typical features of Indian (not only Hindu) religious practice is the existence of veritable "sound rites," and of categories of text which are not texts at all as per Western understanding. Most pronouncedly, this is found in the "seed" (*bīja*) *mantras* of Tantrism, which consist of nothing other than (strings of) monosyllabic sounds, such as HRAUṂ and AIṂ HRĪṂ ŚRĪṂ, or the nasalized alphabet (AṂ ĀṂ etc.). These non-lexical sounds were a new type of *mantra* introduced by the Tantra, which became exceedingly successful. Tantric *mantras* differed not only in form from Vedic *mantras* (mostly semantically transparent short texts of different contents) but also in terms of content (mostly monosyllabic sounds which embody a deity). What is most characteristic of Tantric *mantras* is the idea that they incorporate — like a "seed" — in their mere sound pattern the respective god or goddess (or another numinous force) in a very real sense: for instance, HRAUṂ the Supreme Śiva (*Paramaśiva*), or AIṂ HRĪṂ ŚRĪṂ the Great Goddess in her mild form (*Lalitā-Tripurasundarī*). Tantric deities are invariably *mantra* deities. Uttering a Tantric *mantra*, thus, will make the divinity and all its powers immediately present. This idea was also absorbed by devotional *mantras*, that is, formulas containing God's name (such as *namaḥ Śivāya*, "prostrations to Śiva," or *Rām Rām*). The various Tantric (and *bhākta*) initiation lines generally feel superior to the Veda, to whom they attribute less (or no) soteriological force.

Although Vedic and Tantric *mantras* and devotional ones can be distinguished, there is one very essential and most basic feature shared by them: namely, the typical *mantric* idea of an agency and inherent power of the utterance independent of the speaker's intention. Following on from speech act theory, one can speak of "language acts." The idea of inherent power, coupled with the immediacy of access to the cherished deity at any time and place, the possibility of direct empowerment without any priestly mediation, and the openness of Tantric and devotional *mantras* (*mantra* initiation) to all groups of society, irrespective of caste, gender, or creed, easily explains why they became immensely successful. One can understand the new empowerment which the Tantric and devotional *mantras* offered to social groups who had been excluded from Vedic initiation, but also to Brahmins who had turned their attention to the gods of classical Hinduism (and who were accused in the initial phase of Tantrism of having left the Vedic path). Between the 5th and 13th century, Tantra established itself as a religious mainstream in India, across traditions and religious boundaries (the Śaivas played a leading role in this; see SANDERSON 2009). There exist a large variety of Tantric traditions, some also including heterodox features (such as sexual rites); but *mantra* practice will invariably be common to all, and their difference is primarily due to different *mantra* systems (*mantra* deities). With the spread of Tantric and devotional *mantras* throughout India, *mantra* power became common cultural knowledge even in the remotest villages. The recitation of *mantras* (non-semantic or semantic sacred formulas), and the constant repetition of one of God's names, are still among the most widespread religious practices today.

In *mantras*, the phonetic structure is more important than the literal meaning (if there is any), and the performative context is all that counts. Only in a traditionally defined speech act (language act) do they become effective and powerful. Above all, *mantras* have a ritual efficacy, that is, they exert an effect. *Mantras* are used, not interpreted (PADOUX 1991; WHEELOCK 1982 and 1991). The language of ritual does not transport information but creates participation, and seeks to transform the state of the speaker and his reality.

Since the sonic aspect is so important and the semantic is so unimportant in many Hindu rites, in Western research it has sometimes been suggested that *mantras* should not be viewed as language at all, but rather as "meaningless sounds," where the important thing is not the understanding but the composition of the sounds, and the use and the function within the ritual; in other words, the pure form replaces the content (STAAL 1979, 1991, 1996). However, this very formalist theory forgets an essential thing: the sensory aesthetics of sounds. Even if *mantras* do not have any semantic meaning, they still are sounds that are received by the senses. Sounds can be felt physically. They are expressive characters which elicit emotive and intuitive associations. This is very obvious in the Tantric *bījas*, in which the sensory aesthetics of sounds is very essential and plays a powerful experiential role. They are indeed without lexical meaning; but they are invariably known as bearers of a powerful divinity and her potential. Moreover, they create a very direct bodily knowledge. The nasalized sound at the end leaves a strong impression in the body, reverberating in the head like the echo of a gong. What *mantras* mean becomes known only by their use. And naturally, those who use the *mantras* do not consider them to be meaningless. It is, therefore, also not surprising that attempts exist to semantize the sound sequences and find deep esoteric sense in each phoneme. Such hermeneutics were not only transmitted orally by the *guru* but also codified in the traditional "*mantra*-science" (*mantra-śāstra*). This means, in addition to the sound impression, the lexically meaningless sound combinations hide secret messages for the initiated.

Mantras — whether Vedic, Tantric, or devotional — are invariably powerful sacred formulas of high symbolic value. They are coded with cultural and group-specific imaginations: connotations fixed by tradition, particular functions, specific experiential fields, and an array of expectations resulting from the global connotation of *mantra* power.

There is a commonly shared field of imagery about *mantra* power which was greatly informed by the Tantra, and also projected on Vedic and devotional *mantras*. Above all, *mantras* are charged with the power of transformation and change. They not only make the ritual work and bring about its effects but are also able to change the world from one moment to the next. *Mantra*s are the most important instruments for getting immediate and direct access to the godhead, warding off any danger, getting all that one wants, and absorbing all the deity's powers and protection. The array of cultural imaginations surrounding *mantra* practice has very much to do with personal empowerment and self-transformation. It is a "technology of the self" (FOUCAULT 1988) to cope with daily life and to reach "the other shore" within this very life, that is, liberation while living. In various ways, *mantra*s are used as gateways to the divine and the cosmic whole, and as powerful medium to transcend the limited frames of the ordinary human condition. Depending on the tradition, lineage, and also personal motivation, *mantra*s are instrumental for disciplining the wandering mind, and bringing about emotive immersion, healing, self-transformation, supernatural powers, and liberation. *Mantra* practices include verbal and mental (and often also breathing) techniques, appealing to both the outer and inner senses. *Mantra*s may be recited, sung, and chanted alone or in groups, may be muttered or silently repeated, and may be contemplated upon. In the Yogic–Tantric traditions, they are often experimented on, for example, by concentrating on the sound vibrations and their resonance in the body. Sound in all Tantric traditions was a very powerful holistic symbol, and a perfect connector of exterior and interior space. It was used to arrive at and channel non-ordinary experience (visions and auditions, de-differentiation of duality, out-of-body experience, ecstasy, possession trance, healing, and wonder-working) and make the body a "sounding-board" of the Divine. The sources enforce constant *mantra* practice, so that the Sādhakas ("those who strive") become Siddhas ("perfected ones") — supermen on earth who enter the fabric of unseen cosmic forces, perceive the universe as a world of light and sound, and attain a cosmic mind, that is, become all-knowing and almost omnipotent. This image of the Tantric superman is very widespread.

Such virtuosi practices and imageries, which are deeply rooted in the cultural memory, should not make one forget the most common *mantra* reception: namely, the calling of the name of God, and constant remembrance (*smaraṇa*). For the *Bhāktas*, what is most important is surrender, loving participation, and strengthening of the emotive ties to God. In actual practice, *mantra* repetition may be just a daily duty. There is no need to think consciously of the divinity or discursively ponder over it. *Mantra* muttering can be done quite thoughtlessly, and even be experienced as boring (which is also true for the Vedic and Tantric fold). However, even then, the *mantra* will invariably be charged with the knowledge referring to the divine subject (of one's choice). The *bhakti* mode of loving surrender produced its own *mantra* styles and imageries of perfection. Characteristically, many devotional *mantra*s contain not only the name of God, but also a formula of surrender and praise, and they are often set to music. *Bhākta*s seek shelter in the Lord, protection, peace of mind, and emotional absorption. Typically, the ideal of perfection of the Bengali Vaiṣṇavaite virtuosi of *bhakti* was not a body of sound, but a body of emotion.

To sum up: these various experiential fields are hard to capture with merely formalistic theories like the one of Frits Staal. We have to take into account the sensory–aesthetic dimension, along with the cognitive and emotive associations and highly symbolic value connected with the *mantra*s. *Mantra*s need not have, and often do not have, any meaning in the usual sense of the word; but this is definitely not to say that they are not full of meaning for those uttering them.[6] In Vedic and Tantric *mantra*s, and very often in devotional *mantra*s as well, the acoustic aspects are exceptionally important (including the number of syllables, rhythms and tonal modes, etc.). In *mantra*s, an inherent power is ascribed to sound, but this is by no means limited to *mantra*s alone, as seen earlier.

Linguistics and metaphysics

In order to understand phenomena such as the *bīja-mantra*s and the recitation of the Sanskrit alphabet, and to honor them in their own contexts, it is expedient to use indigenous ritual literature and its explanations. But, maybe it is even more fundamental to take into account native language theories and language philosophies since they best reflect culture-specific views of language, and reveal fundamental ontological criteria and values. Apart from the many and varied performative functionalizations of language and sound that we find in Hinduism, perhaps no other culture has turned so much of its mental attention to language and sound.

The importance of language is not least expressed in the fact that the cosmologies of the early *mythos*, and of the later philosophical *logos*, see in language a force that opens up the world — and sometimes even creates the world. We have seen that the late hymns of the *Ṛgveda* already sing of the Goddess Language (*vāc*) as the creator of the universe — a notion that is continued in ever-new forms, and culminates in highly elaborate philosophical concepts in the Middle Ages. It is remarkable that, almost as a by-product, Indian language theoreticians had hereby anticipated the "linguistic turn" of Western philosophy by hundreds of years. Even in the early Middle Ages, the linguistic philosopher Bhartṛhari (5th century AD) noted in his famous linguistic work *Vākyapadīya* the fundamental dependence of perception on language: "In this world there is no perception of things that is without language [and our] whole perception appears permeated by language."[7]

Bhartṛhari seems decidedly modern with his thesis of the indissoluble connection between language and thought. But interestingly, this is only a subordinate aspect of a holistic and "re-mythifying" program of metaphysics inspired by the old cosmo-genetic notions of language (*vāc*) in the Veda. The

---

[6] PADOUX (1991, p. 313); WILKE/MOEBUS (2011, pp. 89–91, 280–285, 406–409, 665–668, 690–762).

[7] *Vākyapadīya* 1.123 (1.131); WILKE/MOEBUS (2011, pp. 287, 624).

originally mythical idea that language was the actual basis of existence and possessed cosmogonic relevance is developed further by Bhartṛhari using systematic philosophy. His philosophy teaches that the phenomenal world is nothing but a "metamorphosis" (*vivarta*) of an eternal, transphenomenal linguistic principle (*śabda-tattva*). At the same time, this principle is equivalent to an integral world consciousness (*brahman*) that, on the phenomenal level, becomes the meaning aspect of language. In Bhartṛhari's assessment, meaning takes place only because there is a global network of meaning to which all words must refer to become meaningful. Viewed in its cosmic dimension, this global linguistic network goes beyond both time and space, and does not recognize either individual words or individual things. However, in its worldly form, it is splintered into time and space, and its fragments — the individual words and their meanings (that is, individual things) — form the whole phenomenal reality. This idea of a linguistic basis for the world's existence (*śabda-brahman*) — which some commentators again interpreted as sound — set in motion a real revolution of thought in India. It has strongly influenced many other philosophers, and determined quite fundamentally the ritual practice of later Tantrism. The ritualistic Lakṣmaṇa Deśika, whom I quoted earlier, actually built on Bhartṛhari.

An important conception of Bhartṛhari, which is most relevant in the Tantric discourse, is the idea that language/speech/voice (*vāc*) has three dimensions,[8] of which the first is "corporeal" speech (*vaikharī*); the linguistic expression that is uttered and heard (along with all individual characteristics of speech like modulation and tempo). The next is the "middle" or "mediating" one (*madhyamā*), that is, interior speech, the dimension of thought in which the apprehension of the sound sequence as a meaningful word takes place, and where words are not articulated as aerial vibrations but rather as mental processes. However, there is still a subtler dimension which exists beyond the sequences of sound, the mental labelling and the linearity of discursive thought: namely, the sudden comprehension of meaning. Bhartṛhari describes this immediate insight of the meaning-whole as the "seeing" or "visionary" dimension of speech (*paśyantī*). What is so vital in Bhartṛhari was the insight that language works in both the verbal and non-verbal sphere, and that understanding meaning always happens in a holistic way of sudden insight. Speech and consciousness exist in a continuum.[9]

---

[8] *Vākyapadīya* 1.159, crit. ed. Rau 1.134; Wilke/Moebus (2011, p. 646).

[9] It is noteworthy that the verse following the one on the three dimensions of language (*Vākyapadīya* 1.160) and the (auto-) commentary of the section refers to the "Language Cow" to describe the nature of speech in a poetic way; the commentary also quotes Yogic–Tantric sources, and alludes to the mysterious Ṛgvedic riddle verse of the four levels of language (RV 1.164.45), which reach, according to Bhartṛhari, into a sphere, which cannot be measured at all.

In Tantric discourse, Bhartṛhari's three dimensions of language appear further differentiated and radicalized into four dimensions: the fourth one being *parā*, the "highest" dimension, a cosmic language which is identical with a perception of the whole. This synthetic view was the very backbone of the non-dual Śaivism developed by Abhinavagupta (10–11th century AD), the great Kashmiri philosopher, left-hand Tantrist, theorist of aesthetics, and poet (WILKE/MOEBUS 2011, pp. 771–792). Abhinavagupta's starting point was *mantra* practice and the unbrokenness of sound extending from the physical to the non-physical stages. He built on Bhartṛhari when distinguishing four levels of language: 1) the spoken word, with which intersubjective communication takes place; 2) discursive thought; 3) the sensory and affective overall impression of an object; and 4) the integral perception of the whole. To Abhinavagupta, this all-encompassing perception of the whole (*saṃvid*) represents the gaze of God upon the world, and the "cosmic language" (*parā vāc*), which is crystallized most perfectly in the Sanskrit word *aham*, meaning "I." To him, *aham* is the central *mantra* of the universe, for "I" contains all levels of language within itself, from the synthetic vision of the whole to the judgment "[t]hat is that" (*idantā*, literally "that-ness"). The levels of language arise solely out of the increasing differentiation between I and That, and between message and sign. So they are nothing other than a continuous self-formulation and self-expression of AHAM. This esoteric teaching is rationally credible, for it has impressive philosophical support:

> [We claim that every form of] discursive perception requires an integral perception of the whole. [For discursive perception] consists [not of an integral impression, but is based on] complementary [terms] such as 'black' and 'white,' it considers the appearances as opposites [of one another] and subsequently understands [them] to be separate in space or time. [But it is always a form of an integral perception of the whole, which] puts the complementary phenomena, which are declared to be opposites, such as 'black' or ['white'] in relation to each other in the first place. [That is] comparable with looking at a painting or the view from a mountain-top … (*Pāratrīsikā-Vivaraṇa*, vs. 1; WILKE and MOEBUS 2011, pp. 316, 772).

Abhinavagupta shows that language includes not only linear and discursive modes but also simultaneous presentational modes. And, he is not only contrasting these two modes but also deriving one from the other. Discursive perception only works because of a holistic perception surrounding it. Holistic perception includes not only the logical, discursive aspect, but the sensory and emotive dimension which is also interwoven with the logical and discursive aspect. On the concrete level, the aesthetic impression is coincident with the intuitive overall impression of an object before its analytical dissection by discursive thought. This integral overall impression is compared with the view from a mountain-top, and at other places with enjoying music. The overall impression is, in a way, pre-linguistic since it is not and cannot be verbalized, just like the experience of music. But this does not necessarily mean that it is not communicable. Sounds do not have to be translated into something else — one can receive them sympathetically and spontaneously. Abhinavagupta conceives of language from a starting point totally embedded in the audible aspect because the perception of audible sound is the most holistic. All linguistic signs develop from a preceding sound language ("Klangsprache") and oral communication, and not vice versa. Only complete intersubjective participation in the actual sound creates an opportunity for linguistic communication.

For Western readers, Abhinavagupta's argumentation simply seems foreign because their world contains so little experience of language as sound, whereas for the Kashmiri author, it is no problem to have sound and its perception as the basic paradigm of all communication. Here, he correlates communication with participation in a remarkable manner, for audible experiences are basically pure participation. Most sonic phenomena are received in a purely sensory and emotional way, and this applies, first and foremost, to the musical and semi-musical forms of sound, which can also include the metrical and alliterative aspects of poetry.

Pure sound is ultimately the model for Abhinavagupta's contention that a perception of the whole must always exist between two discursive perceptions. He uses the term *saṃvid* for this holistic perception and apparently does not so much mean a focused perception and conscious registering, but much more an intuitive impression or a feeling. The term *saṃvid* can mean both: on the one hand, an "integral vision" or "complete awareness" as a requirement for the logical and objective (*samam+vid*) — here Abhinavagupta refers to Bhartṛhari's linguistic pre-reflexive intuition (*pratibhā*); but, on the other hand, the word also connotes "feeling" and "physical sensation" in the realm of the emotive and aesthetic (*samyak+vid*) — which for Abhinavagupta is more basic. He uses *saṃvid* synonymously with *camatkṛti*, the "wondering astonishment," the aesthetic awe-struck emotion of the connoisseurs and authors of poetry and drama. For this reason, Abhinavagupta regards aesthetics as an essential part of communication. In line with his theory of cosmic language, in which the perception of objects crystallizes out of the perception of the whole, the objective dimension of language (which relates to the external world) is also a reification of the pure audible and expressive aspect. The expression comes first, and then the semantics. For Abhinavagupta, the fundamental basis of communication can never lie in semantic language because his integrative theory of language can only be conceived starting from the much more general and more sympathetic contents that are communicated at the level of pure sound.

Looking at Abhinavagupta and Bhartṛhari (and also Śaṅkara's soundless Advaita-Vedānta) — ultimately the same program becomes clear: the search for a myth(os) that encompasses the whole world, that is, a "universal myth." But still, the manner in which this is attempted shows that India is not at all more strongly participation-oriented and "irrational" than Western societies. Quantifying statements of this type are unworkable in a differentiated culture and complex society. The Sanskrit culture in which Bhartṛhari and Abhinavagupta grew up was supported by a highly rationalized and highly technical society, with a considerable share in world trade, a society that also postulated the law of gravitation, invented the first automated machine in the form of the water wheel, and started to tackle differential equations. But despite these strongly emancipatory elements in the culture, the myth was never devalued in contrast to Greek society which set *mythos* and *logos* against each other. In India, there is no Socratic *logos* program spanning the whole culture and engaging in a dialectic search for the truth. The Indian academic program works differently: one expects relatively little from the dialectic (*tarka*), but a great deal from a pragmatic ability to differentiate and make judgments (*viveka*), that is, the ability to identify the correct approach for solving a particular problem. Perhaps what characterizes Indian culture most of all is the steadfast refusal to subordinate its participatory world orientation simply to an absolute, atomistic rationality whose purpose is to emancipate the individual. As Indian culture progresses, it always works additively and inclusively.

Conclusion

The coincidence of text, sound, and ritual with the performance culture and phonocentric life-world in Hindu India brought about many social and religious practices and symbolic forms which are distinctly specific to this cultural area: from the great value given to orality and sonality to the Language Cow and cosmos-sustaining Language Goddess, who appeared in ever new forms and ritualizations, to alphabet recitation and mantra power. Besides such highly performative fields, we find at a very early age also highly analytical systems of grammar and linguistics. Although the traditional Indian sciences produced some outstanding scientific results which appeared only centuries later in Europe, the Indian scientific practice reveals quite different aesthetic styles from those in the Western intellectual culture of both the past and the present. This has much to do with a life-world of sonic perception in which abstract thought and sensory awareness were able to combine. A good example is the alphabet, which has appeared again and again in various contexts in this essay. Strictly speaking, the alphabet does not consist of "letters," but of an acoustically structured series of sounds whose order becomes apparent via hearing and not via seeing. Likewise, in the sciences such as mathematics and astronomy, the notation of abstract subjects was not bound to the graphical and visual but included the acoustic, and often favored it since the time of Pāṇini. In the Āgamas and Tantras, sound even becomes the basis of the universe. This idea was further topped by the Nāda-Brahman of the musicologist Śārṅgadeva in the 13th century, whose theses that the world is sound, and listening to music a pleasant form of yoga, could not be discussed here.

A fundamental theme of the essay has been the Veda. The Vedic liturgical model (a canon of acoustic signs) had great influence in various ways, not so much as a ritual canon but as a cultural canon of authoritative speech and sacred auspicious sound, which was re-produced and re-interpreted or rather, newly re-invented in a variety of completely different texts and contexts, some of them far beyond the Vedic–Brahmanic milieu. Maybe the Vedic model, which was not a discursive model but a liturgical one, can explain that, in Hindu India, there seems to be a much more participatory orientation towards world and language than the Europeans are used to. Just as orality and literacy have not been broken apart, there was never really a split between *mythos* and *logos*.

An important question in this essay is one of world-view. I do not pretend that there exists only one world-view in the Hindu India of the past and the present. This already became very clear with the shifting views of language and reality in the Vedic world, and the sacred and profane spaces and the plurality of options and traditions which developed in post-Vedic times. My remarks are rather general, and pertain foremost to the evaluation of the senses versus rationality. The philosophical positions discussed in the previous chapter made clear, in a more reflexive way than the preceding observations that, unlike in Western philosophy and discourses on sensory awareness which devalued the senses in favor of the mind and consciousness, we find in Hindu India and Sanskrit culture a model of an unbroken continuum of the sensory and the mental, and no split between physical sense perception and the non-sensory spirit (this is true even for the later Yoga tradition). We can extend this observation to *mythos* and *logos*, human and divine, ritual and contemplation, intellect and emotion, mathematics and poetics, and last but not least, orality and literacy. It seems, indeed, that the spaces of sonic perception and acoustic communication, that is, the phonocentric life-world which remained so pronounced in Hindu India (even after writing was widely in use) had a distinct influence on world-view formation, or at least were supporting it. Some things suggest that the Indian predilection for inclusivism and holistic world-views correlates directly with the sound-centered life-world, and was promoted by the paradigm of sonic perception. In Sanskrit Hinduism, language and sound are among the most significant holistic symbols of non-dual reality. However, sound was not only a good model of unitary vision and non-dual world interpretation (shared by important and otherwise quite different cultural policy makers like Abhinavagupta and Śaṅkara), and not only a very effective means of tuning into the deity and melting with the divine, but also a means for structuring and organizing abstract ideas in the traditional sciences and training formalistic thinking. Sonic awareness was able to produce and re-produce diverse forms of "third space-habitus" which are so characteristic of Hindu India and Sanskrit culture: from the understanding of the term "word" (*śabda*), in which the meaning aspect was never detached from the sound aspect, to the fusion of aesthetics and the sensory with abstraction in analytical science (like mathematics) and in speculative metaphysics (like Abhinavagupta's philosophy).

References

Beck, G. L. (1993): Sonic Theology. Hinduism and Sacred Sound. – Columbia.

Cassirer, E. (1994): Philosophie der symbolischen Formen. Erster Teil: Die Sprache. – Darmstadt.

FALK, H. (1990): Goodys for India – Literacy, Orality, and Vedic Culture. In: RAIBLE, W. (Ed.): Erscheinungsformen kultureller Prozesse. – Tübingen, pp. 103–120.

FOUCAULT, M. (1988): Technologies of the Self. In: MARTIN, L.H., et al. (Eds.): Technologies of the Self: A Seminar with Michel Foucault. – London, pp. 16–49.

HALBFASS, W. (1991): Tradition und Reflexion: Zur Gegenwart des Veda in der indischen Philosophie. In: OBERHAMMER, G. (Ed.), Beiträge zur Hermeneutik indischer und abendländischer Religionstraditionen. – Vienna, pp. 123–146.

LIPNER, J. (1994): Hindus: Their Beliefs and Practices. – London.

LYONS, J. (1968): Introduction in Theoretical Linguistics. – Cambridge.

MICHAELS, A. (1996): Das Buch als Fundament von Religion. In: RUSTERHOLZ, P. and MOSER, R. (Eds.), Die Bedeutung des Buches gestern – heute – morgen. – Berne and Vienna, pp. 111–146.

MICHAELS, A. (Ed., 2001): The Pandit: Traditional Scholarship in India. – New Delhi.

MICHAELS, A. (2005): Rituelle Klangräume. In: LANDAU, A., and EMMENEGGER, C. (Eds.): Musik und Raum: Dimensionen im Gespräch. – Zürich, pp. 33–44.

PADOUX, A. (1991). Mantras – What are They? In: ALPER, H. P. (Ed.): Understanding Mantras. – Delhi, pp. 295–321.

POLLOCK, S. (2007): The Language of the Gods in the World of Men: Sanskrit, Culture and Power in Premodern India. – Delhi.

SANDERSON, A. (2009): The Śaiva Age. The Rise and Dominance of Śaivism during the Early Mediveval Period. – Tokyo.

SINGER, M. (1972): When a Great Tradition Modernizes: An Anthropological Approach to Indian Civilization. – New York and London.

STAAL, F. (1991): The Meaninglessness of Ritual. In: Numen, Vol. 26, 1, pp. 2–22.

STAAL, F. (1996): The Fidelity of Oral Tradition and the Origin of Science. In: Mededelingen der Koninklijke Nederlandse Akademie van Wetenschappen, NR 49, 8, pp. 3–40 (251–288).

STAAL, F. (1996): Ritual and Mantras: Rules without Meaning. – Delhi.

STAAL, F. (1991): Vedic Mantras. In: ALPER, H. P. (Ed.), Understanding Mantras. – Delhi, pp. 48–95.

WHEELOCK, W. (1982): The Problem of Ritual Language: From Information to Situation. In: Journal of the American Academy of Religion, Vol. 50, 1, pp. 49–71.

WHEELOCK, W. (1991): The Mantra in Vedic and Tantric Ritual, In: ALPER, H. P. (Ed.), Understanding Mantras. – Delhi, pp. 96–122.

WILKE, A. (2008): Sound and Sense: Sonic Perception in Hindu India. In: GUZY, L. (Ed.), Religion and Music. – Berlin, pp. 15–59.

WILKE, A. (2011): Der Veda als Kanon des Hinduismus? Neue Aspekte zur Kanondebatte. In: DEEG, M., FREIBERGER, O. and KLEINE, C. (Eds.): Kanonisierung und Kanonbildung in der asiatischen Religionsgeschichte. – Vienna, pp. 1–56.

WILKE, A./MOEBUS, O. (2011): Sound and Communication. An Aesthetic Cultural History of Sanskrit Hinduism. – Berlin and New York.

Karsten Lichau

"Noise" or "Silence?" Listening to Sacred Sound in 20th-century Europe

Between "dense silence" and ear-deafening noise

Soundscapes of human–divine encounter in Serres and Schafer

In their interpretations of soundscapes of the human–divine encounter, Michael Serres and R. Murray Schafer seem to be in opposition with each other, when hearkening "dense silence" or ear-deafening noise in these soundscapes. This is evident in the following discussion:

> For the last two hours this morning I have been tasting the sun in the theatre at Epidaurus, alone, reclining against one of the steps. [...] Peace in the transparent air, yellow and blue. Silence. The countryside awaits the gods — it has been waiting for two thousand years. Silence. The gods will descend, healing will come. A question mark on the sky's axis, visible from passing planes, an immense ear bathed in the precisely tuned acoustic properties of the amphitheatre. I listen, I wait, in the dense silence. [...] The silence within the theatre and in the surrounding scrub seeps into my skin, bathes and penetrates it, vibrates and drains it, in the hollow of the empty ear. [...] Alone on this step, sitting in silence for the last two hours, little by little the world gives me its gods (SERRES 2008, pp. 85–86).

According to Michel SERRES' *The Five Senses* (2008), spaces or scenes that allow for divine presence stand out due to a special kind of silence; they are designed to enable such a silence since, in the absence of this, the human–divine encounter becomes impossible. The gods, like shy and timid small wild animals, vanish at the slightest acoustical nuisance in the silent moment — and it takes a long time for the required silence to be re-established:

> Silence returns like a modest veil.[1] Slowly. The immortals are hesitant to descend to such an easily sullied place. The gods pass us by, weightless, insubstantial, flanking non-existence, evanescent spirits; the least wrinkle in the air will chase them away. They have long since fled our deafening world (ibid., p. 86).

[1] The French original uses the word "pudeur," which means "shame" or "sensitivity" rather than "veil."

The encounter proceeds in a synesthetical mode ("tasting the sun," "ear bathed in the precisely tuned acoustic properties"), characteristic not only of the spatial and architectural framing as well as of the bodily perception of the human–divine encounter in general, but also of its very particular silence. This silence is at once fragile and powerful, slowly taking possession of the acoustic world and of the sojourning human bodies: It "seeps into my skin, bathes and penetrates it, vibrates and drains it" (SERRES 2008, p. 85).

This sensuous, hesitant silence, troubling the border between the perceiving subject and the perceived (sound-)object, has its counterpart in the irruption of a sudden, fast-moving, and loud noise — a phenomenon totally isolated from, or even hostile to, its surroundings:

> Horror. Here comes a group. I can hear it in the distance, coming this way. It projects itself across space as filthy noise. It is deafening, disturbing the transparency of the air, even before I can see it from my vantage point, coming out of the tunnel of green branches. Two, ten, forty people are encased in a shell of language and then in a rumbling outer hull which precedes, flanks and follows them like the prow, sides and stern of a bulky ship. The sea vibrates around the vessel, overwhelmed. It is here. A whole orchestra. They talk, squawk, discuss and exclaim, admire out loud, call to each other, give explanations, point out this, describe that, read the guide book, lend a distracted ear to its explanations and test, for the hundredth time, the location's exact acoustic properties. A din in the great ear of society. The fearful gods have fled from this eruption (ibid., pp. 85–86).

For Serres, this "filthy noise" summons up the acoustic sphere of the profane, the deaf "mass" and the everyday business (with the described tourists representing the everyday business of trying to escape everyday business) — all that can't keep silent.

We find quite another opposition of silence and noise with R. Murray SCHAFER's description of human–divine encounters and their acoustics. In his *The Tuning of the World* (SCHAFER 1994), the constellation of the sacred and the profane, noise and silence, is an inversion of SERRES' model. SCHAFER associates sacred spaces with loud, sometimes ear-deafening acoustics:

> [L]oud noises evoked fear and respect back to earliest times, and [...] they seemed to be the expression of divine power. [...] [T]his power was transferred from natural sounds (thunder, volcano, storm) to those of the church bell and pipe organ. I called this Sacred Noise (1994, p. 76).

Even if we take into account that SCHAFER mainly explores the *production of Sacred Sounds* (as expressions of the presumed Gods' "divine power" or as the earthly means to invoke or transfer this power), and SERRES listens for the arrival of the Gods emphasizing the human *perception* of Sacred Sounds, the two descriptions are constructing acoustical spheres of the human–divine encounter — sacred soundscapes[2] — that emerge from the processes of sound production as well as sound reception.

In SERRES, silence is the crucial quality of this soundscape of divine beings as well as of their encounter with profanity — the latter being the realm of noise, haste, and lack of sensitivity. Inverting this topology, SCHAFER, for whom the divine presence is distinguished by a tremendous *Sacred Noise*, attributes silence to the realm of the profane world. Under somewhat questionable reference to Claude Lévi-Strauss,[3] he suggests

> placing noise in parallel with the sacred, and silence in the same relationship with the profane. [...] The profane world was, if not silent, quiet. [...] Sacred Noise [.] was not only absent from the lists of proscripted sounds which societies from time to time drew up, but was, in fact, quite deliberately invoked as a break from the tedium of tranquillity (SERRES 2008, p. 51).

We seem to be confronted with an insurmountable contradiction. Does the acoustical staging of the Sacred, the soundscape of the human–divine encounter, stand out due to *Silence* (which in this case, in analogy to SCHAFER's "Noise," takes on a capital letter)? Or, is exactly the opposite true, and this soundscape reverberates with "Noise" whereas silence belongs to the profane world?

The unheard complexity of sacred sounds

A critical reflection on the acoustical stagings, the practices of producing and perceiving Sacred Sounds as well as on the ways in that they are conceived of in different cultures, may take some hints from the apparently irreconcilable opposition between loud, violent "Noise" and vague, fragile, yet overwhelming *Silence* that sacred soundscapes transmit to SCHAFER's or SERRES' ears.

We may read the opposition as a trace of the historical, cultural and social differences in sensual, in our case auditive, practices. While both Serres and Schafer — despite the fact that they draw their conclusions from specific

---

[2] While SCHAFER's concept of the soundscape tends to emphasize the study of acoustic environments and sound objects ("The soundscape is any acoustic field of study. We may speak of a musical composition as a soundscape, or a radio program as a soundscape or an acoustic environment as a soundscape" [1994, p. 7]), it does not totally ignore the unconturnable interdependency between the objective and subjective dimensions of sound — the soundscape also comprehends "the relationship between man and the sounds of his environment" (ibid., p. 3).

[3] SCHAFER himself admits: "I must warn the reader that Lévi-Strauss informs me that the Sacred Noise theory developed in this book bears 'little relationship, if any' to what he has written" (SCHAFER 1994, p. 51). This is probably due to SCHAFER's precipitated and rather un-reflected court-circuit of Strauss's reconstruction of mythical semantics with material soundscapes.

epochs and cultures (the Epidaurus theatre, built during the late classical period of Greek antiquity in the 4th century BC; the transformations of religious and profane culture in western European countries after 1500, and especially the process of modernization and the industrial revolution) — are more interested in sensitizing their readers for sensual perception than for the latter's historical variability, recent anthropological studies about the senses emphasize the need for a historical-cultural approach.[4] The perception of sounds is learned in and by cultural training, and the habitualization of the aural sense which varies highly in time, culture, social group, and even from one individual to another; and this also accounts for those sounds embodied in utterances of, or invocations for, the Sacred.

Just as is true for aural perception in general, the listening for silence or noise is far from being a universal phenomenon resisting historical and cultural change — like SCHAFER and SERRES tend to suggest.[5] The historical and social variability of auditive cultures is not only at stake with the distinction between noise and silence. We also find this historical and social variability in examining the properties and aural qualities of noise and silence: "What is 'noise'?" and "What is 'silence'?" are questions haunted by further distinctions that fill each of these two phenomena with cultural meaning. And, without raising such questions, neither "noise" nor "silence" may be adequately explored (not to mention their relationship to each other and to the Sacred).

The recent interest in exploring sensory cultures has given rise to a new field of research in auditive cultures, and the phenomenon of loud, "filthy" noise and acoustical nuisance is being given special attention in this emerging field. Several studies on "Lärm" (filthy noise) and noise abatement (BIJSTERVELD 2008, MORAT 2010, TOYKA-SAID 2009) have shown how an acoustic environment may well be perceived as an acoustical nuisance by one person, while another individual with historically, culturally, or socially different experiences and habitus forms may react to it with quite another attitude — not at all incited by nuisance, but by amusement, indifference, or functional interest. Well-known forms of acoustical "din" — like street music, market criers, children's voices, or traffic noise — may have disturbed intellectual workers, writers, or philosophers from the 16th to the 20th centuries (like Theodor Lessing, founder of the German "Lärmschutzverband," cf. MORAT 2010, pp. 177–179) — while

[4] Cf. CORBIN (1998); HOWES (2003); SMITH (2007); on historical-cultural anthropology WULF (2010); on the need for a historical-cultural exploration of auditive cultures: MORAT (2011).

[5] SCHAFER does not totally ignore historical dynamics: he assumes a rise in "noise pollution" from the pre-modern tranquility of everyday life to modern times — a thesis that cannot be easily denied. But, his approach is, historically, neither differentiated nor does it account for the historical changes in the cultural and social distinctions in noise perception, and hence in noise phenomenon in general. For that reason, noise and "Noise" remain largely ahistorical and universal categories in SCHAFER's studies.

his co-citizens next door, or outdoors, have scarcely felt disturbed by the same acoustic sounds or events.[6] Or, to take another example, there is good reason to have noise protection campaigns against the very loud, even ear-deafening and sickening sounds of industrial machines and production processes; but these are prone to fail if they do not reflect the working men's attachment to these sound(scape)s that have serve(d) as important means of controlling the production process as well as marks of a special male working class culture.[7] In other words, "filthy noise" or acoustical nuisance is an outcome of social and cultural struggles on the ever-moving threshold between allowed and not-allowed (loud) noise.

The same distinction between noise and acoustical nuisance, legal and illegal profane noise, recurs in the realm of (sacred) *Noise* — which may also be legal or illegal. SCHAFER himself points to that struggle — and to the political implications of religious rules on soundscapes — when he argues that Noise is an acoustical exemption, enabled by the non-prohibition of what in other, more profane circumstances, is supposed to be prohibited:

> I called this Sacred Noise [with a capital letter] to distinguish it from the other sort of noise (with a small letter), implying nuisance and requiring noise abatement legislation. [...] The important thing to realize is this: to have Sacred Noise is not merely to make the biggest noise; rather it is a matter of having the authority to make it without censure. Wherever Noise is granted immunity from human intervention, there will be found a seat of power (SCHAFER 1994, p. 76).

To make it even more complex, even the special permission to make loud *Noise,* which has long been granted to the Christian Church, was a set of well-defined rules of periodical restrictions. Sacred *Noise* may be legal during one period of the liturgical year and illegal during another. So, for example, the exclusively Christian *Noise* of ringing the bell was not allowed from the beginning of the Sacred Triduum (Holy Thursday) until Holy Saturday. During this period proscribing the bells' ringing, we find liturgical as well as folklore traditions of sounding the instruments of darkness — a set of rough musical instruments in use from the Middle Ages until the late 19th century which were permitted only in times when the bells were not, with the latter taking over the acoustic regime again with the beginning of Easter (cf. VAN GENNEP 1998 [1947], pp. 1016–35).

All these various oppositions and distinctions — between noise and acoustical nuisance, legal and illegal profane noise, (profane) noise and (sacred) *Noise*, or even between prohibited *Noise* and allowed *Noise* — do not follow the same concepts or aural perceptions in different cultural, historical, or social contexts.

---

[6] Cf. the illustrative analysis of Hogarth's painting *The Enraged Musician* in MISSFELDER (2012, pp. 40–46).

[7] Cf. the groundbreaking study by BIJSTERVELD (2008).

And, we must be aware of such historical, cultural, and social differences for any exploration of Sacred Sounds, for what applies to the distinctions in the perception and production of noise(s), also applies to the opposition between *Noise* and *Silence*. We find both terms on either side of the cultural cleavages between the Sacred and the Profane. What is at stake is often rather the distinction between (sacred) *Noise* and everyday noise, between (sacred) *Silence* and everyday silence or "quiet."

Thus, I suggest exploring *Noise* and *Silence* not as a stable binary opposition, but as a dynamic chiastic structure. In doing this, we may sharpen our senses for another, less obvious hint to be drawn from reciprocally challenging SCHAFER's and SERRES's phenomenological approaches: sacred soundscapes may even in one historical, cultural, and social context — namely, in our own — turn out to be internally divided and highly ambivalent — and not at all as monolithical and homogeneous as they pretend to be. If we focus our ear on the practices of staging, sounding, and perceiving Sacred Sounds — ear-deafening *Noise* or dense, fragile *Silence* — we may detect tensions that counter the overwhelming and violent effects that Sacred Sounds often reclaim — effects that both SCHAFER's and SERRES's auditive perception succumbed to, but that can be subverted by joining their nevertheless inspiring auditive encounters.

In the following exploration of a mute or unheard dimension of uncertainty and ambivalence that is inherent to Sacred Sound, I will confine myself to listening to one of its two poles, the silent one; and to tracing the ambivalences of *Silence* only within the limits of a certain epoch and region, by analyzing a specific and well-defined, yet scarcely examined ritual of modern auditive cultures — a ritual emerging in early 20th century Europe — the Minute of Silence.

And within these historical and geographical limits at least, the Sacred Sounds of *Silence* reverberate with ambivalence.

"For the brief space of two minutes": A short (history of) silence

Before going deeper into some details of the cultural history of the Silent Minute, I will provide the reader with a brief orientation about the yet unwritten history of this modern ritual.[8]

The first ever Minute of Silence staged in the form known to us — as a large-scale ritual joining huge crowds up to the size of a whole nation — took place on February 9, 1919, in the United States of America. Being held in honor of Theodore Roosevelt, who died on the January 6 of the same year, it comprises all important elements of the modern Silent Minute ritual: a silence of — in this case — exactly one minute, marked by acoustical signals, and going along with a nationwide interruption of traffic as well as with an immobilization of

[8] The author is currently working on writing this yet unwritten history as the central issue of a larger project on the "acoustics of the political body."

people in public places. But, it was another event that was decisive for the Silent Minute's breakthrough and its later spread to various countries and memorial cultures: in November 1919, on the occasion of the first anniversary of the ceasefire signed in Compiègne on November 11, 1918, King George V asks for all the British people to commemorate the dead soldiers of World War I.

The decision to have a ceremony climaxing in a Minute of Silence was taken by the war cabinet only on November 5, leaving the time for preparation and organization rather short (cf. GREGORY 1994, pp. 8–11). On November 7, George V addressed his people with the following call, which was published in many newspapers:

> The King invites all his people to join him in a special celebration of the anniversary of the cessation of war, as set forth in the following message: To all my People. Tuesday next, November 11, is the first anniversary of the Armistice, which stayed the world-wide carnage of the four preceding years and marked the victory of Right and Freedom. I believe that my people in every part of the Empire fervently wish to perpetuate the memory of the Great Deliverance, and of those who have laid down their lives to achieve it. To afford an opportunity for the universal expression of this feeling, it is my desire and hope that at the hour when the Armistice came into force, the eleventh hour of the eleventh day of the eleventh month, there may be for the brief space of two minutes, a complete suspension of all our normal activities. During that time [...] all work, all sound, and all locomotion should cease, so that, in perfect stillness, the thoughts of every one may be concentrated on reverent remembrance of the Glorious Dead. [...] At a given signal, which can easily be arranged to suit the circumstances of each locality, I believe that we shall all gladly interrupt our business and pleasure, whatever it may be, and unite in this simple service of Silence and Remembrance (GEORGE 1919, p. 12).

The performance following this appeal four days later became a great success. A great part of the population (though it was not very popular with certain social groups or in some British regions, colonies, and dominions) joined the public staging of *Silence*. In the following years and decades, the ritual has been regularly repeated, and from Great Britain it has spread to various countries. A short account of the most important traditions of this silent ritual would have to mention the French *Jour de l'armistice* (the equivalent to the British *Armistice Day*, established in 1922, but which adopted the Silent Minute some years later). Amongst other adaptions of the Silent Minute commemorating the war dead (most often dead soldiers), we have important traditions in Belgium and Poland (after 1920). Then, there is the Soviet *Minuta molčanija* on May 9 honoring the dead soldiers of the *Great Patriotic War*, starting in 1965 and transmitted via radio broadcast throughout the entire Soviet Union (it still exists in today's Russian federation); or the Israeli version on *Yom Ha-Shoah* (inaugurated in 1953 and, since the early 1960s, accompanied by the wailing of sirens) commemorating the Jews who were murdered during the Shoah and the Jewish resistance. These transfers into different national — and later, inter- or transnational — memorial cultures have transformed the *Silence*'s emotional, acoustical, mediatic, or political stagings (as well as the historical contexts it refers to). In Germany, too, there have been attempts to establish the tradition of the Silent Minutes, the first initiated in 1925 by *Reichskunstwart* Edwin Redslob; but in the end, the ritual has not become part of a national memorial culture as it has in many other European countries. Today, the Minute of Silence has crossed the national, often chauvinistic context that it originally came out of, and in which it still plays an important role; important international Minutes of Silence took place after the death of Lady Diana, or in the days after 9/11 (this expansion does not necessarily eliminate the Silent Minutes' chauvinistic attitudes).

In general, the national (and international) Minutes of Silence are ordered and organized by state organs or other institutions of political domination, mostly in a hierarchical, top-down process, and are generally staged in a political and secular context. But, despite the secular attitude of these stagings, the shared acoustical gesture of *Silence* brings with it a scent or vibration of the Sacred. And this sacred dimension is not the least important element for the success or failure of the Silent Minute — whether it is employed willingly and consciously or not: the ritual must either succeed in re-appropriating the *Silence*'s sacred sphere for modern, seemingly profane political representations of national unity and homogeneity — or succeed in getting rid of the sacral or religious aura and in establishing *Silence* as a "purely" political, non-religious practice of power, which is far from being an easy task. There is something like a persistent religious heritage inherent to the rituals of *Armistice Day*, *Minuta molčanija*, or *Yom ha-Shoah*, and which stems from the historical traditions that have established (sacred) *Silence* as an acoustical staging of the human–divine encounter, reverberating with practices of sacralizing power, incorporated by political bodies over the centuries. Even the staging of *Minuta molčanija* in the Soviet Union reverberates with this *Silence* — the broadcast is ironically entitled "the prayer" in the vernacular language.

Thus, the Silent Minutes turn out to be Minutes of *Silence*. And this *Silence* implies several moments of ambivalence — political, acoustical, emotional, and religious — whose traces may already be grasped in the early days of the Silent Minute in Great Britain.

In order to follow these traces, my exploration of the Silent Minute as a staging of (sacred) *Silence* and its ambivalences will take into account three aspects. The first step ("Sounds of Silence") will focus on the Silent Minute's acoustic events and "sound objects" — that is, the technical devices, the material sound objects and phenomena, and the human practices forging a special soundscape. However, this production of an "outer" or "objective" *Silence* is intrinsically linked with the perception of *Silence* — the complex process of listening in which, and by which, individual as well as social distinctions become sensuously manifest. The second point ("Mute [E-]Motions") will analyze some of the emotional and political contexts merging into the culturally formed perceptions of *Silence* and its ambivalences. The third and last aspect

("Re-enchantment or anachronism?") will especially focus on the transformation of the gestures and rituals of *Silence* stemming from a religious tradition, and on the ambivalent anachronistic attitude that this tradition has bequeathed to the modern Silent Minute ritual.

"Sounds of silence": The fragility of a modern hi-fi soundscape

Let us listen to, and with, Michel SERRES once more. In his description of Noise — as a counterpart of *Silence* — Noise appears as a sort of medium allowing for the emergence of an acoustically unified community: "The collective only believes in its own noise [...], the collective believes that the world is given to us [...] in the midst of pandemonium" (SERRES 2008, p. 86). We find this kind of (loud) "noise" (the French word is "bruit") or acoustic "pandemonium" as a synonym for idle talk, as also for human beings cut off from their sensual and reflective capacities and from the surrounding world throughout the whole of SERRES's writings (in which we also find SERRES's constant fight against these phenomena).

However, SERRES also alludes to other sounds allowing for the formation of an acoustically unified community — sounds that also make the "collective believe:" *Silence,* to which the whole architectural structure of the Epidaurus theatre is consecrated; or music which may also evoke a sacred sense of unity in an individual as well as in a collective body.

> A sacred word will silence those assembled there; it need not even be a word, sometimes a wordless gesture is all it takes to render them silent: a kind of ritualized mime, and silence overtakes the collective hearing as all eyes focus as one. Transfixed, one's organs are at peace: this is healing. Sometimes music is all it takes, and nestled in the hollow of hearing the orchestra listens and watches, the assembled throng heals itself by listening to its own harmony, observing it in silence, nestled inside the immense marble ear; what it hears is its own social contract (SERRES 2008, p. 87).

These lines make two points that are crucial moments for today's sensual explorations not only of ancient Greek theatres but also of the modern Minute of Silence. First, we have to deal with a crowd of acoustically connected bodies who are listening silently to themselves, and who are thereby interwoven to a *body politic*[9] — or this is at least what the ritual program aims for. Second, the Minute's *Silence* is not to be misunderstood as a "perfect stillness" as George V announced: the whole ritual is not a total absence of sound, but a complex

[9] The textual, ritual, or pictorial representation of a political and social community as a corporeal unity — a *body politic* — has been an important figure in political theory and discourse over centuries (cf. FRANK et al. 2007; KANTOROWICZ 1957; SASSE and WENNER 2002; for a historical survey, see HARVEY 2007).

acoustical setting made of various and very different acoustical phenomena comprising "word," "mime," or "music."

On the one hand, there is the acoustical framing of the Silent Minute ritual, which is full of keynote sounds, signals, and soundmarks. These are the terms that SCHAFER introduces for the description of soundscapes. The musical concept of *keynote sound* is transformed to a general quality of acoustic environments and the effect they have on their inhabitants.

> Keynote is a musical term; it is the note that identifies the key or tonality of a particular composition. It is the anchor or fundamental tone and although the material may modulate around it, often obscuring its importance, it is in reference to this point that everything else takes on its special meaning. [...] The keynote sounds of a given place are important because they help to outline the character of men living among them (SCHAFER 1994, p. 9).

Signals, in contrast, have a much more limited, precise, and institutional character. "Signals are foreground sounds and they are listened to consciously [...], they are figure rather than ground" (ibid., p. 10). As for the soundmarks, they aim at the manifestation or expression of a group identity: "The term soundmark is derived from landmark, and refers to a community sound which is unique or possesses qualities which make it specially regarded or noticed by the people in that community" (ibid.).

In a Silent Minute, keynote sounds, signals, and soundmarks play an important role. We have horn and trumpet *signals* (e.g., the military calls "The Last Post," "The Rouse," or "Reveille"), or non-musical signal sounds (like church bells, gun or artillery fire, the wailing of sirens or the sound of maroons), which mark the beginning — and in general also the end — of the Silence. Music pieces, chants, national anthems, and Christian hymns (the two most regularly played are "O God our help in ages past" and "The son of God goes forth to war") serve as soundmarks.

However, sounds are not only important elements of the ritual's acoustical and musical frames. The moment of *Silence* itself sounds in its proper, very specific, and variable way and, thus, creates a keynote sound — for "it is in reference to this point that everything else takes on its special meaning" (ibid., p. 9). An assembled crowd performing a collective *Silence* produces and perceives a lot of sounds coming from inner or outer movements of the assembled bodies: that is, sounds produced by breathing and digestion, the rustling of fabric, the shuffling of feet, or the crying of children. All these sounds are perceived in a particularly clear and distinct way. And then, there are other sounds merging with these: the blowing of the wind, animal sounds (dogs barking or birds singing). All these low sounds create a special keynote sound whose special attitude comes from its opposition to another keynote sound characteristic of modern metropolises: the constant and noisy hissing sound produced by traffic and far-reaching industrial noises, or by usual, non-silent crowds which usually dominate and superposes a whole bunch of other sounds in public places of big cities. All these are suddenly suspended, and cede to a new acoustical environment. Borrowing from SCHAFER's concepts once again, we could interpret this break as a shift from a *lo-fi* soundscape to a *hi-fi* soundscape. While in the first "individual acoustic signals are obscured in an overdense population of sounds" (SCHAFER 1994, p. 43), in the latter "discrete sounds can be heard clearly because of the low ambient noise level" (ibid.).[10]

Where the staging of "Silence" succeeds to a certain extent is when the *lo-fi* soundscape gives way — "for the brief space of two minutes" — to a *hi-fi* soundscape, and this sudden change allows for the emergence of sound objects normally drowned by the dominating layer of keynote sounds of big modern cities. In addition to this "objective" gain in audibility by an altered acoustic environment, the subjective aural perception is also refined. In a Silent Minute, each participant is obliged to keep immobile and silent, and to control the sounds (and movements) produced by himself as well as by the surrounding participants in the ritual. And this may incite — though it does not automatically produce — a sharpened auditive perception.

Thus, reports about the first *Two Minute Silence* in 1919 often describe the hi-fi experience of *Silence* by referring to the perception of fine, low-volume acoustics or strangely amplified sounds. In a letter to his family, Bill Grant (a former soldier) describes his impressions during the 1919 ritual: "A child started to cry but was quieted by his mother — but that cry sounded 100 times louder than ordinary because of the great hush" (cited in: GREGORY 1994, p. 15). This children's cry is a break of the Minute's Silence — but one that is not necessarily opposed to the aimed-for *Silence*. As a sound object typical of a *hi-fi* soundscape, the child's cry performs what could be called a "Sound of Silence," thus staging — and perhaps even creating — an acoustically unified political body whose cohesion depends at the same time on a collective emotional effect.[11] However, the unity of this acoustically staged political body of *Silence* is fragile, and prone to be disrupted by any sort of disturbance. And indeed, the history of Silent Minutes is full of other acoustical disturbances that do not fit the *Silence*, resulting in a breaking of the unified soundscape that the soundmarks or signals have aimed for.

[10] This rather general thesis is not easily to be rejected; but it has led to several critiques, with Emily THOMPSOM's book *The Soundscape of Modernity* (2004) being the most instructive one. She shows that the emergence of modern acoustics and of the growing concern of architects with sound — hence the emergence of or the listening for something like a *hi-fi* soundscape — may also be conceived of as a particularly modern phenomenon. Then, a Minute of Silence could be interpreted as a simulation of a *hi-fi* soundscape *avant la lettre* — a test that was surely far from satisfying, with noise not being totally suppressed, as we will see. But this is also true even for the most sophisticated architectural techniques of building a structure absorbing modern noise: even in a silent chamber, there are sounds, as John Cage reports from his first visit to an anechoic chamber (cf. CAGE 1961, p. 8).

[11] See later for the emotional dimension of the Minute of Silence.

The soundmarks framing the silent ritual (anthems and hymns of national, local, or religious provenance) often hint at differences rather than at national unity. In London, Dublin, Belfast, or Edinburgh, the sound of instrumentally performed or sung pieces of music is not at all the same. In Ireland, for example, the number of lines of the national anthem varies remarkably from one region to another, as do the chosen Christian hymns (soundmarks articulating adherence, submission, or opposition against the hegemonic political–religious power) or the language (Irish Gaelic, English) in which they are sung.

On another, rather technical level, the signals also pose other serious problems. Thus, the acoustic devices marking the beginning of the Silence are not at all "easily to be arranged" as George V suggested in his call. In the early years of the Minute of Silence, the relay joining locally installed clocks to a web of centrally adjusted devices of time measurement had not yet been built to a sufficiently fine degree (cf. GALISON 2003); and thus, while the Silence had already begun in one town district, maroons or gun fire from neighboring districts disturbed this silence. Town officials have faced more and more complaints and, since 1924, the use of maroons for signaling the beginning of the *Silence* was forbidden in London. However, due to the lack of an alternative, we see — or rather hear — this signal back on the scene only one year later, in 1925 (cf. GREGORY 1994, p. 42).

With progress in the centralized synchronization of time measurement and in mass-communication media (first of all, the spread of radio broadcasting in the late 1920s and early 1930s), the problem of (mutely) synchronizing huge crowds (up to the size of a whole nation) becomes easier to deal with. At the same time, a new problem arises: Silence constitutes a big problem for the radio — notably in its early days — since usual radio sound consists of a constant continuum of voices or music. Any interruption of this continuum creates a soundscape which is not at all a *hi-fi* soundscape similar to that of a locally performed Minute of Silence. Silence on the radio makes audible exactly that sound which the radio strives to minimize and to withdraw from the listeners' perception (and which in the 1920s and 1930s was particularly strong)[12] — that is, the constant hissing noise.

What is more, Silence evokes a second, very serious problem in early radio broadcasting services: technical failure of transmission processes leading to interruption in reception — that is, a sudden silence in the middle of a program. Thus, Silence is very closely related to the two big phantasms of early radio culture: the poor quality of broadcasting and reception devices and the total breakdown of transmission. For Walter BENJAMIN, who worked a great deal

[12] Even if local stagings of the Silent Minute sound themselves with another "hissing sound," which is characteristic of modern metropolises, the effect of the radio's hissing sound on aural perception is likely to be a much stronger and disturbing one.

both for and in radio, Silence in early radio programs sounds "the silence of death" (2002 [1934], p. 406).

To be sure, mass communication media systems of noise reduction have seen enormous progress during the last 80 years, and they have become much more fail-safe. But, Silence continues to be a problem. It is still the case today that automatic circuits instantly start playing some music whenever there is an interruption of more than several seconds in a radio program (and radio technicians must remember to switch off these systems whenever there is something like a Minute of Silence or pieces such as John Cages' 4'33" on the air).

Mute (E-)motions

A collectively performed *Silence* may well be a powerful acoustical gesture; but it is not an end in itself. It also provides an acoustical medium for the production of emotional effects — or at least has some potential[13] of doing so. Only if the staging of an acoustic unity succeeds in evoking an emotional unity at the same time does the Silent Minute become the powerful "Service of Silence and Remembrance" that George V wants it to be. Thus, we may conceive the Silent Minute as a means of emotional articulation — in fact, in the double sense of articulation: it is at once a cultural expression of emotions and a ritual of joining a crowd to a political body that allows for the emergence, manipulation, or change of emotions.

On the emotional level too, the Silent Minute proves highly ambivalent. This is due to its bodily performance having a twofold orientation. The double order given to the crowd of individual bodies — to keep silent and to keep immobile — stimulates a collective, socially shared (e-)motion and at the same time an individualizing, socially isolating (e-)motion.[14] What distinguishes the individual gestures of the Silent Minutes from other acoustical articulations of crowds or political bodies is their strong inward orientation, which is not to be found to the same extent in chants, jubilation, or ecstatic exultation. Or, to be more precise: only a double (e-)motion that turns inwards and outwards at the same time makes the individual's silent gestures become gestures of a collective political and emotional body, whose individual parts are listening inside and outside of their own bodies. In order to perceive and to control the Silence (of the own body as well as of that of the others), the bodies' perception must necessarily be turned outside. But this is not sufficient. Only when it is accompanied by an inner (e-)motion does the silence become *Silence*. And, such an inward-orientated emotional practice is far more difficult to verify as true, or to unveil as being feigned than are other emotional expressions and bodily gestures.

[13] For an elaborated theoretical discussion of the Silent Minute's "emotional potential," see LICHAU (2012).

[14] For more on emotion and movement, kinaesthesia, and empathy, cf. BRANDSTETTER in this volume.

We do not know — and will probably never know — how far different performances of the Silent Minute really succeed(ed) in evoking the emotional effects they are aiming at — for example, sorrow and grief, awe, solemnity, or even — as we will see — anger. But one thing seems to be evident: if all stagings of ritualized emotions can never be sure of reaching their (hegemonic) goals, this is particularly true with the Silent Minute. The emotional articulation it proclaims may turn out to have powerful political effects; but it may also fail. Both the success and the failure of the Silent Minute ritual are due to the close interdependency of emotional practices and socio-political contexts and, thus, the aimed-for *Silence* is highly dependent on these contexts (and their contradictions).

One year after the First World War, the national political body addressed by George V was far from being a unity. There was political conflict in different fields: the war was not entirely over, with military operations going on in northern Iraq and in the Soviet Union. On the inner political scene, social conflicts were sharpening. This was being caused by the post-war economic situation, and by revolutionary movements in Germany and Russia, and by the rise of the Labour party — not to forget the Ireland conflict passing through a crucial period in these years, with the Anglo-Irish War beginning in 1919 and resulting in the foundation of the Irish Republic and, in 1922, of the Irish Free State.

It is these political circumstances — or at least some of them — that the left-wing journal *Daily Herald* was alluding to in an anonymous article (on page one) on the first Armistice Day, November 11, 1919. The emotions it appeals to are quite different from those that George V pronounced:

> You are asked to be silent for two minutes to-day, to be silent and to pause in your labours, to remember this day and this hour last year. At 11 a. m. a year ago this day the guns that had made the days hideous and the nights hell ceased firing along all the Western front. The war that seemed endless had come suddenly to an end. [...] And today, at the same hour, you are to be silent for two minutes; you are to stand bareheaded wherever you be; you are to remember the Glorious Dead. What will you remember and what will you forget? You will remember, mothers, the gay sons you have lost; wives, you will think of the husbands who went out in the mist of the winter morning — the mist that sent cold chills round the heart — never to come back. And brothers will think of brothers, and friends of friends, all lying dead today under a tortured alien soil. But what will you forget? The crime that called these men to battle, or the fond, glorious and tragic delusion under which they went? The war that was to end the war, and that in bitter reality did not? The lies, the hatred, the cruelty, the hypocrisy, the pride; and the agony, the tears of the innocent, the martyrdom of the weak, the hunger of the poor? Make the most of this day of official remembrance. By the sacred memory of those lost to you, swear to yourself that never again, God helping you, shall the peace and happiness of the world fall into the murderous hands of a few cynical old men (GEORGE 1919).

Interestingly, while the unknown author of these lines claims a political and emotional articulation quite different from the official one, he does not call on his readers to break the *Silence*. He differs in the type of affect attributed to the ritual — but respects or adopts the *Silence* as a means for keeping "the sacred memory of those lost to you."

"There will be service enough": Re-enchantment or anachronism?

In addition to the acoustical, political, and emotional dimensions — and yet interwoven with these aspects — it is the religious dimension inherent in the Minute of Silence that accounts for a great part of its ambivalences. The Silent Minute and its corporeal practices exploit silent gestures and rituals stemming from various historical traditions and social classes. Gestures of silence figured — in different ways — as forms of distinction in courtly or in bourgeois culture; mute practices also came out of the modern military, school, or industrial institutions; or we have traditions of silent rituals of political protest (for example, the workers' movements' silent march (cf. MOSSE 1976, p. 190). But the religious-born gestures and rituals of *Silence* are, without doubt, of particular importance.

In borrowing gestures of *Silence* stemming from a religious — mainly Jewish-Christian — sphere, the Silent Minute transfers them to a secular or profane scene (for example, to the public places of modern cities or to modern mass media). There they are bereaved of their sacral framing: in Christian liturgy and homiletics, silent practices are embedded in a complex set of discursive, ceremonial, and sensory practices which result from long corporeal exercises and training processes. The modern ritual of the Silent Minute strips these practices from their contexts, and uses them as the centre of a ritual that scarcely bears religious character. The Minute of Silence may, therefore, be perceived as a pure *profanization* — a transfer of a sacred practice into a secular context, destroying its sacral aura (cf. AGAMBEN 2005). In this case, the isolated but obviously religious-borne gestures easily appear anachronistic and are prone to fail, or at least do not produce the intended results (as we can suppose for "the prayer" [cf. earlier section]).

On the other hand, the Silent Minute's anachronistic attitude offers a big potential, because it may also serve as a means for a re-sacralization or re-enchantment of political rituals originally free from religious attitudes. On the modern, disenchanted urban scene, the anachronistic religious character may turn into a promise, and make the silent ritual a reaction or antidote to the loss of a religious-based community — a loss often deplored in early 20th century discourse on a disenchanted civilization or culture. And, it is not by pure chance that the Minute of Silence emerges in the same epoch when concepts of political theology (Carl Schmitt), or political religion (Eric Voegelin), or calls for a new "Kultursynthese" (TROELTSCH 1922, p. IX) replacing older religious bonds, get attention from very different political currents and scientific disciplines.

This ambivalence between profanization and re-sacralization, anachronism and re-enchantment, adds to the ambivalences of modern *Silence*. And, we find this ambivalence already in one of the first texts proposing such a ritual. On May 8, 1919, the London newspaper *Evening News* published a letter sent by the Australian Journalist (and war veteran) George Edward Honey, whose important role in initiating the British Silent Minute tradition has been recognized in recent years:[15]

> Five little minutes only. Five silent minutes of national remembrance. A very *sacred* intercession. *Communion* with the Glorious Dead who won us peace, and from the *communion* new strength, *hope and faith* in the morrow. *Church services*, too, if you will, *but in the street, the home, the theatre, anywhere, indeed*, where Englishmen and their women chance to be, surely in this five minutes of bitter-sweet silence *there will be service enough* (HONEY 1919 [my italics]).

Here, the religious heritage is graspable as are its ambivalences: when Honey takes up the (church) "services" and, at the same time, transfers them to the profane places ("in the street, the home, the theatre, anywhere, [...] there will be service enough"), the textual movement gets rid of and re-appropriates the *Silence*'s religious heritage, oscillating between profanation and re-sacralization.

Conclusion

The Sacred Sound of the Silent Minute is at the center of a ritual laden with acoustical, emotional, political and religious cultures, and their ambivalences. Being haunted by all these ambivalences, its specific *Silence* stages a fundamental ambivalence underlying all the other cultural dimensions: it is at once modern *and* anti-modern.

The anti-modern aspects are obvious. The religious anachronism inherent in the Silent Minute is probably the most striking element of this anti-modern attitude. However, one may even go further and take the Minute of Silence as a ritual synopsis of the three main topics of the anti-modern discourse on the problems of modern civilization. A recurrent diagnosis that most of the very different, often opposed positions inside this discourse share, states that modernity suffers an overkill of circulation and breathless speed, of (loud) noise, and of disenchantment or loss of religious bonds. And, a Minute of Silence counters these three topics point by point with immobility and interruption (vs. circulation and speed), *Silence* (vs. loud noise), and re-enchantment (vs. disenchantment).

---

[15] Adrian Gregory, in his *The Silence of Memory*, does not mention Honey's influence; according to Gregory, the inspiration stemmed mainly from Sir Percy Fitzpatrick, whose memorandum to the war cabinet on November 4th is with no doubt an important incitement for the emergence of the British Armistice Day, but not the only one (cf. GREGORY 1994, pp. 8–11).

But these obvious anti-modern features should not make us ignore the modernity of the Silent Minute. First, it is not just a Silence, but one Minute of Silence — or sometimes two. So it is itself — the problem of synchronization notwithstanding — a ritual meticulously measured and calculated on behalf of the rationalized regime of a linear and homogenous space–time continuum[16] which is often associated with modern civilization. Hence, the Silent Minute originates in the same rationalized culture that it tries to suspend for a moment.

Secondly, it is performed by large crowds whose capacity to keep silent is itself the product of modern disciplinary power. So the seemingly (re-) enchanted collective or political body is, at the same time, the product of body politics that individuals were subjected to by specifically modern institutions: the factory, the school, the national army — or modern means of transport (SCHIVELBUSCH 1979, p. 70).

And finally, fine ears — like those of Georg SIMMEL — may detect in the Silent Minutes' muting device a keynote sound of modern life, marked by industrialized working processes. For, one of the central characteristics of these processes is the interruption of acoustical exchange, as described by SIMMEL when he asks for the emergence of the modern concept of the "worker."

> This enormously powerful concept, which embraces that which is common to all wage labourers [...], was inaccessible to previous centuries, whose guilds were often much closer and more intimate, because they were essentially based on personal and spoken communication, but lacked the factory workshop or the mass meeting. Only *there, where one saw innumerable people without hearing them* [my italics], did there occur that high abstraction of everything that is common to all of them, which is often hampered in its growth by all the individual, concrete and variable material which the ear transmits to us (SIMMEL 1997 [1908], pp. 732–733).

If we ask for the spaces and spheres of *Silence*, one would probably not think of factory workshops, or halls and mass meetings. These are, rather supposed to be modern temples of loud *Noise.*[17] But with SIMMEL, we may come to hear silence or *Silence* — understood as the interruption of acoustic circulation in communication processes (the German original uses the word "akustischer Verkehr," which connotes circulation and traffic) — lurking in the heart of modern *Noise*.

By exploring the senses in a historical-cultural anthropology approach, things and sounds often gain a much more complex and sometimes even ambivalent

[16] That does not mean exact chronological prescriptions of political rituals are exclusively modern or European.

[17] "During the Industrial Revolution, Sacred Noise sprang across to the profane world. Now the Industrialists held power and they were granted dispensation to make Noise by means of the steam engine and the blast furnace, just as previously the monks had been free to make Noise on the church bell" (SCHAFER 1994, p. 76).

attitude. Up to the point, when not only *Silence* emits lots of noisy sounds, but when also *Noise* gets in touch with *Silence*, as remarks Simmel. Both *Noise* and *Silence* turn out to be complex acoustic articulations, staged by heterogeneous political bodies, and reverberating with acoustical, religious, emotional, and political cultures and histories — and with all their ambivalences.

References

AGAMBEN, G. (2005): Profanierungen. – Frankfurt/M.

ANONYMUS (1919): Rememberance Day. Will you ever forget? In: Daily Herald, No. 1.186 (No. 193 New Series), November 11, 1919, p. 1.

BENJAMIN, W. (2002 [1934]): Auf die Minute. In: BENJAMIN, W.: Medienästhetische Schriften. – Frankfurt/M., pp. 405–407.

BIJSTERVELD, K. (2008): Mechanical Sound. Technology, Culture, and Public Problems of Noise in the Twentieth Century. – Cambridge/Mass.

CAGE, J. (1961): On Silence. Lectures and Writings. – Middleton/Conn.

CORBIN, A. (1995): Die Sprache der Glocken. Ländliche Gefühlskultur und symbolische Ordnung im Frankreich des 19. Jahrhunderts. – Frankfurt/M.

CORBIN, A. (1998): Zur Geschichte und Anthropologie der Sinneswahrnehmung. In: CONRAD, C. and KESSEL, M. (Eds.): Kultur and Geschichte. Neue Einblicke in eine alte Beziehung. – Stuttgart, pp. 121–140.

FRANK, T., Koschorke, A., LÜDEMANN, S. and MATALA DE MAZZA, E. (Eds.) (2007), Der fiktive Staat. Konstruktionen des politischen Körpers in der Geschichte Europas. – Frankfurt/M.

GALISON, P. (2003): Einstein's Clocks, Poincaré's Maps. Empires of Time. – New York.

GEORGE, R.I. (1919): The Glorious Dead. King's Call to his People. Armistice Day Observance. Two Minutes' Pause from Work. In: The Times, No. 42215, November 7, 1919, p. 12.

GREGORY, A. (1994): The Silence of Memory. Armistice Day 1919–1946. – Oxford.

HARVEY, A.D. (2003): Body Politic. Political Metaphor and Political Violence. – Newcastle.

HOWES, D. (2003): Sensual Relations. Engaging the Senses in Culture and Social Theory. – Ann Arbor.

KANTOROWICZ, E. (1957): The King's Two Bodies. A Study in Medieval Political Theologie. – Princeton.

LICHAU, K. (2012): "This moving, awe-inspiring silence": Zum emotionalen Potential der Schweigeminute. In: KWASCHIK, A. and JARZEBOWSKI, C. (Eds.): Performing Emotions. – Göttingen.

MISSFELDER, J.-F. (2012): Period Ear. Prospects of a Modern Sound History. In: Geschichte und Gesellschaft, Vol. 38, No. 1, pp. 21–47.

MORAT, D. (2010): Zwischen Lärmpest und Lustbarkeit. Die Klanglandschaft der Großstadt in umwelt- und kulturhistorischer Perspektive. In: HERRMANN, B. (Ed.): Beiträge zum Göttinger Umwelthistorischen Kolloquium 2009–2010. – Göttingen, pp. 173–190.

MORAT, D. (2011): Zur Geschichte des Hörens. Ein Forschungsbericht. In: Archiv für Sozialgeschichte, Vol. 51, pp. 695–716.

MOSSE, G.L. (1976): Die Nationalisierung der Massen. Politische Symbolik und Massenbewegungen in Deutschland von den Napoleonischen Befreiungskriegen bis zum Dritten Reich. – Frankfurt/M.

SASSE, S. and WENNER, S. (Eds.) (2002): Kollektivkörper. Kunst und Politik von Verbindung. – Bielefeld.

SCHAFER, R. M. (1994): The Soundscape. Our Sonic Environment and the Tuning of the World. – Rochester.

SCHIVELBUSCH, W. (1979): Geschichte der Eisenbahnreise. Zur Industrialisierung von Raum und Zeit im 19. Jahrhundert. – Frankfurt/M etc.

SERRES, M. (2008): The Five Senses. A Philosophy of Mingled Bodies I. – London and New York.

SIMMEL, G. (1997 [1908]): Sociology of the Senses. In: FRISBY, D./FEATHERSTONE, M. (Eds.): Simmel on Culture. – London etc., pp. 109–119.

SMITH, M.M. (2001): Listening to Nineteenth-Century America. – Chapel Hill.

SMITH, M.M. (2007): Producing Sense, Consuming Sense, Making Sense: Perils and Prospects for Sensory History. In: Journal of Social History, Vol. 40, No. 4, pp. 841–858.

THOMPSON, E. (2004): The Soundscape of Modernity. Architectural Acoustics and the Culture of Listening in America, 1900–1933. – Cambridge/Mass.

TOYKA-SAID, M. (2009): Von der "Lärmpest" zur "akustischen Umweltverschmutzung". Lärm und Lärmwahrnehmung als Themen einer modernen Umweltgeschichte. In: HERRMANN, B. (Ed.): Beiträge zum Göttinger Umwelthistorischen Kolloquium 2008–2009. – Göttingen, pp. 253–276.

TROELTSCH, E. (1922): Das logische Problem der Geschichtsphilosophie. In: TROELTSCH, E.: Gesammelte Schriften. III/1. Der Historismus und seine Probleme. –Tübingen.

VAN GENNEP, A. (1998 [1947]): Le Folklore Francais. Tome 1. Du Berceau à la tombe. – Paris.

WULF, C. (2010): Anthropologie. Geschichte, Kultur, Philosophie. Zur Einleitung. In: WULF, C. (Ed.): Der Mensch und seine Kultur. Hundert Beiträge zur Geschichte, Gegenwart und Zukunft des menschlichen Lebens. – Cologne.

Holger Schulze

The Sonic Persona: An Anthropology of Sound

You begin reading this chapter. As you do so, you are in a specific spatial situation: maybe you just received this volume (by mail, at the bookstore, or in the library), and now you are just browsing the pages and reading selected articles which catch your attention. While you are doing so, there is a specific sonic environment around you that is present all the time as you are browsing. Maybe even your attention is zooming in and out, framed by the sounds around you — and suddenly, reading these words, you notice this one special and strangely annoying or surprisingly remote sound: a sound which you did not hear before — but now seems to be at the front of your auditory awareness.

Maybe you start browsing now in the auditory environment you are sitting or standing in: you listen to the movements of other people around you; you listen to the cooling sounds of laptops or video projectors in the room you are in; you are listening to the sounds of outside noises, sounds of birds and of cars, sounds of people talking, or sounds of official announcements and commercials.

Introduction: Bodies in sound

In each situation of our existence, we stand and move and act in an environment that resonates. We are in such an environment all the time. Any physical situation is a situation in resonance; we are bodies in sound. Or, as the last ever printed version of the ENCYCLOPEDIA BRITANNICA (2003) defined the phenomenon of sound: "Sound: Mechanical disturbance from a state of equilibrium that propagates through an elastic material medium".

Any vibration is a slight disruption and, as such, a slight transformation of our surroundings in their material shape; this happens in every moment, many times. When we do research on how different human beings in diverse cultures or historical eras lived with this sonic fact, and how they perceived themselves as sounding and resonating creatures, we find that sound is nevertheless not *only* physical or corporeal. The corporeality of sound is not separated from our self-perception, our actions, our emotions, and our sensory setup. Being a *body in sound* means you are neither an object nor a subject of individual sound events; but you are — and I quote the previously mentioned definition — an *elastic material*, reacting and acting.

So, how can we adequately theorize and analyze the existence of human beings under the condition of sound? What is the specific position of human beings in a culturally and historically shaped sonic environment? How can we speak about sensory experiences in research? In this chapter, I will try to unfold a few of the main research findings, research methods, and terminologies of a strand of study that has evolved in the last decade. It is known under such terms as *Auditory Culture, Sound Culture, Auditory Research* or, most prominently: *Sound Studies* (cf. BIJSTERVELD and PINCH 2011, BULL 2007, COX 2004, SCHULZE 2008, STERNE 2012). This rather young tradition of research seeks to understand how different cultures in different historical times have lived with, lived through, and lived by performing and hearing sounds — and how this focus on the sonic and the auditory transforms our interpretation of culture, history, and *la condition humaine*. Research has been done on the sounds of church bells (CORBIN 1994), on the listening practices in history (JOHNSTON 1995), of mechanical sounds in urban environments (BIJSTERVELD 2008), on the history of technological inventions to reproduce sound (STERNE 2003), on the science history of resonance (ERLMANN 2010), on the narratology of sonic experiences (ESHUN 1998), and on the history and possible future of warfare related to sound (GOODMAN 2010).

It is a fundamental change in perspective that takes place when we apply an auditory approach to culture, history, artifacts, and practices: we switch from a seeing perspective to a *hearing perspective* (AUINGER and ODLAND 2007), as the Austrian sound artist Sam AUINGER has coined it. Thus, I will try to give you in the following paragraphs of this chapter a very brief and condensed insight into the ramifications and resonances of sound and sensory studies in general — and especially into my own research findings in the field of sonic anthropology.

Performing the Sonic: Sound practices in auditory dispositives

When we speak about sound, we do not merely speak about music. And, we do not speak at first of immaterial sonic imaginations. We speak about sound as a sensory element of every action in our lives. So how can we understand the specific performativity in place when we explore the field of the sonic?

On the one hand, research in the last decade has shown that there are recurring formats or dispositions of situations in which we are listening and hearing, in which we are engulfed and transformed by sound: these are so-called *auditory dispositives*. On the other hand, the specific sonic performativity has been described by research in recent years: sound can only be manifest and actualized when bodies are in motion; I pointed at this fact with the introductory quote from the ENCYCLOPEDIA BRITANNICA.

Silence in the strict sense of radical, static non-vibration is (in our time–space-continuum at least) epistemologically not possible unless our cosmos is dead. Thus, *sound practices* (ALTMAN 1992) are at the centre of every sound event. Human beings live and act — and as they do so, they actualize sound. The film studies scholar Rick ALTMAN coined the term *sound practice* in the early 1990s — and the German musicologist and media studies scholar

Rolf GROSSMANN (2008) coined the term *auditives Dispositiv* a few years ago: both terms, sound practice and auditory dispositives, have been more prominently used in recent years by sound studies researchers.

The two terms provide a genuine terminology, in tune with a broader and widely known discussed theoretical context, which takes speaking about sonic experiences out of the realm of the esoteric and eccentric. For instance, in this moment right now, you or I find ourselves in a very specific auditory dispositive (referring to the history of the dispositive since BAUDRY 1970, 1975, FOUCAULT 1994, 1977, AGAMBEN 2006): we are probably sitting in an office, at our desk — or perhaps, we are reading this text in a more mobile or personal situation (at home, on the subway), or in an even more specified auditory dispositive: in the library. Take the situation of the library: this spatial arrangement as an auditory dispositive is related to the history of designing and building places for philological research, for detailed close reading and an intensely, if not intimately, executed analysis of texts and documents. The architecture of shelves and tables, lamps and stools, of draperies and aisles, all of these spatial arrangements provide an essential element to the auditory dispositive of a library. This spatial arrangement with all its material, its geometrical and its ornamental necessities, provides a sort of specific *aural architecture* (BLESSER 2006) that frames, distorts, and focuses our listening and reading activity. The silence postulated in each building for storing books and analyzing texts, is of a very specific, historical quality.

The auditory dispositive of the library implies and demands from us, its visitors and users, the bodily tension of a concentrated reader who might be easily irritated because of being so focused; and it implies also that a state of non-silence, of noise and babble, would distract the reader, and that this distraction would provide an inadequate form of concentration to analyze a text. The silence of the library — having its origins in the history of monasteries and prayer — is a moralizing silence, a silence with almost the character of worshipping the individual text, the author of a text, and the whole archive of stored texts, and their corresponding authors. It is the most prominent religious activity of Western writing culture (besides writing itself, of course). When in a library (and being educated how to behave in such an edifice and institution), we try to concentrate and focus our bodily movements and our mind to grasp the meaning of the words we are reading in the current moment. We try not to distort our reading (and in my case right now: the writing) activity by making noises, moving the body, whistling, or finger snapping. There are other times where we, perhaps, love those sound practices, but at that moment we try to refrain from indulging in them.

This sound practice of silenced bodily tension while reading is also very specific, and obviously historically and culturally anchored, in the history of reading and the specific habitus of Christian monasticism, Western poetry, and modern humanities. In brief: even an activity like reading that is likely to be regarded as completely soundless these days has its characteristic sound practice which, in this case, is mainly a practice of non-sound.

So, these two terms of auditory dispositive and sound practice are useful and rather central contributions to the broader discussion of the spatial and performative aspects of sensory studies. Specific sonic performativity, with its characteristic and highly detailed reference to the effects of material resonance in specific spatial arrangements as well as its reference to personal practices with a characteristic temporal quality, is implied in the concepts of auditory dispositive and sonic practice. By introducing these two terms into the transdisciplinary discourse of cultural studies and anthropology, the new and emerging research field of sound studies may prove their transforming and progressive quality.

The Sonic Persona: An anthropology of sound

From the approach of anthropology, the main question in sound studies is: *What is the position of human beings in a specific sonically shaped environment?* In my research, I decided to concentrate on the specific bodily self-perception and the corporeal appearance of human beings in sound. In the cultural history of sound, it is a rather recent discovery that sound is corporeal. Over centuries and millennia of at least Western history, sound has recurrently been coined as an ethereal and fundamentally non-physical, heavenly phenomenon. But, via acoustic research on sound in experimental physics of the 19th century (HELMHOLTZ 1863), and the body and performance theories of the 20th century (NANCY 1992), it has become clear that our individual body as a whole — and not only our ear, or even our brain, or specific brain regions — is the stage where a sound event takes place, and has an effect. Experiencing sound is a corporeal experience which affects various different areas of our bodies, according to our individual biographies concerning sonic experiences. We listen with our bodies — and not only with selected organs alone, for example, our ear or brain.

This position is by no means a dualist view that would separate the psychological from the physical in human beings; but the corporeal and the spiritual elements in listening and sounding are interpreted as just two emergent and deeply interwoven aspects of human life. In cultural anthropology, they are both regarded as culturally and historically anchored categories that have evolved over specific strands of cultural and science history to describe different aspects of human life. Our individual bodies are historically and culturally determined to serve us as a medium by which we perceive sound — and with which we perform sound. In any given moment, we are in a corporeally resonating and a situationally performing state. My current research summarizes all these situational and corporeal qualities of living with, living through, and living in sound under the term of a *sonic persona*.

What is a sonic persona? The sonic persona of a human being — but also of larger groups of people, even of organizations and institutions — is shaped and constituted by the sonically perceptive, performatively generated traces that any vibrating entity leaves in a specific culture and historical era as well as in a situational sonic environment. These sonic traces materialize the situational agency as well as the individual idiosyncrasy of the entity in question. What does this definition mean? When I enter a space, you can hear my steps, the moving of my hands, my clothes, my jewelry (if I am wearing some), and my hair (if it were longer than mine right now), among other things. If your sensory perception is largely focused on hearing, you would be able to auditorily recognize a rhythm of either more hectic or more relaxed movements that could be symptomatic of my habits while I'm moving through space. You would, then, probably immediately interpret or categorize my actions and my habitus according to these sonic practices that I apply, either intentionally or involuntarily.

The character of such a sonic persona is, of course, mainly dependent on its differentiated cultural and historical significance which is scripted by our auditory appearance. And it is also scripted by our individual, biographical, and instantaneous sensory (especially its auditory) set up: for instance, are we right now neglecting to listen to certain sounds? Are we focusing on a specific spectrum and category of ephemeral and peripheral sounds? Are we listening only to the spoken arguments and propositions of a person, neglecting all other auditory signals? Or, are we responding only to dancing moves and rhythmical patterns on this dance floor right now? That is to say: we hear our own culture and our own historical time in our sonic performance in any given moment — and our interpretation thereof.

These auditory qualities of an individual persona can be heard; but they can also be recognized in a fictitious or legal person. I follow here the concept of a boldly *symmetric anthropology* (LATOUR 1999), which acknowledges how the multitude of objects, performative actions, structures, and dispositives in human cultures constitutes also the existence of individual human beings and all of their activities. Following the symmetric anthropology concerning sound studies such aforementioned institutions as a whole can and must also be recognized as coherent, acting, performing, and effective entities, and they do leave their own, very specific auditory traces in space and time.

So, what is the benefit of such an approach to our sensory appearance and sensory performativity? First of all, this approach allows us to analyze individual characters, institutions, and organizations following the shape of their sonic persona. Thus, an interpretation of rhythms and syncopations, of sounds and swings, is by definition a completely different approach to human beings than understanding human culture from its monuments and institutions, social orders, and cultural artifacts which are stable, constant, defined, and not in constant resonance and transformation. In contrast, a sonic analysis understands any entity in our world as being always in motion, as oscillating, and as transforming all the time in relation to any given situation and its material, as well as in relation to a personal setup (which is likewise in transformation all the time). Of course, such an analysis is not objective in a simple, straightforward sense. It is necessary to provide at least intersubjectively understandable and interpretable material for analysis. However, the model of the sonic persona helps us understand human beings and characters in their time-based and time-critical dynamics.

By applying a sonic persona approach to human culture, we as researchers can find a way to analyze specific events, environments, actions, and rituals from a *hearing perspective*. This change of approach, thus, accentuates completely different aspects and phenomena in human culture. Many scholars have been arguing in favor of this change in methodology and epistemology for decades (SCHAFER 1977, AUGOYARD and TORGUE 2003, ESHUN 1998, ERLMANN 2010); but only the more recent publications on sound studies allow us to try a bit harder in establishing a methodologically grounded and systematically executable path for integrating sonic experiences in our research strategies. By this effort, we may hopefully be able to adjust and correct one major dysfunction in contemporary research in natural sciences, technical sciences, but also in cultural studies. It was the famous cultural historian and mathematician Michel SERRES who vigorously drew attention to this dysfunction already in the 1980s. In his groundwork for sensory anthropology, he stated: "L'emission l'emporte sur l'écoute, nous savons comment lancer un son et comment il se propage, nous pouvons le relayer, nous savons mal recevoir" (SERRES 1985, p. 147). Almost 30 years and a full generation later, it is no longer necessary to draw attention only to the bare necessity for a theory of listening and perceiving; by now it has become important to take all the highly refined elements of research in sound and sensory studies and try to form them into a coherent research strategy: a strategy that allows the research activity of *listening*, mere and non-recorded listening in a specific situation, listening to the sounds of a specific sonic environment or a sonic artifact as a form of empirical research, to be an accepted and respected method in any research in the field of cultural studies.

Narrating the sensory: Sensory fictions about sensorial techniques

In recent years, the quest for an epistemological transformation of cultural studies towards an integration and incorporation of the concepts of sound and the senses has repeatedly returned to one fundamental question of simple description: *How can we describe the sonic or auditory shape of a person or an artifact?* What is the empirical fundament, the sort of source documents that allows us to analyze, to criticize and to conceptualize sonic experience in a meaningful and insightful way? I will try to rephrase this question to its methodologically crucial point: How can we articulate the specific character of an individual sonic experience in terms that exceed the highly specified and culturally as well as historically contaminated terminology of experts and acousticians? Or, in simpler words: How can we speak about sound?

This question directs us to science history and to a critique of science. Traditionally, Western cultures have evolved a rather specific and strangely focused way of communicating sound experiences in music: a system of notation, transcription, and translation of orders for instrumentalists or singers to tell them what musical practices they shall execute to achieve the manifestation of an intended sound event. We call this whole a *writing culture* which is at the core of Western musical practices and all its institutional emanations — the concert hall, the chamber music ensemble, the classical standard orchestra, the conservatoire, even the recording studio, and the traditional education of sound engineers — we call this specific *discourse network*, this *Aufschreibesystem* (KITTLER 1985) our *musical notation*. Actually it is a highly particular if not amazingly weird fact that such an elaborate culture of writing and interpreting, exercising and examining, perceptual as well as discoursive critique evolved just around the instrumental performance practice of playing tones, melodies, rhythms, songs and organized sound. Maybe this could be a genuine and structurally necessary way of Western cultures to domesticize the destructive and transformative energies in musical and sonic performances as Jacques ATTALI did suggest (1977)?

In this strand also the discipline of physical acoustics developed — rather late in the Western history — another very specific form of notation for the frequency oscillations of sound according to established and proven laws of physics. This further led to the creation of a model for sound, the *sonogram*, which is represented in graphs or three-dimensional images that represent the specific sound of anything you hear. All these cultural techniques, these *Kulturtechniken*, have been developed over centuries and millennia (in the case of notation), and they form the dominant corpus, the referential fundament, when we speak today about sound scientifically. However, what about the individual and the experiential side of sound events? What about a side that is truly idiosyncratic and rather non-reproducible strictu sensu? How can we represent this situational, corporeal, and highly biographical quality of sound and listening?

Obviously, there is no simple access to any experience of human beings. But there is growing doubt in the scientific community regarding whether this should really lead us to neglect research regarding sensory experience. There are many questions that arise. Could there not be better ways of representing individual sensory experiences? Would we not be losing the very specific core of any individual experience if we remained satisfied with just describing those elements which could be described anonymously and objectively? Does the objectification and reification of sound really help in understanding the experience of sound? How can we enhance research on individual sensory experiences — and sonic experiences in particular?

Though we may not have access to the individual imagination as such, we can nevertheless access the imaginary representations of auditory experiences. We can get hold of these in their representations in narrations and the elaborations of listeners: that is, what are known as "sonic fictions" (ESHUN 1998). This very concept brings us to the core of sonic experiences. It takes up the notion that experiences are not only physically and materially grounded in "percepts" (DELEUZE/GUATTARI 1991) and sensory data, but reflect — especially if it is a substantial experience — the realm of our individual, idiosyncratic imagination. At the same time as it is rooted in the material world and in physical encounters, any experience is also rooted in our imaginarium, our bits and pieces of fiction and fantasy. As long as we neglect this fact and exclude this element from our description and definition of sound, we are not actually speaking about sound; we are, then, only speaking about the mere physical emanation of a sonic experience. What is a *sonic fiction*? British DJ and music critic Kodwo ESHUN (1998) explored this methodological concept and its possible application in a volume called *More Brilliant Than the Sun: Adventures in Sonic Fiction*. In this volume, he narrates, in an advanced style, his listening voyages into the realms of free jazz, of advanced electronic dance music, and of imaginary and factual new technologies. He draws connections from his narrations to the history of electronic warfare, to the invention of new musical instruments, to new life forms, and to extraterrestrial creatures. Thus, the whole volume consists of a highly idiosyncratic and very joyful selection of topics. Moreover, all of this is narrated in a rather unconventional, cut-up, stream of consciousness, and rhapsodic kind of way. Surely ESHUN presents here no orderly, scholarly writing; but it is, nevertheless, a truly insightful, inspiring, and sonically deeply informed account of his individual (but not at all arbitrary) listening experience. Or, as I like to call it: a black *Finnegans Wake* of sound and technology studies.[1] "The African drumchoir complexifies the beat into distributed Polyrhythmachines, webbed networks of poly*counte r*contra*cross*staggered rhythms that function like the dispersed architecture of artificial life by generating emergent consciousness" (ESHUN 1998, p. 5).

ESHUN's sonic fictions might be regarded as mere tales or fantasies, imaginary theories or aphorisms, aroused rhapsodies; but they could also be interpreted as dancing movements, hand gestures, mimicry, and even as sound events themselves — as in finger snapping, tapping, humming, singing, and onomatopoetic sounding. Such sonic fictions leave many if not all basic assumptions of traditional research methods behind that — following ESHUN — need to be historicized and scrutinized in their main and often compulsive concern with a rather culturally-specific urge for linear, almost obsessive consistency, with anonymous reproducibility of results and with a decontextualized objectification, all often contrived and morally-executed categories, for which ESHUN proposes an alternative way of relating to. But these highly personal articulations about sound and the senses are not arbitrary. On the contrary, they are focused on specific sonic experiences in a given historical period, as experienced by

[1] Being a co-founder of *CCRU*, the *Cybernetic Culture Research Unit* at the University of Warwick together with Sadie Plant, Nick Land, and many others in the 1990s, ESHUN especially refers to popcultural examples from the strand of *afrofuturism* (JAMES 1954; BERNAL 1987).

specific and nameable beings: beings that do not hide behind the all-too-well-known rhetorical figure in academia of an anonymous subject with insight. Beings that are specific even in their corporeal practices and in their individual tastes. Thus, sonic fictions strive for an analytical strength and a subtlety that can be achieved only in the genre of the essay — a highly fantastic genre that affects our bodies via personal narrations of sensory, often-imagined experiences and experienced imaginations. To sum up: sonic fictions are corporeal, sensory fictions. They incorporate our embodied and corporeally sensed, auditorily triggered imaginations. Sonic fictions are focused on the auditory; but they unfold a rich spectrum of fictions and formulations that touch all the other senses, and represent a very specific perspective on our individual corporeal and sensory setup. They are the most genuine articulations of a sonic persona that might even name a selection of 10 specific criteria that define and describe a sensory and sonic fiction. In this chapter, this selection will not be discussed in detail (which I do extensively in this chapter: SCHULZE 2013) — but the 10 postulates are listed as follows, starting with the most general and ending with the most specific one, as an ambitious inspiration for you, the reader, to write a sonic fiction of your own sonic environment and sound practice.

10. Sonic fictions are empirical
9. Sonic fictions are imaginary
8. Sonic fictions are sensory fictions
7. Sonic fictions articulate auditory experiences
6. Writing sonic fictions can help to unfold the experiential depth of auditory experiences
5. Sonic fictions are epistemological insightful
4. Sonic fictions inspire other sonic fictions
3. Sonic fictions tell the untold tales of theory
2. Sonic fictions are narratologically generative
1. Sonic fiction is a heuristic to transform and expand our contemporary speaking about sound

At this point I would like to emphasize one aspect of researching a sonic persona and then narrating a sonic experience: the sonic fiction of a specific persona in a specific sonic environment with specific auditory experiences is, on the one hand, idiosyncratic to a great extent; on the other hand, it sheds light on the individual *sensorial* and *audile techniques* (STERNE 2003) a person has learned to live with and has learned to perform in his or her life. The term *audile technique* was coined by Canadian cultural historian Jonathan STERNE. However, while he defines this term rather narrowly in respect to Western technological developments in audio technology, I wish to expand his terminology. Thus, in my reading of STERNE, broader terms such as *sensorial technique* can be applied to a full range of culturally formed and historically anchored practices, inventions, and cultural forms concerning the senses in everyday life. These sensorial techniques are a crucial element in any sonic and sensory fiction.

In sensorial techniques, we may find a whole range of new phenomena and constellations in human cultures which ground our lives in a transversal way. With this category in mind, we can reconstruct, narrate, interpret, and analyze the whole sensorial set-up of any historical culture. We can then analyze specific recording and listening technologies. We could also analyze highly differentiated media constellations and their situational usages as a whole — for example, concerning web 2.0 or social networks. We could extend this analysis to the specific sensorial quality in the use of certain substances in a cultural strand — for example, the consumption of coffee and on forms of espresso in contemporary culture. And, we may even expand this analysis to the point where we may analyze the apotheosis of a single-apartment life in the early 21st century — for example, working at a laptop in an almost monastery-like situation which obviously provides the counterpart to the contemporary (and to me, rather alienated and estranged) praise of families and having kids. Such sensorial techniques, crucial to a specific culture, can then be analyzed by applying the sonic fiction approach by being extended to a broader form of sensory fictions. In telling sensory fictions about our everyday life we might gain a certain and amazing access to the experiential side of human beings in highly diverse cultures, to specific sonic personae.

Conclusion: The corporeality and relationality of sound

I come to the end of my rather compressed overview of the research questions, issues, and methodological approaches in sound and sensory studies these days. As you saw — and maybe also heard — sound is a quality in the lives of human beings that cannot easily be reduced to one physical, stable, manifest, or even linear phenomenon. It is a dynamic, moving, transforming, and transgressing quality that defines the sonic. It is a relational and a corporeal element.

The sonic is (a) *relational*: in what ways you perceive a sound event — and what exactly you do perceive in a sound event — depends to a large extent on you and your sensorial biography as well as your cultural and historical background. The sonic is also (b) *corporeal*: it is related to the very idiosyncratic and individual bodily and sensorial set up of how you or I hear and sense what we sense, how we focus, how we zoom in and out, and how we experience sound in a subtle relationship to all our other senses.

Through the terminologies of *auditory dispositive*, of *sound practices* and *sensorial techniques* accessed by the method of *sonic fictions*, this combination of corporeality and relationality of the sonic makes it possible to access a sonic and sensorial aspect of human existence which, until now, was rarely researched in all of its subtlety: that is in the *sonic persona*. The sonic persona as a highly plastic yet integrating concept for cultural analysis allows us to speak about individual yet historicized and culturalized experiences by referring explicitly to individual body concepts and technological set-ups. Thus the experientiality of the sensory might finally be represented in adequate concepts of the sonic and the sensory — beyond reductive concepts just following the technologically most advanced inventions of the researcher's contemporary era. Such an anthropology of sound is a culturally reflexive and self-historicizing approach to auditory cultures of human beings.

Needless to say, this methodological and sensorial focus on the auditory, in the end, paves the way to research which could then proceed in a rather similar way: conceptualizing *individual sensory personae* via the analysis of specific dispositives, practices and techniques, and via inspiring new sensory fictions in the realms of the olfactory, the gustatory, the tactile, or the kinaesthetic. The biggest goal for cultural anthropology and sensory studies would be that the senses could provide a point of access to research cultures — historical and present — by their precise practices in everyday life and their specific perceptual constellations. Now: what do you smell at this very moment, at the place where you are? How warm is this place? Do you feel hungry? What would you love to taste right now? You might even tell me your sensory fiction of this very moment:

References

AGAMBEN, G. (2006): Che cos'è un dispositivo? – Rome.

ALTMAN, R. (Ed. 1992): Sound Theory, Sound Practice. – New York.

ATTALI, J. (1977): Bruits. Essai sur l'économie politique de la musique. – Paris.

AUGOYARD, J.-F. and TORGUE, H. (Eds.) (2005): Sonic Experience: A Guide to Everyday Sound. – Montreal.

AUINGER, S./ODLAND, B. (2007): Hearing Perspective (think with your ears). In: SEIFFARTH, C. and STURM, M. (Eds.): Sam Auinger. Catalogue. – Vienna and Bozen, p. 17.

BAUDRY, J.-L. (1970): Cinéma: effets idéologiques produits par l'appareil de base. In: Cinéthique 7–8, pp. 1–8.

BAUDRY, J.-L. (1975): Le dispositif: approches métapsychologiques de l'impression de réalité. In: Communications 23, Psychanalyse et cinéma, Éditions de Seuil Paris, 1975 (Eng. Translation: Camera Obscura, Fall 1976, Trans. ANDREWS, J. and AUGUST, B.; also in: ROSEN, P. [Ed.] Narrative, Apparatus, Ideology. – New York 1986).

BERNAL, M. (Ed.) (1987): Black Athena: The Afroasiatic Roots of Classical Civilization. – New Brunswick.

BIJSTERVELD, K. (2008): Mechanical Sound. Technology, Culture and Public Problems of Noise in the Twentieth Century. – Cambridge (MA) and London.

BIJSTERVELD, K. and PINCH, T. (2011): The Oxford Handbook of Sound Studies. – New York.

BLESSER, B./SALTER, L.-R. (2006): Spaces Speak, Are You Listening? Experiencing Aural Architecture. – Cambridge (MA) and London.

BULL, M./BACK, L. (2003): The Auditory Culture Reader. – Oxford and New York.

BULL, M. (2007): Sound Moves. iPod Culture and Urban Experience. – London.

CORBIN, A. (1994): Les cloches de la terre. Paysage sonore et culture sensible dans les campagnes au XIXe siècle. – Paris.

COX, C./WARNER, D. (Eds.) (2004): Audio Culture. Readings in Modern Music. – New York.

DELEUZE, G./GUATTARI, F. (1991): Qu'est-ce que la philosophie? – Paris (Eng. translation: What Is Philosophy? 1994 Trans. by BURCHELL, G. and TOMLINSON, H. – New York).

ENCYCLOPEDIA BRITANNICA (2003): – London.

ERLMANN, V. (2010): Reason and Resonance. A History of Modern Aurality. – New York.

ESHUN, K. (1998): More Brilliant than the Sun. Adventures in Sonic Fiction. – London.

FOUCAULT, M. (1994): Le jeu de Michel Foucault (1977). In: DEFERT, D. and EWALD, F. (Eds.) (1994), Dits et écrits. Vol. 3 (1976–1979). – Paris, pp. 298–329.

GOODMAN, St. (2010): Sonic Warfare. Sound, Affect and the Ecology of Fear. – New York.

GROSSMANN, R. (2008): Verschlafener Medienwandel. In: Positionen – Beiträge zur Neuen Musik (2008), H. 74 – Dispositiv(e), pp. 6–9.

HELMHOLTZ, H. von (1863): Die Lehre von den Tonempfindungen als Physiologische Grundlage für die Theorie der Musik. – Braunschweig (Eng.: On the Sensations of Tone as a Physiological Basis for the Theory of Music. 2nd Eng. translation by ELLIS, A. J. – London 1885).

JAMES, G.G.M. (1954): Stolen Legacy: The Greeks Were Not the Authors of Greek Philosophy, But the People of North Africa, Commonly Called the Egyptians. – New York.

JOHNSON, J.H. (1995): Listening in Paris. A Cultural History. – Berkeley.

KITTLER, F. (1985): Aufschreibesysteme 1800/1900. – Munich.

LATOUR, B. (1999): Politiques de la nature. Comment faire entrer les sciences en démocratie. – Paris.

NANCY, J.-L. (1992): Corpus. – Paris.

NANCY, J.-L. (2007): Listening. Trans. MADELL, Charlotte. – New York.

SCHAFER, R.M. (1977): The Soundscape. Our Sonic Environment and the Tuning of the World. – New York.

SCHULZE, H./WULF, C. (Eds.) (2007): Klanganthropologie. Performativität – Imagination – Narration. – Berlin.

SCHULZE, H. (Ed.) (2008): Sound Studies: Traditionen – Methoden – Desiderate. – Bielefeld.

SCHULZE, H. (2013): Adventures in Sonic Fiction. A Heuristic for Sound Studies, In: Journal of Sonic Studies. – Leiden and Nijmwegen (in preparation).

SERRES, M. (1985): Les Cinq Sens: philosophie des corps mêlés. – Paris (Eng. translation 2009: The Five Senses. A Philosophy of Mingled Bodies. – New York.)

STERNE, J. (2003): The Audible Past. – Durham and London.

STERNE, J. (Ed.) (2012): The Sound Studies Reader. – London.

Alain Montandon

Taste as an Aesthetic Sense

The gustatory organ is concerned with the physical perception of the savor of food. It allows us to distinguish the good from the bad through a sensation of pleasure.

> I notice first that the latin word *gustus*, from which our *goût* is derived, is seldom taken figuratively. Quintilian is about the only writer that used it in the sense we give to the word goût. It is indeed the definition he gives of Roman urbanity, *proprium quemdam gustum urbis* — a certain taste of politeness that can only be acquired in Rome. As for us, we fortunately (and often) use the word *goût* figuratively (GÉDOYNS 1767).

Although seldom used in the figurative sense in classical antiquity, it gradually acquired this meaning from the 16th century to designate the ability to discriminate socially as well as aesthetically. Like the MÉRÉ (1981, Vol. II, p. 128), Norbert ELIAS (1978) mentioned the link between the formation of taste and table manners. Others explain the formation of taste by the development of an elaborate gastronomy and culinary habits involving a quest for discrimination. Voltaire wrote:

> This sense, this capacity for discriminating between different foods, has given rise, in all known languages, to the metaphorical use of the word *taste* to designate the discernment of beauty and flaws in all the arts. It discriminates as quickly as the tongue and the palate, and like physical taste, it anticipates thought. In common with physical taste it is sensitive to what is good and reacts to it with a feeling of pleasure, it refuses with disgust what is bad; it is frequently uncertain and misleading, at times it cannot even tell whether something is pleasant or not, and sometimes it needs practice to develop discrimination (ENCYCLOPÉDIE, 1757).

The figurative senses of taste are discrimination, shrewdness of judgment, sensibility, the pleasurable or profitable appreciation of something, pleasure, but also, by extension, the manner in which a thing is made (a tasteful object), and the character of its owner (a man of taste). Guez de Balzac writes in a letter to Boisrobert: "I have for melons the same relish as for verse," thus highlighting the universality of the pleasure of savoring.

Taste is, at the same time, a physiological, psychological and socio-cultural phenomenon. In the ENCYCLOPÉDIE of d'Alembert and Diderot, CHEVALIER

DE JAUCOURT explains its physiological mechanism in detail in the following words:

> Taste in general is the excitation of an organ that delights in its object and feels its goodness; this is why taste pertains to all sensations — one has taste for music and painting, just as for ragouts, when the organ of these sensations savors these objects, so to speak (ENCYCLOPÉDIE, article "goût").

He defines taste as a finer and subtler kind of touch. And, for him the principal organ of this delicate sense is the tongue, on which savors operate, and where three kinds of cells may be discerned. The taste buds, which are the organs of taste, are not only found on the tongue, but throughout the mouth and the palate. Yet, for the writer, the tongue is the principal organ whose various movements "excite the secretion of lymph that irrigate the buds, open the pores leading to them, and induce the sapid juices to penetrate them." The chewing movement is essential:

> In order to taste the sapid objects properly, you must not keep them still on your tongue, but you have to move them around to divide them; the salts must be melted to be tasted; the tongue only perceives what is tiny enough to penetrate the pores of the nervous buds (ibid.).

In the following century, BRILLAT-SAVARIN distinguished three kinds of movements in his *Physiologie du goût*: *spication*: first, when the tongue, like a spike, comes against the lips which repress its *rotation*; second, when the tongue rotates around all the space between the interior of the jaws and the palate; and third, *verrition*, when the tongue curving up and down gathers the particles of food. The kinds of excitement are, however, very changeable and diverse according to one's temperament, diseases, sex, age, and habits — a fact he attributes to the shape, texture and disposition of the nerve buds.

> The same object produces different tastes according to age; Rhenish wine, which is so agreeable to adults, irritates young children because of their delicate nerves. Sugar and sweet things, that the latter relish, seem too insipid to those who like salty, pungent, spirituous flavors and strongly seasoned ragouts. All these discrepancies can be explained by the difference between the more sensitive nerves of childhood, and the more callous and less responsive ones of adults (ibid.).

Yet, other factors come into play: sight, hearing and especially smell and imagination — and to such an extent that taste seems to depend on all the senses. The sense of smell seems to account for nine tenths of the powers of tasting; an often-cited example is that of a person without a tongue that still enjoys flavors quite well. Conversely, everyone knows that the sense of taste vanishes when one has a cold and the nose is obstructed.

> Let a man, for instance, eat a peach, and he will first be agreeably impressed by the odor which emanates from it. He places it in his mouth, and acid and fresh flavors induce him to continue. Not, though, until he swallows it and the fruit passes under the nasal cavity, does the perfume reveal itself, thus magnifying the sensation a peach is expected to produce. Finally, it is only after he has swallowed it that, reflecting on the whole experience, he says to himself: "This is delicious!" (BRILLAT-SAVARIN 1965, p. 56).

To the sense of smell we must add the tactile quality of the food, its shape, consistence and temperature. The fact that it can be soft, or sticky, or unctuous, or mellow, or hard, or brittle is an essential feature that determines the pleasantness or unpleasantness of such and such a dish. Some people can experience a jubilant attraction to the viscous or, conversely, an absolute disgust — like Sartre. One may enthuse over the irresistible combination of the crisp and the tender in meat hardly browned, and remaining firm and juicy under its crunchy surface, or over the airy mellowness of sashimi, "that velvet dust, almost turned to silk" (BARBERY 2000, p. 73).

Also relevant is temperature, which, if inadequate, can render food unpleasant, like cold soup or tepid beer.

The sense of hearing is also involved. Eating is hardly performed in perfect silence, or in a tremendous uproar: any sound interfering with the consumption of a dish can facilitate or hamper it — and to such an extent that a meal is a kinesthesic experience. The crunching sound participates in the savouring of a vegetable or a biscotte. So do the surrounding noises, such as chinking cutlery or the confused hum, "the rumbling inside large restaurants, with the clatter of dishes and the clink of silver, the noise of the rapid steps of waiters muffled by the carpets of corridors" (MAUPASSANT [1885] describing the atmosphere of Café Riche in *Bel-Ami*).

The appearance of a dish, such an essential feature, reminds us that the sense of sight is also involved in the operation of taste. The eye, first of all, allows us to appreciate the degree of freshness of the food. Marguerite DURAS tells an anecdote about a green-looking steak bought by Yann Andréa and placed by the author on his plate: "He came in, saw the green steak, yelped with horror and threw it forever into the dustbin" (DURAS 1987, p. 117). But, in most cases, the eye discovers food that is attractive and appealing. Thus, during his stay in Italy in 1850, Théophile GAUTIER, that wonderful colorist, did not fail to marvel at the appetizing hues on the Italian market-places he visited:

> The tomatoes mingle their brilliant scarlet with those golden tints and the watermelon shows its rosy pulp through the cleft in its green skin. All these lovely fruits, brightly lighted by gas-jets, show rarely well against the vine leaves upon which they are laid. It is impossible to regale one's eyes more agreeably, and often, without being hungry, I purchased peaches and grapes through sheer love of color. I recall also certain fishmongers' stalls covered with little fishes so white, so silvery, so pearly, that I felt like swallowing them raw, after the manner of the ichthyophagists of the Southern seas, for fear of spoiling their tints. I could

> understand, on seeing them, the barbarous custom of ancient banquets, which consisted in watching the death of murænas in crystal vases in order to enjoy the opal tints which they assumed in their death throes (GAUTIER 1860, p. 257).

The Romans used natural colorings such as fig syrup or saffron, and added perfumes, as Eastern people still do. Today, dealers polish or even add color to vegetables or fruits to make them more attractive, although they may be tasteless after being raised in hothouses. MOSKOWITZ has shown that the thresholds of gustative responses to basic flavors are altered if their conventional color is modified: thus, the green color increases sensitivity to sugar, while red lowers sensitiveness to the bitter, etc. (1978, p. 319). And, one knows how much attention is paid to the appearance of the dining table, to its decoration, its silver, its linen, its flowers, in order to flatter the eye of the guests and signify the refinement of the dishes served.

It is clear that the "stage" of the table, like a show or performance, is essentially festive; the importance of objects corresponds less to practical necessities than to an æsthetic culture, related to *decorum* and expected to produce that *je-ne-sais-quoi* that is the recipe of successful conviviality. The table is covered with a cloth "of very white, very fine linen, artistically folded (ironed in squares, so that once unfolded the cloth retains the pattern of ironing with its ridges and hollows)." Napkins can also be folded in very complex shapes, imitating birds, flowers, fishes, animal of all sorts. There have always been specialists of that technique, and in baroque Germany — the foldings of Harsdörffer, for example — testified an incredible refinement.

Ornamented plates, vessel-shaped cases containing napkins, cutlery and spices, sideboards, knives and forks, crystal glasses, decanters, epergnes (elevated dishes garnished with spices, sugared almonds, fruit, etc.), and "centre-dishes" are much in demand for their rich decoration. The plates, formerly made of tin or silver in the 17th century, were later made of china, then of *faïence* — the latter, once mass-produced, was rejected.[1] Salt-cellars with original shapes have also inspired numerous decorative features.

The æsthetic enhancement of food occurs throughout the world, in eastern as well as western cookery. In *Vie et passion d'un gastronome chinois*, W. LU puts the following words in the mouth of a cook at Suzhou:

> Your cooking is imperfect, the knuckle-joints are insipid. We will cook them longer at home, setting them on a small cushion of young broccoli: vivid red against jade green. We will serve them on a china plate white as snow. And then, there will be everything: color, aroma and taste (LU 1996, p. 2).

[1] "China has once more superseded *faïence* whose long reign came to an end because of its shoddiness; still, very fine dinner sets in *faïence* artistically ornamented may still appear, even on an elegant table" (DELORME 1901, p. 151; quoted in Claudine Marenco, *Manières de table, modèles de moeurs*, 17e-20e siècles, ENS Cachan, 1993).

And, in his essay *In Praise of Shadows*, the Japanese writer J. TANIZAKI explains why one should serve meat stock in a lacquer bowl: "because a ceramic bowl is far from giving similar satisfaction" (1977).

To these multi-sensory connections one must add the naming of dishes which plays an important part in the ability to relish food. Antonin Carême, the author of *Le Cuisinier Parisien ou l'Art de la Cuisine Française au XIXe siècle* (1828), among other books, paid much attention to the relations between signifier and signified, being aware that a word induces a meaning, and that a common appellation may discredit and depreciate a dish. This is why words like fart, arse, heel, sole, must be prohibited. In menus poetic elegance is the key to happy eating (DUPUY 2009).

More generally, conversation appears to be an essential feature of any feast. Roland BARTHES rightly points out that "conversation, so to speak, is the law that protects culinary pleasure from the risk of psychosis and preserves the healthy rationality of the gourmet: speaking — and conversing — at the same time as he eats, the guest confirms his singularity and forestalls any subjective escape, thanks to imaginative discourse" (BARTHES 1995, p. 283). If conversation is expected at the dining table, it must be said that for some people their favorite subject, is in fact, the food being eaten, which arouses detailed as well as passionate comment.

We find that taste is not just a physiological operation, but that it involves a large range of psychological and sociological representations, the produce of history and experience. One rightly speaks of the education of taste, a process that consists in learning gustative discrimination. The authors of 17th- and 18th-century cookbooks do not hesitate to describe the history of cookery in terms of improvement and gradual refinement: "The Italians have polished all the European nations, and were doubtlessly our masters in the art of cookery" (*Les Dons de Comus* 1995, p. 2).

Experience also plays a part — above all, in the remembrance of flavors. Many works of fiction, such as the film *Ratatouille* or Muriel Barbery's novel *Une Gourmandise* are based on the quest for the remembrance of a long-lost flavor. The most famous example is Marcel Proust's *madeleine*, when the experience of a particular flavor conjures up a train of memories and transports the hero into the past:

> No sooner had the warm liquid, and the crumbs with it, touched my palate than a shudder ran through my whole body, and I stopped, intent upon the extraordinary changes that were taking place. An exquisite pleasure had invaded my senses, but individual, detached, with no suggestion of its origin. And at once the vicissitudes of life had become indifferent to me, its disasters innocuous, its brevity illusory — this new sensation having had on me the effect which love has of filling me with a precious essence; or rather this essence was not in me, it was myself. I had ceased now to feel mediocre, accidental, mortal. Whence could it have come to

> me, this all-powerful joy? I was conscious that it was connected with the taste of tea and cake, but that it infinitely transcended those savors, could not, indeed, be of the same nature as theirs (PROUST 1954, p. 45).

Quivering within him is a visual memory connected with that savor, a trace of a remote past to which the taste is linked. Taste as the language of memories is praised by Maryline DESBIOLLES through her heroine in *La Seiche* whose memory is saturated with the odors of yore:

> Tasting cooked food, and, even better, cooking it precisely means bringing one's memories to the mouth, masticating them over again, distilling what they are made of and not just having them on the tip of your tongue, but salivating and submitting them to your tongue. Once they are kneaded over and over in your watering mouth, memories get to the heart of the matter (1998, pp. 72–73).

There is a history of taste, just as there is a history of the social representations that play an important part in the operation of taste and distaste. In fact, taste itself is socialized:

> If there is a connection between *œufs à la neige* and a modest income, it is not just because this dessert is inexpensive, but because taste is a social construction whose values are not defined in an absolute way, but in a given context. Therefore, it is always on the basis of culture, not of needs, that Brillat-Savarin discusses food as a social practice (BARTHES 1995, p. 293).

There are many illustrations of this culinary sociology (only think of the numerous meals described in French naturalist novels like those of Maupassant or Émile Zola), and they all clearly reveal the diversity of tastes and the process of *distinction* analysed by BOURDIEU (1979).

Well-known, for example, are the fluctuating relations between sugar and salt — they were combined in the Middle Ages, and separated in the modern period, until the influence of Eastern cuisine gathered them again. The notion of a progress of taste, parallel to the progress of art and civilization, contributed to the rejection of former tastes. Thus, in the modern period people, stopped using spices generously, as was done in the Middle Ages: saffron, ginger, galingale, mace, herb mastic, nutmeg practically disappeared. This historical mutability is also geographical, and we could here adopt Michel de Montaigne's dictum in Pascal's dictum "Truth this side of the Pyrenées, error beyond" (*Pensées*, 294), since the eating habits that underlie taste differ from one country to another, from one culture to another. The Burgundy snails and frogs' legs *à la Provençale* — symbols of French cuisine according to Philip HYMAN (2005) — are found disgusting in other cultures, just as some insects or worms that are relished in sub-Saharian Africa are found repulsive by the French. The list of such tastes and distastes, in the context of intercultural exchanges, would be a long one.

For this reason, defining taste often amounts to invoking a *je-ne-sais-quoi* since tastes are so fluctuating. Leibniz finds its perfection confusing, and requiring many explanations. And Voltaire, writes in *The Temple of Taste*: "'Tis easier to say what the Temple is not Than to describe what it really is."

In *La Science du Maître d'hôtel cuisinier* (1749), we can read that savors can be infinitely varied: "Milk, sugar and honey are sweet, yet each sort of sweetness has its particular character, its differences and special nuances; and who will dare fix the bounds of such variety ?" And, Abbé Du Bos wrote: "One tastes ragout, and at once decides whether it is good, without knowing the rules of its preparation" (1770, Vol. 2, p. 341). The list of savors is infinite. In Western countries, we principally distinguish what is salty, sugary, bitter, sour, spicy, astringent; but the Encyclopédie of d'Alembert and Diderot finds many more varieties:

1. Salty.
2. Sour; the taste of several summer fruits, of wine and vinegar.
3. Alkaline; like the urinous salts smelling of putrefied urine.
4. Sweet; such is the taste of most vegetables when they are ripe; also that of sugar, honey, manna, etc. Whatever is sweet belongs to the class of acids.
5. Vinous; the taste of all wines and beers, etc.
6. Bitter; the taste of the two sorts of biles, of absinthe, aloes, colocynth, and rancid oil.
7. Aromatic; the adequate term for all plants giving off a strong smell or taste when you chew them.
8. Pungent; for example euphorbia, garlic, onion, and other plants with an unpleasant smell, unlike aromatic ones.
9. Austere, as in gall-nuts from which ink is obtained, ink itself, oak, green oranges, etc. The austere taste is a kind of pungent or sour taste, very astringent.
10. Finally, all other savors combining those mentioned, offering an infinite variety of tastes, and with effects impossible to describe.

In India, the four fundamental Western savors (sugary, salty, sour, and bitter) are complemented by the pungent and the astringent. In Burma, they distinguish six savors: sweet, sour, pungent, salty, astringent, and bitter; but they are rarely found alone, and are often combined. China identifies five savors (sweet, sour, pungent, bitter, salty). In his *Huainan Zi*, Liu An points out the importance of the number 5 in his chapter on "Terrestrial forms:" five sounds; five color tones, all governed by yellow; "in savors there are five varieties of taste, all governed by sugar."

> When the sweet is refined, it produces the sour; when the sour is refined, it produces the pungent; when the pungent is refined, it produces the bitter; when the bitter is refined it produces the salty; when the salty is refined it reverts to the sweet (Liu An 2003, p. 178).

The five components control each other.

According to Chinese rituals, the insipidity of the "great soup" represents a kind of state of nature. Yet insipidity, that non-savor, is an essential feature of Chinese cuisine as well as art, a testimony of authenticity and interior detachment.

> Savouring what is without savor (*wei wu wei*). (Lao Zi, § 63)
> Dao is tasteless and without savor.
> It cannot be perceived,
> It cannot be heard,
> But it is inexhaustible. (ibid., § 35)

While music and delicacies are full of appeal and stimulation, and yet cannot procure any delight capable of expansion (they are only a "stop" for the passer-by), the insipidity of Dao is a paradoxical sign of wealth and abundance that are all the more inexhaustible as they do not appear to be so, have no visibility ("It cannot be perceived"), and remain self-contained. In this way, "insipidity" (*wu wei*) or tastelessness prevails radically over the too immediate, too ephemeral value of the sapid. The less easily a savor can be perceived and appreciated, the less it can be actualized and, therefore, exhausted in the here and now of concrete experience. And, it remains the richer in potential, preserving its internal capacity for development, since any actualization means a limitation.

Both in the East and the West, there exists an aesthetic of savors sublimated by the art of cooking. "Cuisine renders the grosser parts of food subtler, rids its composite ingredients of the terrestrial juices that they contain: it perfects, purifies and spiritualizes them, so to speak" (*La Science du Maître d'hôtel cuisinier*, xxii). Gastronomy pertains to the fine arts, and to the cultural practices of a given period. It is an art of the ephemeral, doomed to destruction by ingestion. The cook as artist is a sculptor of time, "in order to make the ephemeral a little less so" (Barbery 2000, p. 38).

It used to be the fashion to have recourse to musical metaphors to describe savors. In his *Chimie du goût et de l'odorat* (1760), Polycarpe Poncelet wrote:

> Savours consist in the more or less intense vibrations of the salts acting on the sense of taste, just as sounds consist in more or less intense vibrations of air acting on the sense of hearing. There can be music for the tongue and palate, just as there is for the ear (1760, p. xix).

Just as in the realm of sound, one may then discern generative, dominant, major, minor, high and low pitches, with their consonances and dissonances. And, if seven keys are the basis of music, one will identify seven primitive savors that are "the basis of the music of savors and their harmonic combination" (ibid.).

For Cartaud De La VILATTE (*Réflexions sur la délicatesse du goût*, 1751), a refined mouth can break down the most subtle ragout, just as a trained ear can distinguish the components of a great musical piece. FONCEMAGNE (1749)[2] insists on the notion of harmony and unity in diversity: "Can one be blamed for maintaining that there is a harmony of savors, just like a harmony of sounds, and perhaps of colours and odours?" There exists an aesthetic of savors comparable to the harmony of sounds. The author of *Chimie du goût et de l'odorat* sees the cook as a composer, "a symphonist of a kind" (PONCELET 1760, p. xxii) who has to know the principles of harmony.

> Would you compose an aria of savors in a sharp key? Then take as dominant acid, pungent, austere or bitter tastes; on the contrary if you select as dominant insipid, sugary, sweet and sour tastes, with a touch of the pungent, in order to give zest to your composition, you will get a savory aria in a flat key (ibid.).

Poncelet gives precise examples:

> In music for the ear, thirds, fifths and octaves offer the finest consonances; there are precisely the same effects in the music of savors, when you combine acid with sweet and sour (...). With lemon combined with sugar, you will obtain a simple, but charming consonance, like a fifth major (ibid.).

And, he also adds a chart showing the scale of savors. Taking as a model the ocular harpsichord of Father Castel, Poncelet imagines a new kind of organ on which could be played all kinds of arias (ibid., p. xxv) — an organ that prefigured Joris-Karl Huysmans' mouth-organ in *A Rebours*[3] or Boris Vian's cocktail-piano in the film *L'Écume des jours*.

E.T.A. HOFFMANN[4] was one of the writers that defined parallels between music and beverages. One reads in *Kreisleriana*:

> One could posit certain principles concerning beverages. For example, I would recommend old Rhenish or French wine for church music; very fine Burgundy for opera; champagne for comic opera; heady wines for Italian canzonette; for a work of high romanticism, like *Don Giovanni*, an average glass of that drink produced by the salamander and the spirit of earth (meaning punch).[5]

---

[2] Étienne Laureault de Foncemagne, *Dissertation préliminaire sur la cuisine moderne*.

[3] "Each liqueur, according to him, had a taste corresponding to a musical instrument. Dry curaçao, for example, evoked the clarinet, whose tone is thin and velvety; for kummel it was the hautboy whose sound is loud and nasal; for mint and aniseed it was the flute, whose notes are both sweet and spicy, plaintive an soft" etc. (HUYSMANS 2004, pp. 83–84).

[4] See MONTANDON (1983, pp. 159–166; 1981, pp. 51–70).

[5] "Man könnte ordentlich rücksichts der Getränke gewisse Prinzipe aufstellen. So würde ich z.B. bei der Kirchenmusik alte Rhein- und Franzweine, bei der ernsten

Nerval, Musset, Vigny, and Maupassant approved (sometimes with modifications) such correspondences between champagne and comic opera, Rhenish wine and religious music, etc. And, BAUDELAIRE (1860) writes: "It seems to me there is an obvious affinity between this psychic barometer and the explanation of the musical qualities of wines." Like the perfumer Septimus PIESSE (1865) who used a scale of odors to discuss fragrances (C: sandalwood; E: acacia; G: orange blossom), when we discuss savors we have recourse to pictorial metaphors (we speak of a delightful hot-potch of colors to refer to the beauty of colors), to musical metaphors and a whole range of synaesthesias.

F. T. MARINETTI had a futuristic conception of gastronomy which was supposed to change, even revolutionize, the world. Although his ideas are not really new, they still rightly stress the synaesthesic nature of taste, giving pride of place to the gaze (harmony in the display on the table), but also to the touch (knives and forks are discarded, and replaced by the fingers which assess the temperature, the consistence, the texture, or smoothness of food). He designed small plaques covered with diverse cloths or other materials intended to be fingered, the tactile sensation being associated with savoring. Odors, perfumes as well as music are here expected to stimulate taste sensitized by

> the concoction of gobbets of food to be eaten together or alternately, and containing ten or twenty savors to be tried within a few moments. In futuristic cuisine, these gobbets will have the function of amplification by analogy, much like images in literature — a gobbet being able to sum up a slice of life, the unfolding of a love affair, or a journey to the Far East (MARINETTI 1982, P. 48).

The difficulty in discussing taste, and of translating the inexpressible, entails an upsurge in images and metaphors rich in flavors. Of a wine one will say it is gallant, or that it is cuddly, or that it is sweet like baby Jesus.[6] Its fragrances will conjure up ideas of flowers (rose, lilac, jasmine, sweet william), of fruit (peach, raspberry, almond, apricot, red berries), of dead leaves, resin, moist earth, hare's belly, etc. Taste, then, seems to be a synthesis and sublimation of the five senses, controlled by imagination and a multitude of representations (personal, cultural and social).

References

BARBERY, M. (2000): Une gourmandise. – Paris.

BARTHES, R. (1995): Lecture de Brillat-Savarin. In: Œuvres Complètes – Seuil (Eng. Reading Brillat-Savarin, In: On Signs, BLONSKY, Marshall [Ed.]).

Oper sehr feinen Burgunder, bei der komischen Oper Champagner, bei Kanzonetten italienische feurige Weine, bei einer höchst romantischen Komposition, wie die des 'Don Juan' ist, aber ein mäßiges Glas von eben dem von Salamander und Erdgeist erzeugten Getränk anraten !" (HOFFMANN 1963, p. 915).

[6] The literal French phrase is "baby Jesus in velvet pants."

BAUDELAIRE, C. (1860): Les Paradis artificiels. – Paris.
BOURDIEU, P. (1979): La distinction. Critique sociale du jugement. – Paris (Eng. Distinction: A Social Critique of the Judgement of Taste – London 1984).
BRILLAT-SAVARIN, J.A. (1965): Physiologie du gout. – Paris (Eng. The Physiology of Taste. – Philadelphia 1854).
DELORME, M. (1901): Une Maison bien tenue. – Paris.
DESBIOLLES, M. (1998): La Seiche. – Seuil.
DUPUY, J.-P. (2009): Rhétorique du menu gastronomique. In: Communication & Langages, Vol.160, pp. 19–33.
DURAS, M. (1987): La Vie matérielle. – Paris.
ELIAS, NORBERT. (1978): The Civilizing Process: The History of Manners. – Oxford.
ENCYCLOPÉDIE ou Dictionnaire raisonné des sciences, des arts et des métiers, LE ROND D'ALEMBERT, J.B. and DIDEROT, D. (Ed.). – Paris 1751–1781.
DE FONCEMAGNE, É.L. (1749): Dissertation préliminaire sur la cuisine moderne. – Paris.
GAUTIER, Th. (1860): Italia, 3rd edition. – Paris.
GÉDOYNS, N. (1767): Réflexions sur le gout. – Paris.
HOFFMANN, E.T.A. (1963): Kreisleriana. In: Romantiques allemands, Bibliothèque de la Pléiade. – Paris.
HUYSMANS, J.K. (2004): A Rebours, Flammarion. – Paris.
HYMAN, Philip. (2005): *Larousse des cuisines régionales*. – Paris.
LES DONS DE COMUS (1995): In: Les liaisons savoureuses. – Saint-Étienne.
LA SCIENCE DU MAÎTRE D'HÔTEL CUISINIER (1749). – Paris.
LAO ZI (1995): Tao Te Ching. – New York.
LIU AN (2003): Bibliothèque de la Pléiade, Philosophes taoïstes, Vol. II, Huainan Zi. – Paris.
LU, W. (1996): Vie et passion d'un gastronome chinois, Picquier poche. – Arles.
DE MÉRÉ, Antoine Gombaud Chevalier (1981): Œuvres completes. – Paris.
MAUPASSANT, Guy de (1885): Bel-Ami. – Paris, Ollendorf.
MONTANDON, A. (1981): les fantastiques bouteilles d'un buveur enthousiaste. In: La Correspondance du vin. – Paris, pp. 51–70.
MONTANDON, A. (1983): L'imaginaire du vin dans le romantisme allemand. In: L'imaginaire du vin. – Marseille, pp. 159–166.
MOSKOWITZ, H. (1978): Taste and food technology: Acceptability aesthetics and preference, In: C. Carterette and Morton Friedmann, Handbook of perception: Tasting and smelling, Vol. 6. – Paris.
PIESSE, Septimus (1865): Des odeurs, des parfums et des cosmétiques. – Paris (2nd edition 1877).
PONCELET, P. (1760): Chimie du goût et de l'odorat ou Principes pour composer facilement, and à peu de frais, les Liqueurs à boire, and les Eaux de senteurs. A Paris, Le Mercier.
PROUST, M. (1954): A la recherche du temps perdu, Bibliothèque de la Pléiade, I, MONCRIEFF, Scott (Trans.). – Paris.
DE LA VILATTE, C. (1751): Réflexions sur la délicatesse du goût. – Paris.
TANIZAKI, J. (1977): In Praise of Shadows. – New York.

Astrid Zotter

Scent of a Flower: Notes on Olfaction in Hindu Worship*

jāīphūlko basanā, na bole ni hāṃsi rākha na
(See) the scent of the jasmine flower — keep smiling,
even if you do not speak.
(From a Nepalese wedding song)

As Gérard COLAS has noted in his contribution to this volume, Sanskrit devotional traditions lay stress on vision, audition, taste, and touch when discussing the role of divine and human senses. In contrast, smell seems to be considered of minor importance in the interaction of humans and deities. Mudagamuwe Maithrimurthi, a colleague of mine, spontaneously remarked when he heard that I was invited to contribute a paper on the ritual significance of smell: "In South Asia you can see (*darśana*) the truth (or the Divine), you can hear it (*śravaṇa*), you can taste its flavor (*rasa*), you can touch it (*sparśana*), but you cannot smell it." What, then, can be said about the role of smell in addressing a deity?

Pūjā, the ritual I will be concerned with here, is perhaps the most popular form of worship in South Asian religious traditions. The exact period of formation and early history of the ritual are matters of discussion amongst scholars (see COLAS 2006, pp. 354–55; EINOO 1996; THIEME 1939). There are many forms of (and norms for) *pūjā*; but, at its core, it consists of treating a deity (usually present in or incarnated as an icon) or another revered being as one would treat a respected guest. This consists of several activities including: the welcoming; a series of offerings, such as water to wash; articles for decoration; food offerings; entertainment; and finally the bidding of farewell. These services (*upacāra*) rendered to the divinity can number in the hundreds, but can also be reduced to giving water, some rice grains, or a flower (BÜHNEMANN 1988, pp. 63–66).

Rules pertaining to the latter, viz. the offering of a flower (*puṣpa*), are found in Sanskrit texts and text passages of different genres, some of which have recently

* For their helpful corrections and comments I would like to thank Gérard Colas, Mudagamuwe Maithrimurthi, Axel Michaels, and Christof Zotter. Moreover, I am grateful to James Hegarty for revising the English of this paper.

been studied more closely.[1] In the following, I will focus on the discourse on *pūjā* flowers as developed in late medieval Sanskrit digests (*nibandha*) of non-sectarian (Smārta) Brahmanism as well as Śaiva and Śākta Tantric traditions. I will try to relate this evidence, which is technical and prescriptive in character, to other branches of Sanskrit religious literature.

It is very often stated in these prescriptive texts that flowers fit for offering should be fragrant (for example, *surabhi*, *sugandha/°i*), whereas the use of scentless (for example, *nirgandha*, *gandhavarjita*) and strongly fragrant (*ugra°* or *utkaṭagandha*) flowers is prohibited. No further specifications are made; neither are individual flower species classified as fragrant or unscented, nor are types of scent distinguished. This observation on rules for *pūjā* flowers concurs with James McHugh's broader findings (2007, 2012) on the notion of scent in South Asia. He states that in Sanskrit texts in general, there is a two-fold classification into fragrant and non-fragrant (*surabhi* vs. *asurabhi*) or favorable and unfavorable odor (*iṣṭa°* vs. *aniṣṭagandha*). In contrast to the classification of taste, color, touch, and sound, there seems to be no attempt to establish objective categories of scent (Bhattacharya 1983), but such classifications are rather an aesthetic judgment (McHugh 2007). In describing particular smells, Sanskrit authors mostly resort to comparisons, likening the smell of one thing to that of another,[2] or they borrow terms from the description of taste. The smell of flowers, both in general and of particular species, figures prominently in the comparative characterization of scent. Thus, the scent of flowers is viewed by McHugh as one of the major landmarks of the South Asian "smellscape." Moreover, he notes a tendency to attribute "fragrance" to plant smells, whereas animals and flesh tend to be associated with the idea of a "stink." Accordingly, only rarely does the idea of an unpleasant odor feature in descriptions of *pūjā* flowers.[3]

[1] Petr Duda (2005, 2006) has analyzed Puranic text passages on the topic; James McHugh (2012, pp. 219–232) has dealt with a passage from the *dānadharma* section of the *anuśāsanaparvan* of the *Mahābhārata* (13.101.1–43). In my doctoral research, resulting in a textual edition and study of the *Puṣpacintāmaṇi* (Zotter 2013), I have been studying the Nepalese textual tradition on *pūjā* flowers, but have also drawn on other relevant passages.

[2] The "tendency to name odours by pointing to objects in the real world" (Lawless 1997, p. 157) seems to be widespread, and is listed among major impediments to universal scientific systems for the description and classification of odor. The fact that humans, unless specially trained, usually perceive odors as "unitary perceptual experiences" (ibid.) — and are unable to decompose them — complicates matters further, as does the much larger number of basic odors in comparison with primary colors or basic tastes (ibid, pp. 156–57).

[3] A rare instance of mentioning bad smelling (*durgandha*) flowers is *Puṣpacintāmaṇi* 1.5b, where they are said to be suitable for the Dānavas, the enemies of the gods. Otherwise, even among the prohibited flowers, usually only the strongly fragrant are listed, and never the malodorous flowers.

Apart from flowers as offerings, I will review some other examples concerning the smell, or the smelling of, flowers in *pūjā* in order to gain a deeper insight into the Brahmanical conception(s) of the ritual use of flowers. I do not aim to establish a single, nor a dominant, or a historically primary, interpretation. There is no absolute answer to the question as to the significance of the scent of flowers in *pūjā*. Instead, I will explore some of the connotations prevalent in Sanskrit texts on this topic.

Consuming flowers

The prohibition against the offering of flowers that have previously been smelt (*āghrātapuṣpa*) is a standard one which is to be met with in most treatments of *pūjā* flowers. The sniffing at offering material is, in general, deemed to be a ritual flaw:

> The man who offers a flower (*puṣpa*), incense (*dhūpa*), fragrant substance (*gandha*) or other offerings after having sniffed at shall suffer hell.[4]

A flower that has been sniffed at is equated with a flower that has already been offered; both are considered *nirmālya*:

> *Nirmālya* is said to be twofold, namely (already) presented and sniffed at. It is not to be used in another ritual, under all circumstances it is to be left aside.[5]

Nirmālya technically denotes flowers and all other material remains of the offerings to a deity. The term can either be related to *mālya*, "garland" — perhaps hinting at an extension from the remains of flower garlands to other offerings — or to *nirmala*, "spotless," in which sense it would denote stainlessness or purity.[6] The latter might point to the quality the offerings are said to have achieved by

---

[4] *Puṣpaṃ dhūpaṃ ca gandham ca upacārāṃs tathāparān | ghrātvā nivedya devebhyo naro narakam āpnuyāt* (*Kālikāpurāṇa* 69.149); cited with variant readings in a recent handbook: *gandhapuṣpadhūpāś ca ghrātvā devebhyo na deyāḥ kālikāpurāṇe* — "*gandhaṃ puṣpaṃ ca dhūpaṃ ca upacārāṃs tathāparān | jighran nivedya devebhyo naro narakam āpnuyāt*" (*Pūjāpaṅkajabhāskara* (1997: 32); cp. *Śāktānandataraṅginī* 14.49: *puṣpaṃ ca pañcagavyaṃ ca upacārāṃs tathāparān | ghrātvā nivedya deveśi naro narakam āpnuyāt.*

[5] *Nirmālyaṃ dvividhaṃ proktam utsṛṣṭaṃ ghrātam eva ca | na kriyāntarayogyaṃ tat sarvathā tyajyam eva ca* (Miśra and Miśra 2004, p. 112, citing the *Tattvasāgarasaṃhitā*).

[6] Cf. Brunner (1968, p. 274); Nowotny (1957, p. 154, fn. 209). In the so-called *Petersburger Wörterbuch*, the word *nirmālya* is equated with *nirmala* on the basis of its use in *Gṛhyasaṅgraha* 2.85–87 (Böhtlingk 1865: s.v. *nirmālya* 1.). When the dictionary was republished in an abridged version, the entry on *nirmālya* appears to have been reworked (Böhtlingk 1882 s.v.: 1. Adj. (aus einem Kranze ausgeschieden) ausrangiert; unbrauchbar, nicht hingehörig). This is perhaps due to M. Bloomfield's

their contact with the deity. Hence, when the offerings are redistributed to the worshippers, they are also called *prasāda*, "clarified substance."[7] The term used synonymously with *nirmālya* in the technical literature under consideration is *ucchiṣṭa*, "leftover." This word commonly designates the remains of food offerings in the Vedic fire as well as the remains of human food.[8] Food touched or consumed by another person is considered polluted and, therefore, a highly polluting substance. Sanskrit authors on *dharma*, the religious, social, and political order of the world, forbid the eating of one's own leftovers as well as those of another person. And yet, consuming *ucchiṣṭa* can at times signal submission, respect, or even intimacy. For instance, in the marriage ritual, a bride is to eat food that has been tasted by her groom; a student of the Veda should feed on the *ucchiṣṭa* of his preceptor; and a mother may eat the food left over by her child. In like manner, receiving a *nirmālya* flower as the *prasāda* of a deity and carrying it on one's head is a way to show one's respect. At the same time, it provides the possibility of prolonging physical contact with the deity, of experiencing her "grace" (*prasāda*) even after the actual worship is over. The similarities between *prasāda* and human leftovers are limited, however, because the divine "consumption" of offerings is not polluting, but rather has the opposite effect.[9] It is also the case that presenting human *ucchiṣṭa* to a deity would be an affront. Indeed, a flower that had been smelt prior to its presentation stands on a par with food polluted through it having been eaten by an inferior.

The notion that to smell is akin to eating seems to be very widespread in South Asia. A popular Sanskrit saying goes: "(something is) half-eaten by smelling" (*ghrāṇenārdhabhojanam*). Smelling, as an act similar to eating, and yet to be distinguished from it, is known from Brahmanical ritual as well. Part of the regular ancestor worship (*śrāddha*) as it is carried out today — at least among some Brahmin groups in Nepal — is to sniff at the sacrificial balls of rice flour (*piṇḍa*) after they have been offered to the ancestors (Figure 1). The

---

note (1881, p. 584) on *Gṛhyasaṅgraha* 2.85, in which, on account of the commentaries' gloss of *nirmālyatā* as *nivīryatā* (powerlessness, ineffectiveness), he doubts the relation to *nirmala*. Obviously there are diverse conceptions of *nirmālya* found in Sanskrit texts of different ritual traditions that deserve to be studied in more depth and detail; see, for example, BRUNNER (1968, pp. 266–88; 1969), who discusses the consumption of Śiva's *nirmālya* in the Śaiva Siddhānta tradition.

[7] The Sanskrit verb *pra-sad-*, "to settle down," signifies the becoming bright or clear, as for example, a body of standing water does once all the particles of dust have settled to the ground. Derivatives of *pra-sad-* are figuratively applied, amongst others for the human mind as becoming free of thoughts. Offering material that has become *prasāda* in this sense can be understood as having been "clarified" by contact with the divine, yet the semantic range of the term includes purity, transcendence, or grace as well (MALINAR 2009, p. 22, fn. 6). For *prasāda* in general, see also, FULLER (1992, pp. 74–75).

[8] For *ucchiṣṭa* see GONDA (1975) and WEZLER (1978).

[9] Likewise the *ucchiṣṭa* of Vedic sacrifice is considered the purest form of food as the fire (*agni*) has removed impurities that might have remained (MALINAR 2009, p. 22).

Figure 1: Towards the end of the annual ancestor ritual (*śrāddha*), the sacrificial patron smells the sacrificial ball (*piṇḍa*) he has offered to his forefathers. Photograph taken by the author on February 25, 2012, at Matatirtha, Nepal.

need to smell the remains of food offered to one's forefathers, prescribed in Śrauta- and Gṛhyasūtras, is already discussed in the Brāhmaṇas (GONDA 1975: 455–56). There, it seems to be held as a form of ritual compromise, a way not to eat what is meant for others, but yet partake of it:

> Those who expound the Veda say: 'should (the remains of the oblation) be eaten, (or) should they not be eaten? If he should eat (of them), he would eat food which belongs to other creatures (and) he would be liable to an early death; if he should not eat (of them), he would not share in the oblations and estrange himself (cut himself off) from the Fathers. (The remnant) should only be smelled at; thus it is on the one hand not eaten and on the other hand not not eaten.[10]

Smelling is not only described as a way in which humans may ritually consume food and drink; but — and more relevant for the present discussion — deities are said to consume flowers by smelling them. This view is variously expressed by modern day worshippers in India and Nepal, and is also found in literary sources:

> By the odor (of the flowers) deities are satisfied, spirits (*yakṣa*) and demons (*rākṣasa*) by the sight, the snakes (*nāga*) by eating, but humans by these three things.[11]

At first glance, this statement from the epic *Mahābhārata* seems to be a rather schematic grouping of classes of beings with forms of sense perception, perhaps serving to order them according to their ability to establish more or less direct bodily contact with offerings. In such a scheme, the deities would be furthest removed, and would thus perceive flowers from a distance by smelling them. More specifically, the pairing of deities and smelling makes one think, as MCHUGH (2012, pp. 230–232) did, of the world of Vedic ritual. The Vedic fire sacrifice has been described as a food exchange between the gods, who had gone to heaven, and men on earth. Agni, the (god of) fire, has the role of

---

[10] *Brahmavādíno vadanti | prā́śyā̆3ṃ ná prā́śyā̆3ṃ íti | yát prāśnīyā́t | jányam ánnam adyāt | pramā́yukaḥ syāt | yán ná prāśnīyā́d | áhaviḥ syād | pitŕ̥bhya ā́vṛścyeta | ávaghréyam evá | tán ná iva prā́śitaṃ ná iva áprāśitam* (*Taittirīyabrāhmaṇa* 1.3.10.6, translation by GONDA 1975, p. 455). In the *Kaṭha Āraṇyaka*, a text that like the *Taittirīyabrāhmaṇa* belongs to the tradition of the Black Yajurveda, the same question is posed and answered in similar wording in regard to the consumption of the remains of the offerings of the *pravargya* ritual. There it is also the case that smelling is commended as the way not to eat but still have a share in the oblations (*havis*): *prā́śyā̆3 ná prā́śyā̆3ā́? íti mīmāṁsante | yát prāśnīyā́t prākā́rukas syād yán ná prāśnīyā́d áhavis syād | ávajighred | ubháyam evá karoti* (*Kaṭha Āraṇyaka* 2.143; cf. WITZEL 1997, p. 511).

[11] *Gandhena devās tuṣyanti darśanād yakṣarākṣasāḥ | nāgāḥ samupabhogena tribhir etais tu mānuṣāḥ* (*Mahābhārata* 13.101.34.); cf. *Gandharvatantra* 9.8c (see fn. 16 below).

the go-between, who carries the oblations burnt on earth to heaven. There they are consumed by the gods, perhaps by smelling the smoke.[12] Caution must be exercised when trying to account for notions pertaining to *pūjā* by drawing on the fire sacrifice (*yajña/yāga*), which has been the centerpiece of Vedic ritualism and was treated in textual sources long before *pūjā* made its appearance in Brahmanical literature. *Yajña* and *pūjā* have often been seen as competing, if not mutually exclusive, ritual modi,[13] but in this case it may be permissible to speak of a continuity of thought concerning the means whereby the gods are able to perceive and consume offerings. McHugh suggests that the author of the statement in the *Mahābhārata* may actually have intended to allude to the prestigious world of Vedic sacrifice in order to furnish "the use of flowers in ritual . . . with orthodox Vedic resonances" (2012, p. 232). But this interpretation might be too narrow, as the ability of deities to smell at offerings might have been a very common idea not limited to the Vedic tradition.

Admittedly, the explicit mention of deities smelling flowers is hard to find in the kind of literature dealt with here. In the prescriptive texts on *pūjā* flowers, it is mostly said that the deities are satisfied or pleased, the verbal roots *tuṣ-* and *prī-* being frequently used. Before discussing how the satisfaction or delight of a deity can be linked to smelling, I will now look at some other ideas associated with the scent of flowers.

Effects of smelling

Purification

Ritual purity is a central concern of the Brahmanical tradition, as it probably is of most, if not all, ritual traditions. Each thing and each body employed in Vedic ritual has to be made fit (*medhya*) by acts of purification or with the help of special substances (cp. Malinar 2009, pp. 22–27). Vedic texts, amongst others, prescribe certain plants as a means of purification. The *kuśa* grass (*Desmostachya bipinnata* [L.] Stapf) is reckoned as *pavitra*, a "purifying agent." Ropes, the seat of the ritual patron, or instruments to strain or sprinkle water are made of this grass, and are ascribed the capacity to render things

[12] For a short summary of how one may conceive of food as a medium of exchange between humans and deities in Vedic and post-Vedic religion, see Witzel (1997, pp. 509–12). In her detailed study of the development of different strands of thought about the *Kreislauf der Opfergaben im Veda* ("Circulation of sacrificial gifts in the Veda"), Wilden (2000) has demonstrated that the notion of exchange between gods and humans is complex. It is less coherently expressed in the Vedic texts, as my general statements suggest.

[13] Actually, there are more interrelations and continuities between the two kinds of ritual than one might expect, given the contrastive rhetoric in academic discourse. See Colas (2006) for an illuminating discussion of this issue.

and bodies *medhya*.[14] The same holds true for a ring of *kuśa* grass worn by the sacrificial patron throughout the ritual, which secures the purity of his ritually prominent right hand (Figure 2).

Figure 2: Throughout the ritual, the sacrificial patron wears a ring of *kuśa* grass on his right hand. Photograph taken by the author at the Rāma temple in Battis Putali, Deopatan (Nepal), on February 3, 2006.

In *pūjā* as well, all material, including the body of the worshipper, needs to be made suited for ritual. An example of this, telling in the present context, is to be found in a Smārta *pūjā* tradition followed by *Ṛgvedic* Brahmins in Maharashtra (1988): when the worshipper takes his seat, he invokes the earth as his support, drives away evil spirits (*bhūtotsādana*), and removes his human odor (*manuṣyagandha*) by the recital of two mantras from the *Ṛgveda* (BÜHNEMANN 1988, pp. 118–121).[15] As for all other ritual acts, the power of the mantras is decisive in purification. However, in a way that is comparable to *kuśa*

[14] For references on instruments of *kuśa* from Vedic texts (mostly Brāhmaṇas and Kalpasūtras) and their application in purification measures, see GONDA (1985, pp. 30–32, 65–69). For the concept of *pavitra* in a more general perspective, see MALINAR (2009, pp. 23–25, 35–36) and following sections.

[15] As a Vedic background to this act, BÜHNEMANN quotes the *Aitareyabrāhmaṇa* (3.30.4.), where it is said that the deities abhorred the Ṛbhus on account of their human smell. This passage from the *Aitareyabrāhmaṇa* is related by MALINAR (2009, p. 32, fn. 28) to the gods' general disgust for humans smelling of desires and fears, which eventually led to quitting their original habitation on earth.

in Vedic rituals, later texts on *pūjā* also refer to the purifying effect of plants. For example, in Tantric *pūjā*s, the use of a flower is sometimes prescribed in the purification of the hands (*karaśuddhi*), which is also called the "grinding of flowers" (*puṣpamardana*).[16] *Karaśuddhi* is one of the preliminary rites that are intended to purify the worshipper's body: to the accompaniment of mantras, a flower is taken with the fingers, rubbed between the palms, ground between the back of the hands, and smelt. Afterwards it is cast away:

> When it has been carried out in this way, there will be complete purity of both hands; if leeches, snakes, etc. have been touched, one will be pure after this rite of purification. A defect of both hands on account of contact with evil-smelling things or remnants of food (*ucchiṣṭa*), without knowing, all these defects will be caused to disappear, if (this rite) has been performed according to the rule. The fingertips will be pure because of the grasping of the flowers, the two hand-palms become pure because of the rubbing; the back because of the grinding, the utmost point of the nose because of the smelling; and (all) the holy places converge in the tip of the nose, and in the hand.[17]

In this passage, the touch of a flower removes the effect of contact with impure and bad-smelling things. Some texts even add that the flowers used should be smeared with sandalwood paste (*candana*),[18] which is the most important representative of one of the *pūjā* offerings, the *gandha* (fragrant substance).

---

[16] For example, *Gandharvatantra* 9.5–10; *Kālikāpurāṇa* 57(59).48–55; *Śāktānandataraṅginī*, 17.38–45 (pp. 81–82); *Tārābhaktisudhārṇava*, pp. 149–50. According to most authorities, the flower should be red and cast away into the north-eastern direction. According to other Tantric texts, *karaśuddhi* is achieved by mantras alone.

[17] *Evaṃ kṛte tu karayor viśuddhir atulā bhavet | jalaukāgūḍhapādādisparśāc chuddhir viśodhanāt || durgandhyucchiṣṭasaṃsparśād dūṣaṇaṃ karayos tu yat | ajñātarūpaṃ tat sarvaṃ nāśayet suvidhānataḥ || aṅgulyagrāṇi śuddhāni puṣpāṇāṃ grahaṇād bhavet | taladvayaṃ mardanāt tu viśuddham abhijāyate || nirmañchanāt pāṇipṛṣṭaṃ ghrāṇāt nāsāgram uttamam | tīrthāni ca samāyānti nāsikāgraṃ* (ed. °*kāyāṃ*) *karaṃ prati*. (*Kālikāpurāṇa* 59.52–55, trans. K. Rijk van Kooj). In the Chowkhamba Sanskrit series edition consulted, these verses appear as *Kālikāpurāṇa* 57.52–55. The passage on *karaśuddhi* in the *Gandharvatantra* (partly quoted in the *Śāktānandataraṅginī* 7.42c–44) has a very similar text. Notably in this version, the smelling at the flower is said to please the deities. Moreover, it is added that all hindrances are removed by throwing the flower away: *aṅgulyagrāṇi śuddhāni puṣpasya grahaṇād bhavet | mardanāt karayoḥ śuddhir nirmañchanat tu pṛṣṭhayoḥ | ghrāṇād devāś ca tuṣyanti tīrthānāṃ ca samāgamaḥ | prakṣepāt* (*Gandharvatantra* 9.9a: *kṣepanāt Śāktānandataraṅginī* 7.43c) *sarvavighnānāṃ dūrasaṃsthānam eva ca | durgandhocchiṣṭasaṃsparśadūṣaṇaṃ karayos tu yat | ajñātarūpaṃ tat sarvaṃ nāśayet vidhināmunā* (*Gandharvatantra* 9.7c–10b); cp. *Tārābhaktisudhārṇava*, p. 150 (citing the *Uttaratantra*).

[18] For example, *Mahānirvāṇatantra* 5.91–92 (without smelling the flower); *Puraścaryārṇavatantra* 3.150–153, *Tārābhaktisudhārṇava*, p. 149 (see next fn.); Tripathi 2004, pp. 148, 177–78 (without smelling the flower).

Thus, a bad smell is removed by a pleasant one, and the hands themselves are rendered fragrant.[19] Not only the hands, but also the nose (and perhaps the breath) are purified by floral scents. It would be useful to investigate the extent to which the Tantric rite of *karaśuddhi*, mostly prescribed after taking one's seat and before proceeding to the "purification of the elements (of the body)" (*bhūtaśuddhi*), is related to the abovementioned Smārta rite of the removal of human scent, both conceptually and structurally. It is sufficient for the purposes of the present study to note that the ability of a flower to purify is intimately linked to its fragrance.

Some flower species are particularly famous for their power to purify. One of the prime examples is the *tulasī* plant, the fragrant holy basil (*Ocimum tenuiflorum* L.), worshipped in many Hindu households and regarded in Hindu mythology as an emblem of purity.[20] The *Padmapurāṇa*, usually considered a late representative of Puranic literature, devotes much space to praising this plant. It is said that wherever the wind blows after having caught the fragrance of *tulasī*, the directions and elements are purified (*Padmapurāṇa* 6.23.33). Various other benefits are detailed, which include the following: when a follower of Viṣṇu smells a leaf of *tulasī*, all sin that exists in his body disappears; bodily ailments suddenly perish when the fragrance of *tulasī* enters the nose; and joy stays in the house of one who takes delight in smelling the leaf of *tulasī* (*Padmapurāṇa* 7.11.135–137).

Flowers in general, and certain species in particular, may be considered pure; but in most cases their purity is vulnerable. Apart from very prominent species for which exemptions are made, some of which are even ascribed the status of *pavitras*, "purifying agents," which theoretically cannot therefore be polluted (MALINAR 2009, p. 35),[21] the general rules for *pūjā* flowers feature long lists of circumstances, actions, and substances that can afflict the purity of flowers or, more precisely, their suitability as offerings. Flowers are considered unfit for worship in the following circumstances: when torn or faded; when they have stood over night; when they have been carried with the left hand or carried when greeting someone; when they are packed in a garment or in certain leaves; when they have previously fallen to the ground or on one's seat; when they have been touched by the lower parts of the body; or spoilt by insects, worms, or hair (ZOTTER 2013, pp. 297–98).

[19] Cf. *sraggandhapuṣpāṇy ādāya candanāktāni mantravit | mardayitvā karau samyak surabhīkṛtya sādhakaḥ* (*Tārābhaktisudhārṇava*, p. 149, citing the *Uttaratantra*).

[20] For further details on myths and rituals related to the purity of the *tulasī* plant, see ZOTTER (2013, p. 238).

[21] The ritual purity of the *pavitras* is not completely inviolable. According to the *Gṛhyasaṅgraha* (2.85–87), some of the classical "purifying agents," namely the Brahmin, the fire, the mantra, and the *kuśa* grass (here called *darbha*), which generally do not turn into *nirmālya* by ritual use, do so on certain occasions.

From the above examples, we may conclude that the purifying quality flowers possess is transferrable, amongst other means, by smelling them. Their fragrance itself is possibly at the foundation of their purity. However, in contrast to the *pavitras*, the Brahmanical instruments for creating purity that resist pollution, the purity of most of the flowers can be exhausted and is easily spoilt. For this reason, it must be carefully guarded.

Bewildering the senses

Apart from the notion of the purity of a flower and its ability to purify, there is another, actually more prominent association in Sanskrit literature, which might even be understood as opposed to the former quality. Flowers are associated with the intensification of bodily sensations far more often than with the downplaying of the carnal character of the body and its associated impurities. Associations between the reproductive organs of plants and human bodily pleasures are widespread and multifaceted in different "Cultures of Flowers" (Goody 1993). Very typical in epic and Puranic literature is to read of charming forests in spring, their trees covered with flowers, replete with the buzzing of bees, and resounding with the calls of mating birds. In such depictions, Kāmadeva, the Indian cupid, striking his targets with arrows made of flowers (*puṣpabāṇa*), is not far away, either explicitly or implicitly. In some of these stories, the scent of various flowers figures prominently, and is said to have a profound effect on living beings.

The 9th chapter of the *Viṣṇupurāṇa* relates the story of the seer Durvāsas, who is a partial incarnation of the god Śiva and is notorious for his violent temper. He curses the king of the gods and overlord of the three worlds, Indra, because the latter has disregarded a garland of flowers presented by the seer.[22] Durvāsas had taken the *unmattavrata*, probably meaning that he followed an observance that featured transgressions of socially accepted behavior and purity rules (as some Śaiva ascetics do in imitation of the *unmatta* aspect of Śiva). The story starts with an account of how the seer himself obtained the garland in question, and how he presented it to Indra:

> Durvāsas, who was a partial incarnation of Śiva, wandered the earth. The seer saw a divine garland in the hand of a Vidyādharī (a semi-divine being), by the smell of which, O Brahmin, that forest of heavenly trees[23] was thoroughly

[22] The garland is considered to be the abode of good fortune (*śrī*). Accordingly, Durvāsas puts a curse on Indra to be deprived of *śrī*. Thereafter, all righteousness and prosperity in the three worlds over which Indra rules fades away, and is only restored after the gods and demons have churned the milk ocean for the nectar of immortality (*amṛta*).

[23] *Santānaka* is one of the five trees said to grow in Indra's heaven.

> perfumed and became extremely enjoyable for those who roamed the wood. Seeing this magnificent wreath, the Brahmin who had taken the *unmatta* vow, then asked the nicely-hipped bride of a Vidyādhara for it. Upon his request, the large-eyed spouse of the Vidyādhara with delicate limbs handed him the garland, greeting him respectfully. The Brahmin who had assumed the form of a lunatic (*unmattarūpadhṛk*) took hold of the wreath, put it on his own head, and went on roaming the earth. He saw the overlord of the three worlds, the husband of Śacī (i.e. Indra) together with the (other) gods approaching, standing on the mad (*unmatta*) Airāvata, (his elephant). And the seer, behaving like a mad man (*unmattavat*), grasped the wreath, full of intoxicated (*unmatta*) bees, from his own head and threw it towards the king of the immortals. Seized by the king of immortals and placed on Airāvata's head, the wreath shone like the river Ganges on the peak of mount Kailāsa. The elephant, his eyes blinded by passion (i.e. ruttish), threw the wreath with his tusk, which had been attracted by the smell, to the ground as soon as he had smelt it.[24]

In this account, as in the passage discussed earlier, there is a conspicuous use of words formed from the Sanskrit verbal root *mad*, to "gladden," here more often prefixed to *unmad*, "to madden." On the one hand, while describing Durvāsas, the line between the ascetic modus of the *unmattavrata* and the genuine lunatic (*unmatta*) is played with. On the other, the animal's reaction is revealing: Indra's elephant, and the precise word chosen here is "the resisting" (*vāraṇa*), is conquered by the smell of the garland, which renders him *madāndha*, that is to say, "ruttish." A similar effect is described in another Puranic story concerning the scent of the *damanaka* plant. Questioned by Yudhiṣṭhira as to the proper form of the worship of deities with *damanaka* in one of the spring months (Caitra), Kṛṣṇa recounts the legendary origin of the plant:

> Formerly on mount Mandara, the abode of the gods, grew the *damanaka* tree, rich in fragrance, licked by swarms of bees. When the divine maidens smelt its scent, which should not be smelt, they sang and laughed being subject to intoxication (*unmāda*) by passion (*madana*). The seers abandoned their penances and hurried home. They took no more delight in studying the Veda or in contemplation. And

[24] *Durvāsāḥ śaṅkarasyāṃśaś cacāra pṛthivīm imām | sa dadarśa srajaṃ divyāṃ ṛṣir vidyādharīkare || santānakānām akhilaṃ yasyā gandhena vāsitam | atisevyam abhūd brahmaṁs tad vanaṃ vanacāriṇām || unmattavratadhṛg vipraḥ sa dṛṣtvā śobhanāṃ srajam | tāṃ yayāce varārohāṃ vidyādharavadhūṃ tataḥ || yācitā tena tanvāṅgī mālāṃ vidyādharāṅganā | dadau tasmai viśālākṣī sādaraṃ praṇipatya tam || tām ādāyātmano mūrdhni srajam unmattarūpadhṛk || kṛtvā sa vipro maitreya paribabhrāma medinīm || sa dadarśa samāyāntam unmattairāvatasthitam | trailokyādhipatiṃ devaṃ saha devaiḥ śacīpatim || tām ātmanaḥ sa śirasaḥ srajam unmattaṣaṭpadām | ādāyāmararājāya cikṣeponmattavanmuniḥ || gṛhītvāmararājena srag airāvatamūrdhani | nyastā rarāja kailāsaśikhare jāhnavī yathā || madāndhakāritākṣo 'sau gandhākṛṣṭena vāraṇaḥ | kareṇāghrāya cikṣepa tāṃ srajaṃ dharaṇītale* (*Viṣṇupurāṇa* 9.2–10).

the sulky women's mind, which had broken off from the lover on account of a transgression, was consoled again by the smell.[25]

The behavior of animals, divine maidens, and seers under the spell of the literally "overpowering" (*damana*) fragrance of the plant is described in terms that carry strong connotations of sexual excitement. More explicit in this regard is a passage in the *Mahābhārata* (1.57.38–40) with the actual forest scene as an interpolation.[26] According to this story, King Vasu went hunting for an animal to be offered in ancestor worship. He set out in order to fulfill his ritual duty; but his mind stayed back home as he knew his wife Girikā to be in her fertile period. Having wandered through a forest in spring, he rested under an *aśoka* tree, and "having smelled a delightful perfume from the flowers, mingled with sweet smells, carried along by the wind, he attained joy"[27] and shed his semen, which he collected with a leaf.

In all three examples, the intense scent of flowers renders living beings what we would call "out of their senses." However, taking into account what Angelika MALINAR has said in this volume about the conception of senses in the Sāṃkhya philosophy, it would perhaps be more appropriate to speak of senses "on the loose," with the loss of control of the senses resulting in states of intoxication or sexual arousal.

A flower seems to be a very suitable item for such an attribution. Far from being limited to scent, a close connection between flowers and women — and eroticism in general — is attested in Sanskrit literature. The sending of flowers as gifts and the decoration of oneself or beds with flowers are all standard tropes of lovers' interaction. In religious traditions as well, especially in those of the Kaulas, a particular movement within the Śaiva Tantric traditions, the identification of human reproduction and plant reproduction is highly developed. In such comparisons, the bodies of goddesses or women are identified with flowers or trees, and anatomical analogies between flowers and human genitals are drawn.[28] The *aparājitā* flower's (Figure 3) striking physical appearance speaks for itself, and finds an echo in both its Sanskrit and Latin names as

---

[25] *Purā surāṇāṃ āvāse mandare cārukandare | gandhādhārī kulālīḍho* (*gandhāḍhyālikulālīḍho* conj. J.J. Meyer) *jāto damanakas taruḥ || tasya gandham anāghreyam āghrāya surayoṣitaḥ | madanonmādavaśagā gāyanti ca hasanti ca || ṛṣayo niyamāṃs tyaktvā prādravanta gṛhān prati | na vedādhyayane dhyāne ratis teṣāṃ babhūva ha || aparādhād vighaṭitaṃ yad babhūva priye param | mānasaṃ māninīnāṃ tu punar gandhena saṃdhitam* (*Bhaviṣyottarapurāṇa* 133.4–7; for a German translation see MEYER 1937, p. 51).

[26] For a translation and analysis of this passage, see MCHUGH (2012, pp. 98–99).

[27] *Madhugandhaiś ca saṃpṛktaṃ puṣpagandhaṃ manoramam | vāyunā preryamāṇaṃ tam āghrāya mudam anvagat* (text and translation cited according to MCHUGH 2012).

[28] See DYCZKOWSKI (2004, pp. 279–81), WHITE (2006, pp. 115–22), ZOTTER (2013, pp. 345–49).

Figure 3: Due to its characteristic appearance the flower of the *aparājitā* plant (*Clitoria ternatea* L.) is intimately associated with the female body in Hindu Tantric traditions. Photo taken by the author in Allahabad in January 2002.

yonipuṣpa (Sanskrit) and *Clitoria ternatea* (Latin), might suffice to illustrate this point. The aforesaid might be related back to flowers as *pūjā* offerings, and in so doing add another layer of connotation to the flower and its smell therein: the moment of sensual arousal.

Smell and breath

The following is little more than a marginal note; however it may be taken as illustrative of the range of connotations that the smelling of flowers in *pūjā* can assume, especially when this act is considered in relation to a closely related action, namely breathing.

Breath (*prāṇa*) and breath control (*prāṇāyāma*) form vast topics of their own. Suffice it here to say that *prāṇāyāma* occupies much space in the guidelines for *pūjā*, especially in those of the Tantric schools. As with the revered deity's body, the devotee's body also needs to be ritually constructed and divinized. According to a famous Tantric dictum, one should worship a deity only if one has become a deity oneself (*devo bhūtvā devaṃ yajet*). Hence, the practitioner's body is prepared by acts of purification, such as the *karaśuddhi* treated above, and is ritually recreated. What specially sets Tantric *pūjā* apart from its Smārta counterpart is the awakening of the deity in the practitioner's heart, and its projection into the image from where it will be retrojected at the end of the worship. Theological positions may differ; but all descriptions of the technical procedure of which I am aware follow a common model, according to which the deity is drawn from the heart of the worshipper and exhaled through the nose. In many accounts, a flower plays a central role in this procedure.[29] The practitioner holds a flower under his nose, meditates on the

[29] The description follows TRIPATHI (2004, pp. 296–97, 367), who has studied the temple ritual in the Jagannātha temple in Puri (Odisha). For similar accounts, see for example, DAVIS (2000, pp. 128–33); DIEHL (1956, pp. 117–18); GUPTA (1979, p. 149); and VAN KOOJ (introduction to the translation of the *Kālikāpurāṇa*, p. 19). The *Kālikāpurāṇa*

deity in his heart, and speaks a mantra. The deity emerges in the heart and is led through the central channel (*suṣumnā*) to the point between his eyebrows, the *ājñācakra*. From there it is made to descend through the right nostril, and by exhaling enters the flower, which is then placed on the head of the image or into the diagram (*yantra*), depending on the type of icon employed. With another mantra, the deity is made present in the *yantra* or the heart of the image. When retracting the deity, the process is inverted: by means of a flower, the deity leaves the icon, is inhaled through the left nostril, and is sent back to the heart of the practitioner.

In Tantric *pūjā,* the worshipper makes his body a vessel for the divine presence after extensive purifications. Flowers can be instrumental in the purification process, but can also serve as a vehicle for the deities imbued with their presence, or again, be emptied by smelling them. Thus, at least according to the Tantric conception of the human body, deities seem to be able to travel by means of the divinized worshipper's breath.

Flowers beyond smell, smell beyond flowers

Dealing with the smell and the smelling of flowers in a religious context offers interesting insights. However, smell is not everything. Flowers address more than one sense. Actually, more often than being depicted in the act of smelling flowers, deities are said to see flower offerings or someone worshipping them with flowers. Accordingly, flowers are much more categorized according to their visual appearance. Moreover, the texts request that the flowers to be offered should have color, flavor, *and* odor.[30] In this light, the authorities' demand for smell may more aptly be understood to guarantee the offering of a "complete" flower.[31]

A flower can be seen, tasted, touched, and smelt. Except for audition, all senses are addressed (cf. McHugh 2012, 228). That a flower applied in *pūjā* is appreciated as a synaesthetic ritual object is also mirrored in the aforementioned passage in the *Mahābhārata* (13.101.19–21). There, another Sanskrit word for "flower," *sumanas*, is verbally played with — establishing a link between a flower and a good (*su-*) state of mind (*manas*). Neither the sense of smell nor sight alone is in focus here; rather, it is the mind, *manas*, the organ superordinate to the sense faculties (cf. A. Malinar's contribution in this volume). The passage in the *Mahābhārata* states very clearly that it is the deity whose *manas* is

---

describes an alternative method according to which the deity exhaled through the nostril is transported with the help of a specific gesture (*mudrā*) and mantras alone (ibid.).

[30] For example, *Puṣpacintāmaṇi* 2.22cd, 2.80cd.

[31] Thus, an expression like: "only by smelling *tulasī* Sundarī gets angry" (*tulasīghrāṇamātreṇa kruddhā bhavati sundarī; Puṣpacintāmaṇi* 4.95, citing the *Vārāhītantra*) implies the warning that the goddess will become furious at the least notice of the *tulasī* plant, underlining Tripurasundarī's extreme aversion to it.

attended to by the gift of a flower.[32] When the deity has been treated respectfully and is satisfied (*tuṣṭa*) or happy (*prīta*), the devotee may expect to be favored. The worship is then considered to be "fruitful" (*saphala*). As commonly stated in digests on *pūjā* flowers, the worship is "fruitless" (*niṣphala*), or the deity may even get angry, if wrong flowers or impure flowers are employed.

The sense perceptions of the devotee, on the other hand, are not the concern of the Sanskrit texts under discussion. But, if one was allowed to step a bit further from textual evidence, one may view a flower as a material link that sensually stimulates the relationship between deity and worshipper. It enhances and beautifies the ritual atmosphere. The worshipper is exposed to material perceptible by all of his senses, which he perceives in communion with the deity worshipped. In that sense, a flower may be supportive in realizing the presence of, or the worshipper's identity with the deity, depending on the theological position adopted.

However, flowers are not the only means to delight the senses in *pūjā*. Many other services offered to the deity beautify, stimulate attention, induce bodily pleasure, and satisfy. The deity is duly welcomed, washed, dressed, decorated, fed; the deity is circumambulated; bells or conch shells are rung. Singing and dancing may form part of the *pūjā*. Very common — and possibly a kind of historical nucleus (see EINOO 1996) — is a set of five services (*pañcopacāra*): *gandha* — fragrant substance, *puṣpa* — flower, *dhūpa* — incense, *dīpa* — light, and *naivedya* — food.

Gandha is a paste serving as body ointment (*anulepana*) that is made of scented substances, mostly of sandalwood (*candana*). The offering of *dhūpa* consists of the burning of fragrant material. In contrast to the latter two perfumery products, the scent of a flower diffuses by itself. It needs neither preparation as in the case of a fragrant paste nor activation as in the lighting of an incense stick.

Overall, while scent cannot be separated from the flower, it presents but one aspect of its role as a sensual object employed in *pūjā* for the satisfaction of the deity's mind. Without scent, however, a flower is incomplete, at least according to Brahmanical reasoning.[33]

Conclusion

The scent of flowers is central to the discussion of the role of smell in South Asian religious tradition. The smelling of a flower in *pūjā* can be linked to

[32] For example, *tasmāt sumanasaḥ proktā yasmāt tuṣṭanti devatāḥ*; *Mahābhārata* 13.101.20cd.

[33] In this context, it might be worth noting that some of the flowers very popular in worship traditions are scentless. Some, but not all, of these are accounted for by exceptional rules. Such inconsistencies suggest that the rules for *pūjā* flowers do not constitute a monolithic system but rather a pool of homogeneous traditions for which different arguments are found to synchronize them with Brahmanical scholasticism.

consumption: it can be compared to eating, be it in the context of abstinence from consumption by the worshipper or that of consumption by the deity. It may also be linked to acts of ritual purification: to this end floral scent is smelt, is applied to the limbs, or pervades the very air of a *pūjā*. There are stories in Hindu mythology that tell of floral scents provoking the loss of control of the senses and stimulating erotic arousal. Deities not only smell flowers but may themselves be transported by human breath, with a flower serving as their vessel. However, a treatment of the aesthetic effect of a flower cannot be limited to its scent alone.

The cultural understandings of flowers treated here by no means exhausts the range of dispositions and interpretations that may or may not come into play in ritual performances, where they might pre-configure the actual perceptions of a worshipper. Moreover, it can be expected that the stress will be laid differently depending on many factors, from personal taste to traditional background. Hence, an orthoprax Smārta Brahmin may see the purity of the flower, whereas in Bhakti traditions the scent of a flower may point to simplicity; to something that is available for all; to something that distributes its fragrance "for free" in contrast to costly perfumery products. It is also imaginable that a Tantric practitioner might emphasize the sexual connotation of flowers.

Thus, the present analysis in no way claims to be a comprehensive treatment of the semantics of floral scent when it is part of an act of Hindu worship. At best, I have caught some of the "aromas" that surface in verbal expressions of the role and power of floral scent. In closing, I shall return to the Nepalese song with which I began. This song is sung at marriage, at the point when a mother turns into a mother-in-law and a girl into a bride and daughter-in-law. In this socially dramatic situation, the women praise the scent of the jasmine flower. The line invites several interpretations. It may be taken as advice to follow the example of a flower's scent — silent and smiling — or to think of the pleasing effects of the scent of a flower. In either understanding, the result is the same. The scent of a flower captures a cultural ideal. However tense the emotional situation may be, a woman should keep smiling. In this way, from *pūjā* to euphoria amongst gods and men, from a vehicle for the gods to an exemplar for the Nepalese bride, flowers and their scent are appreciated and cultivated in South Asian religious traditions.

References

Sanskrit texts

Aitareyabrāhmaṇa (2008): Haug, M. (Ed. and Trans.): The Aitareya Brahmanam of the Rigveda. Containing the Earliest Speculations of the Brahmans on the Meaning of the Sacrificial Prayers and on the Origin, Performance, and Sense of the Rites of the Vedic Religion. – Delhi.

Bhaviṣyapurāṇa (1959): Kṛṣṇadāsa, K. (Ed.): Bhaviṣya mahāpurāṇa. – Bombay.

Gandharvatantra (1986): Rai, Ram Kumar (Ed.): Gandharvatantram. – Varanasi.

Gṛhyasaṅgraha: See Bloomfield 1881.

KĀLIKĀPURĀṆA (1972): ŚĀSTRĪ, V. (Ed.): Kālikāpurāṇam. – Varanasi.
KĀLIKĀPURĀṆA (1972): KOOIJ, Karel Rijk van (Trans.): Worship of the Goddess according to the Kālikāpurāṇa, Vol. 1, A Translation with an Introduction and Notes of Chapters 54–69. – Leiden.
KATHA ĀRAṆYAKA (2004): WITZEL, M. (Ed.): Kaṭha Āraṇyaka. Critical Edition with a Translation into German and an Introduction. – Cambridge (MA).
MAHĀBHĀRATA (1933–68): SUKTHANKAR, V.S. et al. (Eds.): The Mahābhārata. For the First Time Critically Edited. 35 Vols. – Poona.
MAHĀNIRVĀṆATANTRA (1929). WOODROFFE, J.G. (Ed.): Mahānirvāṇatantra with the Commentary of Hariharānanda Bharati. – Madras.
PADMAPURĀṆA (1984): The Padmamahāpurāṇam. Vol. 3. – Delhi.
PARAŚURĀMAKALPASŪTRA (1999): SASTRI, M. et al. (Eds.): Paraśurāmakalpasūtra: With Rameśvara's Commentary. – Baroda.
PŪJĀPAṄKAJABHĀSKARA (1996). – Bombay.
PURAŚCARYĀRṆAVA (1985): JHA, M. (Ed.): Puraścaryārṇava of His Majesty Shri Pratap Singh Sah Dev King of Nepal. A Treatise Dealing with Theory and Practice of Tantric Worship. – Delhi.
PUṢPACINTĀMAṆI. See Zotter (2013).
ŚĀKTĀNANDATARAṄGIṆĪ (1987): TRIPĀṬHĪ, R. (Ed.): Śāktānandataraṅgiṇī of Brahmānandagiri. – Varanasi.
TĀRĀBHAKTISUDHĀRṆAVA (1940): BHAṬṬĀCHĀRYA, P. (Ed.): Tārā-bhakti-sudhārṇava: With an Introduction in English. – Calcutta.
VIṢṆUPURĀṆA (1997): PATHAK, M.M. (Ed.): The Critical Edition of the Viṣṇupurāṇam. Vol. 1. – Vadodara.

Secondary literature

BHATTACHARYA, R.S. (1983): A Purāṇic Objective Division of Smell (*gandha*) not Found in the Works on Philosophy. In: Purāṇa, Vol. 25.2, pp. 246–53.
BLOOMFIELD, M. (1881): Das Gṛhyasaṃgrahapariçishṭa des Gobhilaputra. In: Zeitschrift der deutschen morgenländischen Gesellschaft, Vol. 35, pp. 533–87.
BÖHTLINGK, O. (1865): Sanskrit-Wörterbuch. Vol. 4: n – ph. – St. Petersburg.
BÖHTLINGK, O. (1882): Sanskrit-Wörterbuch. In kürzerer Fassung. Vol. 3: ta – na. – St. Petersburg.
BRUNNER(-Lachaux), H. (1968): Somaśambhupaddhati. Vol. 2: Rituel Ocassionels dans la tradition śivaïte de l'Inde du Sud selon Somaśambhu. I: Pavitrārohaṇa, Damanapūjā et Prāyaścitta. Texte, Traduction et Notes. – Pondichéry.
BRUNNER(-Lachaux), H. (1969): De la consommation du nirmālya de Śiva. In: Journal Asiatique, Vol. 257, pp. 213–63.
BÜHNEMANN, G. (1988): *Pūjā.* A Study in Smārta Ritual. – Vienna.
COLAS, G. (2006): Jalons pour une histoire de conceptions indiennes de yajña. In: COLAS, G./TARABOUT, G. (Eds.): Rites hindous, transferts et transformations. – Paris, pp. 343–87.
DAVIS, R.H. (2000): Worshiping Śiva in Medieval India. Ritual in an Oscillating Universe. – Delhi.
DUDA, P. (2005): Flowers and Leaves in the Worship of Hindu Deities. In: VACEK, J. (Ed.): Pandanus '05. Nature in Literature, Myth and Ritual. – Prague, pp. 113–120.

DUDA, P. (2006): Flowers in Hindu Ritual Literature. In: VACEK, J. (Ed.): Pandanus '06. Nature in Literature and Ritual. – Prague, pp. 287–97.

DYCZKOWSKI, M.S.G. (2004): A Journey into the World of Tantras. – Varanasi.

EINOO, S. (1996): The Formation of the *Pūjā* Ceremony. In: Studien zur Indologie und Iranistik, Vol. 20, pp. 73–87.

FULLER, C.J. (1992): The Camphor Flame. Popular Hinduism and Society in India. – Princeton.

GONDA, J. (1975): Atharvaveda 11, 7. In: GONDA, J., Selected Studies. Presented to the Author by the Staff of the Oriental Institute, Utrecht University, on the Occasion of his 70th Birthday. Vol. 3, Sanskrit. Grammatical and Philological Studies. – Leiden, pp. 439–74.

GONDA, J. (1985): The Ritual Functions and Significance of Grasses in the Religion of Veda. – Amsterdam.

GOODY, J. (1993): The Culture of Flowers. – Cambridge.

LAWLESS, H. T. (1997): Olfactory Psychophysics. In: BEAUCHAMP, G.K. and BARTOSHUK, L. (Eds.): Tasting and Smelling. – San Diego (et al.), pp. 125–74.

MALINAR, A. (2009): Reinigung und Transformation von 'Unreinem' im Hinduismus. In: MALINAR, A. and VÖHLER, M. (Eds.): Un/Reinheit. Konzepte und Praktiken im Kulturvergleich. – Munich, pp. 19–45.

MCHUGH, J.A. (2007): The Classification of Smells and the Order of the Senses in Indian Religious Traditions. In: Numen, Vol. 54, pp. 374–419.

MCHUGH J.A. (2012): Sandalwood and Carrion: Smell in Indian Religion and Culture. – Oxford.

MEYER, J.J. (1937): Trilogie altindischer Mächte und Feste der Vegetation. Vol. 1, Kāma. Der altindische Liebesgott als Vegetationsdämon und sein Fest. – Leipzig.

MIŚRA, R. and MIŚRA, L. (2004): Nityakarma-pūjāprakāśa. – Gorakhpur.

NOWOTNY, F. (1957): Das Pujavidhinirupana des Trimalla. In: Indo-Iranian Journal, Vol. 1, pp. 109–54.

THIEME, P. (1939): Indische Wörter und Sitten. In: Zeitschrift der deutschen morgenländischen Gesellschaft, Vol. 93, pp. 105–23 (the section on pūjā was published in English as: Pūjā. In: Journal of Oriental Research Madras, Vol. 27 [1957–58], pp. 1–16).

TRIPATHI, G.C. (2004): Communication with God. The Daily pūjā Ceremony in the Jagannātha Temple. – Delhi.

WEZLER, A. (1978): Die wahren "Speiseresteesser" (Skt. vighasāśin). – Mainz.

WHITE, D.G. (2006): Kiss of the Yoginī. "Tantric Sex" in its South Asian Contexts. – Chicago.

WILDEN, E (2000): Der Kreislauf der Opfergaben im Veda. – Stuttgart.

WITZEL, M. (1997): Macrocosm, Mesocosm, and Microcosm. The Persistent Nature of 'Hindu' Beliefs and Symbolic Forms. In: International Journal of Hindu Studies, Vol. 1 (1997), pp. 501–39.

ZOTTER, A. (2013): Von Blüten, Göttern und Gelehrten. Die Behandlung von pūjā-Blüten im Puṣpacintāmaṇi. Text, Herkunft und Deutung eines nepalischen Kompendiums. Leipzig (http://nbn-resolving.de/urn:nbn:de:bsz:15-qucosa-102174, accessed September 1, 2013).

Axel Michaels

Untouchability and Tactility in Hindu Death Rituals*

Touching and pollution

"We should expect the orifices of the body to symbolize its specially vulnerable points," notes Mary DOUGLAS (1966, p. 121). In the Hindu context, all liquid excretions — sweat, saliva, semen, blood, especially menstrual blood, excrement — but also hair, fingernails, and toenails, can indeed be polluting if someone else comes in contact with them. Thus, touch and pollution are intrinsically linked in India. As a consequence, bodily contact between people who are not of the same age, gender, family, sub-caste, or status group is often avoided. Until recently, social kissing, for instance, was not allowed, and it is still taboo among the more traditional groups. It is still not fully accepted even among the middle class:

> Not so long ago, kissing was regarded as a disgusting western habit (like taking tub baths, or using toilet paper instead of a *lota*), violating our deeply ingrained taboos about *chhua-chhoot* and personal hygiene, and blamed for spreading viruses, pimples and other infections. Remember the time it was banned in Bollywood and other regional films? In romantic scenes, censors allowed the kiss only through coy suggestion — usually depicted through a butterfly alighting on a flower, or two blossoms bending towards each other. Until the early '90s, for most Indians kissing was an intimate act, not for public display unless you were

---

*This article deals with the notions of untouchability and tactility in Hindu death rituals, especially the *sapiṇḍīkaraṇa*. It also includes in the appendix the translation of chapter 95 of the Nepālī law text *Mulukī Ain* of 1854 in which the rules for touching and removing a dead body are laid down in a detailed form that one does not find in the Sanskrit sources, although the text is based on them (on [un]touchability in general, see HARPER 1964; DUMONT 1980; MARRIOTT 1976 and 1990 [introduction]; MARRIOTT and INDEN 1973 and 1977; ALEX 2008). My contribution is partly based on previous publications (GUTSCHOW and MICHAELS 2005; MICHAELS 2004, pp. 178–180). Gutschow and Michaels 2005 also contains a DVD film by N. Gutschow, A. Michaels, and Ch. Bau on the *sapiṇḍīkaraṇa* ritual in Nepal, called "Handling Death: A Death Ritual of the Newars in Bhaktapur, Nepal." This film shows how intensively the deceased (*preta*) is touched and shaped in the form of balls (*piṇḍa*) made of flour.

> kissing babies and chubby-cheeked kids. Acquaintances were greeted with a *namaste*, handshake or just a smile; friends with a hi or, if you were seeing them after a long time, a hug (MEHTA 1990).

The extent of the pollution depends on status, age, sex, and kinship proximity of the persons in question. In Hinduism, it is generally not only the individual body that is polluted, but, under some circumstances, the whole extended family (MANDELBAUM 1970, pp. 192–93; DAS 1985).[1] In the case of death, for example, the extended family is afflicted with impurity by degrees. Pollution, in the Indian context, therefore, is generally contagious. Thus, the pollution of the body is not a question of personal sensuous perception and feelings, like disgust, but rather the violation of purity norms of an extended family and the position of the individual in it.

The Western dualistic separation between material and spiritual, substance and attribute, is not appropriate for India (see MICHAELS and WULF, and MALINAR, both in this volume). Emotional qualities like sorrow, hatred and love, or the senses are understood as subtle substances and, thus, as material. The same holds true for other substances that the body excretes through its "windows," the sense organs — that is, the view, the smell, the sound, etc. All this is part of the essence and nature of the individual, and if somebody sensuously perceives it, it is regarded as touching and potentially polluting. "Untouchables,"[2] therefore, had to keep a suitable distance and live outside the village in some cases. Even their name is an expression of status:[3] they are "untouchable" because they are regarded as impure and, thus, inferior. Any form of touching them would pollute somebody from a higher caste. The *Mulukī Ain* (Ch. 87, p. 28) is clear about this: members of the pure castes are allowed to cross a river over a bridge or in a boat together with "untouchables" only if they do not touch them. The term for untouchables in this text is *achuti* — literally, "somebody who may not be touched" — or *pāni nacalnyā choyi chimo hālnuparnyā jāt*: "the caste from whom water cannot be accepted and a touch (of its members) requires water purification (*chiṭo* literally means 'a drop of water')" (cf. HÖFER 1979, pp. 45 and 67).

Any form of gross and subtle "physical" contact can, therefore, be problematic. To give some examples from the Dharmaśāstra for such subtle "physical" contact (cf. also AKTOR 2010 with more references): Touching even the shadow of an "untouchable," nowadays generally called *dalit*, could

---

[1] Just as pollution can be passed on, religious merit (*puṇya*) can also be transmitted: the wife who goes to the temple every morning, brings back *puṇya* for her husband and family. But this is another topic.

[2] DUMONT (1980, pp. 131–37); MOFFAT (1979); MENDELSOHN/VICZIANI (1998); AKTOR (2008, 2010); AKTOR/DELIÈGE (2010).

[3] On the term "untouchability," which was introduced by Sir Herbert Risley in the 1901 Census of India, see CHARSLEY (1996), and later.

previously make a traditional Brahmin immediately take a ritual bath. Touching the ornaments or cloths of a woman or sitting on her bed could be regarded as adultery (MANU VIII. 357). An "untouchable" (*caṇḍāla*), a pig, a cock, a dog, menstruating woman, or a eunuch should not look at eating Brahmins because such a "touch" by an illegitimate view would spoil or destroy the sacrifice (MANU III. 239–41). For the same reason, one should not accept cooked food which has been touched by feet or at which the killer of a Brahmin has looked (MANU IV. 207–8).

These examples show that pollution is regarded as a substance or a quality that cannot be separated from its originator or bearer. Dust and sweat on the feet are not impure in principle; it is only so depending on the person in question, and the relation to another person who touches him or her. Touching somebody is, therefore, only possible under certain circumstances. These are periods of emergency (*āpad*),[4] as well as intimate and hierarchical relations. And, one also has to differentiate between "permanent untouchability of caste and the temporary untouchability of the home in connection with death, menstruation, and childbirth" (AKTOR 2010, p. 877).

In intimate, especially familial and matrimonial relations, the members of a group share and transfer bodily substances without getting polluted. This concerns, for instance, the marriages or parentage, baby massage, sharing cigarettes among males, and bodily proximity and closeness, especially among young children (ALEX 2008). The biologically related kin group forms one social body (DAVID 1973). Gabi ALEX (2008, p. 532) provides an intriguing example from Tamil Nadu: after a period of seclusion with her mother, a new born baby is placed naked on the floor in the centre of the house, and by this physical act, it establishes a relationship with the members of the household; in Tamil this ritual act is called *totu*, "to touch." Direct proximity, however, is not intentional touching. Being close together in buses or trains does not necessarily create problems, but intentionally touching women in public would be an affront and insult.

In hierarchical relations, the rule mostly is the following: a younger person touching the feet of an older person, a woman the feet of her husband, or a pilgrim the feet of a statue of a god, are all signs of subordination and respect. Touching the feet is, then, a sign of reverence by self-imposed pollution, "respect pollution" (HARPER 1964, p. 158); otherwise touching somebody with one's foot could be an offense. The handshake was not a usual greeting in India, and has appeared only through Western influence. Conferring a forehead mark (*ṭīkā*) as a gesture of blessing is a significant feature of the purity and higher rank of the one granting the blessing. But here too, the pure gives the impure *grosso modo* the *ṭīkā*, the higher ranking one the lower ranking one, the older the younger, the man the woman. Thus, a little girl (*kumārī*) who is worshipped

[4] Even an "untouchable" woman can act as a mid-wife in the case of an emergency: MA, Ch. 87, p. 10.

as a goddess in the annual Indrajātrā celebrations grants the Nepalese king (or now prime minister) the legitimizing *ṭīkā*, demonstrating her religious superiority, while the king or prime minister presses the forehead sign on certain selected soldiers, officials, and subjects.

Since any form of contact is potentially polluting, liberation-seeking individuals, especially ascetics, try to avoid contact with normal people to a large extent — following the prescriptions of the *Mānavadharmaśāstra* or *Manusmṛti* for the celibate Vedic student who is also a temporal ascetic:

> When a man feels neither elation nor revulsion at hearing, touching, seeing, eating, or smelling anything, he should be recognized as a man who has mastered his organs. Of all these organs, however, if a single one slips away, through that his wisdom slips away, like water through the foot of a skin.[5] By bringing the full range of his organs under control, and by restraining his mind, a man will achieve all his goals without having to shrivel up his body through yoga (MANU 2. 98–100, Trans. P. Olivelle).

Ideally, ascetics do not even greet. The danger in greeting resides in what is given, what produces contact: the hand, the word, the gesture, the look. Greeting (MICHAELS 1997) is not only words. It concerns a world in which speech and names acquire a subtle materiality. And, if something is given, the obligation exists to return the gift, which creates dependence and can, thus, pollute.

Even when a person has ritually purified himself personally after a pollution, he or she is still not pure for all other members of his or her caste. The caste status of purity of the extended family as a whole, can only be elevated collectively and not through the virtuous behavior of the individual.

Biological intervals imply extreme changes of the body and, thus, are extremely polluting. For example, menstruation: it is a common notion among the southern Indian Haviks (HARPER 1964, pp. 158–59) that red ants come into the house (not only to the polluted persons) if a family member touches a menstruating woman; there (and in other sub-castes), a menstruating woman is isolated for days in a separate room without any contact. The *Manusmṛti* is full of prescriptions for menstruation women to avoid any form of contact.[6] Or birth: according to the Dharmaśāstras,[7] the woman in childbirth is on the same level as corpse-bearers or dogs. The prescriptions for birth impurity in the *Mulukī Ain* are the following:

> If the wife gives birth to a child whether a male or female, the others shall not touch the child till the husband performs a ritual bath. The pregnant [mother] shall not be touched for 10 days. If she gets sick during those days and for the medical treatment it becomes necessary to touch her or if she is accidently touched by a

[5] Referring to the water bag made of animal skin.

[6] See for example MANU (3.47; 4.40–42, 57, 208; 5.66, 85, 108; 9.93; 11.88, 174).

[7] MANU (5.58*ff.*); *Vāsiṣṭhadharmasūtra* (5.4–9); *Gautamadharmasūtra* (13.30*ff*).

> person, he shall take a ritual bath and drink a mixture of the five kinds of cow products (*pañcagavya*) for purification if he belongs to a cord-wearer caste.
>
> The kins-men of seven generations of same caste (*dasāhā bhāi*) shall observe the birth impurity for 10 days. [Other] known paternal relatives (*tīn dinyā jñāti bhāi*) shall observe the birth impurity for 3 days. If the news of the birth of a child is heard within those days, one shall observe the birth impurity for the remaining days [only]. The father who gives birth shall observe the birth impurity for [only] 3 days for the birth of a child from the wife taken from the rice unacceptable caste (*bhāta nacalnyā*). The other kins-men shall also observe [it] for 3 days. If the news [of the birth] is heard after passing the time [of the duration of observing the birth impurity], the birth impurity shall not be observed. There is no transgression for observing birth impurity (*Mulukī Ain*, Ch. 96, pp. 13–14).

It is the physical and biological changes that pollutes. Life-cycle turning points like initiation and marriage are also changes that require special purification. In them, the social body changes to a certain extent. A child becomes a Twice-Born, a virginal daughter becomes a wife. These are rites of passage in which the extended family changes because the family roles have to be redefined. The most polluting case is touching a polluted corpse or person after a death incident.

Touching the corpse

Hindu rituals of dying and death do not fundamentally differ from those found in the death ceremonies of other cultures. Although death is feared, the dying person should accept death, should not resist, and should be ritually prepared. Often, there is a special path of death for the corpse — almost a kind of secret path — so that the deceased cannot find his way back. The path of the dead after cremation is uncertain and dangerous; the deceased is dependent on the help and nourishment of the survivors. There are, thus, provisions for his journey, accompanied by prayers and blessings, laying out, and a kind of wake: a funeral procession, special clothing for the dead and for the survivors, a gathering for the dead, death knells, a funeral meal, and a period of mourning that implies the pollution of the extended family members. Death means a certain period of impurity (*aśauca, mṛtakasūtaka, sūtaka*) for the survivors. This generally lasts from 10 to 13 days for close relatives, requires various purification measures, and is "contagious," that is, polluted persons may not be touched. According to the Brahmanical legal texts, only a few persons cannot be polluted or can be polluted only for a short time: these include ascetics, Brahmins who maintain a sacrificial fire, and occasionally the king. The chief mourner, however, remains impure for at least 10 to 13 days, during which he is not to shave, cut his nails, or comb his hair, and is to sleep only on the floor, have no sexual intercourse, and wear no shoes or sewn garments. He is to cook his food by himself on a separate fire, eat only once a day, and use no salt.

On the 10th or 11th day only, he is shaved, bathes, and receives a new Sacred Thread. During this time, the chief mourner is treated almost as an "untouchable," clearly separated from his relatives. And anything touched by him is polluted as well.

> In order to take salt, oil, ghee, honey, brown sugar, sugar, syrup, meat, fruit, herbs, medicine, wooden pot, leaf, clay, curd, milk, dry skin, uncooked grains, metal, untouched water, cloth, cattle, tobacco, spices from the house of a person affected by the impurity of death, one shall not take edible things if touched by him or her. If given by the hands of others but without touching by the hand of such affected person by impurity of death, it shall be allowed to be taken (*Mulukī Ain*, Ch. 96, p. 65).

Hindu rituals of death and dying are a gradual removal of impurity and mortality as well as the new creation of a body in the next world. For a certain period, the deceased (*preta*) still has vital energy, which again will bring death. He, thus, needs a body and a place to live so that — according to the traditional belief — he is to be reborn after temporarily being in heaven(s) or hell(s). If he had no vital energy — like an ascetic — he would not have to be reborn. But, he also leaves behind or transmits this death — bringing negative energy to the survivors, who must protect themselves and the deceased mainly by the purifying forces of water and fire, especially the cremation fire, but also by other means, such as water, gifts, oil, vermilion, new clothes, or, in Nepal, the *āmvaḥ* (or Nepālī *amalā*) fruit. Moreover, special forces and substances (for example, Brahmin, *kuśa* grass, basil, gold, fire offerings, Veda recitations) are seen as eternal, immortal, and indestructible; they therefore can neutralize and filter the death — bringing vital energy. "Knowledge, austerity, fire food, earth, mind, water, smearing with cow dung, wind, rites, sun, time — these are the agents of purification for embodied beings" (Manu 5.105, trans. P. Olivelle). However, despite all ritual measures of caution, they cannot completely dissolve or remove it. The deceased also retains a remnant of it, which lets him become the almost deified ancestor, but also leads to his rebirth.

Pollution, thus, represents a constant threat that calls for techniques to return to the state of purity. Food enters the state of impurity if it is either touched or is left over: such food has to be discarded; others cannot eat it. In case an individual is impure, it is the physical body that has to attain purity again in most cases by taking a bath. He or she washes the feet, hands, the face or the entire body, or rinses the mouth.

Traditionally, it is the business of the "untouchables" to handle the corpse. It is by this duty (as well as by removing waste, skinning animal carcasses, tanning leather, the execution of criminals, etc.) that they are believed to pollute people. They have, therefore, been ostracized and segregated, forced to live outside the settlements, barred from using wells, and prohibited from entering temples.

According to the MANU (5.64*ff.*), anybody who touches the corpse becomes polluted and, therefore, needs special purification. However, there are differences:

> Those who touch the corpse are purified in ten days, but those who offer [water] libations in three (64). A pupil who performs the funerary rites of his deceased teacher, on the other hand, is on par with those who carry a corpse and is purified in ten days (65).[9] ... When someone touches a Divākīrti,[9] a menstruating woman, an outcaste, a woman who has given birth, or a corpse — as also a person who has touched any of these — he is purified by bathing (85) ... After touching a human bone, a Brahmin is purified by bathing if the bone was greasy, but simply by sipping water, touching a cow, or gazing at the sun, if the bone was dry (87) ... After completing the required rite, a Brahmin is purified by touching water, a Kṣatriya his conveyance or weapon, a Vaiśya his goad or reins, and a Śūdra his staff (99) ... If someone willingly follows a corpse, whether it is that of a paternal relative or of someone else, he is purified after he has bathed with his clothes on, touched the fire, and eaten some ghee (103). When one's own people are present, one should never let a Śūdra carry a Brahmin's corpse, for a sacrificial offering defiled by a Śūdra's touch does not lead a person to heaven (104) (MANU 5.64–65, 85, 87, 99, and 103–4; Trans. P. OLIVELLE).

The *Mulukī Ain* of 1854 is even more precise with regard to rules of touching the corpse. This text written in Old Nepālī was the Legal Code of Nepal enacted during the reign of King Surendra Vikrama Śāha (1847–81) and promulgated on the 5th or 6th of January 1854 under the red seals of King Surendra Vikrama Śāha and Crown Prince Trailokya Vikrama Śāha, and the yellow seal of ex-King Rajendra Vikrama Śāha. It was prepared at the initiative of Prime Minister Jaṅga Bahādura Rāṇā (1846–57 AD). Thereafter, it has been amended and enlarged several times. The name of this code itself reveals the influence it underwent, namely, the Persian *ā'īn* together with the later addition of *mulukī*, "royal." The sources of the text, however, are not only Islamic and include the maxims of the Indian Moghul administration, but also Dharmaśāstras and much customary law.

Chapter 95 of the *Mulukī Ain* is titled "On carrying a corpse (*murdā uthāunyā*)." To the best of my knowledge, it is the most detailed traditional legal text on this issue. The translation of this chapter (see Appendix) confirms that touching and carrying the corpse to the cremation ground is polluting and, thus, requires purification, especially if the deceased person is from a different caste. Since, in Nepal removing the corpse is not left to "untouchables" but to the common ancestry (cf. MANU 5.64 mentioned earlier), the text regulates touching the corpse for other caste and family members. It states, for instance, that the lower castes get more polluted than the higher castes, and if somebody

[8] According to most commentaries, he is equal to common ancestry (*sāpiṇḍa*).

[9] Most probably a barber or an "untouchable" (*caṇḍāla*).

from the water-acceptable alcohol-drinker castes[10] carries the corpse of a twice-born class — called cord-wearer caste — he even has to pay a fee (*godāna*) to a Brahmin (p. 1). However, since it is not regarded as an individual offense, it is not a sinful action that needs rehabilitation (*patiyā* or *prāyaścitta*) by the religious judge (*dharmadhikārin*; see MICHAELS 2006, pp. 1 and 7). The *Mulukī Ain* also levies fees on officials if they do not care for a corpse because nobody dares touch it (pp. 2–3, 5), and cares about the beginning moment of death pollution:

> If anybody dies in the house of a *jajamāna* (employer of a priest) and death impurity occurs while a feast to a Brahmin is going on, the Brahmin who is eating shall leave the remaining food. Do not eat again. If (the feast) is not [performed] in the house and news of the death impurity is heard by other kins-men, the Brahmins shall eat after expelling the *jajamāna* out from the kitchen, letting him touch nothing because the food was cooked before the news of impurity was heard (*Mulukī Ain*, Ch. 96, p. 55).

Touching the deceased

The rules for purification after having touched the corpse are in a sharp contrast to how the deceased is treated in the death ritual (*sapiṇḍīkaraṇa*) that is performed to help the departed person (*preta*) to reach the word of the ancestors.

Between the 10th and 13th day, mostly on the 12th day — but sometimes on the 45th — after the death, sacrificial balls or *piṇḍa*s[11] are offered to celebrate the dead person joining the forefathers. It is believed that the messengers of Yama will lead the deceased on his one-year-long journey, during which he will get no water and food; thus, the mourners have to supply him with it. Along with this rite, a bed (*śayyadāna*), water (*jaladāna*), cooking utensils, and food are offered to a Brahmin after which the chief mourner and other mourners bathe, and are ritually purified. New clothes — or sometimes only a new cap — are given to the chief mourner. Among the Newars, on the 13th day, relatives, members of the sub-caste, and neighbors are invited and fed; this marks the conclusion of the intensive period of impurity.

It is believed that the deceased has no fixed realm, and that the rituals carried out build places of refuge for him. He or she is believed to reside in the *piṇḍa*, animals, the wind or air, stones, cotton stripes, or the *liṅga*. The goal of the

[10] For the caste system in the *Mulukī Ain*, see HÖFER (1979, p. 45).

[11] Round balls made of a mixture of cooked rice, barley, or wheat flour. The *piṇḍas* also constitute a social body: "Bound by the sacrificial ball" (*sāpiṇḍa*) is a sign of kinship, which is taken into account at birth, in determining endogamy and exogamy, and heirship. *Sāpiṇḍya* relatives form a common body because one is linked by forefathers (normally seven generations on the paternal side and five on the maternal side).

sapiṇḍīkaraṇa ritual is the composition of a body for the deceased to allow him or her to reach the forefathers and ancestors. This process is complicated, and is carried out in several steps.[12] The number of *piṇḍas* which have to be offered during the death rituals, and their functions, vary considerably. According to the influential *Garuḍapurāṇasāroddhāra,* three sets of 16 *piṇḍa*s have to be offered. With reference to the gradually decreasing impurity, the first set is called *malinaṃ ṣoḍaśaṃ*; the second *madhyaṃ ṣoḍaśaṃ*, and the third *uttamaṃ ṣoḍaśaṃ* (*Garuḍapurāṇasāroddhāra*, 12.66*ff*).

The first six *piṇḍa*s of the first set are given on the way to and at the cremation grounds; the other 10 of the first set are given during the first 10 days, or collectively on the 10th day. *Piṇḍa*s are often meant to create a transcendental body for the deceased. Through them, the dead person receives a new body, for the 10 *piṇḍa*s mostly stand for various parts of the body. This composition corresponds to Ayurvedic ideas of the development of the embryo, and the formation of the foetus in the mother's womb.

The second set of 16 *piṇḍas* is offered to the gods, and only one is offered to the *preta*. And the final set of 16, called *māsikaśrāddha*s or *māsikapiṇḍa*s, are meant to be food for the one-year-journey to Yama's world, after which the *preta* becomes a forefather (*pitaraḥ*). The term *māsikapiṇḍa,* thus, refers to the monthly offerings for the deceased during the first year after his death, before the *sapiṇḍīkaraṇa*. Previously, the *sapiṇḍīkaraṇa* was apparently to be held after 12 days. In most normative texts, however, it is prescribed after a year, but in practice this period came to be shortened again to 12 or 13 days; or, among the Newars, 45 days (= *traipakṣe*, Nevārī *latyā*) which, according to the ritual handbooks, is another possible point of time for the *sapiṇḍīkaraṇa*. The 16 monthly *piṇḍa*s are meant to feed the deceased during his one-year-long journey to Yamas world, passing 16 different cities, where he eats the *piṇḍas*. During the ritual giving of a bed (*śayyādāna*) to the priest, he also receives several gifts for his journey: for example, a seat, sandals, an umbrella, a ring, a water pot, Sacred Thread, ghee, clothes, food, and a plate for food. The number 16 includes the 12 months and four additional points of time. These 16 *piṇḍa*s are mostly offered on the 10th or 11th day in advance for the following year.

The third set of 16 *piṇḍa*s should be distributed throughout the year of mourning; but in fact, this ritual takes place, if at all, as a preliminary rite for the *sapiṇḍīkarana* with which the arrival of the deceased among the ancestors is celebrated. In the process, the chief mourner divides one of the *piṇḍa*s, which is somewhat lengthened, into three parts using gold (or money) and *kuśa* grass to separate the parts, and mixes the whole thing with three *piṇḍa*s, which represent the father, the grandfather, and the great-grandfather (Figures 1–34).

[12] For more details see BUSS (2005); and GUTSCHOW/MICHAELS (2005).

Figures 1–3: The large *piṇḍa* representing the deceased (*preta*) with black sesame is torn into three pieces and merged with three other balls representing the father, grandfather and great-grandfather. Photograph: N. Gutschow (2002). Used with permission.

Here again, the chief mourner and the Brahmin priest take the balls as representatives of the forefathers (*pitaraḥ*), ancestor-gods (*viśvedevāḥ*), and the deceased (*preta*). This is the crucial moment when the deceased, abandoning his former name, is brought into the band of forefathers (*pitaraḥ*), and forms a commensal community with them; now he is no longer a helpless outsider as a *preta*. All this is done by the hands of the chief mourner. He most carefully kneads the dough for the *piṇḍas*, which are the deceased and his forefathers, assisted by the priest who repeatedly instructs him how to shape them, and not to hurt them. Through kneading the dough, pasting it, pouring water, or scattering sesame seeds over it, the deceased becomes a new body. The deceased is then treated as if he or she is present in the *piṇḍas*.

During a *sapiṇḍīkaraṇa* ritual that took place in Bhaktapur on August 22, 2002, the priest said to the chief mourner:

> Don't worry that the *piṇḍa* will be broken. — Now this way, move it around. — Make (it) a little thinner upside. Now fold it on like this. Now move it around again. Keep pressing in this way (demonstration). (Be careful), it is going to be broken. Don't hurt him. It is not allowed to break the *piṇḍa*.

Tactility is one of the most significant features of this ritual. Death is literally taken into the hands. United with the other deceased, the dead person can now live on his own, and is provided with a divine body (*divyadeha*). At the same time, the father of the great-grandfather moves into the band of the generalized, half-divine forefathers (*viśvedevāḥ*). Thus, whether one reaches this place depends not only on one's own *karma* and one's own acts, blame or merit, but also on if and how the descendants perform the death and ancestor rituals. In handling death this way, emotions are going from the inside to the outside; from imagination to form. For, the transformation from a living human being into an ancestor, the deceased has to be newly formed, and shaped by the hands of the chief mourner. After all, it is the son who, in this ritual, touches his father in an intensive and intimate way that is impossible during lifetime, when the son normally keeps physical distance from his father and *vice versa*.

Conclusion

Touchability in death rituals is normally related to pollution and, thus, is prohibited. This mainly concerns touching the corpse or the chief mourners. However, in the after-death rituals, substitutes such as the *piṇḍa* balls in the *sapīṇḍīkaraṇa* represent the deceased person and the forefathers; these can and must be touched by the chief mourner. Thus, death is taken into human hands in a way that makes it possible to give a form to emotions. Thus, death is not untouchable. On the contrary, only by this form of touching and revitalizing the deceased "symbolically"— for the bereaved the situation is quite real — is purity restored.

Appendix[13]

On the Observation of the Mourning *(āsauca vārnyāko)* in the *Mulukī Ain* of 1854, Ch. 97

1. If anybody from the cord-wearer castes like Brāhmaṇa, Rājaputa, Kṣatr(iya), etc., dies, and there is nobody from the same caste to carry (*uṭhāuna*) the dead body [to the cremation ground, in such a case], among the cord-wearer castes, it shall be allowed to touch and carry the corpse of a higher caste by the lower caste and the corpse of a lower caste by the higher caste. If there is no [body from the] cord-wearer caste[s], anybody from water-acceptable alcohol-drinker caste[s] shall also [be allowed] to carry [the corpse of a cord-wearer caste]. If a dead body from the cord-wearer caste is touched or carried by a person who is from the water-acceptable alcohol-drinker caste, a fee (*godāna*) shall be offered to a *brāhmaṇa* [expending] five *ānā* to five rupees in the name of the dead person, according to the ability by the person who performs the death ritual (*kriyā*). It is not necessary [to perform] either *patiyā* or *prāyaścitta*.
2. If any poor and bankrupt (*kaṃgāl*) person, who does not have any money or property dies, and nobody comes to carry the dead body [to the cremation ground to] perform the death ritual (*kājakriyā*), [in such a case] the local officer (*amālī*), representatives of the noble families (*thari*), the administrator (*dvāryā*), revenue officer (*mukhiyā*), and contractor (*ṭhekaijārādār*) of the same village or locality where the person has died shall arrange to carry the dead body [to the cremation ground and to perform] the death ritual (*kāyakriyā*) by spending two and a half rupees from the income (i.e. taxes) of that village. If it is confirmed that a corpse remains there for more than two or three days in the village without its being carried [to the cremation ground], the local officer (*amāli*) and the representatives of the noble families (*thari*) shall be fined two and a half rupees. If the rupees are not paid, imprisonment for 15 days [and] release. The expenditure of carrying the dead body shall be compensated (*minhā*) to the contractor (*ṭhekadāra*) [of the land where the person has died] by the government if the land is owned by the government, by the *jāgirdār* if it is the land of a serviceman (*jāgirdār*), and by the owner of the *birtā* land if it is the *birtā* land with tax exemption.
3. Any *amāli* (local officer) who does not appoint a person to carry the dead body of the person who dies in his village (locality) [to the cremation ground] shall be fined five rupees [and] the person who does not go [for the cremation work] after his appointment by the *amāli* shall be fined two and a half rupees. If the rupees are not paid, imprisonment according to the *Ain*.
4. If any unidentified and unknown outsider (*paracakri*) person comes and dies in a village [whereinsoever], the local officer (*amāli*) and the representatives of the noble families (*thari*) of that village shall cause somebody to carry the corpse. If the corpse remains there for two or three days in the village without it being carried [to the cremation ground], the local officer (*amāli*) shall be fined five rupees [and] the representatives of the noble families (*thari*) shall [also] be fined two and a half rupees. If the rupees are not paid, imprisonment according

[13] I gratefully acknowledge the help of Noutan Sharma in translating the text.

to the *Ain*. If no confirmation of an heir [of the dead] is made [and] some money [and] property [tied] on his wrist are found, the remaining money shall be for the *amāli* after it is spent on the cremation ritual (*satagati*) [of the dead person as] if he was the resident (citizen) of our country. If the heir [of the dead person] is found, the property remaining after the cremation is paid for shall be given to the person to whom it belongs after an investigation is carried out. If it [the money] is of a foreigner [or] traveler who is an outsider of our country, the remaining property, after his cremation ritual (*kājakriyā sadgati*) is paid for, shall be for the government. Deposit [it] with the court (*adālata*).

5. If any person, from the employees of the civil administration (*nijāmat*), [or] other men [or] woman from the commons, of the three cities (Kathmandu, Patan, and Bhaktapur), except from the villages of the Nepal valley (Nepālakā *gāmal*), dies and, since there is nobody from his or her kin nor any social trust (*goṣṭhī*) to cremate [the corpse], the corpse remains there in the city [without any cure] and [even] after the appointment of a person for the cremation of the corpse by the court [or] police station if the corpse remains there in the city for two or three days without the corpse being taken out [in time], a fine of twenty rupees shall be imposed on such a person. If the rupees are not paid, imprison [him].
6. If anybody from the water-unacceptable alcohol drinker (*pāni nacalanyā matavāli*) [or] untouchable (*achuti*) caste dies in somebody's house, [or] in the neighborhood [or] in the village, cause the dead body to be carried [to the cremation ground] by the main person (*moṣya*) if found from the equal caste [of the dead person]. If a person from the equal caste is not found, anybody even from water-acceptable castes like Brahmana, Rajaputa, Kṣatṛ, Magar, Gurung, etc., shall carry the corpse to a cremation *ghāṭ*. If a Brahman touches [such] a corpse of an untouchable caste, he shall be purified after taking a ritual bath [and] fasting at a pilgrimage site (*kṣatropavās*). The others belonging to cord-wearer castes and others shall be purified after [simply] taking a ritual bath.
7. If anybody from lower than his or her caste [like] Śudra caste, water-unacceptable caste (*pāni nacalanyā jāta*), or untouchable caste (*choyā chiṭo hālanu parnyā jāta*) touches the corpse of the cord-wearer etc. caste who died while going to the countryside, [a foreign country,] drowning in the water, being eaten by a wild animal like a tiger in the forest, or falling or jumping down into a slope, ditch, pond, well, or from a suspension bridge, a bridge, or into a bend of a river or of a sea (*ṣāḍi*), the brothers and sons have to give a fire (*dāga vatti*) to the corpse if it is found. Later on, the death ritual (*kājakriyā*) has to be performed after doing *patiyā* of *kriyā suddha*. If the death is confirmed but the corpse is not found, his or her brothers and sons have to perform the death ritual (*kājakriyā*) after performing the *Nārāyaṇa Bali* rite. The *prāyaścitta* shall not be necessary [to perform in this case].

References

Texts

GARUḌAPURĀṆASĀRODDHĀRA (1921): ABEGG, E. (Trans.), Der Pretakalpa des Garuḍa-Purāṇa (Naunidhirāma's Sāroddhāra). Eine Darstellung des hinduistischen Totenkultes und Jenseitsglaubens. – Berlin and Leipzig.

MANU (2005): Manu's Code of Law. A Critical Edition and Translation of the Mānava-Dharmaśāstra. OLIVELLE, Patrick (Ed.). – Oxford.

MULUKĪ AIN (1965): Śrī 5 Surendra Bikram Śāhadevakā Śāsanakālamā Baneko Mulukī Ain. Ed. Śrī 5-ko Sarkāra [H.M.G.]. – Kathmandu: Kānūna tathā Nyāya Mantrālaya, V.S. 2022.
Le Code Népalais (Ain). FEZAS, Jean (Ed.). – Torino 2000 (Corpus Juris Sanscriticum, Volume II)

Secondary literature

AKTOR, M. (2008): Ritualisation and Segregation: The Untouchability Complex in Indian Dharma Literature with Special Reference to Parāśarasmṛti and Parāśaramādhvīya. – Turin.

AKTOR, M. (2010): Untouchability. In: Brill's Encyclopedia of Hinduism. – Leiden and Boston 2011, pp. 876–81.

AKTOR, M./DELIÈGE, R. (Eds.) (2010): From Stigma to Assertion: Untouchability, Identity and Politics in Early and Modern India. – Copenhagen.

ALEX, G. (2008): A Sense of Belonging and Exclusion: 'Touchability' and 'Untouchability' in Tamil Nadu. In: Ethnos, Vol. 73.4, pp. 523–543.

BUSS, J. (2005): Gieriger Geist oder verehrter Vorfahr? Das 'Doppelleben' des Verstorbenen anhand des newarischen latya-Rituals. In: ASSMANN, J., MACIEJEWSKI, F. and MICHAELS, A. (Eds.) Abschied von den Toten. Trauerrituale im Kulturvergleich. – Göttingen, pp. 181–198.

CHARLSEY, S. (1996): 'Untouchable': What is in a Name? In: Journal of the Royal Anthropological Institute (N.S.), Vol. 2.1, pp. 1–23.

DAS, V. (1982): Structure and Cognition: Aspects of Hindu Caste and Ritual. 2nd edition. – Delhi and Oxford.

DAVID, K. (1973): Until Marriage Do Us Part: A Jaffna Tamil Account of Categories for Kinsmen. In: Man (N.S.), Vol. 8.4, pp. 521–535.

DOUGLAS, M. (1966): Purity and Danger: An Analysis of the Concepts of Pollution and Taboo. – London.

DUMONT, L. (1980): Homo Hierarchicus: The Caste System and Its Implications. 2nd edition. – Chicago.

GUTSCHOW, N./MICHAELS, A. (2005): Handling Death: The Dynamics of Death and Ancestor Rituals among the Newars of Bhaktapur, Nepal. – Wiesbaden.

HARPER, E.B. (1964): Ritual Pollution as an Integrator of Caste and Religion. In: Journal of Asian Studies, Vol. 23, pp. 151–197.

HÖFER, A. (1979): The Caste Hierarchy and the State in Nepal: A Study of the *Muluki Ain* of 1854. – Innsbruck.

MANDELBAUM, D. (1970): Society in India. 2 Vols. – Berkeley.

MARRIOTT, M. (1976): Hindu Transactions: Diversity without Dualism. In: KAPFERER, B. (Ed.), Transaction and Meaning. – Philadelphia, pp. 109–142.

MARRIOTT, M. (Ed.) (1990): India through Hindu Categories. – New Delhi.

MARRIOTT, M./INDEN, R. (1973): Caste Systems. In: Encyclopedia Britannica, macropaedia. – Chicago: Vol. 3, pp. 982–991.

MARRIOTT, M./INDEN, R. (1977): Toward an Ethnosociology of South Asian Caste Systems. In: DAVID, K. (Ed.) The New Wind: Changing Identities in South Asia. – The Hague and Paris, pp. 423–38.

MEHTA, N. (2009): Mouth Ke Saudagar. Out with the Mwahists! Social kissing is anti-national! In: http://www.outlookindia.com, January 19, 2009 (accessed September 9, 2012).

MENDELSOHN, O./VICZIANI, M. (1998): The Untouchables: Subordination, Poverty and the State in Modern India. – Cambridge.

MICHAELS, A. (1997): Gift and Return Gift, Greeting and Return Greeting in India. On a Consequential Footnote by Marcel Mauss. In: Numen, Vol. 44, pp. 243–69.

MICHAELS, A. (2004): Hinduism: Past and Present. – Princeton, NJ.

MICHAELS, A. (2006): The Price of Purity: The Religious Judge in 19th Century Nepal. Containing the Edition and Translation of the Chapters on the Dharmādhikārin in Two (*Mulukī*) *Ains*. – Torino (Comitato "Corpus Juris Sancriticum et fontes iuris Asiae Meridianae et Centralis;" and Vol. 6).

MOFFAT M. (1979): An Untouchable Community in South India: Structure and Consensus. – Princeton, NJ.

Gabriele Brandstetter

Senses of Movement: Kinesthetics and Synesthetics in Contemporary Dance Practices

Exploring the senses is an important part of dance as a movement research in modern, postmodern, and contemporary dance. Which senses are addressed in doing and in watching movement? Movement research, as well the theory of movement and dance, has shifted from a perspective that concentrated primarily on the visual to a perspective that is concerned with kinesthetic awareness. Kinesthesia is now understood as a basic sense — the sense of sensing ("spüren"), or sometimes even the *sixth sense* — and is associated with modes of synesthesia: a cross-modal process of perception which interweaves the sensual and the aesthetic aspects of experience. Kinesthesia has been a much discussed issue in phenomenological and psychological theory since the early 20th century. The relation of the bodily sense of positioning in space and the sensing of movement are linked with questions of empathy: these issues have also found significant place in recent debates on the role of the movements of the body as underlying aesthetic experience (GALLAGHER 2005, GIBSON 1966).

Within the field of research in dance, the exploration of the sense of kinesthesia is closely linked with the sense of touch (and the field of the haptic perception) and with the experience of *listening*. Listening even becomes a kind of master trope that covers the kinesthetic and synesthetic modes of sensing in different movement practices in contemporary dance. This is why this chapter chooses to focus on "listening" as a mode of sensing movement within the exploration of kinesthetics and synesthetics in dance.

Listening

"Listening" is a term belonging to the basic vocabulary of contact improvisation. The following remarks are intended to investigate the use of this concept, and see how it ties in with the discussions and practices of "kinesthetic awareness." In her introduction to "contact improvisation" as a "dance form," Cheryl PALLANT remarks that "listening," or "listening to motion," is a term

> regularly used in contact improvisation. Listening, according to contact improvisation's metaphorical use of the word, refers to paying attention to all sensory occurrences arising from touch, from the play of weight, as partners move through space, and from the event of one body encountering the presence of another. Listening refers to noticing stimuli not only within oneself but also from another (2006, p. 31f).

The range of meanings covered by the word "listening" refers to one of those — open — scenarios of the metaphorical which LAKOFF called "metaphors we live by" (LAKOFF and JOHNSON 1999). Thus, the image of a summons to an act of "listening" refers to a field of perception of the sensory that is not just limited to acoustics: it is a syn-aesthetic network of experiences of the body, of its internal and external states at rest and in movement. It involves awareness which, in contact improvisation, is exercised and refined in a multitude of ways in, and through, the synesthetic-kinesthetic addressings of perception. A selection of sentences that act as a guide to such (synesthetic) perception may illustrate the range covered by "listening:"

> – Listen to the click of cartilage, the slap of skin, of the whisper of your will typically silenced by a shout.
> – Notice a part of your body for which you have no name, no history, no awareness.
> – Feel weight push into your stubbornness, your expectations, against your habit of always yielding to aggression or constantly fighting it.
> – Sniff the circumstances, the leg extending into view, the hand urging direction.
> – Watch time dissolve.
> – Follow the sound into the garden past the bench in the corner on.
> – Tend your body as if it were the body of a lover.
> – Drink the elixir of expansion, the release within repose.
> – Find the edge between comfort and discomfort, the familiar and the unknown. Balance there, however precariously.
> – Devolve into protozoa.
> – Let your body call you back into yourself (PALLANT 2006, pp. 7*ff*).

From this list of addressings of a sensory awareness that is important for the preparation and setting of contact improvisation, it can be seen that "listening" refers not so much to *hearing* as a sensory form of registering acoustic events (although this is part of it), but to a very broad and open state of sensuous/ sensory perception. It also includes the sensing, the tactility of touching. Thus "listen" does not refer primarily to a hearing event. It refers, rather, to an intersection of action and event (EREIGNIS) —which in German breaks down into the terms *zuhören*, *hören auf*, *horchen*, and *lauschen* — thus implying the reference to the self as well as the reference to the other, and to space.[1] In contact improvisation, "listening," and "listening" to motion refer to synesthetic and kinesthetic forms of *awareness*, which embrace both conscious and unconscious "subliminal" perceptions.

In this context, one is reminded of John Cage's postmodern and contemporary performance of *4′33″* — that silent piece in which the solo instrument,

[1] Cf. NANCY (2010, pp. 15f. and pp. 38*ff*.). Nancy argues that "listening" relates to the whole register of the senses, being touched, and within a difference of the interior and the exterior.

the piano, was *not* heard. What happened instead was that a space of attention was opened for the numerous noises and sounds heard inside and outside the concert hall. The reduction of sensory attention to an "act of hearing" was used in yet another way by Xavier le Roy in his solo performance *Self Unfinished* (1998). Le Roy began the piece by entering a vacant white space, and going towards a tape deck and pressing a button, as though starting the music for a (dance) piece. However, not a sound was heard — neither music nor noise. Le Roy made the *gesture* of opening a sonic dimension and, thus, brought about an act of "listening." The drawing of the audience's attention to a "*possible*" hearing event changed the hearing and the attention. This kind of focus on an act of "listening" helped to facilitate — synesthetically speaking — a *different* perception of space and movement. "*Listen!*": listening to the movement, hearing the body–space movement, means that the seeing receives a different, an additional sensory (kinesthetic) quality. As Paul VALÉRY, for whom the ear was the preferred sense for conveying attention, said, the ear "keeps watch, so to speak, at the frontier beyond which the eye does not see".[2]

Contact improvisation and kinesthesis

Contact improvisation is a dance practice in which two (or more) moving partners, always in contact, explore the possibilities of their movement. Curt Siddall, an "early exponent of contact improvisation" defines this dance form as

> a combination of kinesthetic forces: Contact improvisation is a movement form, improvisational in nature, involving two bodies in contact. Impulses, weight, and momentum are communicated through a point of physical contact that continually rolls across and around the bodies of the dancers.[3]

Historically, this movement *praxis* goes back to Steve Paxton's movement and improvisation explorations at Oberlin College in 1972. Since then, this dance form has established itself internationally, and assumed different forms, whether as performance improvisation or social dance in the shape of regular jams, or as a means of exercise in combination with various release techniques, which in turn determine the aesthetics of contemporary dance. "The physical training of contact improvisation emphasizes the release of the body's weight into the floor or onto a partner's body (...)," writes Ann Cooper ALBRIGHT. "The experience of internal sensations and the flow of the movement of two bodies is more important than specific shapes or formal positions."[4] In an early article

---

[2] VALÉRY (1974, p. 934, my transl.); cf. WALDENFELS (2004, p. 198).

[3] Quoted in ALBRIGHT/GERE (2003, p. 206).

[4] Ibid., p. 206. This is not the place for a more detailed examination of the historical development and aesthetic structures of contact improvisation. Cooper Albright has pointed out that it is a "tricky business" to give a coherent description of contact improvisation: "the form has grown exponentially over time and has travelled through many

in *The Drama Review* (1975), Steve Paxton identifies the six main elements of contact improvisation: "attitude, sensing time, orientation to space, orientation to partner, expanding peripheral vision, and muscular development, which includes centring, stretching, taking weight, and increasing joint action."[5]

The emphasizing of the motor aspects of movement — such as working with "momentum," "gravity," "mass"/ "weight," "chaos," "inertia," the attention to highly differentiated states of muscle tone between release/inertia and contraction, and finally the shifting of spatial perception between the focus on the interior of the body and the exterior of space — makes clear that an accent of the overall concept of contact improvisation lies on the conscious work with the "sixth sense," or kinesthesia. This is where two fields of the kinesthetic mesh together: kinesthetic proprioception and working with kinesthetic communication — that is, the contact and shifts of weight and spatial position which are shifts of the dynamically interacting dancer-bodies.

"Both the gross motor awareness of kinesthesia and the less conscious sensory feedback mechanism of proprioception form the basis of the physical dialogue which is so pivotal to creating dance," writes Cheryl PALLANT (2006, p. 32). That is why experienced "contacters" like Nancy Stark Smith constantly stress the spatial orientation created not only by vision but by the entire physical perception, a condition which she calls "telescoping awareness" (ALBRIGHT/GERE 2003, p. 153), a "shifting between narrow and wide views, from up-close sensation to perceptions of the wider world," (ibid., p. 154) accompanied by the "sensation of dropping through space," "the forces of gravity, momentum, and mass" (ibid., p. 157).

There has been a delay between the highly differentiated *praxis* with kinesthesia in dance and theoretical references to the results of physiological, phenomenological, and neuroscientific research in kinesthesia. This research has only recently attracted more attention in the field of dance studies (cf. MONTERO 2006, COLEMAN/MONTERO 2007). The initial impetus for this discussion was provided in the 1980s by an article by Mary M. SMYTH (1984). The research and discoveries connected with "kinesthesia" (from SHERRINGTON, 1906 to GIBSON 1966) as the ability to feel the movement of the limbs and body, are examined by Smyth to see if they yield an answer to the question as to how "watching someone dance could link to the movement system of the observer" (SMYTH 1984, p. 19). For Smyth, this question ultimately remains unanswerable.[6] Her work reviews several hypotheses, all of which arose before

---

countries and dance communities. Although it was developed in the 1970s, contact improvisation has recognizable roots in the social and aesthetic revolutions of the sixties" (ibid. p. 205). On the history of contact improvisation, see NOVACK (1990).

[5] Steve Paxton, quoted in PALLANT (2006, pp. 12*ff*).

[6] SMYTH (1984, p. 22) notes that *Somehow* remains as a gap in the process. "Even if dancers were happy that such a process could in any way relate to the experiences which they called 'kinesthetic communication,' we still do not know how it is effected [...] We do not yet know how seen movement can do this."

the more recent research findings on the function of "mirror neurons" which came to be discussed in dance and dance studies (RIZZOLATTI et al. 2008). The subject of "kinesthesia," on the other hand, is a topical one in dance research, since recent interest is focusing on the meaning of "energy," "rhythm," and the "synchronization" of movements in modern and contemporary dance. Thus, Dee REYNOLDS (2007) has devoted her study of *Rhythmic Subjects* to the "uses of energy" and the question of kinesthesia not only in relation to bodily position, muscle tension, and movement, but also with regard to the kinesthetically "embodied" cultural "imaginations" of, and attitudes toward, the kinesthetic. Rudolf von Laban's concept of "effort" and Edmund Husserl's and Maurice Merleau-Ponty's phenomenological theories inform her approach. By using the concept of "kinesthetic imagination" — which refers not only to the subjective aspects of proprioception, but also to questions of cultural imprint and the transfer of energy — she manages to detach the phenomenon of kinesthesia from the issue of self-perception in dancer *praxis*, and open it up to questions of (syn-)aesthetic perception by the observer (FOSTER 2008, cf. FOSTER 2010).

In the practice of various body techniques which are of relevance to contemporary dance (though not only to it), the subject of kinesthesia is of increasing importance, even if the term itself is not part of the vocabulary of the discourse. Thus, in a newly held series of interviews, several representatives of body techniques — such as Feldenkrais and proponents of the Alexander technique and Body–Mind Centering — admitted to having worked with the basic principles of kinesthesia long before they became aware of the term, and the research associated with it. The dancer Julyen Hamilton, for example, stated that his work was very spatially oriented: "This spatial sense is highly informed through the kinesthetic sensing of the inner body" (cf. CORPUS 2010, p. 2). Moreover, the "choices," which are always movement decisions, are influenced by the fact that they are not made from outside — that is, "via an outside eye" — but are "choices made from the proprioceptive abilities within the body as it senses itself and its environment." The result is a "radically spatial event permitted by the public and performers sharing of space" (ibid.). Susan Klein, the founder of the *Klein Technique*™, stresses the extraordinary importance of "kinesthetics," both as a "tool that allows us to understand the body," and as an aid to artistic work (ibid.).

> For me the beauty and excitement in kinesthetics is bringing a body-felt understanding of movement to consciousness. It is fine-tuning our ability to feel, on subtle levels [...] Kinesthetics is our tool to bring the body into a deep state of balance, to its optimal state of movement potential (ibid.).

The associated "process of discovery" which is able to trigger a periphrasis of fixed blockades, of postures of muscles, bones, and tissue, leads to a kinesthetically informed "internal knowing" (ibid.). The aim is — as in most concepts of body techniques which operate with Body–Mind Centering, "ideokinesis" or "functional integration" (such as the Feldenkrais method) — "body alignment, ease of movement and overall body harmony in dance," as Linda Rabin puts it.[7] Here, as in all works of kinesthetically oriented practices, it is not a "beautiful" bodily form resulting from a course of training dictated by an aesthetic style or movement code that is the guiding principle of the idea of dance and choreography. It is to be found in the answer to the question posed by Linda Rabin: "What would dance performance be like if dancers drew from this essential source?" (CORPUS 2010).

Attention: Kinesthetic awareness

A key concept that plays a pivotal role in nearly all texts and discourses of the above-mentioned body techniques and contact improvisation is that of attention — in the double sense of attention and awareness, of directed attention (perception), as well as "noticing" — a distinction made by the philosopher Bernhard Waldenfels on the basis of the phenomenological theory of Husserl and Merleau-Ponty (cf. WALDENFELS 2004).

"It all starts with paying attention," says Linda Rabin (CORPUS 2010, p. 5). "Kinesthetics, the sense that tells us where and how we exist in our internal environment and how we connect and relate to our external environment," (Interview with Susan Klein, in CORPUS 2010, p. 3) can lead to a conscious perception. Of particular interest in this connection is the *division* of attention. According to Susan Klein:

> It requires a split level of consciousness: one level is doing while the other level is observing what is done. Kinesthetic awareness allows us to keep track of what we are doing with our bodies as well as how we are doing it (ibid.).

Attention — as attention and awareness — embraces the entire sensory and action scenario which is addressed, for example, in the movement explorations of contact improvisation. Attention implies attentiveness — both to the processes of one's own physicality and to the experience of contact with the Other. Attention, thus, opens up the entire range of the concept as it might be described in an anthropological-phenomenological specification. Waldenfels points out with recourse to Immanuel Kant that the boundaries between the deliberate direction of attention (*attentio, abstractio, distentio*), noticing (*animadvertere*), and observing (*observare*), are fluid (WALDENFELS 2004, pp. 230*ff*). To this must be added the mode of self-affection, i.e. "the affection of the inner sense by ourselves with an 'Actus of attention'" (ibid., p. 231). It is this doubling of only partially controllable awareness and self-affection by images in the (inner)

[7] CORPUS (2010, p. 4). Linda Rabin worked with Lulu Sweigard on "ideokinesis," learned the Alexander technique (through Rika Cohen), practiced "Body-Mind Centering®" (founded by Bonnie Bainbridge Cohen) and, finally, became a teacher of the "Continuum Movement" founded by Emile Conrad.

perception that marks the potential of kinesthesia and the "kinesthetic imagination" (REYNOLDS 2007). This is where the key formula "*listening*" opens the synesthetic-kinesthetic spectrum of possible modes of attention: perception and awareness. A small episode may serve to illustrate the shifts and transfers between movement and (observer) perception.

In the context of my movement research on contact improvisation, I drove with two colleagues through the Brandenburg landscape to a village where there was a kind of "Dance Land" farm called "Ponderosa," where a workshop on contact improvisation was being held by Nancy Stark Smith, one of the best-known personalities in this field. We had announced our arrival, and had permission to observe the workshop as a small research team. The workshop was taking place in a large, somewhat dilapidated barn set amidst an overgrown, elderberry-scented "Paradise" — like a relic of the hippy 1970s. It was in a large, light-filled room, supported by wooden beams, whose atmosphere had put all the "participants" into the right mood, thanks to its spaciousness, openness, conduciveness to concentration, calm *and* dynamic character, and the rhythmical division of the space by windows and beams. The 19 participants in the workshop — and we as observers — distributed ourselves about this space. What was striking was how much this space and its divisions actually helped to promote the whole process of the workshop, with its various action centers of movement and "contact." Here *participation* was not just about "sharing" the place, but also and equally about constituting "space" in (inter-)action, in motion, and in watching-listening. The question of the relationship between movers (workshop participants) and observers was in the air throughout the entire process — and it changed! Relationships transform perception.

The workshop was intended "to pay special attention to the delicate transition from intimate, private authenticity to making art intended to be viewed by the public [...] Are the subtle experiences of perception and action inside improvised dance visible to the watcher?"[8]

These *experiences* and these *questions* were shared. At the end, we were asked: "What did you see?" The question was posed with regard to the process of movement involving constant changes between "dancing, watching, listening, and being watched." It is remarkable that all themes and processes that occurred in the workshop were linked with the question of "attention": attention as a sensory-kinesthetic mode of participation.

In reply to the question that all participants put to us in the closing interview: "What did you see?" one participant in our research group said that the entering into (and sharing of) this workshop on *space* and *framework* had been a striking experience. Why? The answer lay, as the participant pointed out, in the difference between his everyday stress situation (one's normal job, university life, an arduous journey) and the workshop space offering opportunities for meeting people, lots of peace and quiet, freedom to organize one's own

[8] Nancy Stark Smith in the Program note of the workshop.

affairs, and the release from perfection constraints. This feedback was very well received by the workshop participants. It was clear that the experience of the release from the tensions in everyday life, scope for selective contacts, and the remoteness of output-oriented tasks unconsciously responded to the concept of the workshop and contact improvisation. In addition, however, it was the experience of difference itself in this case, which caused the outside observer to be accepted as a participant — in the sense of "sharing" — in the group of "movers" that made the experience so special.

Our questions lead us to reflect on whether, and in what way, the parameters which constitute this kind of *kinesthetic sharing* could be reconsidered. In this case, this would also mean, for example, that the mutual "responsiveness" between workshop-movers and workshop-observers was not the "answer" to the question of participation. But it did raise a question concerning context-dependent changes. The question that arose is: What does this tell us about forms of kinesthetic and synesthetic empathy if the relaxing of tension or a change in breathing is seen as an emergent effect of such a transference? And in what way are different dimensions of experience and knowledge addressed in such processes? Was this, in the case of our example, addressing a "tacit knowledge" (Michael Polanyi) of a liminal attention? It is hard to describe a state in which one is receptive to signals on which one is not — intentionally — focused and which are received in a distracted, casual manner.[9]

Sensing the movement: "Small dance"

The questions which were to be illuminated by this episode of a "contact" between dancers and observers at a contact improvisation workshop are complex. Neither in a neuroscientific nor in an aesthetic-theoretical sense is the multiplicity of aspects easy to solve. There is, for example, the question of *how* the intricate and microscopic kinesthetic processes which take place during an hour of work with the Susan Klein technique, or in a sequence of contact improvisation, are perceived by an observer.

[9] Our questions, on the other hand, focus on modes of participation with such formulas and criteria that are difficult to describe. Thus, in the contact improvisation workshop in "Dance Land" in Ponderosa, in what way did I as "audience," observer, spectator belong or was "included" in the process of actions, exercises, movements? I was "there," and yet was "outside." And yet, this was a situation that would not accurately be reflected in the words "exclusion," or "not belonging." Does this not show how potentially interesting it might be to rethink participation on the basis of experience and performance theory? Should we not recognize that the attributions of active and passive, and the semantic range of the concepts of action and performance cannot ultimately be determined, and that the shifting nature of relationships (e.g. between performers and spectators), and the changes in the background against which they play out, give rise to all sorts of temporary possibilities of participation? (Cf. Rancière 2009). Such questions need to be examined more thoroughly in further research.

In the context of contact impro-visation discourse, it is "listening" — as a quality of attention *and* awareness — in which "voluntary" and "involuntary" movement processes that is open both to *mover* and *observer*. In other words, "Remaining present and listening go hand in hand" (PALLANT 2006, p. 34).

Figure 1: Ease in stillness: Susan Singer and Keith Winston (PALLANT 2006, p. 23)

Figure 2: Giving full weight and support: Jessica Wright and Heather Shrock (PALLANT 2006, p. 40)

Figure 3: Extending support: Eric Ortega (bottom) and Courtney Cooke (PALLANT 2006, p. 41)

As the phenomenological studies by Husserl, Merleau-Ponty, and Waldenfels show, kinesthesia is a physically embodied space–time experience. As such, it assumes a particular shape within a hear–sound space (WALDENFELS 2004, p. 199; cf. TAYLOR 1999). This implies an "acoustic epoché," that is, a breach (in) the resonance. "Listening" thus means (to follow WALDENFELS, ibid., p. 194) that a "different kind of hearing" (*ein "Andershören"*) is needed to break through the hearing order and reach the synesthetic-kinesthetic quality of that "*movere*" (in the sense of a sensory and emotional "being moved") which is involved in the "contact," the touch play of contact improvisation. Thus, the concept of "*Kinästhese*," as Edmund Husserl introduces the term, is not

> to be understood as a sensation of movement that is only distinguished from other sensations by a special sensibility, but 'Kinästhese,' which the ego ascribes to itself, means a moving sensation before a sensing movement, the chiastic formulation indicating that kinesis and aesthesis are not fully congruent either in a phenomenal or a neuronal sense (WALDENFELS 1999, pp. 68*ff*).

This hesitation, this delay — that kinesthetic epoché that keeps open a gap in the relationship between movement and (self-)perception (WALDENFELS 2004, p. 221) — is constantly registered in the descriptions of kinesthetics and contact improvisation. Linda Rabin poses the question: "What is movement within the movement?" (CORPUS 2010, p. 5) Nancy Stark Smith constantly emphasizes the elementary significance of the kinesthetic experience of "disorientation" for contact improvisation, and of a "gap" which interrupts the control of movement orientation. At this point the question — long since obsolete — may be raised again as to where the boundary of kinesthetic perception between the praxis of "social dance" and artistic performance runs, shifts, and becomes diffuse. According to her, the orientation to "flow," to "coordinating falling, following momentum, blending with 'partner's movement'" turns into a game of being "against" all these. She believes in

> making myself heavy instead of light when a lift starts, [...] insisting instead of yielding, adding no to yes [...] I've been in the harmony business a long time now. [...] As much as I love running around, I think I'm going to try running *into* things more often, or at least against them.[10]

This refraction, this counterforce, or kinesthetic resistance reflects the pendulum, the balancing between motion and stillness, in which the potentiality/reflexivity of the kinesthetic is articulated. In Linda Rabin's experience, the extreme reduction of movement results in a "deep inner dance"— and "by reducing the outer movement to a minimum, and by slowing down the speed to a degree, I continued to explore the *inner* world of the dance," (CORPUS 2010, p. 5). She was eager to learn "what the audience would perceive when all extraneous movement was removed, if the simplicity of a dancer's walk, sitting or raising an arm, could communicate the intriguing world of sensations and feelings coursing through the performer" (ibid.). Even if this inner journey, this "inner dance" cannot be comprehensible in every detail, there are links in kinesthetic perception — a "sharing" between "mover" and "observer" — which is a vital aspect of a syn- and kinesthetic (empathic) movement synchronization in contact improvisation and other body practices mentioned here. This reduction, this attention to the microscopic "inner dance," opens a specific field of (kin-)aesthetic movement experience bordering on "standstill;" a standing still that is not a standstill, but a scenario full of risky inner movement: "Even standing, we execute a continuous fall."[11] Where would we find beginning and end, rest and movement in a dance which consists of nothing but a standing still? Nancy Stark Smith describes that "dance" as the one that Steve Paxton invented in the 1970s, and which he called "*small dance*."[12]

[10] Stark Smith in an article in *Contact Quarterly*, 1984, quoted in ALBRIGHT/GERE (2003, p. 162).

[11] Ann Woodhall formulated this central paradox, quoted in ALBRIGHT/GERE, (2003, p. 157).

[12] On Steve Paxton's instructions on "small dance," see the "reconstruction" by Nora HEILMANN (2006): in *Rupture in Space* (http://www.ruptures.wordpress.com); cf. Erin Manning, who comments on "A Mover's Guide to Standing Still," referring to Steve Paxton's "Small Dance," in MANNING (2009, pp. 43–49).

One might well ask: a dance that consists of nothing but "standing"? Nancy Stark Smith comments on her experience as follows:

> Relaxing erect, the intelligence of the body is revealed as it fires the appropriate muscles just enough to keep the body mass hovering within the range of its vertical supports. The micro movements that occur to keep me balanced are so tiny and yet so magnified, and arise from such a deep feeling of stillness and space, that I get giddy, tickled by the impossible magnitude of such subtle sensations. The disorientation in the stand comes from the feeling that inside the apparent solidity and stillness of standing, there is nothing but movement and space![13]

Disorientation, the intensity of movement, a tumult in the heart of standing still — such moments of the kinesthetic experience of an act of "listening" are what open and transmit the potential for inventing movement in contemporary dance.

References

ALBRIGHT, A.C. and GERE, D. (Eds.) (2003): Taken by Surprise: A Dance Improvisation Reader. – Middletown.

COLEMAN, J. and MONTERO, B. (2007): Affective Proprioception. In: Janus Head, Vol. 9.2, pp. 299–317.

CORPUS (2010): Kinesthetics: Four Questions. http://www.corpusweb.net/kinesthetics-four-questions.html, pp. 2*ff*.

FOSTER, S. (2008): Movements Contagion: The kinesthetic impact of performance, online publication of: University of California, International Performance and Culture Multicampus Research Group, June 2008. http://uc-ipc.com/wp-content/uploads/2008/06/movementscontagion-11.pdf (accessed December 19, 2012).

FOSTER, S. (2010): Choreographing Empathy. Kinesthesia in Performance. – London.

GALLAGHER, S. (2005): How the body shapes the mind. – Oxford.

GIBSON, J. J. (1966): The Senses Considered as Perceptual Systems. – Boston.

MANNING, E. (2009): Relationscapes. Movement, Art, Philosophy. – Cambridge, MA, London.

JOHNSON, M. (1987): The Body in the Mind: The Bodily Basis of Meaning, Imagination and Reason. – Chicago.

LAKOFF, G. and JOHNSON, M. (1999): Philosophy in the Flesh. – New York.

MONTERO, B. (2006): Proprioception as an Aesthetic Sense. In: The Journal of Aesthetics and Art Criticism, Vol. 64.2, pp. 23.242.

NANCY, J.-L. (2010): À l'écoute, German: Zum Gehör, VON DER OSTEN, Esther (Trans.). – Berlin and Zurich.

NOVACK, C. (1990): Sharing the Dance. Contact Improvisation and American Culture. – Madison.

PALLANT, C. (2006): Contact Improvisation: An Introduction to a Vitalizing Dance Form. – North Carolina and London.

POLANYI, Michael (1966): The Tacit Dimension. – London.

[13] Quoted in ALBRIGHT and GERE (2003, pp. 16*ff*).

RANCIÈRE, J. (2009): The Emancipated Spectator. – London.

REYNOLDS, D. (2007): Rhythmic Subjects. Uses of Energy in the Dances of Mary Wigman, Martha Graham, and Merce Cunningham. – Hampshire.

RIZZOLATTI, G. et al. (2008): Mirrors in the Brain: How our Minds Share Actions, Emotions, and Experience. – Oxford.

SHERRINGTON, C. (1906): The Integrative Action of the Nervous System. – New Haven.

SMYTH, M.M. (1984): Kinesthetic Communication in Dance. In: Dance Research Journal, Vol. 16.2, pp. 19–22.

TAYLOR, C. (1999): The Body in Husserl and Merleau-Ponty. In: Philosophical Topics, Vol. 27, pp. 205–286.

VALÉRY, P. (1974): Cahiers. Vol. II. – Paris.

WALDENFELS, B. (1999): Sinnesschwellen. – Frankfurt/M.

WALDENFELS, B. (2004): Phänomenologie der Aufmerksamkeit. – Frankfurt/M.

Jayachandran Palazhy

Memory, Experience and Imagination in Performance

In this chapter, I am particularly concerned with the conceptualisation, creation, and experience of contemporary movement arts in India. This chapter attempts to shed light on some of the thoughts and concerns that have influenced the evolving training methodologies for movement arts. As this is, in many ways, closely linked to my own artistic practice, I will be sharing some life experiences and the underlying beliefs that govern them. In an effort to draw on multiple sources that have colored my artistic journey, the chapter refers to a few examples of the workings of some of the physical and performance traditions of India, as well as thoughts and practices from other cultures, including contemporary and digital cultures. I hope this will give some insight into the processes that are involved in the making and receiving of a performance work.

The chapter is divided into eight sections — some ideas have been given an entire section whereas others form a subsection of a main section. In sections one through three, I attempt to establish the context for contemporary performing arts in India by looking at conceptions of time, space and the body. In sections four through six, I attempt to look at the creation and reception of performance. I try to supplement this with ideas on improvisation, structure, abstraction, metaphor, empathy, and synaesthesia. And, in sections seven and eight, I include samples of my own work and collaborations at Attakkalari Centre for Movement Arts to elaborate the ideas discussed in the paper.

Mapping human resonances

Through a continuous engagement with bodily practices and choreography, I often think of human experiences as being a series of resonances. These resonances appear to be created by layers of memories, constant sensory inputs from daily life (the empirical world), and the imagination. In other words, the human experience can be thought of as a product of the inter-relationships between the body's histories and residues, the emergent memories of the present, and the images produced by the imagination. Moreover, these resonances could occur in multiple realms or spaces: the empirical (visual, auditory, tactile/somatosensory, gustatory, olfactory), imaginary, temporal and digital, among others. Through this chapter, I attempt to map such resonances experienced by the body (the choreographer's, the performer's, and the spectator's) in the performative context to open up new possibilities.

Before I explore these performative mappings further, I would like to include a note on multiplicity in the Indian context. In a country such as India, multiple strands of identities exist due to differences in caste, religion, social and economic status, education, gender, language, region, history etc. Therefore, there are huge differences amongst individuals in terms of their practices, customs, beliefs, values, aspirations, and artistic expressions etc. These differences are crucial, and are to be kept in mind as we investigate the genealogy of physical and performance practices in India today. We do not have a history of embracing modernity through a continuous and organic process; rather, modernity was abruptly thrust on our society. Moreover, the knowledge and ownership of physical and performance traditions has often changed hands from one community or section to another, and there has been a lot of cross-pollination between these forms as well, often resulting in new expressions.

The vital energy and inspiration for creating contemporary arts often stems from unique individual experiences. Within an individual too, I often see the contradiction of time and evolution in some of the strands mentioned above. This maybe because the genealogies of these strands are complex, and defy chronology; and, because individuals have not invested enough in processing their own histories, memories, and imagination; or indeed, have not had the opportunity of doing so. Interestingly, the realm of performing arts in India can aid in processing these unexplored bodily capitals, and can help bring out original expression.

In a country such as India, several strands of traditional cultural streams and syncretic traditions coexist with rapidly changing contemporary life practices. Particularly in India, and for myself, there is hence an exciting emerging multitude of hybrid artistic expressions.

Spatialization of memory, experience and imagination: Understanding time and place making in the Indian context

While examining the "body" in dance in its current as well as its historic state, it is important to look into the spaces and contexts in which the body is placed; the modes of expression that were, and are, available to it; and the ways in which those expressions are received by an audience. I will first examine some aspects of time and place making in traditional Indian architecture, iconography, literature, and martial arts to bring other dimensions to our perception of space and time, and their implications on the performer's body.

The idea of interchangeability and transposition between time, landscape, architecture, and human bodies is found in various Indian traditions. These traditions include the *Siddha* philosophy of southern India, the *Vastu Shastra* (the science of traditional architecture of ancient India), the *Shilpa Shastra* (the science of sculpting), and the martial art traditions such as *Kalarippayattu*.

The late V. Ganapati STAPATHI, an internationally reputed architect and a master sculptor of traditional idols, made great contributions in the contemporary understanding of *Vastu Shastra* and *Shilpa Shastra*. He had suggested in an interview:

> The science of Vastu is based on the concept of space (subtle energy) as a dynamic element out of which all objects of nature come into existence and into which all disappear ultimately. The frequency of vibration of this subtle energy, which is based on a particular rhythm or time measure, causes the birth and development of all objects of nature. So time is the causal element of all material forms (STHAPATHI 1998).

STAPATHI elaborates on this idea in a talk (1997):

> This time-measure has come to de designated in the scientific field by a peculiar term called "Kaala maanam" and in the technological domain as "Taala maaman", each of which means "time-measure". The "Time" that is known to the Vaastu Science is independent or absolute, not solar time, which is physical or relative.

This notion of rhythm as a pattern or scale of measurement for both time and space is a key concept here. Here in a way, physical forms are considered as the materializations of time. In the same talk, STAPATHI continues:

> In India, the Tala measure is most familiarly applied to the field of music and dance, but that same Tala system has been in force for centuries in the domain of sculpture, architecture and poetry. This Tala measure is also denoted by another term, rhythm, which is used in the fields of music and dance all over the world. This Tala rhythm is used in the design of residential buildings, temple structures and sculptural forms. In the past, it was also used in designing furniture, vehicles and household utensils (ibid.).

I often come across the incredible power of architecture and landscape to invoke complex thoughts and memories. Numerous instances of place making through the the metaphors of landscape and architecture are found in literature, film, visual arts, martial traditions, and the performing arts. These instances have often influenced me during the creation of multimedia dance productions. I would like to briefly explore three examples of place making by looking at the following: a) Indian iconography and architecture; b) the treatment of landscape in Tamil poetry; and c) conceptualizing space in a *Kalarippayattu* pit.

Indian iconography and architecture

In this subsection, I look at Indian iconography, architecture and monuments in order to find their relationship to space making in performance. The idol of *Nataraja* (the iconic image of Shiva as the God of Dance) is a profound example of a single symbolic representation of multiple attributes and concepts. Often, by the roadside in India, an insignificantly shaped, ordinary piece of granite is transformed into an idol or shrine through acts of attribution, rituals and an investment of energy by devotees. In the performance improvisation process, objects or human bodies, or indeed their inter-relationships, become abodes for memory, experience and imagination; often metamorphosing into dynamic images. In turn, these images may find their way into the making of performance. I have talked more about these ideas in section 7 of this chapter.

In his book, "Making Space: Sufis and Settlers in Early Modern India," Nile GREEN suggests how spaces and their relationship to time and reality could be transformed:

> The ritual buildings . . . were transformed through ritual and narrative into other temporally and spatially different places . . . descendants in successive generations continued to make present these connections of new homelands and old ones, whether these 'homelands' were factual spaces of physical ancestry or the imaginary homelands (2012, p. 120).

In my full length dance production *MeiDhwani — Echoes of the Body* (2011), I try to evoke the sense of an "imagined land". A continuously emerging landscape of images and associations is created by the suggested presence of the five elements; the physical and emotional relationships of the dancers amongst themselves; as well as the use of metallic pots and cylindrical lamps. These dynamic images create multi-layered movement trajectories and traces; often intersecting, overlapping, juxtaposing, displacing and contrasting with each other, forming symbols and metaphors in the process.

According to Green, iconography invokes spaces which invite one to listen. In historic spaces, the visual presence is muted and, instead, a meditative quality is invoked which invites the onlooker to pause and listen. Unlike the clear presence of a body that is seen in European iconography, in certain Hindu and Buddhist traditions, idols are often sculpted with cloth or flowing continuous surfaces covering the body in order to remove any hard edges and mute the empirical presence of a body. This gives the idol an internal sense, and urges the viewer to listen rather than simply see.

In the performative context also, this idea of inviting the audience into the inner dynamics and spaces of a performance assumes importance in certain productions, depending on the theme and approach. The use of eye focus either linked to, or detached from, any particular body movement; the specific use of breath to modulate the intensity, intention and quality of specific movement; a shift of weight and center of gravity; the articulation of the spine and its relation to other body parts, etc. can play a role in determining the nature of space a dancer is constructing through a performance. The specific approach adopted by the choreographer and the performer influences whether a sequence or a section of choreography is inviting the audience into its inner spaces, or indeed projecting the action on to them. The making of internal landscapes in performative contexts, is further explained in this chapter in the context of some of my choreographies.

Historic monuments in India — such as Hindu temples and Sufi shrines — indicate facets of life from the past, including the history and memories from a particular period in time. These facets act as a trigger for the imagination. One can feel this spatialization of memories through the organization of space in the monuments. For example, spaces in Hindu temples are often constructed to reveal themselves in stages of progression as devotees go through rituals and perambulations in the edifice. The inner sanctums of Hindu temples allow a more private experience of the Divine, with space for a relatively smaller number of people. Thus, these spaces provide different sets of images and sensations for the devotee (cf. PANDYA 2005). Similarly, navigation through a performance is often influenced by a change of vantage points, perspective, texture, light, color, sound, energy, and dynamics, etc. Certain images, events, sonic elements etc., get prominence and emerge from the field, demanding the attention of the audience.

In his book, Nile GREEN (2012) writes that spaces in Sufi shrines are created through rituals as well as the investment of memory. For GREEN, "architecture or an object can give us visual, tactile and olfactory clues about memory," and can be conceived as "a movement fixed in space." As a choreographer, I am fascinated by these ideas of architecture as the spatialization of memory. I attempt to explore these aspects in my choreography.

Treatment of landscape in Tamil poetry

Tamil *Sangam* poetry, particularly the love poems or the poetry of the interior (*Akanaanooru*), classify poems into different modes called *Tinai* according to the relationship between elements and the mood of the poem. The presence of codified symbols in the poem reflects the inner emotions of the characters. According to this classification system, each *Tinai* has an associated landscape populated with particular flora and fauna, presiding deities, a certain climate, and time of the day, amongst other specifications. These landscapes are named after different flowers: such as *kurinji* for the mountain region, *mullai* for forest region, *marutam* for fertile land, *neithal* for seashore, *palai* for desert or wasteland.[1]

The concepts of *Tinai* were used in 2009 in one of my productions titled *Chronotopia*, in which the interactive scenography changed according to the emotions and events in the choreography. The landscapes of this scenography was produced by the images captured from the events on the stage, which were processed and projected back. This idea is further elaborated later in this chapter.

[1] For more information on Tamil love poems, see RAMANUJAN (1994).

Figure 1: Interactive Scenography and LED Installation in Attakkalari's *Chronotopia*. Photograph: Chris Ziegler.

Figure 2: *Chronotopia*—multimedia dance production by Attakkalari. Photograph: Mohan Das Vadakara.

Figure 3: *Chronotopia* — Scenography depicting internal landscape of the characters in the multimedia dance production by Attakkalari. Photograph: Mohan Das Vadakara.

Conceptualizing space in a *Kalarippayattu* pit

The south Indian martial art tradition of *Kalarippayattu* has a unique body language. It employs some body concepts from the Sidha tradition as well as aspects of Yoga, and is often referred to as dynamic Yoga. It is believed that this martial art tradition has influenced several other Asian martial arts and Indian performing arts. Many masters claim that when the *Kathakali* dance-theatre form was created a few centuries ago, the first performers were *Kalarippayattu* practitioners. The evolution of Indian contemporary dance too owes much to *Kalarippayattu*, and several artists use the embedded body concepts and movement principles of this form in their vocabulary.

The geography of the *Kalari* clay pit where *Kalarippayattu* is practiced is conceived as a symbolic representation of the larger universe and its forces. For a practitioner, it is a place where time, space and the energies of past *gurus* and deities converge. Time — represented by the 12 months of the *Malayalam* calendar — is assigned to 12 designated spots, distributed along the peripheral walls of the *Kalari* arena. Similarly, the energies of past *gurus*, deities, and even the directions represented by the *dikpalakars* (the guardians of the eight directions) are all invoked in the *Kalari* pit. These ideas have been referred to in my production titled *MeiDhwani — Echoes of the Body*, and have been elaborated in section 7 of this chapter.

The human body is placed in this universe where ritualized training and practice heighten the senses and perception. Even the strokes of the herbal oil massage for the practitioners are seemingly designed to aid in constructing this contextualized body. Recycled, circular, and unhindered energy flowing from the *naabhimoola* (the lower abdominal area) is sketched out on the young practitioner's body. This results in the construction of a particular self and body.

In this section, I looked at the spatialization of memory, experience and the imagination by attempting to understand time and place making in the Indian context. We explored examples from architecture, iconography, literature, and martial arts to gain different perspectives. I will now move onto the next section where I share ideas of the performative self and body, with particular reference to contemporary India.

In search of an evolving performative self and body in contemporary India

In this section, I refer to both personal life experiences, as well as pioneering ideas in the field of the performing arts in order to paint a multi-dimensional picture of the performative self and body. While growing up in the southern Indian state of Kerala, with its rich physical and performance traditions, I had the opportunity to experience ritual, folk, classical, and popular performances in a variety of contexts. Massive percussion orchestras during temple festivals; the highly charged snake worship rituals involving trance dances in small village shrines and houses; women's social dances and rituals affirming femininity;

ceremonies for the rites of passage; larger than life characters of the all-night *Theyyam* (ritual performances with huge masks) and *Kathakali* (classical dance theatre) performances; beautiful images from the classical dance forms of *Bharatanatyam* and *Mohiniattam*; the martial energy of *Kalarippayattu* (martial art) and *Kaniyarkali* (martial dance)—all left vivid and indelible impressions on me.

As a young boy, I was keen to learn dance. However, I did not receive permission to learn any dance form, even though most of the performers in the *Kathakali*, *Kootiyattam*, *Theyyam*, and many other forms were male. I was encouraged, instead, to focus on academic studies. Therefore, I had to wait till I went to university, where I stayed in a students' hostel, before I could take my first dance lessons.

As I began learning the classical dance form of *Bharatanatyam*, I started questioning the content of the dance form, even though I was very attracted to its technique and aesthetics. In subsequent years, as I pursued my higher studies in *Bharatanatyam* in Chennai, this urge to find the relevance of the art form to my life, its experiences and concerns, grew, and I started searching for contemporary expressions.

However, this was difficult in the India of 1980s as there were no institutions offering a comprehensive approach to process both the inherited knowledge embedded in our rich physical and performance traditions, as well as contemporary life experiences, in order to create new idioms. Therefore, I sought opportunities to engage with different forms and systems of training in an effort to create an ongoing curriculum of sorts for my own education and artistic growth.

I began exploring theatre practices and experiments in dance in order to find a new path. Working with the contemporary choreographer Chandralekha, and with N. Muthuswamy's Tamil experimental theatre Koothu-P-Pattarai introduced me to new ways of looking at Indian forms. I remember attending a National Theatre festival in Delhi in 1986. I was one of the two performers in a movement adaptation of the play *Suvarottigal* written by N. Muthuswamy, and directed by K.S. Rajendran. The other performer was Sambantham, a practitioner of *Therukoothu* (a form of folk dance-theatre from Tamil Nadu). During the festival, several acclaimed theatre directors and practitioners from all over India presented their training strategies.

These strategies had been developed through an engagement with the traditional forms of their particular regions, including folk, ritual, martial arts, and classical forms. Instead of unearthing body concepts or movement principles from traditional forms, some of these strategies adopted parts of the technique of these forms solely for the training of their actors. This could possibly have been due to a lack of an experiential knowledge of the traditional forms. Nevertheless, for me this experience opened up the world of theatre practitioners such as Stanislavski, Meyerhold, Grotowski, and many others. The exploration of theatre practices from different parts of the world stayed with me when

I continued learning at the London Contemporary Dance School. In the notes below, I have highlighted some of the major influences in the understanding of the performative self and body.

The "extra daily" body

The work of theatre personality Eugenio BARBA — through his years of association with the Polish theatre director and thinker Jerzy Grotowski, as well as, his own research into several performance traditions of the world — was an important part of this journey of learning. BARBA (1991) dealt with the notion of "pre-expressive" layers of knowledge that help to create an "extra-daily" body on stage. These ideas were explained in his pioneering book *A Dictionary of Theatre Anthropology: The Secret Art of the Performer* (1991).

Barba explained the specific ways in which movement can be dilated, and how inherent forces of opposition in movement play a role in creating the "extra-daily" tension on stage. He also articulated the use of breath, eye focus, balance, and so on. This empirical examination of performance art in Barba's work shone a new light on the science of movement embedded in some of the performance traditions he explored. This encounter with the approaches of training and creation by several dance and theatre practitioners helped in furthering my own enquiry into Indian physical and performance traditions. In turn, this has informed and influenced the development of strategies for training dancers at the Attakkalari Centre for Movement Arts in Bangalore, since its inception in 2001.

Manifestations of the body in life situations

Movement artists have to be sensitive to the physical manifestations of thoughts, emotions, and images in daily life. As human bodies are constantly experiencing and communicating much more about life around them than we care to acknowledge, it is important for me, as a choreographer, to access this information and knowledge as part of my creative process.

The pioneering ideas articulated in the 1930s by Marcel MAUSS, in his article "Techniques of the body" (1973 [1935]), include his belief that the techniques acquired by human beings in their lifetimes form a part of their identity. These techniques often assume the role of distinguishing from, or identifying with, a particular group/community/culture etc. MAUSS lists a series of activities — such as swimming, walking, running, dancing, sleeping, waking, and so on — and categorizes them according to the age, profession, gender etc., of the person. These 'techniques' (as he calls them) are part of the *habitus* of the individual, and need to be taken into account in order to help draw a psychological profile of the person and the history of the body. The idea of using physical actions, signs and markings as pointers to the psychological dimensions of an individual, thus, gain importance in the contexts of training, improvisation and performance.

The empirical body and its architecture

Understanding the empirical body, exploring the possibilities of wiring the body in multiple ways, and developing complex inter-relationships and inter-subjectivities among performers have been an essential part of the creation of an evolving body and self. Over the years, contemporary movement art practices developed by many pioneers have dealt with different facets and possibilities of physical manifestations on the stage.

I am particularly drawn to the approaches of the choreographer William Forsythe. The seminal works *Improvisation Technologies* and *Synchronous Objects for One Flat Thing (reproduced)*, based on Forsythe's deep understanding of movement, have greatly influenced recent developments in performance training. Through his works, Forsythe articulates in detail the possibilities and complexities of the constantly evolving, empirical-geometric relationships between different parts of the body of a single performer, and among performers on the stage.

The "symbolic" body

Images, symbols, and spaces play a crucial role in performance training. From my understanding, a "symbolic" body is created by connecting the senses and imagination very closely. Symbols are arrived at through a process of sensation, imagination, abstraction, and stylization. Ideas are transposed from one sensory realm to another. The dancer may have to internalise these images, symbols and spaces, as they may not be empirically available on stage. Appropriate training allows the performer to access the world of symbols and imagination.

The training, importantly, also equips the body to follow the associated syntax and grammar, and enables the performer to articulate these clearly. If the performer does not have the capacity to comprehend and articulate this process of connections and abstractions, or the audience is not sensitized to decipher them, then the movements can seem arbitrary, and sometimes even confusing or meaningless. The codification process is culturally informed and influenced as well. Therefore, performers and spectators have to gain access to particular cultural realms in order to de-codify embedded information and experience works of art.

Ideas of the Body in traditional Indian physical practices

Traditional Indian dance-theatre forms such as *Kathakali*, *Kootiyattam* or even *Bharatanatyam* employ a comprehensive training scheme of physical exercises to give a heightened sense of body awareness, agility, flexibility and strength, as well as an acute sense of music and space. Post training, the performer can execute complicated physical articulations, suggesting multiplicities of evolving spaces — both macro and micro — on the stage at any given time.

Sound and sonic vibrations are often imagined as the core basis of expression in the training process. All other articulations are considered variations of this fundamental core. Even when vibrations are not explicitly audible, they are imagined, and act as the motor behind the physical action. Therefore, breath control attains a very important role in the training process.

Elaborate eye exercises are employed in *Kootiyattam* and *Kathakali* to exploit the enormous potential of the eyes for expressing a range of emotions, when used in conjunction with the appropriate facial muscles. Therefore, eye focus, breath control, a specific organization of body postures and physical movements, accompanied by appropriate music are incorporated to construct a body that suggestively transcends its own physical contours on stage.

The process of acting begins with the construction of a neutral body through training. This neutral body is — interestingly called *Paathra* or a vessel — capable of containing shapes, movements, emotions, and expressions. For example, in *Kootiyattam*, the actor is trained to keep his lips in close contact with the teeth in order to keep his face neutral. In other words, the process of acting involves creating this neutral body first, before enacting a character or a situation. This device is central to the idea of enactment in many Indian performance traditions as it is common for a single actor to handle several characters or situations. Rather than imagining a purely empirical body, aspects of *Sookshma Shareera* or the subtle body, prevalent in other Indian traditions such as Yoga, are at play here as well.

In many streams of philosophy, the body is seen as unclean, and not capable of experiencing the Divine. According to these streams of thought, suppressing bodily urges and experiences seem to be the only path to experience the Divine. In stark contrast, the *Siddha* and *Tantric* traditions in India hold the human body in high esteem. The body and its physical attributes are considered pure, and of a higher level.

In the *Siddha* traditions, the body is often conceived and imagined through the five elements: earth, water, wind, ether, and fire. Several practices in *Siddha* are aimed at fine tuning these elements to reach a desired balance, so that the body can achieve supernatural abilities. It is believed that the body undergoes a purification of sorts through intense physical practices, long meditations, and the consumption of appropriate medicines.

The idea of fine-tuning the body espoused in the *Siddha* traditions and Yogic practices finds a direct expression in the martial art form of *Kalarippayattu*. In *Kalarippayattu*, movements derived from essentialized animal motifs are woven together to create a body language that is earthy, sinuous and cyclical, yet capable of producing high leaps and explosive energy. Weapons become an extension of the practitioner's body, and continuous rigorous practice is aimed at achieving a heightened sense of awareness. This awareness is encapsulated and conjured up in the celebrated *Kalari* notion of the "*body becoming all eyes*" (Zarrilli 1998).

Enhancing kinaesthesia and proprioception

As a choreographer and teacher in my specific situation in India today, I am faced with the need to explore both the empirical spaces so beautifully articulated by Forsythe, as well as the "symbolically" mandated spaces prevalent in many Indian performance traditions. In my works, I often attempt an oscillating presence of the body on the stage. I alternately access and process contemporary experiences, while blending these with the nuances of the "symbolic body" — a product of traditional knowledge systems — in order to create "suspended spaces" of sorts.

Increasingly, contemporary Indian dance artists are recognizing the need to process and mediate experiences and imaginations stemming from complex contemporary life situations, in the ever more interconnected world. Additionally, they have to find ways to access inherited knowledge from our traditions as well.

The training programme developed at Attakkalari Centre for Movement Arts employs a process of creating a body that is capable of inhabiting both the empirical and the imaginary worlds simultaneously. The pedagogic system includes strategies to enhance the physical facilities of the dancers by exposing them to many different styles of dance, martial arts, and body care systems. The dancers simultaneously try to effectively use images, abstraction, symbols, and metaphors to create "symbolic bodies."

An encounter with different movement styles, methods of training, specificities of that particular form, and their unique approaches, helps the dancers to discover different facets of the body. The performers familiarize themselves with different movement systems within specific parameters and rules. Training in different forms, arguably, gives relatively more comprehensive body awareness. However, this needs to be handled prudently and with care, to avoid confusion and conflicting information for the performer.

Dancers have to become increasingly aware of the distribution and use of energy and breath, the transitions and placement of body weight, eye focus, shape of the spine, the relationship to gravity, the starting point and trajectory of a movement in the body, the images and intention of a movement, musicality, as well as the multiple layers of space. They have to be aware of their relationship with objects, scenography, other performers on the stage, as well as the audience.

Dancers are also trained to project their bodies beyond fixed empirical spaces and volumes by extending their bodies and movement to an imaginary space. For example, a dancer imagines a line, a trajectory or a field, passing through his/her body, thus suggesting dynamic spaces beyond the contours of the physical body. The dancer, thus, imagines each molecule of the body as having an individual agency. These molecules can then connect to imagined and evolving spaces, or perceived trajectories of movement in time.

These processes of physical articulation and imagination create a multiplicity of dynamic spaces, depending on the dancer's physical capabilities as well as his/her ability to imagine. At Attakkalari, working towards the creation of this enhanced sense of kinaesthesia and proprioception in the dancer, is part of the training and artistic mediation process.

Improvisation and structuring of emergent bodies and movements

During dance improvisation, dancers often have to access their memories or a set of impressions in a particular realm, in order to abstract and create metaphors resulting in specific body postures and movement sequences. This extrapolation and mediation of experiences, memories, and the imagination from one realm into another through a synaesthetic process is a complex one. If the parameters for the improvisation are chosen very carefully, then the skill set and complex wiring of the body gained through training, along with a cultivated desire of the body to inhabit the spaces provided by the imagination, can often make interesting cross-sensory connections, resulting in the emergence of fresh movement vocabulary. Most of the time though, it is difficult for people to transcend their habitual movements. Therefore, setting the right parameters for improvisation tasks is of utmost importance in order to push the psycho–physical entity of the performer beyond the habitual realm.

For a choreographer, the task often is to be a keen observer. This helps him/her to identify what is fresh in the movement material created, and in making new connections with the material generated by other members of the group. The choreographer has to also envision the possibilities of potential connections that may arise in the creative process subsequently. Unlike classical forms, in contemporary movement arts, the logic of these images, and the cross connection amongst them, often rest within the work of art itself. Therefore, structuring and further modification of the material from the improvisation is necessarily dictated by many factors, such as the sound score, dramaturgy, color story, dynamics and scenography, including interactive scenography etc.

This sensory extrapolation and cross-connection of moving images often results in a multi-dimensional field of perception. Here, any set of relations or events can gain prominence against the larger set of relations which tend to become the field. The field and events are multifaceted, and it is important to keep this aspect in mind, without focusing solely on the visual qualities. Therefore, I am deliberately restraining myself from using the word "foregrounding" and "backgrounding" as that often unfairly privileges the visual aspect of the field and events.

Performance as pattern making and synaesthesia

Performance, like any other art, is pattern making of sorts. Understanding the processes of creating and deciphering a complex set of patterns is important in making sense of a performance. The set of rules used to create the patterns can emerge from i) the empirical world; ii) a specially constructed performance universe with its own parameters; or indeed from iii) the realm of the imagination. The processes of deciphering the embedded information is dependent on one's own understanding of a series of codes employed in any given performance. These codes can be determined by a certain set of conventions (as in the case of many classical performing arts); or by a new or evolving set of relationships — the logic of which might often lie within the framework of that particular art work (as in the case of several contemporary performance works).

These patterns are experienced differently if the vantage points are different or, indeed, if the contexts in which they are presented are different. In other words, the access to patterns in space — both empirical and imaginary — are determined by the ongoing *transitions* (as coined by the renowned cultural theorist Homi K. Bhabha) in the world at large, and in one's own life. The body itself — as choreographer, performer and spectator — has a history, and undergoes constant changes and experiences. The ways in which these experiences are contextualized become significant in the meaning making process during a performance.

In the performing arts, abstraction and stylization are often used to suggest situations and images that are larger than life, or indeed sublime. In his article "Art and Synesthesia: in Search of the Synesthetic Experience", Hugo HEYRMAN writes:

> We can define a metaphor as a figurative expression, which always involves a transfer between two different contexts. This means that metaphors are not only a figure of speech, but also a figure of thought ... A metaphor is like a mental encounter; it can produce a flash of insight. The poetic form of the metaphor allows us to counter-balance rational thinking with a creative potential, by making the words more faithful to their sensual origin. Metaphors are grounded in our bodily experiences in the world. Artists use metaphors to bridge differences between seemingly dissimilar images and ideas. In art, synesthesia and metaphor are united. Through the arts, the synesthetic experience became communicable, and blended with a personal vision (2005).

Quite often, artistic mediation involves a process of reading the impact felt in a particular sensory organ or a combination of a few organs, which in turn might be the transposition of an experience from another sensory organ. Input from one sensory organ can stimulate an experience in another sensory organ and realm. In an interview with Stephen John Sackur for "Hard Talk" (BBC), Composer Philip Glass remarked: "Music is a Place." A musician feeling the taste of the interval between two notes; or a visual artist experiencing the smell of a color; or a dancer feeling the touch of light falling on his or her body, are common.

Traditional Indian practitioners and connoisseurs often transpose measures and qualities from one discipline to another. In Indian musical traditions, experiencing the auditory world of a musical arrangement through the rendition of a particular *raga* can invoke visual landscapes or denote specific times of the day in the imagination of the listener. The making of physical and temporal space in this way through sonic devices is not done in isolation. The treatises governing several performance traditions of India also suggest the relationships of certain rhythms or musical structures or colors to certain emotions. For example, a 5-beat rhythm (*taka-takitta*) is used to show aggression or anger, and red can be the color associated with this emotion in the dance theatre form of *Kathakali*. This extrapolation of certain aspects/qualities from one domain to another in order to affect a materialization with very distinctive and specific characteristics is part of the creative process and codification in the performing arts.

The process of stylization and abstraction inevitably undergoes a series of subliminal yet culturally sanctioned distillations before arriving at acceptable gestures (*mudra*), body postures, lines, or movements. The selection of elements is governed by the notion of *auchitya* or appropriateness. The notion of a complete ideal body is encapsulated in the traditional Indian aesthetic concept of *saushtava* which outlines the 10 essential qualities for a dancer.

How does the audience perceive a performance? Neuroscientists argue that activities of mirror neurons play an important role in identifying oneself with the physicality and movement, as well as the emotional state of another person. French sociologist and philosopher, Pierre Bourdieu's concepts of "habitus and field" have influenced our understanding of receiving and perceiving information in a dance performance. In their lecture titled "Coming Alive in a World of Texture: For Neurodiversity" at the *Thinking — Resisting — Reading the Political* conference (2010), Brian Massumi and Erin Manning state that if one does not have the access to the realm of cross connections, it is possible to miss the emergent multiplicity, and instead opt for easy inference supported by so called factual information.

The resonances of symbols and metaphors depend on the shared access of a sensorial memory, experience, and imagination. Recent discoveries by neuroscientists such as V.S. Ramachandran point to the physiological mechanisms and brain activities that allow us to communicate synaesthetically and metaphorically. He says: "One skill that many creative people share is a facility for using metaphor ... It is as if their brains are set up to make links between seemingly unrelated domains" (RAMACHANDRAN/HEARING 2003, p. 52). This aspect of experiencing the invisible or non-auditory, either symbolically or otherwise, is part of artistic practice.

The role of empathy in the meaning making process

Certain events, actions or individuals on the stage amidst a field of realms, gain importance depending on the structure and nature of the performance; and the "habitus" of the performers and audience. These emergent "experiential immediacies" and "presences" are vital in understanding the notion of empathy in a performative context. The interaction and exchange of kinaesthetic imagination between the performer and the audience as a co-creator is important in understanding the scope of empathy as a major factor in the meaning making process.

By playing with time (altering, stretching and collapsing time on the stage), chronology (breaking empirical chronology), and space (invoking multiple spaces), the performance creates a world of its own. In these emergent environments, fields and trajectories that a dancer has to negotiate, a discerning member of the audience can perceive constantly evolving visual, auditory and even tactile priorities, singling out objects, movements and events from the "field," resulting in a certain kind of navigation through the performance. This navigation is tied to empathy.

Navigation through a performance often involves a dynamic hierarchy of the senses as well a hierarchy of the spaces created in the performance. An extended version of anthropomorphism takes place where the realistic functionality of the body, its movement, emotions etc. get stretched in dance through the creation of an "extra-daily" body on stage. Theatrical structures, conventions as well as devices and approaches that are particular to that production, are used as well. A spectator intermittently distances himself/herself from the performance action by remembering the empirical reality of being in a theatre amongst other audience members. This oscillation between an objectification *of* the performance and a vicarious identification *with* the performance is central to the empathetic experience of dance.

In Indian traditions, the empathy of an actor to a character is a case of an oscillation between identification with the situation and an objective detachment from it. This is often referred in the training process as *Taadaatmiyam* — transitory identification with a character or a situation. In classical Indian dance theatre forms, there are detailed processes prescribed for a performer to continuously be in a state of oscillation. The performer has to identify with the character while retaining a subjective consciousness to relate to other empirical factors. These other factors include the story line, fellow performers, musicality, and a perception of the emotional and motor empathy of the audience, amongst others.

Empathy often allows us to identify with the situation even if these situations have to be mediated through a set of conventions, metaphors and symbols. In the make believe world of performance, movements, gestures, events, or characters are often represented by suggesting their disembodied presence. Through theatrical devices, disembodied and suggested presence can also create an empathetic response in the audience. Examples include an enactment of the play *Ashokavanikaangam* in the Sanskrit dance theatre tradition *Kootiyattam* where Ravana addresses Sita who is physically absent, but symbolically represented by an oil lamp. Similarly, when a character dies in *Kootiyattam* performances of stories such as *Baalivadham* or *Jataayuvadham*, after showing the elaborate process of dying on stage, the actual death itself is left out, but is represented symbolically by laying down the character's costume on stage.

A classic example of disembodied presence is described in an article by Adriano D'ALOIA in the the book "Kinesthetic Empathy in Creative and Cultural Practices" (2012). D'ALOIA explains that in the film *Trapeze* (1956), made by the American director Carol Reed, the death of a trapeze artist is shown by shots of the gasping audience, the empty swinging trapeze, and the empty bouncing net underneath etc. In a performance, the physical reaction of a performer to a situation or action can be experienced by the audience even if the cause of the reaction is not shown. In other words, multi-dimensional streams of empathy are at play when we watch a performance.

Discussing the notions of kinaesthetic engagement, embodied responses, and intersubjectivity, Dee REYNOLDS suggests that conceptualizations of empathy can be too restrictively tied to the category of, and instead proposes to treat it in terms of, the more fluid notion of "affect," which is embodied and not defined by emotional categories. In her article, "Kinesthetic Empathy and the Dance's Body: From Emotion to Affect," she writes:

> I explore kinesthetic empathy as a movement across and between bodies, which, in an artistic situation, can have affective impact with potential to change modes of perception and ways of knowing . . . movement among dancers and between dancer(s) and spectator, rather than any specific, individual dancer constitute 'dance's body' (REYNOLDS 2012, p. 88f.).

For her, this is similar to the assertion of D'ALOIA in relation to films. She writes:

> The camera can include its own movement — that of the 'film's body', which is specific to the film medium — thereby intensifying the spectator's own kinesthetic sensations as they internally 'imitate' the movement of the camera as well as the character (D'ALOIA 2012, p. 88).

Objects as metaphors in performance, and making of places through layering of meaning

During a performance, the audience is invited to various sources of emotional resonance including movement sequences, sonic and pictorial images, objects and color, amongst others. These resonances may be influenced by current or recent experiences, but quite often invoke memories and perceptions of inherited information as well.

In my recent work *MeiDhwani — Echoes of the Body,* my attempt was to create a sensorial narrative, exploring the idea of latent memories in the landscape and the human body. Here, my attempt was to find a symbolic representation on the stage of a transitional place consisting of very limited elements. The empty performance space was conceived as a microcosm. This idea was inspired by the rectangular *Kalarippayattu* clay pit as well as the diagrammatic representation of the universe in the architectural tradition of *Vastu Shastra.*

Then I chose metallic spherical pots (suggesting femininity, water, and earth) and cylindrical oil lamps (indicating masculinity, wind, and fire). The props had certain continuous curvatures and shapes designed to invoke almost primordial memories. The shapes helped to bring to the fore a quality of tactility invoking latent memories, similar to the sculptural characteristics of Hindu and Buddhist iconography.

Improvisation tasks were set to create movement material. One of the ideas was to invest energy in and attribute different images, qualities, and meaning to the props by finding new associations and shapes in conjunction with body movement. In the words of Nile Green, "landscape and objects become spatialization of memories" whereas "human beings are embodiments and carriers of memories." Through constantly evolving dynamic corporeal images, complemented by the use of props, "bodies become impermanent abodes of narrative."

In the process, sometimes pots symbolized femininity or different parts of the female anatomy while cylindrical lamps evoked masculinity and became phallic symbols. On other occasions, the props became utensils or objects in daily life, or simply a part of the landscape. Through these transformations, a complex set of images and meanings were constructed. Humans and props emerged from the landscape only to dissolve into it subsequently, and re-emerge as transient materializations of memories, experiences and imaginations resulting in multiple images, events and trajectories. Here, the original sources of inspiration went into the background, and had only an embedded yet subliminal presence.

Images from memories, life experiences, or the imagination of the dancers, or indeed a set of images given by me or collected from books, cinema, or through our research often became the starting point for structured improvisations to create movement material. The movement sequences thus created by individual dancers was influenced by information from their habitus which included their training as dancers, as well as all the external stimuli given to them as part of the improvisation task.

For dancers, these sequences now became the raw material to communicate and negotiate with other dancers. These chosen movements were then edited, and processed further with a set of body concepts and movement principles that were specially chosen for the production as one of the connecting threads. In creating duets, trios or group pieces, the movement sequences underwent another transformation in relation to the groups' vocabulary. These negotiations and transactions were complex and multi-layered. I wanted to create several layers of experience for the audience. I attempted to do this by developing varied and evolving inter-relationships on the stage by suggesting multiple cross connections.

As a choreographer, I looked very closely for special moments where unique movements and images emerged that offered possibilities for further connections. Slowly, different components of the piece began to have an evolving

Figure 4

Figure 5

Figure 6

Figure 7

Figures 4–8: From the production *MeiDhwani — Echoes of the Body*, 2011. Photographs: Dilip Banerjee, Sudeep Bhattacharya and Peter Christopher.

relationship with each other, within the over-arching conceptual framework set up at the beginning of the process. At some point, each one of those components found new alignments and relationships in terms of space, time and energy.

Ideas of individual, universe and technology as coordinates of transient spaces in performance

A contemporary dance performance is often an act of actualizing a complex set of overlapping realms, relationships, patterns, images, and perceptions. These result in the construction of a multi-dimensional experiences of sorts. Physical movements are embedded with information and energy, becoming capable of motor and emotional empathy. While the body suggests evolving spaces and relationships in a performance through its movement, it is also placed in spaces and relationships created by agencies external to it.

A city street in India can be a site of different life practices, rituals and events ranging from the most cosmopolitan, urban and contemporary to dating back to a few centuries in the past. As contemporary life is immersed in these time frames and belief systems, quite often artists have to find ways in which to process these seemingly fragmented and often discordant experiences, and produce images and a narrative structure that are authentic and relevant. As the "habitus and field" of this world is multi-layered, so will be the expression stemming from it.

I would now like to explore the ways in which emergent spaces in a performance are perceived. Additionally, I want to look at how the audience reacts when technology helps in constructing those transient spaces. In the multimedia performance context, the sensorial experience is constituted by a sense of resonances created in overlapping, often seemingly dissolving, flowing and merging frames and domains. In his article, Hugo HEYRMAN states:

> The complementary power of art and science are extending our horizon of perception. With the use of telematic hypermedia, synesthetic art forms will become much more sophisticated in their own right. There is a future for tele-synesthesia, to bring synesthetic experiences further into our daily awareness (2005).

The idea of an immersed sense of experience involving multiple sensory organs and non-linear interactive modes might become part of creating and experiencing the arts.

When a performance is mediated with interactivity and digital scenography, the notion of non-linearity becomes pronounced. The context which a body inhabits can be changed in a split second. Digital technology allows a change in the scenography, sound-scapes, illumination and color, the sequence of events, the vantage points etc., instantaneously. This change is similar to the way our imagination works.

The Indian psyche has a propensity to immerse itself in the synaesthetic and sensorial experience of *rasa*. It can receive large empirical imagery and internal landscapes. It also has the accustomed capacity to invest in minute aspects of gestures and facial expressions. Simultaneously, it can imagine itself as being a part of a larger universal energy. With these qualities combined, a rapid transition in perception is made possible, thus offering a wide range of options for a contemporary Indian dance artist. Thus, the senses tend to shift focus between specific objects emerging out of the evolving audio-visual-temporal fields created by digital technology and live action on the one hand, and grasping the overall impression of the ambient fields on the other. In my multimedia dance productions *Purushartha* and *Chronotopia*, I try to explore the possibilities of technology to challenge notions of chronology and perception by invoking diametrically opposite realms in quick succession, or even simultaneously.

In *Purushartha* (2006), Japanese collaborators Kunihiko Matsuo, Mitsuaki Matsumoto, Naoki Hamanaka, and I were exploring ways in which to bring in the spirit of the Indian philosophical concept *Purushartha* through a sensorial narrative where technology played a major role. We chose to abstract the notions of *Dharma* (pursuit of duty), *Artha* (pursuit of wealth of any kind, including knowledge), *Kama* (pursuit of desire), and *Moksha* (salvation) etc. to images of the "Dilemmas in Life" and further to the aspects of "Phenomenology of Perception."

In *Purushartha*, dots, lines, spirals, square, and circles mingled with more figurative images to create digitally constructed transient spaces, for live action to inhabit. The interactive projections on a continuous white dance floor and back drop, improvised musical score, and the sequenced LED lights illuminating and defining the borders at the sides of the stage etc. were chosen to create almost austere yet imagined spaces. The musical score (which was processed live on stage), and the accompanying voice announcing the exact ticking of time for the entire duration of the performance, created a sense of altered theatrical time of 60 minutes into which a life story was compressed.

Subsequently, in another production *Chronotopia* (2009), I used movement and technology to explore notions of travel and *Tinai* from ancient Tamil poetry. Technology aided in expressing the emotional landscapes of the protagonist — who was represented by three female dancers. In my discussions with my collaborators, one of the main points of focus was to create an imagined land where the interactive scenography would continuously transform as the positions of the dancers and the dynamics and nature of the choreographic events changed. I collaborated with Professor Chris Salter and his team (Concordia University, Canada) on the light installation, Chris Ziegler (ZKM, Karlsruhe, Germany) for the interactive projections, Thomas Dotzler (Sweden) for light design, and Mathias Duplessy (France) for the electro-acoustic score for the piece.

The neon lights from the installation, as well as the images of the dancers were captured, processed and projected back onto a gauze screen creating an interactive scenography referring to the idea of changing landscapes in a journey. Even when the stage was dark, an infra-red camera captured the images,

Figure 9

Figure 10

Figure 11

Figure 12

Figure 13

Figures 9–14: From the production *Purushartha*, 2006. Photographs: Thilo Beu and Alok Johri.

and projected the processed images back on the stage, thus creating a dream or memory of sorts. During the course of the performance, the landscapes created by the processed images of stage events were recycled, creating a sense of memory, loss, and an alteration of time. Here, an effort was made to collapse and stretch the notion of time, as well as materialize time through images.

The stage itself was divided physically into three horizontal spaces. Upstage was a light installation, emanating sequenced neon lights, consisting of several poles placed in a row. In the middle of the stage was a translucent gauze screen. The stage, thus, had three areas: one around the light installation; the second behind the gauze; and the third in front of the gauze. We used the idea of *Parikramanam* (the perambulations denoting a change of scene used in Indian performance traditions), effectively circling the gauze and the light installation behind it. These three spaces (each sometimes with their own action and stories) existing simultaneously on stage, also disturbed the notion of place and time for the audience.

In both these productions, the physical movement of the dancers, and the different production components (aided by and including stage technologies) often referred to elements from Indian traditions while expressing a contemporary idea.

Conclusion

While keeping the specificity of the Indian context in mind, and by looking at the creation and reception of performance works, I hope that this chapter has aided in better understanding the contemporary movement arts practice in India. My attempt was to chalk out a journey of sorts, in order to explain the different streams that contribute to the making and the experience of a performance. These streams include training, a few conceptual ideas pertaining to the body, its histories, and its locations of inhabitance. I tried to do this through my own personal journey as an artist, while foraying briefly into some of the thoughts and practices that have influenced my approach. My attempt was also to list a few possible strategies to deal with the challenges arising from the multiple streams of time that a contemporary performing artist has to negotiate in India today.

References

Barba, E. (1991): A Dictionary of Theatre Anthropology: The Secret Art of the Performer. – London.

D'Aloia, A. (2012): Cinematic Empathy: Spectator Involvement in the Film Experience. In: Reynolds, D./Reason, M. (Eds.) Kinesthetic Empathy in Creative and Cultural Practices. – Chicago, pp. 88*ff.*

Glass, P. (2012): 'Music is the most eloquent language'— An interview with Stephen John Sackur for 'Hard Talk' (BBC).

GREEN, N. (2012): Making Space: Sufis and Settlers in Early Modern India. – Oxford.

HEYRMAN, H. (2005): Lecture titled "Art and Synesthesia: in Search of the Synesthetic Experience" presented at the First International Conference on Art and Synesthesia. http://www.doctorhugo.org/synaesthesia/art/index.html#5 (accessed January 4, 2013).

MANNING, E./MASSUMI, B. (2010): Lecture titled "Coming Alive in a World of Texture: For Neurodiversity" at the 'Thinking – Resisting – Reading the Political' conference in Giessen, Germany. http://youtu.be/DqUaEc O30T0 (accessed November 17, 2012).

MAUSS, M. (1973): Techniques of the Body. In: Economy and Society, 2:1, pp. 70–88.

PANDYA, Y. (2005): Concepts of Space in Traditional Indian Architecture. – Michigan.

RAMACHANDRAN, V.S./HUBBARD, E.M. (2003): Hearing Colors, Tasting Shapes. In: Scientific American Vol. 288(5), pp. 57*ff*.

RAMANUJAN, A.K. (1994): The Interior Landscape: Love Poems from a Classical Tamil Anthology. – Oxford.

REYNOLDS, D. (2012): Kinesthetic Empathy and the Dance's Body: From Emotion to Affect. In: REYNOLDS, D./REASON, M (Eds.): Kinesthetic Empathy in Creative and Cultural Practices – Chicago, pp. 88*ff*.

SCHECHNER, Richard (2001): Rasaesthetics in TDR: The Drama Review. Vol. 45, No. 3, (T 171), pp. 27–50.

STAPATHI, V.G. (1997): Transcript of a talk on the Tala System of Spatial Measures. Referenced in Vastu Design—Lesson 9. http://www.vastu-design.com/seminar/9.php (accessed November 21, 2010).

STAPATHI, V.G. (1998): In conversation with Savita Rao. Harmonizing Humanity and Nature through *Vastu Shastra* the ancient Indian science of time and space. YOGALife. http://www.sivananda.org/publications/yogalife/spring98/?page=/publications/yogalife/spring98/spring98-4.html (accessed December 19, 2010).

ZARRILLI, P. B. (1990): What Does It Mean to 'Become the Character': Power, Presence, and Transcendence in Asian In-Body Disciplines of Practice. In: SCHECHNER, R./APOPEL, W. (Eds.) By Means of Performance. – Cambridge, pp. 144*ff*.

ZARRILLI, P. B. (1998): When the Body Becomes All Eyes: Paradigms, Discourses, and Practices of Power in *Kalarippayattu*, a South Indian Martial Art. – Oxford.

Jan Weinhold

Family Constellation Therapy: Body Memory and the Sense of Space

"Family constellation" is a ritualized form of counselling or psychotherapy conducted in the setting of a group (SAX/WEINHOLD/SCHWEITZER 2010). Family constellations were introduced in Germany in the beginning of the 1990s (WEBER 1993). Over the following two decades, the approach enjoyed rapid adoption in various settings and fields of therapeutic and counselling practice. It spread to various other countries around the globe (ALONSO 2005; COHEN 2006). In Germany, the method was criticized within academia and psychotherapy, in particular for seemingly patriarchal "orders of love" according to which family dynamics evolve, and the directive method and stance of the founder of family constellation, Bert Hellinger (HAAS 2009).

A distinguishing feature of family constellation compared to conventional forms of psychotherapy is that the client does not speak very much. Instead, after briefly formulating a problem and with the assistance of a family constellation facilitator, the client selects group members who do not have any knowledge about the client's family, and sets them up in a shifting spatial constellation. Distances and angles between representatives, and their body postures in relation to each other, are said to correspond to the client's inner image of his family (COHEN 2006). Although a single constellation process rarely lasts longer than 30 minutes, clients are often deeply affected by the social scenario, and frequently report therapeutic effects, such as improved interpersonal relationships or well-being. How can a short-time group-setting with strangers forming a spatial social scenario contribute to change processes which are usually achieved by long-time psychotherapy? I will argue that, during family constellation seminars, memories and associated insights about the client's family dynamics are induced and elaborated upon, which are based on the sensory stimulation and explication of a specific body memory.

In this chapter, the method of family constellation will be first described, and then illustrated with a case from our research. Next, the concept of body memory will be introduced. Finally, the way in which the interplay of the senses, the body and the condensation of time within body memory contribute to the effectiveness of family constellation will be analysed, particularly in regard to how the sense of spatial perception as an interpersonal sense resonates with the emotions and the body memory of participants.

Family constellation: Origins and process

Family constellation can be seen as a systems-oriented individual therapy within a group setting. Bert Hellinger, a former catholic priest who worked for several years as a missionary in South Africa and who became a psychotherapist after his return to Germany, developed family constellations as a unique method drawing on multiple sources. Family constellation borrows from several established psychotherapeutic methods, including group psychotherapy, systemic therapy, psychodrama, family sculptures, and the intergenerational family relations theory of "invisible loyalties" (Boszormenyi-Nagy and Spark 1973; Cohen 2006).

Family constellations are mostly conducted in a group setting seminar of two or three day's duration. In a typical setup, up to 30 people who are not family members and who do not have any knowledge about each other's families, meet with a facilitator. Usually they meet just at that one seminar, not as part of a long-term therapeutic relationship. Approximately 15 participants have signed up for a constellation of their own family system. Additionally, up to 15 observing participants take part without signing up for a constellation of their own family. All participants sit in a large circle, and active participants take turns creating their own family constellation.

At first, the facilitator interviews the client about his problem or concern — typically health-related or family-related issues. Then, he or she briefly asks for information about the present family and the family of origin. Specifically, it is asked for significant or traumatic events and relationships: for example, "Who belongs to the family?", "Who was or is expelled from the family?," and "What were the traumas and significant events within the family history?" Such events include premature deaths, abortions, suicide, war crimes, fleeing and displacement, and expelled members of the family who were denied their right to belong, such as a child given up for adoption (Cohen 2006, p. 230).

Next, the facilitator asks the client to select individuals from the group to represent family members, including him- or herself, as so called "representatives." The client places all representatives into the large empty space within the circle. To do this, he puts his hands on the shoulders of the representative and guides him into place. Once this has been accomplished, the client sits in the circle and observes the process. Non-personal elements (for example, "depression" or "fate") can also be positioned in the room. After positioning all representatives, the client observes the scene from outside. In the beginning, the representatives stand still without moving or talking. This spatial scenario with its distances, angles and body postures is supposed to correspond to the inner image of the respective family.

Asked by the facilitator, representatives voice sensations and observations from within their positions. They often state obvious sensations: for example, "I don't feel good," "A good place," or "Fine." Further, representatives report interpersonal qualities relating to persons or elements they are supposed to represent: for example, "I can't see my Grandmother," or "My husband is between me and my future," or "I don't seem to belong to my family." Sometimes they express strong emotions and physiological sensations that are assumed to relate to past events in the family. For example, if a representative says "I feel a pain in my back," the therapist may hypothesize that somebody in the family was physically attacked; or, on a more symbolic level, that the actual person had a strong burden to bear.

In a further process, the facilitator rearranges the spatial scenario step by step. Representatives are asked to change their positions, sometimes according to their own impetus. New representatives may be added as well. During the so called "process-work," the facilitator may ask representatives to voice ritualized sentences vis-à-vis one or several other representatives upon: for example, "Dear father, I connect with you by being like you," and later, "You will always be my father [...] but I will choose to live my life in my own way" (STIEFEL/HARRIS/ZOLLMANN 2002). Additionally, ritualized gestures may be prescribed to disentangle so called "enmeshments." The facilitator may suggest to the representative of the client to bow down in front of another person with whom he or she has been in conflict as a symbol of respect, or to ask for forgiveness. A stone may be given back to a person as a symbol of the "fate" that was mistakenly carried for this person; or a scarf may be laid on the ground to set a border between the family of origin and the actual family (partner and children) of the client.

Proponents of family constellations claim that by positioning representatives for family members in a spatial scenario, synchronic and diachronic family dynamics will become visible in a condensed manner. The client is supposed to gain insights into his or her family dynamics by observing the constellation, and to experience those symbolized dynamics directly by stepping into the final arrangement, the so-called "solution picture," a constellation in which the client is supposed to feel less burdened (SCHNEIDER 2009). The method aims for the client to take home memories of the constellation and an inner image of the "solution picture." To illustrate the method, an example from our research follows.

An example of a family constellation process

As part of a clinical study, eight family constellation seminars were conducted in our institute (SCHWEITZER et al. 2012). One family constellation is depicted in a schematic manner in the following pictures. The triangle indicates the viewing direction of the representative. The back of representatives for females is displayed round; the back of representatives for males is displayed angled; and abstract elements are displayed as triangles. Six static and schematic scenes of the dynamic scenario are selected that map the course of the process. Our case describes the individual constellation of Marie, a 40-year-old teacher, who is married and has three sons between the ages of two and 11 years. Marie weeps when the facilitator asks for her concern, which is "to understand what this permanent anxiety means, not to manage it on this planet as a family." In the original constellation, Marie (see Figure 1) sets up representatives (abbreviation = rep. or reps.) for herself (RCL) and the "anxiety not to manage on this planet" (A).

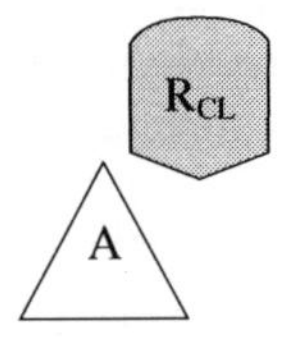

Figure 1: Original constellation of Marie

The representative of the client describes a strong sensation of numbness when the rep. of anxiety enters the scenario. The rep. of anxiety reports he has "something to accomplish here." The facilitator asks Marie to position a rep. for her mother (M) and for her father (F) (see Figure 2).

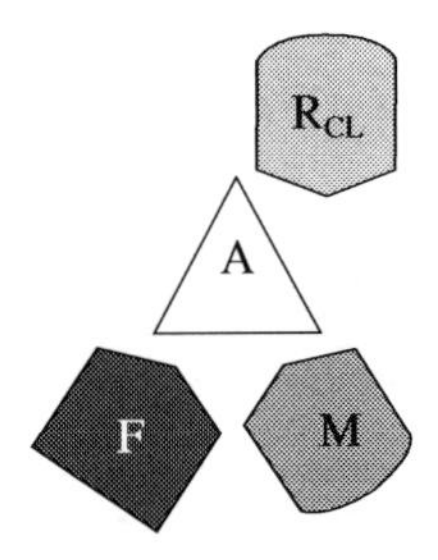

Figure 2: Representatives of Marie's parents are added

Then the facilitator asks all the reps. to move if they feel any spontaneous impulses to do so. Now the rep. of Marie's father stands close to the rep. of the client, they embrace each other, indicating a connection between Marie and her father (see Figure 3).

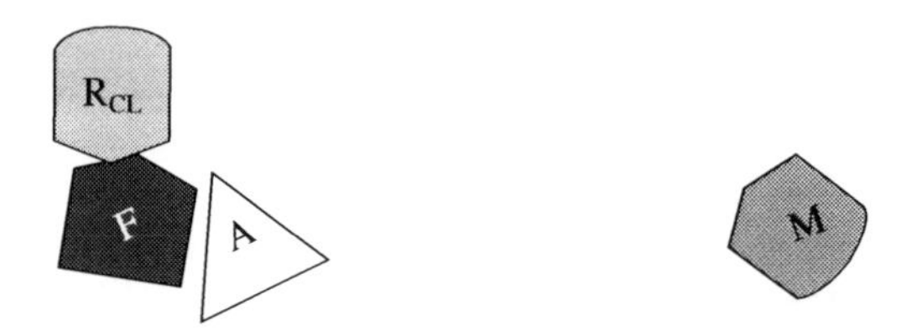

Figure 3: Repositioning of representatives

The rep. of the anxiety says: "It's good to be backed by something." Then the facilitator asks the rep. of the anxiety to turn towards the rep. of Marie and to say to her: "I am a child of your father." Marie mentions that the biological father of her father was a French soldier after World War II in occupied Germany.

The family of the French soldier did not allow him to marry a German woman who was pregnant from him. Marie's grandmother was also pressured by her family to abort the unborn child. The French soldier and Marie's grandmother could not engage in a relationship, but the grandmother of Marie gave birth to Marie's father. Later, she idealized the French soldier and rejected her German husband, Marie's social grandfather. In the course of the process work of the constellation, the facilitator asks the rep. of the client to say to the rep. of Marie's father: "Daddy, I want to be close to you. There's a place for you on this planet." Further, the rep. of the client is asked by the facilitator to say: "Daddy, I am very connected with you and your anxiety. I am carrying it for you." Although Marie reports she had a difficult relationship with her father who was an alcoholic, the facilitator asks the rep. of Marie to say to the rep. of her father: "Daddy, I love you, I am happy that you were born. So I exist, too." Later in the constellation, reps. for Marie's paternal grandmother (MF) and paternal grandfather (FF) are positioned. Now, reps. of Marie's paternal grandparents and parents stand separated from her, indicating the disentanglement of generations (see Figure 4).

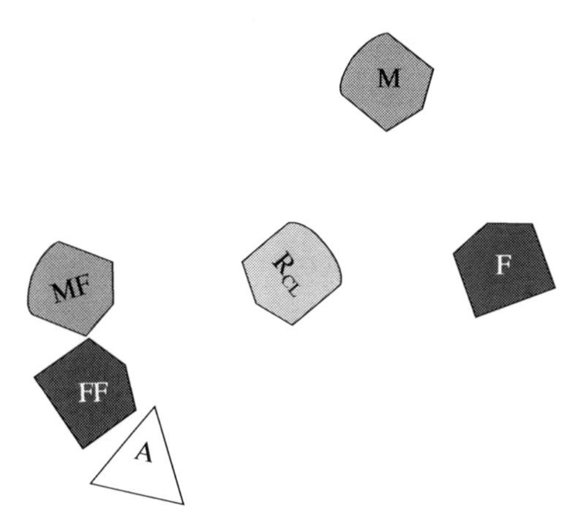

Figure 4: Representatives of Marie's paternal grandparents are added

Towards the end, Marie herself, reps. of her husband (HB), her three sons (S1, S2, S3) and her maternal grandmother (MM), are taken into the constellation (see Figure 5).[1] The facilitator lets Marie, who is now placed herself in the constellation, say to her parents and paternal grandparents: "Be kind when I leave the anxiety with you." Directed to her father, she repeats the facilitator's suggestion: "Daddy, there's a place for all of us on this planet."

In the "solution picture" (see Figure 6), Marie herself, who is now placed in the constellation, turns toward her present family. The rep. of her husband

[1] A rep. of the maternal grandfather of Marie was not placed in this constellation.

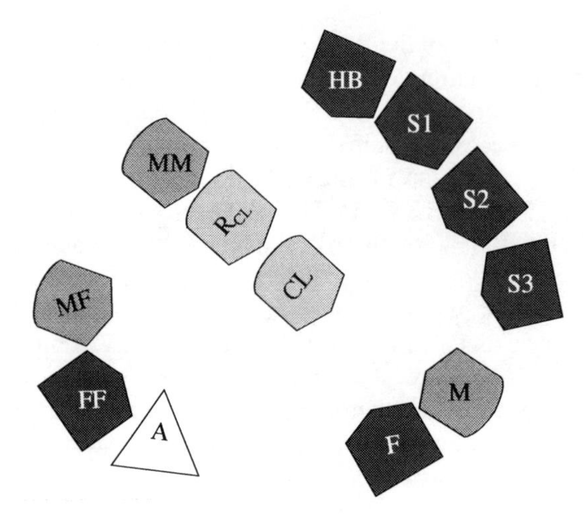

Figure 5: Towards the end of Marie's family constellation

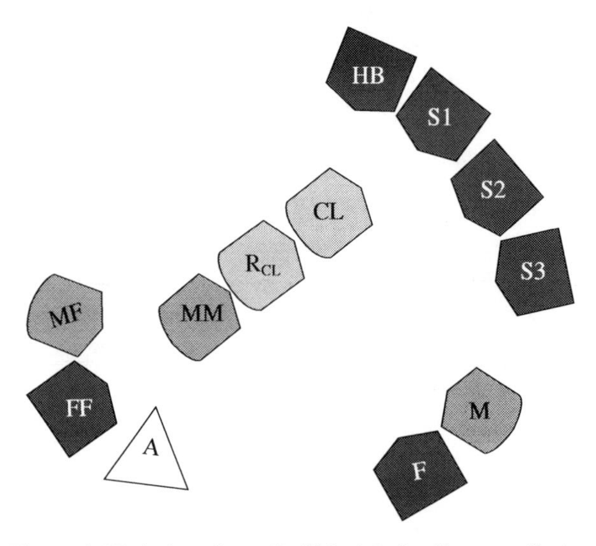

Figure 6: "Solution picture" of Marie's family constellation

says: "Here we are, me and your sons." Marie replies: "Yes, there's a place for all of us on this planet. I will need a little time and then I'll come to you."

The key element in this constellation was that Marie's anxiety to "not manage it on this planet as a family" is associated with her paternal grandparents and her father, who developed strong anxiety and became an alcoholic. In spite of little knowledge about the details of Marie's family history, it seems plausible that an unwanted child from a French soldier in post-war Germany may have grown up in an atmosphere of diffuse anxieties. The example illustrates that family constellations deal with the psychological effects of existential and difficult situations and structures. In this case, the interpretation was offered that Marie unconsciously identified with her father's and grandparents' anxiety. It also illustrates how emotional phenomena can be carried forward over three generations.

Body memory

Structures of human memory

Within psychology, human long-term memory is conceptualized as consisting of two separate systems: explicit and implicit memory. Explicit memory has two forms: episodic or autobiographic memory, consisting of episodes of one's own biography: for example, remembering one's last birthday party or holiday; and semantic memory, consisting of knowledge: for example, the date of one's own birthday or the history of a particular holiday destination. Explicit memory can be accessed consciously: episodes of a birthday party or the name of the capital of a country can be explicitly recalled and verbally reported.

Implicit memory denotes subconscious and preconscious activities.[2] From a phenomenological view point, this form of memory is manifested within the body. Therefore it is called "body memory" (German: "Leibgedächtnis"), and can be defined as "the totality of implicit dispositions of perception and behavior mediated by the body and sedimented in the course of earlier experiences" (FUCHS 2011, p. 86). It manifests in abilities, skills and habits of the lived body. Implicit memory encompasses perceptual and motor skills: for example, activities as reading, upright walking, speaking, painting, or typing on a keyboard. FUCHS (2012) distinguishes several forms of body memory: procedural, situational, intercorporeal, incorporative, pain, and traumatic memory. For family constellations, the intercorporeal body memory seems of special significance. Before I analyse this notion, the principles and processes of body memory are described.

Processes of the body memory

Repetition and habit are the basic processes of body memory. Repetitive perceptions, for example, being in one's own apartment; repetitive practising, for example, playing an instrument; or repetitive interactions, for example, hugging one's partner or child, shape body memory. Repeated perceptual, motor and interpersonal sequences become habits and second nature. In body memory, many similar perceptions, situations, actions and interactions are condensed.

---

[2] See FUCHS (2008b) for differences between the terms "unconscious" and "implicit."

The explicit, autobiographic memory functions in a diachronic time frame. Episodes of the past are recalled in retrospect: for example, an accident when learning how to ride a bicycle. For body memory, the past is synchronically experienced in the present: one simply knows how to ride a bicycle, how to use a computer keyboard, or how to recognize a familiar person. Movements, perceptual qualities and familiar interactions become implicit. How to dance, to type on a keyboard or to recognize a familiar person is not known explicitly; it is simply done. The fact that similar perceptions or actions are indeed experienced as similar is the manifestation of body memory. Explicit memory contains reflexive "knowing what;" whereas implicit memory contains "knowing how." FUCHS (2008) points out that explicit autobiographic memory is reflexive, and includes a first person agency in the sense of "I remember that" In explicit memory, we "have" a past; whereas in implicit memory we "are" past and present. Implicit memory mediates the basic experience of continuity in life; whereas explicit memory contains the biographic narrative.

Implication and explication

Body memory is based on the process of implication, the sedimentation and condensation of explicit perceptions, actions and interactions. For example, trying to ride a bicycle the first time is conscious, intentional and accompanied by difficulties; learning to ride it is associated with increasing ease of movement. After they are learnt, particular movements such as balancing the bicycle, etc., become implicit. Experiencing a particular social situation is consciously perceived in the particular moment. A series of repetitive and similar situations will result in an implicit "knowing how" it is: for example, to greet, to get hugged by a parent, or to feel an unpleasant atmosphere at the family dinner table. In one's life course and the process of implication, repeated experiences or actions are "melted" into body memory. Structures of implication are implicit memory cores (FUCHS 2008).

Explication is the process in which contents of body memory become conscious. In some instances, habitual and implicit phenomena lose their forms when they become explicated. FUCHS (2008) gives the example of proofreading: when looking for typing mistakes, the meaning of the text cannot be understood anymore. However, one of the main goals of most psychotherapeutic processes is to achieve explicit insights into one's biography and family dynamics. Explication then leads to the conscious memory of past experiences. Within the process of explication, an initial vague feeling or impression can become connected to its origin: for example, how it was to be the child of divorced parents, or how it was to have grown up in a foster home. Afterwards, single episodes or associated series of similar interactions are accessible in the explicit, autobiographic memory.

Sensory cues such as smells, tastes, sounds, pictures, or movements enable the unfolding of implicit memory cores into consciously remembered autobiographic episodes. For example, listening to a particular song on the radio may cause the explication of a specific time frame or situation when the song was popular, for example, being in love for the first time. The smell of one's childhood home may cause explication of autobiographic episodes that occurred in the house of one's childhood. A prominent example is an episode in Marcel Proust's "Remembrance of Things Past," where a taste of a biscuit and tea enables the sudden and vivid explication of a whole scene from the past (FUCHS 2008, p. 46).

Similarity, transposition and mimesis

One basic mechanism of body memory is the recognition of similarity. Contents of implicit memory cannot be remembered and reported consciously. Procedural knowledge needs doing instead of understanding. On the sensory level, implicit memory means recognizing something which is familiar. To be precise, it is a "re-recognition" of a familiar certain situation or activity that is already known. Perception means re-recognition according to similar gestalt formations: for example, when reading a text one knows the words and does not mind small typing mistakes; when a friend is met, it is a re-recognition of former contacts. Hence, perception is closely associated with body memory and biographic continuity.

The recognition of familiarity manifests itself in similar forms and shapes, for example, in physiognomy, building styles, or landscapes. Based on a known gestalt, familiar forms can be associated, for example, figures that are recognized within clouds or inkblots. By means of transposition, qualities of a particular gestalt such as form or rhythm can be transferred into other modes. For example, the crescendo of music or the atmosphere of a coming thunderstorm can be perceived as similar since both resemble the bodily impression of a tumescent feeling (FUCHS 2008).

Sensing something with familiar qualities is based on mimesis, the ability to experience something as similar within one's own body. Similarity is perceived when sensations cause resonating bodily feelings, states, postures, or movement tendencies within one's own body. Similarities that are based on the resonance of body memory find their expressions in metaphoric language. For example, one can "be flooded" by water, light, sounds, or joy. Tastes, colors, and persons can possess a "warm" quality. Such metaphors refer to a common bodily basis and mimetic resonance. Thus, by means of transposition and mimesis, different sensations are experienced as similar, based on a bodily resonance.

FUCHS (2008) points out that, without body memory, autobiographic memories would just be empty pictures. Hence autobiographic identity is based on the implicit memory as the carrier of one's own flow of experience and actions. The body memory can be seen as the basis of human identity and of explicit autobiographical memories.

The process of family constellation: explicating family dynamics from body memory

In the following section, I will focus on the relations between family constellation and the intercorporeal memory. Interpersonal encounters are influenced to a large extent by earlier experiences with significant others — often parents and relatives — in one's own childhood and other parts of one's biography. Implicit relational knowledge and interactional styles develop so they become part of the personality. FUCHS points out that each person owns an embodied extract of its past history of experiences with others: "In the structures of the lived body the others are always implied" (2012, p. 15).

Using the concept of body memory, I argue that one core element of family constellations is the explication of the "implied others" and of family dynamics, that is, the memory of repeated interactions of and with other family members and forms of family climate. Different steps and aspects of family constellation work will be analysed regarding their effects on the senses, the body and body memory.

The client's original constellation: externalization

Constellation facilitators advise their clients to not consciously think or reflect upon family dynamics, but instead to set up the original constellation according to their bodily "intuition," and "how it feels right for the moment." Sometimes it is assumed that the "inner picture" of the client is set up in the original constellation. However, since the client moves within the scenario while positioning representatives, and also tests and checks their "right" position, it is more accurate to speak of three dimensional spatial sensations instead of pictures, which are usually looked at from a distance (FUCHS 2000).

It is noteworthy that the spatial position of representatives is not exclusively a symbolic representation. The distance, angle and position of two representatives towards each other may actually match bodily qualities of the real relationship. FUCHS (ibid., p. 15) gives an example: if the father of a client actually was at his back during his biography, maybe with his voice, maybe touching the shoulder or stroking the back, maybe watching the client playing football as a child, then a vague feeling of "father-in-the-back" will develop in the body memory of the client. This implicit bodily feeling then may be set up in a constellation in which the representative of the client's father stands behind the representative of the client.

The externalization of intuitive and bodily sensations in a spatial scenario may have beneficial effects for the client. Externalization as a nonverbal intervention is used successfully in several psychotherapeutic methods: for example, in the form of drawing, using puppets in child psychotherapy or family sculpturing in conventional family therapy. Effects of externalization can be seen in distancing from and "objectification" of a personal problem as well as its translation from language into sensory, mainly visual and kinaesthetic modes. The original constellation also marks a shift from narrative and autobiographic memory to implicit memory. The socio-spatial arrangements of representatives can be understood as expressions of implicit and pre-reflexive sensations, and as externalization of family-related body memory. Positions of representatives can give first hints of family dynamics. For example: if a client positions two representatives of his parents far apart and looking away from each other, it may indicate an unsatisfying marriage. Since the client has set up the constellation, it is not a surprise if the utterances of representatives match the subjective impression of the client about his family. An elaborated explication of the client's position within the family system is usually achieved during the repositioning of representatives and the "process work."

Sensations of representatives and repositioning: The unfolding of family dynamics

In the interplay between representatives' positions and sensations, the facilitators' interventions and the client's recollections about his family, the constellation scenario subsequently changes step by step. This process uses three sources of information: first, the facilitator may reposition representatives according to his theories about family dynamics; secondly, the utterances of the representatives influence the procedure. Representatives are asked if they feel better, worse or equal in different positions, indicating a better or worse position than in the original constellation. Finally, the facilitator asks the client if changes in the constellation or utterances of the representatives appear to be meaningful to him or her. Sometimes clients confirm occurrences that seem to match sensations of representatives: the reported feeling of pain by a representative may be associated with a serious chronic disease that the real person who is represented had in her or his life. If the representative of the client's dead grandfather reports that he feels excluded because he stands outside, the client may confirm that he has never been talked about, since the grandfather was associated with war crimes in World War II.

As the constellation develops, it may enable the further explication of the client's body memory of his family history and dynamics. Since the key principle of body memory is similarity, some cues are needed to activate the explication of implicit memory cores. I propose that the spatial scenario of a family constellation provides such cues. Despite its short duration, a family constellation is dynamic with its repositioning and utterances from several representatives. Changes in positions and utterances may function as cues or stimuli from which the client can better understand his or her family dynamics. It is, however, not so much a conscious understanding, but rather the resonance of the client's body, which reacts to different cues. For example, if representatives of the client's parents look away from each other, the client may find a bodily resonance and sudden recognition of a dominant tension that was present during his or her parents' divorce in the real family history. Prevailing atmospheres that are based on many repeated interactions — or the absence of such interactions — may also be explicated. The spatial properties of a constellation can also indicate the quality of the relationship between family members to each other. The changes of representatives' positions can indicate changes within the family system, for example, the breaking up of a marriage or the exclusion of a family member.

The explication of client's body memory can be achieved by sensory and bodily stimulation. Family constellations use the senses — the kinaesthetic bodily resonance of the client and the visualization of interpersonal relationships — as cues for explication of implicit family-related memory cores. Similarity between the constellation pictures and the client's bodily resonance enables the recognition of interactional schemes, which are somehow "known" but not available in the explicit memory. This is supported by the principle of transposition. For example, distances between representatives in a constellation are translated into qualities of relationships.

Explication and time

Often during their constellations, clients express strong emotions such as anger, sadness or joy. The intensity of emotions can partly be attributed to the ritualization of family constellation seminars (WEINHOLD/SCHWEITZER 2012). However, clients are frequently overcome by sudden and surprising experiences of anger, anxiety or despair — experiences that refer to the explication of emotionally negative implicit memory cores. Explication of body memory represents a coinciding of past and present, partly with similar emotional qualities. It is also worth noting that family constellations do not represent a particular moment of the client's biography, but a condensation of relationships, which are based on many past situations. Intense emotions can be seen as indicators of this process, where accumulated past experiences become conscious and are partly re-experienced in the present.

Process work: Resolving and performing family dynamics

Family constellations also enable the integration of the past and distancing from it, which are common psychotherapeutic goals. While explication of family dynamics may cause strong emotions in the first place, associated insights relating to the client's family dynamics can lead to reflection on this past during a second step.

"Process work" — with its ritualized speech acts, gestures and the change of the constellation towards the "solution picture" — can contribute to a deeper elaboration of the client's position in her or his family. During the "process work," family members are symbolically included, borders between systems are established, and future perspectives for the client are tested. If the client appears "enmeshed" with present or past family members, the facilitator may suggest that he or she addresses that person with speech acts such as, "I acknowledge all that connects me with you. I respect you," and then: "Now I leave the responsibility to you for all the things you did or did not do. I cannot carry it any further for you. It is too much for me." Other sentences might be "Now I will let you go in peace," or "You belong here and I do as well." Ritualized speech acts and gestures are based on fundamental aspects of social systems, such as belonging, autonomy and generational order (SPARRER/VARGA VON KIBÈD 2008).

Whereas the explication of family related complexes of body memory can be accompanied by sudden emotions indicating a re-experiencing of the past to some degree, the "process work" allows an explicit understanding of and coming to terms with this past. During the "process work," clients frequently express forgiveness, relief, joy, acceptance, and reconciliation. These may indicate explicit cognitive-affective autobiographic elaboration regarding their own position within the family system and reflection of their own biography in regard to the present life situation.

An integration of experiences and insights is also enabled by a change in the client's spatial positions. While the client observes the scenario from outside, at the end of his family constellation he may be asked to step into the "solution picture" to allow a direct sensory experience of the "resolved" family dynamics with its "right order." Stepping in and stepping out of the constellation allows experiencing and distancing, involvement and reflection.

While the first parts of the constellation allow for the explication of family related complexes of body memory, the later parts, "process work," and the solution picture create options for the client to get a different view on his past and new perspectives for his future. Such future perspectives are also established by testing hypotheses during the last part of the constellation, for example, when the representative of the client (or the client himself) turns toward the representative of an imagined "future."

It is noteworthy that all components of the constellation work, the spatial positioning, the sentences and the ritualized gestures have performative qualities. Utterances of representatives and ritualized speech acts do not imply talking about the family, but creating a symbolically "new" subjective family structure for the client by means of reconciliation, setting borders, and the acceptance of the past. Similarly, performative effects of ritual gestures are employed. Unlike conventional psychotherapy, where problems are mainly talked about, in family constellations problems and solutions are performed. Since implicit memory is based on "doing" instead of talking, family constellations can be seen as performative action instead of meta-communicative discourse (WEBER/SCHMIDT/SIMON 2005).

Thus, family constellations can be seen as both: they represent not the historical truth but subjective sensations of the client's body memory; and they also performatively create a new system. In some respects, the past is performatively rewritten, with a resourceful and positive image of the client's system.

Conclusion

Family constellation is a ritualized method of group therapy in which interpersonal relationships, transgenerational patterns, and family dynamics are set up in a social scenario. The particular concern of the client is expressed in a spatial performance, and his diachronic biographical experiences are expressed in a synchronic constellation. Compared to verbally orientated psychotherapy, family constellations use several senses, and therapeutic change is brought about with bodily procedures instead of verbal and narrative means. Most steps of this method employ sensory and bodily processes. The externalization of vague bodily sensations into a spatial social scenario, kinaesthetic sensations of representatives, changes of positions, ritualized gestures, and the client's change of perspectives by stepping in and out of the constellation contribute to the performative potential of this method.

Using Fuchs' concept of body memory, I have argued that a variety of sensory cues — mainly the spatial constellation of representatives and their sensations — enable the gradual explication of family related implicit memory cores of the client's body memory. By using performative means, such as ritualized gestures and speech acts as well as the change of the spatial constellations, family constellations aim towards an integration of implicit past experiences into conscious autobiographic memory. Finally, with a "solution picture," clients are given sensory information that indicates hypothetical future perspectives to improve psychological wellbeing and interpersonal relationships.

Family constellations are one prominent example within the range of Western psychotherapeutic approaches that employ the senses and embodied spatial performances to facilitate psychotherapeutic change. However, as argued elsewhere, those processes are also part of healing rituals in non-western cultures (Sax/Weinhold 2010; Sax, Weinhold/Schweitzer 2010). Incorporating the senses and their relationship with body memory into models of ritual healing and psychotherapeutic change may bring about advantages in understanding how both actually are effective.

References

Alonso, Y. (2005): The Family Constellations of Bert Hellinger: A Therapy in Search of Identity [Las Constelaciones Familiares de Bert Hellinger: Un Procedimiento Psicoterapéutico en Busca de Identidad]. In: International Journal of Psychology and Psychological Therapy, Vol. 5, No. 1, pp. 85–96.

Boszormenyi-Nagy, I./Spark, G. (1973): Invisible Loyalties: Reciprocity in Intergenerational Family Therapy. – New York.

COHEN, D. B. (2006). Family Constellations: An Innovative Systemic Phenomenological Group Process from Germany. In: The Family Journal, Vol. 14, No. 3, pp. 226–233.

FUCHS, T. (2000): A phenomenological perspective on family constellations [Familienaufstellungen aus phänomenologischer Sicht]. In: Praxis der Systemaufstellung, Vol. 1, pp. 13–16.

FUCHS, T. (2008): Body memory [Das Gedächtnis des Leibes]. In: FUCHS, T. (Ed.): Body and Lifeworld: New philosophical-psychiatric essays [Leib und Lebenswelt: Neue philosophisch-psychiatrische Essays]. – Kusterdingen, pp. 37–64.

FUCHS, T. (2011): Body Memory and the Unconscious. In: LOHMAR, D./BRUDZINSKA, J. (Eds.): Founding Psychoanalysis: Phenomenological Theory of Subjectivity and the Psychoanalytical Experience. – Dordrecht, pp. 69–82.

FUCHS, T. (2012): The phenomenology of body memory. In: KOCH, S./FUCHS, T./SUMMA, M./MÜLLER, C. (Eds.): Body Memory, Metaphor and Movement. – Amsterdam and Philadelphia, pp. 9–22.

HAAS, W. (2009): The Hellinger Virus: Risks and side effects of constellation [Das Hellinger-Virus. Zu Risiken und Nebenwirkungen von Aufstellungen]. – Kröning.

SAX, W./WEINHOLD, J. (2010): Rituals of possession. In: BROSIUS, C./HÜSKEN, U. (Eds.): Ritual matters: Dynamic dimensions in practice. – London and New Delhi, pp. 236–252.

SAX, W./WEINHOLD, J./SCHWEITZER, J. (2010): Ritual healing East and West: A comparison of ritual healing in the Garwhal Himalayas and "Family constellation" in Germany. In: Journal of Ritual Studies, Vol. 24, No. 1, pp. 61–77.

SCHNEIDER, J. R. (2009): Family constellations. Basic principles and procedures [Familienaufstellungen: Grundlagen und Vorgehensweisen]. – Heidelberg.

SCHWEITZER, J./BORNHÄUSER, A./HUNGER, C./WEINHOLD, J. (2012): How effective are sytems constellations? Reports of an ongoing research project. [Wie wirksam sind Systemaufstellungen? Bericht über ein laufendes Forschungsprojekt]. In: Praxis der Systemaufstellung, Vol. 1, pp. 66–69.

SPARRER, I./VARGA VON KIBÈD, M. (2008): The systemic assumptions as basics for a Systemic Structure Constellation [Die systemischen Grundsätze als Basis für eine Systemische Strukturaufstellung]. In: DAIMLER, R. (Ed.): Basics of Systemic Structure Constellations. A manual for first time users and advanced learners [Basics der systemischen Strukturaufstellungen Eine Anleitung für Einsteiger und Fortgeschrittene]. – Munich, pp. 39–62.

STIEFEL, I./HARRIS, P./ZOLLMANN, A.W.F. (2002): Family Constellation: A Therapy Beyond Words. In: Australian and New Zealand Journal of Family Therapy, Vol. 23, No. 1, pp. 38–44.

WEBER, G. (Ed.) (1993): Capricious good fortune; aka second chance. The systemic psychotherapy of Bert Hellinger [Zweierlei Glück. Die systemische Psychotherapie Bert Hellingers]. – Heidelberg.

WEBER, G./SCHMIDT, G./SIMON, F.B. (2005): Constellation work revisted ... according to Hellinger? With a metacomment by Matthias Varga von Kibéd [Aufstellunsarbeit revisited … nach Hellinger? Mit einem Metakommentar von Matthias Varga von Kibéd]. – Heidelberg.

WEINHOLD, J./SCHWEITZER, J. (2012): Induction and Control of Emotions within Family Constellation Workshops. In: MICHAELS, A./WULF, C. (Eds.): Emotions in Rituals and Performance. – London and New Delhi, pp. 320–329.

Karin M. Polit

Performative Ritual as Sensual Experience of Body, Place and Sociality

In this chapter I explore performative rituals as sensual experiences deeply embedded in social relationships. Possession occurring during the described rituals and connected collective emotions is interpreted as part of a locally shaped repertoire of human existence. I will discuss how movement, as a kinaesthetic sense, in combination with the multisensual experiences common in many ritual traditions of South Asia, is strongly connected to senses of reality and collective emotional responses. These emotions are invoked simultaneously in the moving bodies of the performers, and in the people who take part in the ritual as spectating participants. Ritual performances during which the Divine is called into human bodies, I argue, bring about a special kind of collective emotional and sensual experience. This experience is not only a multisensual one but is also strongly localized, and can only be understood as a part of local people's embodied cultural repertoire. This cultural repertoire enables a collective embodied interpretation of auditive, olfactory, visual, and other sensual experiences which make up much of the atmosphere produced during highly successful ritual events. In the interpretation of my material, I take up ideas from *rasa* theory. The material for my case study is data I collected during a festival held at the end of a six month long divine pilgrimage in the Garhwal Himalayas in North India in February/March 2007.

It was on a sunny but cold afternoon on February 25, 2007, in a village near Gopeshwar, a small urban center in the Chamoli district of the North Indian state of Uttarakhand, close to the great pilgrimage center Badrinath in the Central Himalayas (Figure 1). The homecoming festival of the local deity *Jakh*, who had been on a pilgrimage during the past six months, was coming to an end. My assistant Poonam Semwal and I had been village guests for several days, and I had been observing the deity and his entourage repeatedly during the past months. During my fieldwork, I had learned that *Jakh* was at the same time the god of the Rajput villagers who were responsible for his temple and his pilgrimage, as well as their ancestor. The deity was closely linked to the local version of the *Mahābhārata*,[1] thus linking the villagers themselves to the

[1] The *Mahābhārata* is India's great epic of war and tragedy. It tells the tale of the five Pandava brothers who fight for the throne against their cousins, the ninety nine Kauravas.

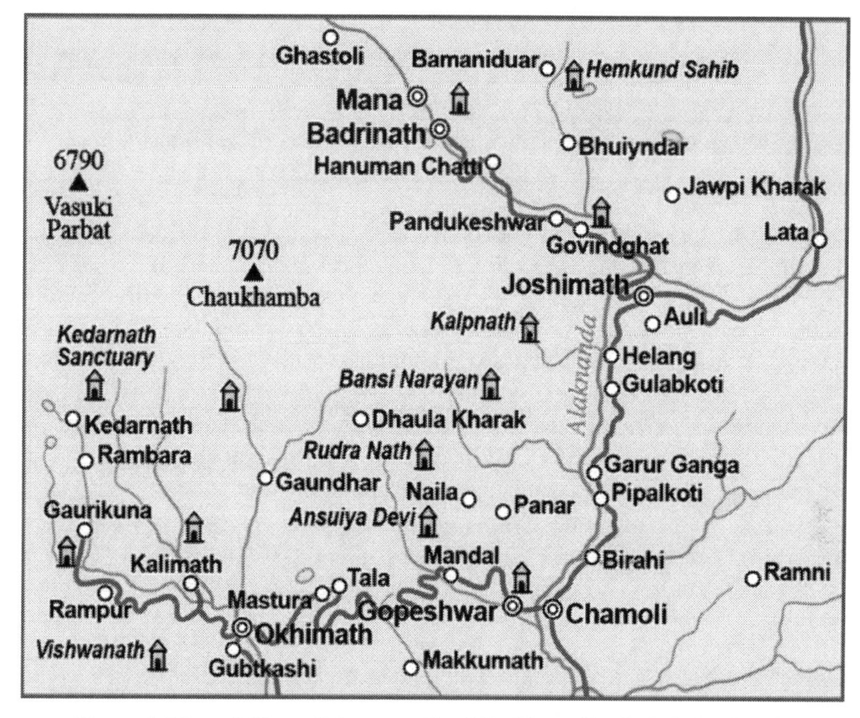

Figure 1: Map of Chamoli (prepared by Nils Harm, South Asia Institute).

ancestry of *Mahābhārata* warriors. People claimed that, in an earlier age, the great warrior Babhru Bahan[2] was tricked by Krishna,[3] and lost his head before he could reverse the course of the great Mahābhārata battle. As compensation for this inconvenience, Krishna offered him the status of a divine king. A local expert on *Jakh's* ritual songs and myths, Govind Singh Rawat, told me the story as follows:

> Krishna said to Jakh: Hey Babhru Bahan! None of this is your fault! It is all my doing! I had my reasons for cutting off your head! In the future, in the age of

It culminates in the great battle at Kurukshetra. In this war, all warriors of the age, except for the five Pandava brothers, are killed (cf. Hiltebeitel 2001, Sax 2002).

[2] The story resembles the myth of *Babrik* in the dominant North Indian versions of India's great epic *Mahābhārata*, but differs from it in important ways. *Babru Bahan* is the name most often used for this particular character in the local versions of the great epic.

[3] Krishna is a subordinate manifestation of Vishnu, one of the high gods of Hinduism. His speech to the reluctant Arjuna at the verge of the great battle in the *Mahābhārata* is better known as the *Bhagavadgītā* (cf. Michaels 2004, pp. 211–215).

> *Kaliyuga*[4] and through all the coming ages, I will make you the god of the land. You will be anointed as a deity in many places. Your people will carry you for six months. All the people who belong to the village where your temple stands will take you on a pilgrimage for six months. You will be worshiped in every home. They will give you sacrifice and take you to holy places and pilgrimage sites. They will take you to all places that can be reached in six months.

According to the local story, this satisfied Babru Bahan, and he became a divine king in the Central Himalayas.[5] Since then, claim his devotees, he is periodically taken on a pilgrimage. At the same time, the deity is recognized within another warrior context. The god king is often also referred to as *Jakh*, which is a modification of *Yaksha*. The Yakshas belong to a group of old South Asian deities who are locally understood to be warriors traveling with the great god Shiva to protect the people, the land and its treasures.[6] *Jakh* is, therefore, understood to be a protector of the village people, the agricultural land used by them, and their livestock. Many forms of *Jakh* reside in the area around the town of Gopeshwar. Numerous small temples are dedicated to different manifestations of *Jakh*, and each temple has a village responsible for satisfying the *Jakh* residing in it. According to his devotees, it is their duty to take *Jakh* on a pilgrimage regularly. If his devotees and ancestors fail to do this, the village will suffer. I was told that the women would have difficulties conceiving male offspring, children would die, cows would stop giving milk, the fields would dry up, and men would start fighting. According to Govind Singh Rawat, a local teacher who became a guru (spiritual teacher) during this particular pilgrimage, all of this began to happen in the village of Maikot Kujaum because villagers had not taken their divine king on his pilgrimage for more than 60 years. After years of trouble and fighting, the villagers finally consulted the god's medium and his priest, and decided to begin the pilgrimage in October 2006. After 69 years, the divine king *Jakh* of Maikot Kujaum visited his land and his out-married sisters (*dhyanis*)[7] again. For six months, the divine king was carried to various

---

[4] The *Kaliyuga* is the last of four ages within the Yuga cycle of Hinduism. In this cosmological model, time follows an endless cycle of creation and destruction, where the yugs follow each other like the seasons (cf. MICHAELS 2004, p. 335).

[5] For a detailed discussion on divine kings in the Central Himalayas, see SAX (2003).

[6] See also ENCYCLOPEDIA BRITANNICA (2012).

[7] Women who have married and left their parents' home to live with their husband and his family, are called *dhyanis*. They play an important role in social relations and ritual practices of Garhwal (SAX 1990, POLIT 2012). On occasions when they visit their natal home, they have all sorts of privileges compared to their unmarried sisters and in-married sisters-in-law. Their rights and obligations are mostly linked to practices that uphold her father's and mother's honor in her *sauryas* (marital home). For example, it is considered highly shameful if an out-married woman's parents let their daughter work in their house. With marriage, a daughter has been given to another family with

Figure 2: *Jakh's* medium in possession (photo: K.Polit)

temples and numerous villages in the region before he came back to his home village and temple of residency. The last 11 days before the deity re-entered his permanent temple were devoted to thanking the accompanying spirits and people and bidding them goodbye. A homecoming festival (*banyat*) took place below the deity's temple and on the village fields. Each day was dedicated to a different divinity. The divinities were worshipped, ritually thanked, and finally sent back home. Such a coming home festival is usually a densely ritualized festivity, which includes many different ritual activities, draws many visitors, and is commonly understood to be a happy social occasion.

The first days of the festival had been very quiet. The ritual activities[8] were performed in short versions only as there were no or very few spectators besides me and my assistant. But on this day, I was excited. The atmosphere

all her productive powers, and she should never again be productive in her father's house (POLIT 2012). The importance of the *mait* (natal home) for the *dhyanis*, the out-married daughters, is sung about in many songs all over Garhwal. Many rituals require their presence.

[8] These were the usual rituals performed for personalized deities in South Asia. The god was woken ritually in the morning, washed, dressed and fed, then danced and received devotees in audience, was fed again and carried around the ritual area, entertained and put to sleep.

had changed, and there was a feeling of pleasant anticipation in the village. We had come up to the ritual grounds with our host early that morning, and watched the ritual wakening of the deity with a ritual song (*jagar*), which I recorded. The crowd of visitors was much greater than on the previous days. The mood had changed. The men were no longer simply doing their ritual duty. Somehow, they were more excited than they had been before. Women, out-married daughters, had come from all surrounding villages and places far away. After the deity had been danced by his three servants (*dharis*), *Jakh's* representation (*nishan*), his golden mask, on top of a long wooden pole, decorated with yaktail hair and cloth, was installed in a field in the midst of the offerings given to him that day (Figure 2). As more and more people entered the ritual ground, the beat of the drums became more and more intense. We could see the deity's medium standing next to the deity's pole (*nishan*), waiting for the deity to enter his body. With a shake of his head, and in accordance with the beat of the drums, he suddenly started moving. He danced for a while, and then picked up a short sword and a heavy wooden board. He danced with the utensils, and then stared, shouting loudly "Zah," hitting the sword hard with the wooden board towards the middle of his stomach (Figure 3).

Once he had started doing this, three men next to him began making loud shrieking noises, and all at once started dancing passionately around *Jakh's* medium. Suddenly, everybody was alert; the spectators put up their hands in respectful greeting positions (the *namaskar* gesture), and moved closer towards the dancing bodies. I was no longer able to record much of what was happening as suddenly the density of the crowd became immense. Everybody wanted to see and hear what the dancing deities were shouting and doing. Everybody hoped to catch hold of one of the deities present to be blessed or ask for divine advice. Women began shaking and shrieking, themselves being filled with different spiritual beings. The four men in the middle of the crowd, who, I was told, were the mediums of *Jakh*, Chandika, Rishi Muni, and Nairsingh, all important local deities, danced for about an hour. They talked to each other, gesticulating wildly, gave out divine gifts (*prasad*) to the people in the crowd, and stopped to talk to selected devotees for short oracular sessions, answering their questions and giving advice for various ritual treatments until the beat of the drums signaled the end of the session, and led the deities back into their world, away from the people. The men and the crowd then proceeded with the daily ritual routine of the event, and the mood changed back to normal.

The dance of the deities temporarily changed the mood amongst spectators and "performers" into one of high sensuality, emotional involvement and excitement. This was not an unusual event for rural Garhwal. As a matter of fact, deities manifest themselves in the bodies of their human vehicles in the Garhwal Himalayas all the time. Such trance dances during ritual occasions are highly regulated. People usually know in advance who will be the vehicle of which deity, and the dances are governed by strict rules prescribing movements, gestures, and the use of the spoken word as well as the spectators' gaze

Figure 3: *Jakh's* medium — in possession (Photograph: Author)

and involvement. They are, therefore, to be understood as performances of a certain kind. Unlike theatrical performances, however, the practice of the rituals discussed depends not on rehearsal, but on *habitus* and mimesis. The ritual requires that those who perform it already possess the embodied skills to do so competently, that those who are present know how to react competently.

People are expected to relate to the divinities in a respectful manner when asking questions, approaching the deity to offer worship or sacrificing and receiving the gift of the gods (*prasad*) in return. At the same time, the ritual transmits this knowledge to the people involved.

In this context, I understand ritual movements such as dance and possession as ways of experiencing and transmitting cultural knowledge and collective memory in a profoundly sensual and embodied way. These rituals are vehicles for forms of embodied knowledge — that is, different from language based knowledge. They are, instead, based on a certain kind of knowledge of the senses. The people involved know intuitively how to move to a certain rhythm, and how to hold their bodies so as to signify a certain deity. In other words, they exhibit what the ritual theorist Catherine BELL (1992), in her influential book *Ritual Theory, Ritual Practice*, calls "ritual mastery." Viewing trance as a performance, therefore, does not mean that I understand trance and performative rituals in which trance occurs as a theatrical enactment of symbolic meaning. Neither do I interpret them to be practices which metaphorically enact the people's relationship to their deities. On the contrary, the presence of spiritual beings in the bodies of humans are not theatrical performances, but rather part of everyday performances which are integrated into the local people's understanding of themselves and the world around them. I argue that the relationship to the deities is not re-enacted metaphorically and symbolically, but created and strengthened through the emotional involvement of spectators and performers alike. The beat of the drums, the rhythm of the dance, the movement of the mediums, the words spoken — all refer to a specific deity which is thought to be present in that particular moment. The rituals, therefore, enable everybody present to engage in a specific relationship with that deity.

The *rasa* theory — as a theory that is both an aesthetic theory and a theory of emotional involvement — seems particularly suited to helping us understand what it means to partake in an experience that is at once individual and collective, social and religious, such as the events described above. The *rasa* theory as formulated in the *Nāṭyaśāstra*, as HECKEL points out, is the theory of a specific experience in the world of theatre: "rasa is described in the *Nāṭyaśāstra* as taking place in the world of theatre which allows a specific experience of the world to arise" (1991, p. 34). *Rasa* theory seems suitable for an interpretation of ritual performances of the kind described above for several reasons. It enables us to realize specific localized sensual engagements with the world.

As Angelika MALINAR (in this volume) persuasively argues, sense perception and notions of the "senses" in Indian philosophy are quite distinct from Western concepts, which are all too often assumed to be natural modes of being in the world. In India, the interpretation of the senses is usually connected to assumptions about reality, and is an important aspect of all kinds of different relationships. These include human-to-human relations, the relationship between a devotee and her deity, the relationship of a deity to a place, and so forth. All these relationships are understood as being deeply rooted not only in an embodied mode of being-in-the-world, but also in a sensual way so that sensual experience can very well be an outside agent entering a person enabling a specific mode of engagement with the world. Engaging with Indian philosophy in general, and *rasa* theory in particular, then, forces me — a German anthropologist with an education and upbringing based on Western concepts of theatre, performance, cognition, and emotion — to step back from these western criteria which cannot, and should not, be applied universally to phenomena encountered in the field. In HECKEL's words, applying the *rasa* theory to performances in India may enable us to "disentangle the western paradigms from the discourse of Indian tradition as far as possible" (1991, p. 34), and instead aid us in understanding the processes observed within the framework of Indian philosophy and tradition. *Rasa* theory also enables us to understand performances of the kind described above not necessarily as re-representations or symbolic performances, but as techniques which bring certain events into the present, enabling people to experience what is being performed as part of their lived realities. HECKEL writes,

> According to the Natyashastra, the first theatrical performance took place on the occasion of the festival of Indra's banner, in which the victory of Indra over the demons is celebrated. The battle is performed in such a way that it appears to be an event which is actually taking place. The demons see themselves defeated once again, and attempt to obstruct the performance. This is a clue to the presence ascribed to a performance: it is not a re-presentation of something not present (1991, p. 35).

While theatre in the Western tradition has indeed become disentangled from both everyday and religious experience and content, theatre in the Indian context has a much broader range of genres. While urban India has all sorts of different stage theatre traditions which are similar to stage theatre found in the urban centers of the global North, the philosophical concept of *natya* remains strongly connected to ritual as well as within paradigms of social relations. Heckel provides a useful translation of the *Nāṭyaśāstra* in this context: "The own reality of the world is called theatre, which is connected with happiness and sorrow and is combined with (various forms of) conveyance (*abhinaya*) like movements of limbs, etc." (ibid., p. 35). This particular form of performance is, therefore, to be understood as part of social life and not a mere representation of social relations.

What I observe during trance performances in various ritual traditions in the Garhwal Himalayas is a merging of embodied sentiments, and I believe that it may be useful to consider the ideas of *rasa* to understand the experiences and emotional involvement of the people during events such as just described. This is so because, in very basic terms, *rasa* occurs when aesthetic and spiritual experience merge. In order to use *Rasa* theory as an analytic tool to understand trance performances, we need to abstract the theory from the literary and artistic context, and look at the possible implications for everyday experiences. In my reading of the theory, the concept is very useful as it combines an embodied notion of knowledge and understanding with reflexive knowledge and aesthetic enjoyment of an event. HECKEL clarifies that *rasa* is, at the same time, deeply rooted in a knowledge about the world (*loka*) that enables people to relate emotionally and intellectually to the experience as well as be part of the process that constitutes this world. It occurs in a successful performance when audience and performers enter into a special relationship: "rasa is realized in the relation and as the relation between audience and stage. It also qualifies this relationship" (HECKEL 1991, p. 36). As such, the experience of *rasa* is quite like tasting juice:

> it is realized completely only when tasted, that is to say, when a relationship is established between what is staged and the spectators. This is not just any relationship, it is the particular relationship of correspondence (or dialogue – *saṃvāda*). *Rasa* therefore has essentially a double character: it is 'taste' and it is 'tasted'" (ibid.).

Thus, *Rasa* enables us to put forward a theory of embodied intellectuality relating to certain emotional relationships — something that would not be possible without a certain kind of sensual as well as reflexive knowledge about the world. The *vibhāvas* as the stimuli of emotion and the medium through which emotion passes from performer to spectator in my ethnographic example are the fields which have temporarily been turned into ritual grounds, the deity's temporary temple, the deity's different symbolic manifestations — in the mask, in the medium, the drums, and the songs. All these create an atmosphere which, to the knowledgeable spectator and performer, transforms the space into a sacred and mythical space in which all the different mythical stories surrounding *Jakh*: as Bhumiyal Yaksh, the protector of the village space; as Babrik, a figure in the Sanskrit *Mahābhārata*; as Babru bahan, a figure in the local versions of the *Mahābhārata*, or as the *Jakh* of Kujaum, the youngest brother of the seven godly kings ruling the region. All the stories about the other deities who traveled with him — and are felt to be present during this festival to re-establish him in his shrine — are as much present as the people's involvement and their relationship to the deities, to whom their hopes and fears are often directed.

In this case, the embodied memory of paradigmatic events contributes to the solidarity of the group, thus reinforcing their collective identity. This is another example of the relationship between collective memory and public acts of "reminding" (cf. CASEY 1987, CSORDAS 1997). And, this memory is based not only on narratives, but also upon embodied experience. In his study of charismatic healing, CSORDAS rightly connected this to Pierre BOURDIEU's concept of *habitus,* remarking that

> revelatory reminders and remindands are not only thoughts and words, but sensuous embodied images, and the memory invoked is not necessarily a reliving in the sense of watching a 'videotape' copy, but one that evokes concrete self presence.

> Second, revelation collapses the duality of self and other by the intersubjective interplay of themes and elements shared within a habitus (1997, p.148).

The relationship between the local people and their deities is per se an emotional attachment. The ritual performance of a trance is not producing emotions within spectators or performers but is the medium through which the emotions are expressed. The latent sentiments towards the deities, I argue, are brought to the foreground during such ritual performances. Especially when deities enter the bodies of their vehicles, the relationship to the deity — and therefore the emotions connected to it — become manifested in the ritual space. However, the emotions are connected to an embodied knowledge, and are only possible in persons whose personhood is in part constituted through the relationship to the deity, the place, and the other devotees. It is a specific mode of engagement with the world.

The anthropologist in the field usually has a different experience. This is not because the anthropologist is a rational and therefore superior human being who can record and analyse the superstitious practices of backward and exotic people. On the contrary, it is because the anthropologist lacks knowledge produced by certain kinds of experiences. She does not share the same sensual capacities with the people she studies and, therefore, has neither the knowledge nor the emotional basis for sharing the experience. The interplay of emotion and ritual practice is not a matter of representations or language; rather, it is best understood as a dimension of people's embodied experience, including their belonging to a particular place and social group, and a particular context.[9]

Pierre BOURDIEU developed the notion of *habitus* into the master concept of what came to be called "practice theory," where *habitus* meant something like the unreflective and thoroughly naturalized set of tendencies and dispositions characteristic of a particular class, ethnic group, occupation, etc. (see BOURDIEU 1990). The important point to note is that BOURDIEU deliberately set out to refute those structuralists, linguistically-oriented theorists, and others who had attempted to reduce culture to a set of explicit rules that can, or should be, formulated in language. Regularized, standardized behavior is not normally learned by memorizing sets of rules, but rather by mimesis or imitation. "Practical belief," wrote BOURDIEU, "is a state of the body" (1990, p. 68). In a similar vein, we may understand memory and sensual experience as a state of the body. Diana TAYLOR (2003) has argued that performances can sustain, transform, and transfer complex embodied knowledge. The immediacy and sensuous impact of an effective, live performance makes it an extremely

[9] It makes little sense to talk of cultural differences here, as many differences we observe actually occur just as frequently within a group of people who share the same language, religion and nationality. When we speak of a particular "culture," we mean a local context with its environment, history, religion(s), language(s), etc.

powerful medium for reinforcing body memory. For example, spectacular rituals and performances may facilitate powerful collective experiences and instigate enduring, collective memories (see below; also CONNERTON 1989).

The most important thing about these sorts of memories for the current discussion is that they are both collective and embodied. Paul CONNERTON (1989) has shown that this is not a contradiction, since most memories are, in fact, socially constructed and practically embodied. Here, memories are understood as mindful representations and integral parts of being in the world in a physical body. Similarly, CASEY (1987) argues that memory is situated neither in the individual body, nor in society at large, but somewhere in between. For example, commemorative rituals maintain memory by referring to a community's "master narrative"— itself a product of commemorative events (ibid., pp. 224–225). While an event requires performers and an audience, and thus impacts their bodies and memories, its effect is usually much larger, since it reaches out to all participants as a community. While such events usually refer to particular memories connected to certain groups, they also recreate these memories in the event itself. In this context, memory is at the same time the product and the producer of practices, located in space as well as time, collective as well as individual.

Further, as Diana TAYLOR says,

> (c)ultural memory is, among other things, a practice, an act of imagination and interconnection. [...] Memory is embodied and sensual, that is conjured through the senses; it links the deeply private with social, even official, practices. Sometimes memory is difficult to invoke, yet, it is highly efficient; it's always operating in conjunction with other memories [...] (2003, p. 82).

Therefore, possession phenomena are less exotic, as they are often represented or perceived. For many people, they are part of everyday experience. In fact, the temporary presence of spiritual beings in the human body is part of the basic experiences of religious practices in many parts of the world, and definitely in South Asia.

Simply because the anthropologist may not be able to see what the local people see does not necessarily mean that the experience is less real, and belongs to the realm of imagination or belief rather than to the realm of sensual experience. In his work on multiple personality disorder, Ian HACKING has made this clear. To Hacking, in examining such phenomena, the problem is that we often make the one mistake that hinders us in understanding the specific phenomenon. We ask: is it real? Of course there are phenomena which are strongly connected to times and places; but does that make them less real? The sufferings of patients of multiple personality disorder or schizophrenia no matter what the history of the phenomenon may be— are, of course, to be considered real. The mere fact that something has been socially constructed does not render it less real. In the same way, the phenomenon we have come to call "possession" is not irrational, unreal or fake. Possessions are real experiences belonging to a particular place and a particular time.

Yet, quite often, the accounts of possession restrict themselves to explaining the social function of the phenomenon, or claiming that possession is a deeply religious experience. But while possession is often a religious experience, it is — at least in the North Indian villages I am working in — also part of an everyday social interaction between persons of variable humanity. It is learned behavior of social interaction that is deeply rooted in the sensual experience of being a Garhwali person. Describing the experience of "possession" to me, the medium of *Jakh* told me:

> Madam, it is like this: When we stand there, there is nothing in the beginning (*abtar hota nahim hai*). And then people come and pressure me. They say, come on, get possessed, what are you waiting for, why are you just standing here, you have done it before, come on . . . That is how the people pressure me. And I stand there and listen to them and I never know when and if the *devta* is going to come. And then it starts in the belly, a prickle in the belly and I know — now he is coming! My hands and feet start to get hot. Then I stop asking myself what will happen. I give myself completely over to the *devta*. I am not worried about anything anymore. The *devta* takes over. Then the *devta* tells us what he wants and needs. He tells us to do his work. He tells us how to do his work. Like, when the *devta* came out, when the *devta* took my body, (*avtar laya*), he told us that we would have to perform his 18-masks performance here to bid them goodbye in the end. And he also told us that those who have carried and danced me for six months, those who fed me and took care of me, we would have to bid them goodbye here, too. He will tell them: You have to leave me now. He will say, those who have taken me out of my place with the *tantras* and *mantras*, those men who have come to me, must leave me now! You have to take me back to my place and use the *tantras* and *mantras* there. This is how we give the *devta* our bodies. I am a vessel, we also go up there, what we call *Nandi Kund*. It is an ordeal for our *shakti*. It is a place that is easy to reach when the god is in you, but when there is no god, when a man goes on his own. When god is in me I can carry everything, when it is just me, I am not that strong. It is that easy!"
>
> Madam this feeling . . . it just happened like this . . . First it was my father, he became old, so one day, I don't know, the devta said, this horse has become old, he is not suitable for me anymore. So he decided to catch a new horse. So at that time I did not know anything. I did know what happened or how it happened. So the god caught me and just got up and danced there. I got up and the Panbhai said. This is our Patwāra. So I went to take my asan and became the new oracle.

In any case, in the point of view of the people in Garhwal, the manifestation of non-human agents within the human body is not an unusual, foreign psycho-emotional state — which may even be pathological — but is part and parcel of being a Garhwali person. Not all of these experiences are necessarily religious; nor are they all part of healing processes. However, all of them seem to be part of the basic experience of a continuum between the supernatural realm and the realm of human beings, of which there are many examples — and not only in Indian Himalayas.

In my case studies, the rituals are performances in Richard SCHECHNER's sense of the term, since they are clearly demarcated from everyday behavior and their particulars — gestures, movements, body postures — are conventionalized and authored by someone other than the performer.[10] In fact, the particulars of these rituals are practices developed in and through the history of the performance itself, shaped, transmitted and transformed by generations of worshippers. These bodily positions and movements transport information connected, for example, to the identity of a deity, its mythical story, the history of its worship and of the group, but also to more complex meanings of social norms and moral obligations. This kind of information is such that only insiders are able to grasp its full content. And even this understanding is based on intuitive, habitual and embodied knowledge rather than on cognitive functioning and symbolic decoding. In this way, rituals enable many people to have a similar sensual experience, to share an embodied memory.

Such rituals are part of a larger system of cultural memory that is deeply rooted in bodily experience, and manifests itself in emotions during these dramatic actions of "possession" as well as in cultural norms and values. Movements, gestures, dances, music, and aromas can be mnemonic devices which, especially in the context of rituals, transmit traditions, such as the way a person should relate to a deity; how the hand should be held when interacting with divine beings; how one is to sit showing respect; gendered and caste divisions of space; and also myths and stories of the past. Since all of this is performed before a live audience, spatial and temporal dimensions are changed in the process. Ritual performances are, among other things, pasts experienced as present. Therefore, TAYLOR claims that it is impossible to think about cultural memory and identity as disembodied. For her,

> the bodies participating in the transmission of knowledge and memory are themselves a product of certain taxonomic, disciplinary, and mnemonic systems. Gender impacts how these bodies participate, as does ethnicity. The techniques of transmission vary from group to group. The mental frameworks — which include images, stories, and behaviors — constitute a specific archive and repertoire (TAYLOR 2003, p. 86).

The sensual experience of participating in performative ritual activities is, to the villagers of Garhwal, a basic social experience. They are part of a locally produced cultural repertoire, which is also the basis for every social interaction. Movement, memory, rhythm, smell, and other kinaesthetic and synaesthetic

---

[10] As SCHECHNER puts it, "performances mark identities, bend and remake time, adorn the body with costumes, and provide people with behavior that is 'twice-behaved,' not-for-the-first time, rehearsed, cooked, prepared" (1995, p. 1).

experiences result in moments of communal joy and excitement that is similar to *rasa* in various ways. The emotional experience connects the performers and the spectators. But the emotional experience itself depends on the cultural repertoire of the people involved. During participant observation, the ethnographer usually experiences a different ritual as compared to the ritual specialist or a young child. Yet, the realization of a certain kind of aesthetic perception, which stems from a sensual and non-discursive understanding of the event, results in a moment of high emotional involvement which may be called *rasa* or, borrowing from Victor TURNER (1969), "communitas." It is the moment when the borders of the individual's egocentric experience are blurred, and merge with the experience of the group.

References

BELL, C. (1992): Ritual theory, ritual practice. – Oxford.

BORDIEU, P. (1990): The logic of practice. – Stanford.

CASEY, E. S. (1987): Remembering: A phenomenological study. – Bloomington.

CONNERTON, P. (1989): How societies remember. – Cambridge.

CSORDAS, T.J. (1997): The sacred self: A cultural phenomenology of charismatic Healing. – Berkeley.

ENCYCLOPEDIA BRITANNICA (2012): Yaksha. Online Academic Edition. Encyclopedia Britannica Inc. http://www.britannica.com/EBchecked/topic/651312/yaksha (accessed January 13, 2013). – London.

HACKING, I. (1996): Multiple Persönlichkeit: Zur Geschichte der Seele in der Moderne. – Munich. In English, (1998): Rewriting the soul. – Princeton.

HECKEL, A. (1991): Rasa: The Audience and the Stage. In: Journal of Arts and Ideas, Vol. 17, No. 18, pp. 33–42.

HILTEBEITEL, A. (2001): Rethinking the Mahābhārata: A reader's guide to the education of Dharma King. – Chicago.

MICHAELS, A. (2004): Hinduism: Past and Presence. – Princeton.

POLIT, K. (2012): Women of honour – Gender and agency among *dalit* women in the central Himalayas. – New Delhi.

SAX, W.S. (1990). Village daughter, village goddess: Residence, gender, and politics in a Himalayan pilgrimage. In: American Ethnologist, Vol. 17, pp. 491–512.

SAX, W.S. (2002): Dancing the Self: Personhood and performance in Pāṇḍav Līlā of Garhwal. – Oxford.

SAX, W.S. (2003): Divine kingdoms in the Central Himalayas. In: GUTSCHOW, N., et al., (Eds.): Sacred Landscapes of the Himalaya. – Vienna, pp. 177–207.

SCHECHNER, R. (1995): The future of ritual: Writings on culture and performance. – London.

TAYLOR, D. (2003): The Archive and the Repertoire. Performing Cultural Memory in the Americas. – Durham and London.

TURNER, V. (1969): The ritual process — Structure and anti-structure. – Chicago.

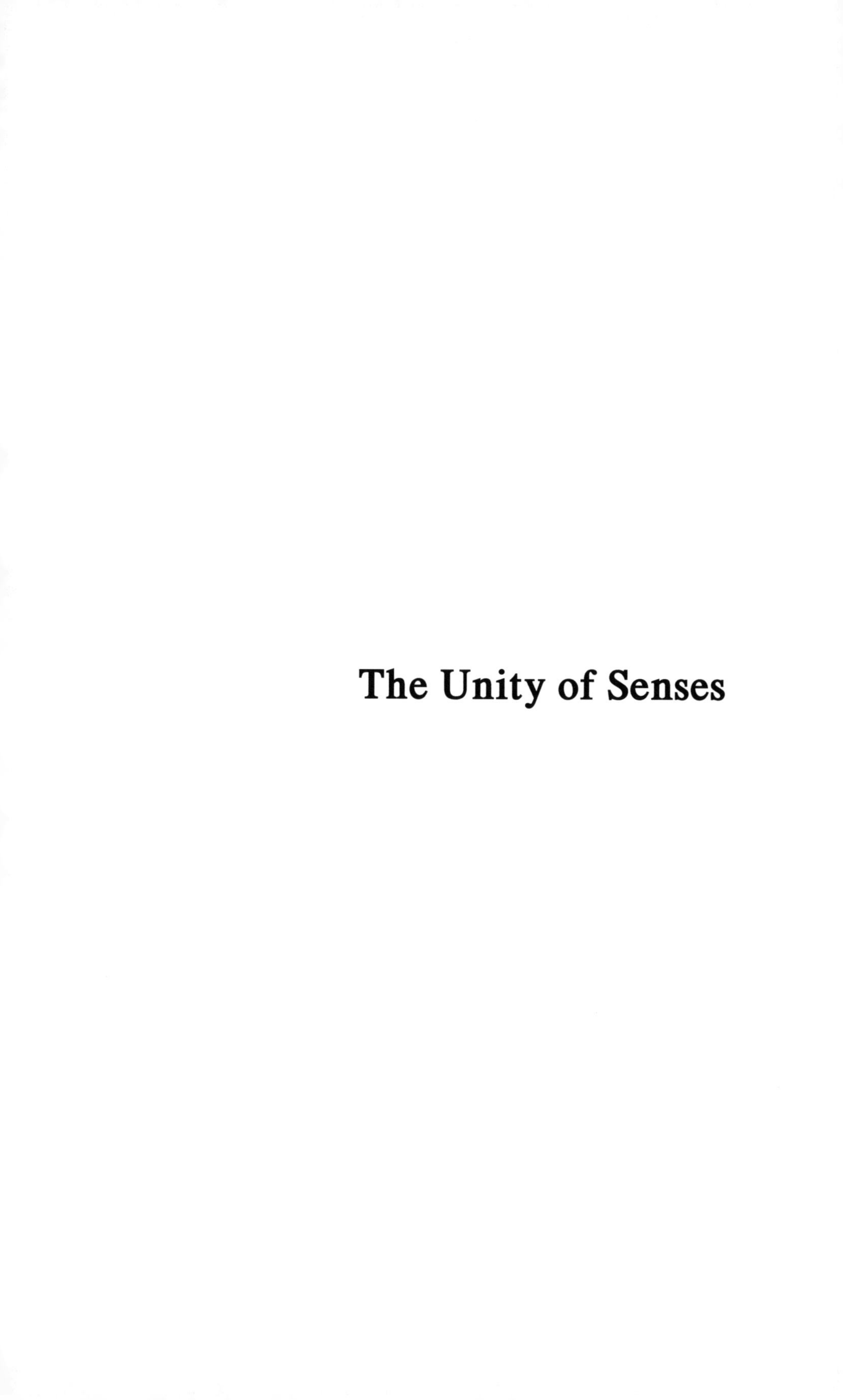

The Unity of Senses

Sundar Sarukkai

Unity of the Senses in Indian Thought

We believe that there are five senses which are the windows to all our experiences. These are the senses corresponding to touch, sight, taste, smell, and sound. These senses are associated with specific sense-organs, although the sense of touch associated with the skin is of a different "kind" as compared to sight, smell and sound. These senses are seen to be independent of each other, although there have also been arguments that taste is akin to the sense of touch. In fact, the independence of these senses is itself a matter of debate, and has been used by philosophers to argue for a variety of conclusions, such as the proof of existence of the self, and even of the world. But there seems to be little disagreement that the nature of these sensory experiences is exclusive. That is, one cannot experience the nature of sound through the eyes; what the ear contributes to that experience is special to that organ. Given this independence, it is natural that, through history, people have associated different "strengths" to these senses. The eye has been the most dominant sense in a number of ways. Sight has been the most dominant metaphor for knowledge and truth: terms such as insight, enlightenment and so on illustrate a universal privilege for the "positive" virtues of sight. But the sense of touch is also essential. As Aristotle suggests, while the sense of sight is important, without the sense of touch existence is not possible. Thus, touch is the most essential sense for human beings since we can live even if we are blind, but if we lose the capacity to touch we will die. Senses, thus, have different functions. Given all this, what does it mean when we say that there could be a unity of the senses?

Let me begin with an anecdote. I have a relative who suddenly lost his sense of smell. He had no idea why it happened, but one day he found that he could not smell anything. Unfortunately for him, he discovered that the loss of smell also meant the loss of taste. In order to get his sense of taste back, he has been trying to get his sense of smell back. What really is the connection between taste and smell? For those who are connoisseurs of good food, they will immediately understand this connection between taste and smell. They can have an idea of the taste of the food by smelling it — deeply and carefully. The fact that smell triggers saliva indicates another interesting connection between taste and smell.

Similarly, we experience a special unity of sound and sight. Culturally, this unity of sight–sound has dominated our aesthetic experience, particularly in the domain of cinema, advertisements and the visual media in general. An interesting way to discover this unity of sight–sound is by watching films by removing background sound and dialogues. Silent films illustrate the complexities of our engagement with sight–sound. Music directors, particularly those who score background music, must be aware of this unity if they are to meaningfully merge sound with vision. One might say that the sound "attached" to vision only serves to heighten certain emotions in the visual, and does not influence the way we see the image. However, to even say this is to accept certain presuppositions about the independence of the visual and the process of meaning-making, or experiencing the visual. For example, one could argue that visual images have the information of emotions within them, but many times we may not be able to access them only visually. The use of sound may serve to extract this information from the visual image and, thus, our emotional experience of the same visuals can radically change under the unified influence of the sound and the image.

These two examples of smell–taste and sight–sound indicate the possibilities of a unification of the senses. From this to move to the unification of the five senses is not in principle difficult because once the independence of even two of the senses is broken, an extension to the others is a matter of detail. There is an obvious idea of the unification of the senses, which is their unification within one entity called the "body." If the body is seen as a unified whole, then the senses function as parts of this unified whole and, thus, the idea that the senses are independent is already a flawed one. Why is it that we do not see the body as a whole and, instead, see it in terms of independent components? Similarly, why would we assume that the senses are independent of the body they belong to? We can look at many examples that suggest the integrity and the unity of the body as the first principle. One such is experiences of synaesthesia whereby one experiences one sense through the register of another sense — such as smelling green (and not just seeing it as green). The very possibility of such trans-sensory experiences challenges a reductive approach to the senses. The second example is the common observation of how emotions influence the senses. The world looks different to us when we are depressed or happy; we hear or not hear depending on what we see, and how intently we see something. If emotions are seen as mental states, then this is a clear indication of how mental states influence the sensory capacity of the body. The way our body reacts when we hear a sound (as best exemplified when kids start spontaneously moving their body to music) relates sound to touch in a fundamental way. (This process is also related to the bodily motility exhibited by Indian musicians when they move their body in all kinds of ways in an attempt to capture certain expressions and notes when they are singing.)

Another example of the non-independence of the senses comes from the common observation of day-dreaming and related activities that suggest the "tuning-out" of a person from her surroundings. Classrooms, for me, are a good illustration of this capacity of human beings to not hear even though the sound waves (from the teacher) fall on the students' ears. What is this phenomenon that makes us not hear sounds even though sound waves fall on our ear drums? If the model of hearing is based on a mechanical process of the auditory sense, which includes the ear drum and other accessories, how then do we explain the process of tuning-out? Something similar also happens with sight: sometimes when we are deeply immersed in something, we do not "see" a person standing right in front of us although the mechanics of vision — such as the light ray falling on our eyes — should entail that we see the person.

These examples illustrate modes of unification among the senses. However, the questions that arise are: what really is their significance? What is the meaning of "unity" here? What kind of unity do these examples imply? I mentioned the phenomenon of synaesthesia earlier. This, as a medical condition, is rare; but the notion itself can be extended in useful ways to understand cultures. SULLIVAN (1986) suggests that the "symbolic experience of the unity of the senses" supplies a culture with a "unity of meaning." His analysis, which is about ritual processes that bring "many or all of the senses into play simultaneously" (HOWES 2006, p. 162), also leads to a way of understanding society in terms of some kinds of unity, and in particular, in terms of "oneness of meaning." Howes finds the idea of the unity of the senses in SULLIVAN's work, with its metaphorical extension of synaesthesia into "cultural synasthesia" limited. Instead of this framework, he finds Kondo's analysis of the Japanese tea ceremony as replacing the notion of synaesthesia with a "model of intersensoriality" (ibid., p. 164) more accurate. This model does not force a synaesthetic experience, and is also not necessarily harmonious. It accepts that the senses are hierarchically ordered; yet it allows the possibility that "sometimes the senses may seem to all be working together in harmony." Howes uses these ideas to emphasize his own argument that even artefacts and places (the sensory experience of places) can be seen as "extensions of the senses" (ibid). Such extrapolations extend the possibility of the unity of senses even beyond the five senses.

A good example of a practice that suggests some form of intersensoriality is the Hindu practice of worship. While this mode of worship may be duplicated in part in other religions, the complexity as well as the extensiveness of this practice makes this unique. The offering of prayers in temples is a process that simultaneously involves different senses. First of all, the idol to whom the prayer is offered is decked with fragrant flowers. To add to the smells, sandalwood and other material are offered as incense. The visual impact of the idol is often striking, given the great detailing of dress as well as the flower arrangements. Along with this visual sense, there is concomitantly a strong sense of smell due to the flowers and incense. The world of smell bccomes much more extensive when we take into account the constant smell of oil and burning wicks from lamps which are normally distributed near the inner sanctum, and sometimes beyond. At the moment of offering the flame, bells will begin ringing. In some temples, sound is created using metallic discs which are struck with a metal rod leading to a loud ringing which accompanies the ritual offering of the flame. At this moment of prayer, at least three senses are simultaneously involved — sight, sound and smell. The experience of touch is also integral to this process, although its dominance is not as much as the other three. Why is it necessary to have a form of prayer that integrates these senses in an essential manner?[1] One possible answer is that the religious experience is heightened, or even sometimes created, as a multimodal experience. Metaphors of religious experience often invoke the idea of submersion, and this is particularly true of Hinduism. Submersion in this context is the submersion into all the senses such that distinctions, which are those which define our ordinary understanding of the world, dissolve, leading to a feeling of oneness. It is remarkable how many discourses of religion hark back to a primal oneness — and this oneness is primarily made possible by the oneness of the senses. This example also points out that the integration and the unity of the senses actually has the capacity to create new experiences such as the religious experience. When all the senses work together, we can indeed see a new world.

In these explorations of the unity of the senses, we have not discussed the nature of the senses which obviously would underlie the possibility, or the impossibility, of such unity. In the following sections, I will explore some aspects of these questions by first drawing on Indian philosophical views regarding the senses. By doing so, I am not implying that these views support the unity of the senses; rather, what I am suggesting here is that these views offer another way of approaching this question, one that may have some relevance to contemporary understanding of the body, and the nature of perception.

Nature of sense organs in Indian philosophies

The notion of sense organs is common to early Greek and Indian traditions. Different Indian philosophical schools use the term *indriya* for sense organs. Broadly, these organs are the "instrumental cause" of perception and, from the very nature of this perception, one can infer the existence of the self since it is the self which is "doing" the perceiving. The word *indriya* itself is derived from *indra* which stands for the self. Both the sense organs and the mind are the ways by which the self has experience.

The Nyāya School describes the origin of the sense organs through the five basic elements of earth, light, water, sky, and air. These elements are seen as the material causes of the sense organs. Each sense organ is associated with one of the elements, and reflects the characteristic of that element (Bothra 1976, p. 56). It is interesting to note how these associations are made: taste — water, sight — light, smell — earth, touch — air, sound — sky. As a consequence, the senses are delimited by these characteristics, and cannot experience the other characteristics unique to the other senses. Jainas disagree with this association

[1] Note that other religions have different approaches to this integration of sensory experience at culminating moments of prayer. For example, the use of flowers in prayer is itself a matter of contention. See Goody (2002) for an insight into the cultural use of flowers. See also Patki (1996) for more on the concept of worship in Hindu traditions.

between the elements and the unique characteristics of the sense organs. They argue that the sense organs are constituted by "matter"/substance. For them, the physical part of the sense organs are made up of "physical matter," and the psychical part made up of consciousness (Bothra 1976, p. 55).

The Nyāya association between the elements and the sense organs is one way to understand the unity of the senses, and this has to do with the unity of the five elements that constitute the world. One can understand the body as the world, and the five senses as the five elements which together constitute everything in the world. However, this view will lead to the following question: how does one view the other organs and other parts of the body in terms of these elements? Why is it that only the sense organs are correlated with the five elements? The Sāmkhya argument would be that the body, and everything in it, is made up of a mixture of the five elements. This would then imply that the Nyāya position identifies the sense organs as being pure representations of the elements. The unity of the senses inherent in this view is that, as elements, these senses have the potential to unite and create something else. This unity of the senses — as elements — is what really constitutes the body. Thus, for Nyāya, the body becomes the locus of the senses.

Although there are many points of disagreement among different Indian philosophical schools on the nature of the senses, there are some basic principles which are accepted. One is that the sense organs are not identified with their location in the body. Thus, the eye is not the physical eye. The Sāṃkhya system, whose theories about the body influence a host of other philosophical systems, describes 11 sense-organs: five sense-organs, five motor-organs and the "mind." These senses are independent of the gross body, and "cannot be identified with anything of this body" (Bhattarcharyya 1988, p. 192). The motor-organs are hands, legs, the organs of speech, excretion and sex. These organs too should not be identified with the gross/physical organs associated with these acts, but are part of the subtle body. Nyāya also agrees with Sāṃkhya that the sense organs are not physical parts of the body, and we have to infer their presence. However, these philosophers do not accept the existence of motor-organs since, for them, sense-organs are the causal agents for producing knowledge, and motor organs do not produce knowledge (ibid., p. 193). We should also note that the association of elements with the sense-organs as described earlier, which is accepted by the Nyāya School, is unacceptable to Sāṃkhya (ibid., p. 195).

Each of the senses has a unique object of sense associated with it. Consider the experience of seeing a jasmine flower. The eyes see the shape and color of the flower; touch discovers its softness; smell captures the unique smell of the jasmine; and, if need be, the tongue can attempt to taste the flower. However, this way of characterizing the function of the senses is not strictly correct. The jasmine is not the object of any of the senses. The eyes can only see the shape and color, which are the correct objects of sense for sight. Smell is merely smell — that it is a smell "of a jasmine flower" is not the experience of smell. In other words, the very act of seeing an object like a jasmine flower is only possible when all the different sensory experiences are collated together, and it is this bringing together of the sensory experiences which creates an experience of an object. The object, as such, is not an object of any of the senses. This unification of experiences has one consequence: it simulates the experience of an object that is being experienced. The constitution of an object happens "internally" and independently of the process of sensation.

Yet another possibility of unification arises from a consideration of the distinction between the outer and the inner sense organs. For Indian philosophers, the outer sense-organs — like the eye or ear — are only a part of a larger system. In this view, the sense-organs are actually not gross like the ear or eye, but are "super-sensible" (Bothra 1976, p. 54). Thus, the five sense organs, for the Jainas, are made up of two parts: one physical and the other psychical.

This distinction between the inner and outer sense-organs problematizes the argument for the independence of the senses. When we say that the organs of sight and sound are independent of each other, are we also saying that the outer organs corresponding to these senses are independent? Or is it that the inner ones are so? Or, that both are independent? Let us say that it is easy to distinguish the outer organs which seem to be independent of each other. However, what about the inner organs? If these sense-organs are not gross but are "super-sensible," then how do we distinguish the independence of these organs? Moreover, if the senses are made up of two parts, the physical and the psychical, what does it mean to say that the two psychical entities are independent just as the physical entities are? In other words, we need a mechanism to distinguish psychical entities if we are to say that senses are independent. This argument is not dependent on any of these ancient philosophies. In contemporary terms, the entity that is central to all notions of experience is consciousness. And, as far as consciousness is concerned, there is only one consciousness. There is no separate consciousness corresponding to sight, and another one corresponding to sound. Another way of understanding this is to say that sensory experiences are unified within one consciousness. This, really, is the gist of some of the claims made by the Indian philosophers.

Yet another challenge to the presumed independence of the senses is supplied by the modality of the perception of these senses. How do the senses perceive? How do they perceive the objects which are special to each sense? The basic debate among the many Indian philosophical schools on this topic is about this: is perception possible through contact between the sense organ and the objects of perception, or can perception happen without contact? The Buddhists argue that all the sense organs perceive without contact; the Jainas that all sense organs perceive through contact, except the eyes; whereas Nyāya and Sāṃkhya argue that all sense organs perceive only through contact. This theory that sense-organs go "out to the object"[2] may seem radically different

[2] There is a difference between the Sāṃkhya and the Nyāya view of going out to the object: for Sāṃkhya, the sense-organs only copy objects which are unclear and vague. These copies are then "presented" to the inner sense (Bhattacharyya 1988, p. 199).

from our present understanding of sight; however, we must note that the description of vision as reflection of light rays from objects, and their falling on the retina is actually a description of perception mediated through contact. As Bhattacharyya (1998) points out, if we accept the view of light rays as falling on our retina, and the eye not being in direct contact with the object, it leads to the problem of the reconstitution of the object in our experience, and this makes perception more a matter of inference. For those who want to hold on to the immediacy of visual perception, then the claim that the sense-organ is in direct contact with the object makes it easier to understand why we see objects directly instead of only sense-data. For the Nyāya, the sense-organ of vision is not the physical eye, for this cannot go out and come in touch with distant objects. For them, the organ is the "ray of light which has its seat in the pupil" (Sinha 2008, p. 27). So, when we say that the eyes are seeing an object, it is the ray of light that goes out to the object.

What is the notion of contact that is so central here? First is the idea that an object of sense is in "contact" with the sense, and this is the cause of perception. Thus, sight involves a contact between the eye and the object of vision. The metaphysics of how this contact is possible can be complex. To understand this complexity, we can look at the Advaitic classification of the types of contact: between object and sense organ, contact between that which is in contact with the object—for example, seeing color which is in prior contact with the object, the contact of the generic color with the specific color in the object, which in turn is in contact with the object, and so on (Gupta 1995). Contact is perceived by two organs, and is a quality that is present in all substances, including the five elements (Guru/Sarukkai 2012, p. 165). These characteristics of contact can be usefully contrasted with the sense of touch.

The argument that contact is the means of sensing in all the senses is another way to understand the unity of the senses. Even if the objects of the senses are different, all senses seem to grasp their object through one common mode called "contact." Given the complex ways of articulating contact in these philosophies, one should not reduce it to a kind of physical contact between the senses and the objects of sense. The unification of the senses through this common mode of contact is a different kind of unification as compared to the unification through the body.

The higher unity: Body and mind

Modern belief in the dichotomy of mind and body is traced to Descartes, whose distinction of body as extended and mind as not, was as much a comment on the distinction between the physical and the non-physical. Thus, mind has no location, no shape and size, and is not made up of matter. The mysterious metaphysics this view engenders is well-known, and has influenced philosophy very deeply. However, there is nothing matter of fact about Descartes' duality. In fact, as many cognitive and philosophical schools argue, there is no need to accept the reality of the mind given the unique characteristics associated with it.

This question of an ontological commitment to mind has led to philosophical positions such as reductionism, nominalism, and so on, with respect to the mind. Briefly stated, the argument is that the mind does not have an independent existence. We postulate an entity called the mind as an explanatory category, one that explains certain kinds of experiences.

Without entering into the merits of this claim, I invoke it here only to point out that Indian philosophical traditions had very different conceptualizations of the mind. For many of these systems, the mind was seen as a sense-organ. It was different from the five sense-organs discussed earlier in that it was referred to as an "internal" sense organ. Moreover, the mind was said to be composed of "matter" and, in a sense, was similar to the other sense organs. The relation between the mind and the other sense-organs becomes almost natural in some of these traditions since the sense-organs themselves are made up of two parts: the physical and the psychical — at least according to the Jains. When other schools, such as the Nyāya, describe the mind, they too describe it as made up of matter. In all these descriptions, the mind has a similar status to the other sense-organs. (Interestingly, there are also debates on *how many* minds there are — and the answers range from four to one.)

These descriptions of the senses and the mind reflect an attempt at a unification of the mind–body complex. In describing the mind as a sense, there is an acknowledgment that there are objects of the sense special to the mind. Just as the eye sees an object, the mind "sees" its objects — for example, thoughts. Even in western philosophy, there is a widely held belief that the mind can perceive more than the senses perceive. This capacity of the mind to perceive what the senses cannot — and by this very process do the "same" job as the senses — is the enduring legacy of the influential tradition of rationalism, one to which Descartes also belongs. Descartes' own invocation of the mind's eye emphasizes this similarity with the senses. However, the important distinction between the other senses and the mind lies in its ontological character. While all the other senses are localized (at least the outer senses, to use the Indian philosophical description), the mind is not. The Indians and the Descartians both make an ontological commitment to the existence of the mind, but the character of this entity differs in both these approaches. However, the function of the mind seems to be similar in some aspects. For example, the Indian classification of the mind into its functions of intellect, will etc., are also those characteristics which describe the Descartian mind.

Since we are interested in developing the idea of the unity of senses, it is useful to consider the views of one of the Indian philosophical systems, Nyāya, on the relation between the body and mind. As BHATTACHARYYA (1988) notes, although the Nyāya system is closest to western theories, its classification of mind and body differs in many important ways. First of all, there are three "substances" for Nyāya: body, mind and self. It is difficult to find clear points of demarcation between these substances: for example, out of the 14 qualities associated with the self, five are common to "material substances" (ibid., p. 177). It is worthwhile to note the differences between the Cartesian conceptualization of the mind–matter dichotomy and Nyāya dualism. Firstly, in the Cartesian view, there are only two kinds of substances, mind and matter. The mind is not extended, while matter's essence is extension. While, for example, Nyāya accepts distinction between self and body, the marker of these types of substances is not extension. The self itself has extension. As CHAKRABARTI (1999) notes, for the Nyāya, there are two types of extension: one is the usual sense of extended matter which is characterized by the fact that something else cannot occupy that space. The second type of extension is that "of being in contact with a substance," which leads to understanding the self as extended (although immaterial) (ibid., p. 20). Nyāya also does not accept the Descartian division of just two kinds of substances and, instead, points out that there are more kinds: those that are not physical nor mental. For example, the self is not the same as the inner sense. As Chakrabarti argues, this metaphysics of Nyāya yields a plausible answer to the insurmountable problem for Descartes, namely, how do two different kinds of mind and matter interact with each other? For Nyāya, the answer is easy since "the self is extended and conjoined with the body, there is no special problem in supposing that bodily states and internal states influence each other" (ibid., p. 26).

On touch as moral sense

These reflections lead us to another way of formulating the unity of the senses. Following a recent work, I want to describe how a unique way of describing the sense of touch can potentially lead to interesting interpretations on the nature of touch. As described above, the idea of contact is very important in understanding the nature of perception. When we see a red rose, for example, the eye is in "contact" with the object; the particular red colour is in "contact" with the rose, and so on. There is a causal nature to this contact. Touch is different. Touch is also a quality; but it is not like contact. Contact is present in nine substances, including the five elements; but touch is a characteristic only of earth, water, fire, and air (GURU/SARUKKAI 2012, p. 165). Contact is a quality for these, and others like space, time, and self. Contact is a quality present in material and non-material substances, whereas the quality of touch belongs only to material substances. We must realize that this metaphysics is not merely a philosophical exploration but one which is central to practice in Indian thought. For example, in the medical system called Ayurveda, which is very popular in India even today, there is a well established theory of the body, the senses as well as health and disease. This system argues that the sense organs are subtle in the sense of the distinction between the gross and subtle body formulated by Sāmkhya. We often mistake the sense organs for their gross body counterparts. For the Ayurveda tradition, what happens in death is that the gross sense organs decay whereas the subtle organs do not.

Moreover, as described in my work on untouchability, the skin — which is the sense organ for touch — is itself understood in a complex manner in

Indian traditions. First of all, there are many layers of skin, with seven layers as a more commonly accepted one. The skin is also the site where sins are inscribed (GLUCKLICH 1994, p. 99). The skin also differentiates between the interior and the exterior, thus leading us to understand tactility not merely as a sense of touch but also "as a way of being in the world" (GURU/SARUKKAI 2012, p. 169). The larger world of touch is also illustrated by the simple observation that touch is the only sense without which an organism cannot survive. If, in the western tradition, touch is the most important sense (for both Aristotle and Kant, for example), the skin is a "map of character" and of "moral disposition" in the Indian tradition (ibid., p. 170).

All this leads us to the claim that the "body is the site of ethics as much as it is the site of action" (ibid., p. 172). As I have suggested elsewhere, the complex narratives associated with touch and the skin in the Indian philosophies allows us to interpret touch not just as a physical sense but also as a "moral sense" (ibid., 173). First of all, this intermingling of the physical and the moral — which might surprise purists influenced by such dichotomies in the Greek and European traditions — is part of the larger worldview of the Indians. Indian philosophy is characterized by a resistance to identifying clear dichotomies between metaphysics and epistemology, ethics and epistemology, metaphysics and ethics, and so on. There is also a reluctance to accept a dichotomy between the physical and mental, as is well illustrated in the many views on the mind, as well as between the physical and the moral. As GLUCKLICH points out, physical dirt is directly correlated to "moral dirt." While this observation can be held by many without the support of a metaphysics, it is nevertheless the case that there is something special in the act of touching, and in the morality of touching. More than any of the other senses, touch is special in that it gives us a model to understand the intertwinement of the sensory and the moral.

In what sense is touch a "moral sense?" I am invoking the metaphorical idea of sense and converting it into the literal when I refer to touch as a "moral" sense. Often morality is talked about in terms of moral sense, a kind of sensibility towards the moral. What is this idea of sensibility? Loosely put, it is a kind of "feeling" that defines *not* what is moral, but *how* to act morally. This view may seem closer to embodied ethics which situate morality in terms of spontaneous action. But my argument is that it is not just about moral action but also about a feeling which signifies a moral sense. Senses are fundamentally about feeling. We experience only through the senses. So, when we see an object, we have certain experiences of shape, color, and size of the object. Seeing a color, for example, is a particular sensation associated with seeing. Similarly, smelling a flower is a particular kind of feeling associated with what we call a smell.

The claim is that we have a special feeling when we act morally or immorally, and this feeling is shared by the sense of touch. This does not mean that whenever I touch an object, I have a moral sense; but the reverse is true: that whenever I have a feeling that is related to my moral and immoral action (and perhaps even moral or immoral thought, although this is a point which I shall not discuss here), that feeling is akin to the feeling of touch. If we want a literal understanding of this, perhaps we can say that the feeling of the "moral sense" arises from a sense of touching the self. The feeling of unease when we do something which we were not supposed to do is a feeling that arises as a sense of touching the self. Religious traditions have often used the notion of conscience to describe the moral sense. This is also another attempt to make morality a sense; but in the case of conscience, it is the sense of sound or of hearing oneself that is associated with it. But hearing oneself only appears as a way to rationalize action. The sense of hearing cannot be the sense of morality — although the Kantian and post-Kantian emphasis on reason as the adjudicator of morality reduces morality to this sense, if reason is understood to be a rational "talking" to oneself. However, before this rational discussion with oneself happens, there is a feeling that catalyzes this discussion. This feeling is a feeling that is special to the moment when we touch our self. The feeling of unease or joy or doubt that arises in these moments of moral confusion is a feeling that brings us most primordially to our self when we — instead of constantly escaping it — reach out to touch and feel the self — literally, thine own self.

In the practice of untouchability in the Indian context, I invoke this example of the moral sense and its relation to touch to illustrate another characteristic of touch: the possibility of an illusion in touch (GURU/SARUKKAI 2012, p. 187). The immorality of untouchability arises through the denial of the real, and the replacement of it by an illusion. An illusion related to vision is the experience of seeing something which looks real, but is really not so. An illusion of touch is the existence of something real but which is occluded to touch and, thus, becoming unreal as far as the sense of touch is concerned. In the case of untouchability, although the person who is untouchable is real and available to the touch, he is not touched or he cannot be touched. This conversion of the real into the illusory is an act of immorality, and this can be asserted when we see how touch functions as a "moral" sense. This bringing together of the physical and the moral, as exemplified in the sense of touch, is — at least for me — a special act of the unity of the senses.

References

BHATTACHARYYA, S. (1988): Some Indian theories of the body. In: BHATTACHARYYA, K. and SENGUPTA, P. K. (Eds.): Freedom, Transcendence and identity: Essays in memory of Professor K. Bhattacharyya. – Delhi, pp. 177–219.

BOTHRA, P. (1976): The Jaina theory of perception. – Delhi.

CHAKRABARTI, K.K. (1999): Classical Indian philosophy of the mind: The Nyaya dualist tradition. – New York.

GLUCKLICH, ARIEL (1994): The sense of adharma. – New York

GOODY, J. (2002): The anthropology of the senses and sensations. In: La Ricerca Folklorica 45.

GUPTA, B. (1995): Perceiving in Advaita Vedanta. – New Delhi.

GURU, G./SARUKKAI, S. (2012): The cracked mirror: An Indian debate on experience and theory. – Delhi.

HOWES, D. (2006): Scent, sound and synaesthesia. In: TILLEY, C., et al. (Eds.): Handbook of Material Culture. – London, pp. 161–172.

PATKI, R.S. (1996): The concept of upasana: Worship in Sanskrit literature. – Delhi.

SINHA, J. (2008 [1958]): Indian psychology, Vol. 1 – Cognition. 2nd Edition. – Delhi.

SULLIVAN, Lawerence E. (1986): Sound and Senses: Toward a Hermeneutics of Performance. In: History of Religions, Vol. 26, No. 1, pp. 1–33.

Theofanis Tasis

The Politics of the Senses: On Vision and Hearing in Hannah Arendt's "Vita Activa"

The human senses usually play a minor role in Western political philosophy. With a few notable exceptions such as Foucault's notion of biopolitics or Agamben's distinction between life and bios, the importance of the human body in politics has been widely ignored. This paper attempts a critique of Hannah Arendt's analysis of the public and private sphere in regard to the human senses. I intend to argue that while Arendt correctly engages with the significance of the public sphere, she ignores the political dimension of the private sphere, which she conceptualizes purely as a realm of necessity. I will argue that the reason for this is, first, a devaluation of the body of the subject and, second, a false primacy of vision over other senses. I intend to show that, as a consequence of this, Arendt establishes (*a*) a problematic distinction between the private and public sphere on the basis of light and darkness, where the political element of the private sphere is masked, and (*b*) a one-dimensional distinction between labor and work that ignores the creative dimension of both.

Exploring the public sphere: Light, vision and immortality

My thesis is that ARENDT's description of the public sphere is exclusively based on two senses, namely vision and hearing. The public sphere is described as the space in which everything "can be seen and heard by everybody and has the widest possible publicity" (ARENDT 1998, p. 50).[1] Light is the primary property of the public space which is opposed to "the twilight which illuminates our private and intimate lives" (p. 51). In Arendt's text, we see the constant repetition of this theme in which the private is identical with darkness and the public is identical with light. For example, in Arendt's discussion of the household: "from the shadowy interior of the household into the light of the public sphere" (p. 38) and "the only efficient way to guarantee the darkness of what needs to be hidden against the light of publicity is private property, a privately owned place to hide in" (p. 71). The theme reappears in Arendt's meditation on individual everyday experience: "where the craftsman in his isolation was exposed to the light of the public" (p. 161), and "The medieval tension between the darkness

[1] If not otherwise stated, all references are from ARENDT (1988).

of everyday life and the grandiose splendor attending everything sacred, with the concomitant rise from the secular to the religious, corresponds in many aspects to the rise from the private to the public in antiquity" (p. 34).

The attribution of light to the public sphere and darkness to the private is followed by an important characteristic of the former which reveals the quality of their relationship. The public sphere is self-illuminated, while the private sphere is not; and the latter is only illuminated by the former. The life spectrum of the subject extends from the light of the "active" public sphere to the twilight or even darkness of the "passive" private sphere, until it vanishes in the Erebos of death. The exemplary experience of the private sphere is pain, which for Arendt constitutes "a borderline experience between life as 'being among men', and death" (p. 51). But, pain does not "appear" either to vision or hearing. Instead, it is felt by the body as whole. The whole body, and not a single sense or a combination of senses, is required in order to experience pain. In this context, the passivity of the private sphere is not only about darkness, but also about the passions of the body. We will discuss the nature of the relationship between darkness and the body later on.

So, if pain is a limit-experience which takes place in the private sphere, how can we think about the body and its importance with regard to politics? When Arendt writes in a footnote that "for the living, death is primary disappearance" (p. 51), she is linking death to vision through image. But how can we actually see the disappearance? In contrast to pain, death has an appearance as old age, which Arendt describes by quoting Goethe as "gradually receding from appearance" (ibid.). In other words, old age constitutes the appearing of disappearance. Arendt pays attention to the great masters and their self-portraits "in which the intensity of the eyes seems to illuminate and preside over the receding flesh" (ibid.). Here it is not vision, but the organ, the eyes themselves, which are illuminating the body in order to make it visible as it disappears. So, vision makes visible through itself what is appearing as disappearance. Let us summarize. For Arendt, vision is the prime sense; at the same time, light is considered positively at the very outset, since what appears is more important than what does not appear. Arendt also introduces a quantitative criterion. According to this, the importance of an appearance is analogous to the number of the witnesses. Hence, all that appears to everybody constitutes reality: that is, the public sphere. In this context, using the notion of the public sphere and the sense of vision, death is defined as disappearance.

The private sphere, on the other hand, mostly harbors the insignificant, with love being mentioned as the primary exception (p. 51). However, it is not clear whether this refers to eros or physical love. Subsequently, human activities are divided "between activities which would be hidden in privacy and those which were worth being seen, heard, and remembered" (p. 85). Nonetheless, if one were to accept the previous hypothesis, the reality of the private sphere becomes fragile. After all, what constitutes the reality of the private sphere? Arendt claims that it is pain. Pain convinces the subject of its reality. Hence, the private sphere is under the sovereignty of necessity in the form of labor which causes pain, that is, the reality criterion for the invisible, since it doesn't appear in public.

Having described death as disappearance from the public sphere, Arendt goes further, making immortality a condition for the existence of the public sphere and of politics in general: "If the world is to contain a public space, it cannot be erected for one generation and planned for the living only; it must transcend the lifespan of mortal men. *Without this transcendence into a potential earthly immortality, no politics, strictly speaking, no common world and no public realm, is possible*" (p. 55; emphasis added). Arendt perceives the public sphere as a space in which the subjects act in the shadow of death, claiming their immortality through the creation of their image, which consists of logos and praxis. Hence, immortality is linked to the senses of vision and hearing, since it is achieved through activities which take place in the public sphere. In this way, the following hierarchy of the senses is established: first comes vision, then hearing, and in the end the sense of the body.

Thus far we have reconstructed the connection between immortality and the public sphere on the basis of vision. We shall now discuss the relationship between immortality and politics on the basis of hearing. The subject can claim its posthumous fame through action as a citizen in the public sphere — that is, political action — which means speaking and being heard in public. Excellent speaking leads to public admiration and resulting fame. Nevertheless, there is a second line of thought linking vision and hearing to politics. Arendt's final argument for the public sphere's superiority is the multiplicity of the points of views it offers. Contrary to the private sphere, in the public sphere "everybody sees and hears from a different position. This is the meaning of public life, compared to which even the richest and most satisfying family life can offer only the prolongation or multiplication of one's own position with its attending aspects and perspectives" (p. 57). But, exactly this multiplicity of possibilities of seeing and hearing, of being visible and heard, is the main feature and precondition of democracy. In conclusion, Arendt perceives reality itself as constructed on being seen and heard — exclusive attributes of the public sphere. In this context, she connects politics to the senses of vision and hearing through democracy while the subject affirms his own reality at the same time through the experience of pain.

Visiting the private sphere: Body and darkness

In contrast to the bathed-in-light public sphere, the private sphere is dark. Darkness is "natural, inherent in the human condition" (p. 119), and identical with necessity and pain. It is interesting that, although Arendt sets darkness as a criterion of difference and value when choosing the positivity of light dominating the public sphere, at the same time she recognizes, up to a certain degree, the dialectics between light and darkness when she writes: "A life spent entirely in public, in the presence of others, becomes, as we would say, shallow. While it retains its visibility, it loses the quality of rising into sight from some darker ground which must remain hidden if it is not to lose its depth in a very real, non-subjective sense" (p. 71). The devaluation of the private sphere which derives from Arendt's negative perception of darkness is mitigated by the existence of the inherently positive "phenomena" of the private sphere like love, and also by the contribution of the private sphere to the "lightening" of the public sphere's image.

However, the private sphere is still "the dark and hidden side of the public realm" (p. 64), and Arendt seems to undermine the difference she introduced earlier between the public and the private sphere as a difference "between things that should be shown and things that should be hidden" (p. 72). I would like to point out that difference was initially defined as a difference between what is not visible, like the experience of pain, and what cannot exist without being visible, like action. Now, the difference is being described in normative terms, since there are things that should or should not be visible. But, if the public sphere has its own dark side, where is it to be found? And, what would be its relationship to the private sphere? Since the darkness of the private sphere is identified with necessity, it should be a necessity which manages to escape to the public sphere. What we usually call "underworld" was initially built on the basis of a biological need that could not always, and for everyone, be satisfied in the private sphere. In brothels, men and women are neither laborer nor worker, since the result of their activity is neither reproduction nor a material product. The brothel's location between light and darkness derives from the fact that sexuality cannot be subsumed to biological reproduction; hence, it cannot be confined to the kingdom of necessity. If, as Arendt claims, "the distinction between private and public coincides with the opposition of necessity and freedom" (p. 73), then, what about the in between twilight zone? What lies between the oikos and the demos, between necessity and freedom? One could say that an architecture of darkness would also be required in order to explore the mostly unseen corners and borderlines of the public sphere.

Before approaching this question, we have to keep in mind that the difference between the public and the private sphere is described, with reference to the body, in both of its versions: a) as a difference between what must be visible in order to exist, and what exists without being visible; and b) as a difference between what must be visible, and what must not be visible. In both cases, the body and its functions remain in the dark. However, the primary sense of communication between the bodies is touch. Therefore, touch is the sense characterizing the private sphere. Now we are closer to an answer; but we still need an intermediate step. What should not be visible? According to Arendt, the appearance and the disappearance of the body, that is, birth and death, should remain unseen. Hence the private sphere is "the realm of birth and death which must be hidden from the public realm because it harbors things hidden from human eyes and impenetrable to human knowledge. It is hidden because man does not know where he comes from when he is born and where he goes when he dies" (pp. 62–63).

Having discussed the difference between the public and private spheres in regard to the senses, it is time to explore what Arendt considers to be their common ground. Regarding zoe as a presupposition of bios, and strictly separating them from each other, Arendt consequently considers the private sphere as the material presupposition of the public in the sense that only someone who has risen above necessity is truly free to participate in the public sphere with the objective of immortality. "To own property meant here to be master over one's own necessities of life and therefore potentially to be a free person, free to transcend his own life and enter the world all have in common" (p. 65). As mentioned earlier, entering the world means appearing in the public sphere, being visible and heard by everyone, and creating a public image as a public figure. Keep in mind that in Arendt's analysis, light presupposes darkness; but, the opposite is not true. The distinction between public and private is based, as shown, on the concepts of light and darkness, in the sense that "the most elementary meaning of the two realms indicates that there are things that need to be hidden and others that need to be displayed publicly if they are to exist at all" (p. 73). I now propose to reformulate this distinction between the public and private sphere as a distinction with regard to the body. Hence, in the next, final section, we shall discuss the notion of labor.

Labor: Body and authority

It is known that in Ancient Greece, those who worked using their whole body were regarded as slaves, while those who worked by using their hands were citizens. Hence, if labor is accomplished through the use of the body and is related to necessity, and action has to do with freedom and is attained through the use of language, the question that arises is: what about work?

According to Arendt, it is clear that work does not relate in any way to freedom, just as action does not relate to the body. Politics becomes disconnected from the mortal body because it implicitly aims at immortality. Bios in contrast with zoe, that is, life which ends in death, may claim immortality in the public sphere. So, we somehow can grasp now the contempt towards labor in ancient times "that left no trace, no monument, no great work worthy of remembrance" (p. 81). I argue that the distinction between labor and work which Arendt proposes is, a) political, b) primarily concerns time, and c) is based on a notion of materiality which is the production of material objects. So, the main feature of labor is that "it leaves nothing behind, that the result of its effort is almost as quickly consumed as the effort is spent" (p. 87). Work, on the other hand, "adds new objects to the human artifice" (p. 88). So, the products of labor are, and are consumed by the equally ephemeral human body.

I regard Arendt's notion of work as highly problematic. Let me provide examples of what I mean by posing the following question. Does a singer labor or work? The song, its lyrics, its melody or rhythm, is not a material product; according to the Arendtian definition of work, the singer is not working. Still, it is possible that the interpretation of the song, taking the criterion of time into account, may be of such a high quality that it remains in the memory of those who listen to it. Hence, that singer could gain immortality with her labor, a fact that is in opposition to what Arendt holds true.

Consequently, Arendt should either interpret the artistic action in relation with the political action, explaining how we could act without speech; or, she should accept the fact that labor contains a creative dimension. Arendt is convinced that work "always requires some material upon which it will be performed and which through fabrication, the activity of homo faber, will be transformed into a worldly object" (p. 91). We could agree that work always demands a material, but this particular material can be the human body itself — as in the case of a bodybuilder, a model, a dancer, an athlete, or a prostitute. On all these occasions, work has to do with the formation of a body, and not, as Arendt claims, the production of a worldly object. What is left unseen for Arendt is that life itself constitutes the material for a work that forms life as zoe into bios.

Taking the above into consideration, we shall discuss now the relationship between labor and life (zoe). Arendt describes the birth and death of the subject as a linear process inside a circular time scale. Furthermore, she makes an interesting choice of terms for the description of the two extreme points in this route: remember that she uses the word "appearance" instead of birth, and the word "disappearance" instead of death. Both words are related to vision. Hence, the subject appears and disappears as an image of limited intensity inside the world. Here, Arendt recognizes the contrast between bios and zoe, describing the former as "full of events which ultimately can be told as a story, establish a biography" (p. 97). So, bios is defined in terms of vision and hearing. Bios, in contrast with zoe, may become a coherent narrative that a subject narrates either to himself or to others, or can be narrated by the others for the subject. Through the hearing of this narrative by the others, bios exceeds its physical dimension inside time, and becomes immortal.

Nevertheless, Arendt is not moving towards a problematic of bios as a project of transforming zoe; neither does she have any alternatives, since she considers work as a material product of a linear activity inside a circular time scale. For her, labor constitutes the circular dimension of human existence, since it corresponds to zoe; while bios, on the other hand, corresponds to its linear dimension. Labor includes the bodily functions, the preparation and consumption of food, personal hygiene, house cleaning, and, of course, biological reproduction, and recovery from injuries or diseases. Due to its circular structure, labor is characterized by repetition, and zoe is therefore monotonous in the same way, in contrast with bios, which is characterized by its creativity and rupture. Although Arendt correctly accuses Marx of subsuming labor under work, the distinction she suggests between labor and work on the basis of the construction of material objects is equally problematic.

However, despite her description of work as the production of worldly objects — hence ignoring the "material" of life — Arendt takes into consideration the meaning of the body for politics in a specific way. Following in the steps of

Locke, who founds private property on the property of one's self,[2] Arendt links the body to the private sphere: "Nothing, in fact, is less common and less communicable, and therefore more securely shielded against the visibility and audibility of the public realm, than what goes on within the confines of the body, its pleasures and its pains, its laboring and consuming" (p. 112). The body is located at the center of the private sphere, where the dominating sense is touch, followed by taste and smell (because of food and sexual intercourse), in contrast with vision and hearing, which condition the public sphere. We should not be surprised by the fact that, in the dark private sphere, touch would dominate vision.

I would like to argue that the devaluation of the private sphere derives from the devaluation of the body, and especially the senses of touch, smell, and taste. For Arendt, the above senses are contrasted with vision, which is "the highest and most noble of the senses" (p. 114). Conversely, the senses of touch, smell, and taste are the "the most private senses, that is, those in which the body primarily senses itself while perceiving an object" (ibid.). Hence, touch, smell, and taste contribute mainly in a negative way to the perception of the external world because they focus a priori on the body. Vision, on the contrary, inherently focuses on the outside of the body exposed to the world. No one can see oneself unless one looks in a mirror which is also a part of the world. Hearing holds an exceptional position, since we can hear ourselves and the world without any external apparatus. Its uniqueness lies in the fact that it is not inherently directed towards outside or inside.

But, let us again turn our attention to the body. For Arendt, in the private sphere, "the animal laborans, driven by the needs of its body, does not use this body freely as homo faber uses his hands" (p. 118). The subject who labors is trapped not only in the activity of labor, but also inside its body. This confinement inside the body induces isolation from the world, because bodily needs or pain can never be visible. Nevertheless, emancipation from labor comes at a high price. While Arendt describes with gloomy colors the situation of the animal laborans, praising at the same time the freedom of those who live in the public sphere, when she tries to describe the condition of those who broke the chains of necessity, she recognizes again the dialectics of zoe and bios. Those who emancipated themselves are alienated, since they are obliged to "see and hear through their slaves" (p. 120). It is the first time that vision and hearing characterize the laborers and, all the more, the participants in the public sphere have lost their vision and hearing. How is that possible? Arendt is forced to recognize through the symphysis of life (zoe) and pain the dialectics of life and bios since "the perfect elimination of the pain and effort of labor would not only rob biological life of its most natural pleasures, but deprive the specifically human life of its very liveliness and vitality" (p. 120).

---

[2] The question is what do we mean by "self" and in what way the self "belongs" to us.

But then again, if bios and life are deeply interwoven, the distinction between labor and work becomes problematic. Labor may constitute a different form of work because it can be performed in different ways, through the use of tools, privately, or collectively, and because it might contain on these grounds both satisfaction and delight. Despite what Arendt believes, there is freedom even in the realm of necessity, during the daily routine in a factory (CASTORIADIS 1974), for example, where, as she claims, "the workers in the factory have always been laborers" (p. 149). What Arendt misunderstands is that labor itself transforms the subject, and the means of labor determine this transformation. Moreover, the attitude of the subject towards labor defines its attitude towards authority and the structures of power, because it is an ingredient of its self-governing. The subject acknowledges that it cannot be truly free because it is obliged to labor; but what is required is not liberation from necessity, but emancipation from the power relations that necessity creates.

In conclusion, due to Arendt devaluation of the body and her problematic distinction between labor and work, the issue of power remains unexplored by her. She sees clearly that the freedom of the subject goes through labor (so through the private sphere as well). Yet, since "man cannot be free if he does not know that he is subject to necessity, because his freedom is always won in his never wholly successful attempts to liberate himself from necessity" (p. 121), she insists on linking freedom to the vanishing of necessity. However, as mentioned above, the issue here is not necessity, but the hierarchy generated from power relations. The fact that woman used to take over labor inside a family — and this still happens even today — has nothing to do with necessity, but with the power exercised by the male. Challenging male authority shall not liberate woman from labor but from the power structure created upon it.

What is more, structures of power in the private sphere remain unseen by Arendt because she believes that "division of labor indeed grows directly out of the laboring process" (p. 123). While she claims that Marx dissolves politics into economics by subsuming work under labor, she fails to see the political dimension of the private sphere by strictly separating labor from work. This situation does not change due to the fact that Arendt regards the political community as a requirement for the division of labor. Gender is instituted in each society in a different way, but men cannot give birth or suckle. Thus, Arendt's claim that "every single member is the same and exchangeable" (ibid.) in the process of labor is not true. As a result, Arendt ignores the role of gender in the process of labor as well as the hierarchy structures due to the power relations which derive from the division of the labor.

References

ARENDT, H. (1998): The human condition (Vita activa), 2nd edition. – Chicago.
CASTORIADIS, C. (1974): L' experience du mouvement ouvrier 2. – Paris.

Mădălina Diaconu

The Sky Around Our Bodies: Climate and Atmospheric Perception

> The question is really about that which lies between the earth and the nearest stars
>
> — ARISTOTLE (1968, 339b 14).

> Die Wolkenzüge geben viel zu denken
>
> — GOETHE (1960, p. 767).

This chapter discusses the concepts of weather and atmosphere from the perspectives of the phenomenology of perception, aesthetics, and environmental philosophy. Its beginning emphasizes a revision of Kant's statement about being filled with awe at the view of the starry sky above him, since the embodied subject has a multisensory experience of the surrounding atmosphere. Three examples then illustrate the broad range of approaches to atmospheric phenomena: while Aristotle focuses on their scientific explanation, the artist–scientist Goethe is interested in the morphology of their appearances, and Cioran regards the weather as the cause of subjective-emotional disorders, and as a symbol of human contingency.

Subsequently, the scientific concept of atmosphere will be contrasted with the phenomenology of atmospheres (BÖHME 2001, SCHMITZ 1967/69). The emphasis here is on the objective–subjective dimension of atmospheres, understood as emotional qualities of spaces, on their multisensory experience, and on spatial structures. The aesthetic appreciation of the weather — whose perception is still regarded as a visual experience although it also entails acoustic, tactile, and olfactory aspects — will be discussed through the examples of a meteorological treatise, and of a study on the "aerial aesthetic." The natural synaesthetic experience of weather undergoes an increasing elimination of non-visual stimuli while flying at high altitudes. This perceptual shift culminates with the astronauts' look back at Earth, which was essential for the outbreak of environmental sensitivity and, as opposed to Kant, of a new form of sublime.

According to the cultural history of climate, humans resorted to various strategies in order to cope with the weather change, ranging from biological adaptation to cultural-symbolic interpretations and from weather-making rituals to geoengineering. More recently, contingency and vulnerability have been extended from the body to the atmosphere; this converted the tragic from an anthropological into an environmental category, and the biological meteosensitivity into the "sensitivity" of the environment itself.

During the last decades, the debate about climate change has converted the weather from being a subject of small-talk into an urgent priority on the agenda of politicians and economists, natural scientists, moral philosophers, and even historians of culture (BEHRINGER 2010) and social scientists (URRY 2011); it is even suspected of being the "Achilles heel of our fossil-fuel-addicted civilization" (FLANNERY 2005, p. 26). In spite of the broad range of disciplines which deal with meteorological phenomena and the evolution of the climate, one dimension still seems to raise hardly any interest (beyond the daily weather forecast): sensory perception. At present, we even witness the emergence of a fissure in the perception of atmospheric conditions: crucial natural events are either *imperceptible* or *unbearable*. On one hand, vital dangers (such as increased radioactivity) are present "in the air" without being felt, but being only abstractly known due to sophisticated measurements. The mistrust in one's own senses goes hand in hand with the suspicion that the agents of knowledge and policy-makers might withhold vital information from the media and the population. On the other hand, natural catastrophes transgress any maximal sensory thresholds, and are downright life-threatening.

Nevertheless, an exploration of the impressions made by atmospheric conditions is, in several respects, indispensable for any anthropology of the senses: in the first place, these are usually multimodal perceptions and, therefore, raise the very question about the unity of the sensibility. They also often consist of perceptual-emotional complexes, given that the weather affects both the body and the affective state. Last, but not least, the weather and climatic conditions cause a multifarious performative responsivity from living beings.

The complexity of the subject obviously requires a specification of the topics to be dealt with in the present essay. After a short prologue on the Kantian sublimity of the sky, three examples — Aristotle, Goethe, and Cioran — illustrate different versions of the interplay between the objective explanation and the subjective perception of the weather conditions. These approaches are also considered, along with an imaginary descent from the sky far above to the sky on the earth. The next section compares two concepts of the atmosphere: the first, which regards it as a continuous physical space in the natural sciences, and second, which sees it as an irreducible plurality of emotionally tuned spaces in phenomenology. Afterwards, the engagement of the senses in the perception of atmospheric phenomena will be analyzed, with a special focus on temperature. At high altitudes, the unity of the senses is split into the mere vision of (atmospheric or cosmic) outer space, and the multisensory perception of the inner space of the flying capsule. Finally, the last section discusses different types of reactions to unfavorable weather and climate change: from the physiological to cultural adaptation, and from weather-making rituals to the technologies of geoengineering. Of particular interest are the changes of mentality in conceiving the relationship between humans and their environment along three major historical stages: premodern representations, the age of modern science, and the rise of ecological awareness.

Meteorology or the sky on the earth

Kant's famous conclusion to the *Critique of Practical Reason* says that "two things fill the soul with ever new and increasing wonder and reverence the oftener the mind dwells upon them: — *the starry sky above me and the moral law in me*" (KANT 2003, p. 215, my translation). This vision of the "sky above me" is described as a dynamic perception which starts from the individual's place in the "outer world of the senses" and expands boundlessly to an infinite number of eternal worlds. The magnificence of this vision fills the human with the feeling of his own insignificance. Lost in the cosmic space, leaving behind the home planet as "a mere point in the universe," the subject becomes aware of his own ephemerality, finitude, but also deep connectedness with the animal world. This disenchantment concerning the human's place in the universe is overcompensated in a second moment by the idea of infinity and the awareness of the moral law within the subject. The same reverence and admiration for the infinity of the universe frees the human from his dependency on nature, and confers on him the dignity of a rational subject. Both moments build together the dialectic psychology of the sublime. Nevertheless, the final impression is that of elevation: the sublime supersedes the tragic of the *conditio humana*.

The following reflections aim to challenge Kant's abovementioned statement in three respects. First, from a meteorological perspective, the sky is not separate from the Earth; but, as atmosphere it envelops the Earth. Second, this sky that surrounds us is not only seen and reflected rationally, as Kant suggested, but its phenomena, called weather conditions are, in a certain way, always at hand, being objects of sensory perception. Moreover, the weather affects the entire body, from outside and from within, in a sensory and affective way. Finally, the change of perspective from the beauty of the aerial world to the multimodal ways of being exposed to the weather on the earth reverts the dynamics of the gaze, too: it is no longer our gaze which seems to cross the infinity of immobile and immutable universes, as in Kant's vision; but, on the contrary, the sky around our bodies exists only as an ever-changing flow of uncontrollable atmospheric phenomena. Before going into meteorological issues, let us examine these three examples in order to make the following correctives to Kant's view more intuitive.

Sky, clouds, mist, smog: Descending the ladder

Aristotle, Goethe, and Cioran here symbolize three different approaches to the topic of weather. Assuming the risk of oversimplification, Aristotle will be regarded in the following, for the sake of a clear contrast, as the philosopher of the sky, Goethe as the artist–scientist of the clouds, and Cioran as the poet lost in the fog. These three moments build together a sort of ladder from the sky above down to the earth (or down to the sky on the earth) and thus provide a kind of counter model to John Climacus's "ladder of the divine ascent" (*Scala Paradisi*).

Aristotle

In *De mundo*, Aristotle analyzes the weather from the perspective of the philosophy of nature and of the elements. His explanations of a wide range of atmospheric processes are based on a cosmological theory that places the coldest and heaviest body — the spherical Earth — in the middle, surrounded in successive concentric circles by water,[1] air, fire ("a sort of fire," ARISTOTLE 1968, 340b 32), and ether; the fifth element is the substance that "Heaven, the abode of the god" and the "divine bodies" of the stars are made of (ibid., 391b 16–17). The sky is in continual motion, revolving eternally in a circle around the immovable Earth. The atmospheric conditions take place in the intermediate space between the Earth and the outermost heaven (cf. ibid., 340a 1–5). It is precisely this in-between or "interval," which seems to be lacking in the Kantian vision of the infinite sky, that is at stake in *Meteorologica* (ARISTOTLE 1968). Unlike the eternal cosmic cycles, the atmosphere belongs to the sublunary world and is, therefore, subject to continuous changes. Nevertheless, in spite of these variations, the whole of the universe is indestructible, being based on the harmony of contrary qualities, such as dry and moist, hot and cold, light and heavy, straight and curved. These are regarded, in the first place, as objective qualia. Moreover, the beauty of the universe — "the fairest thing of all" (ibid., 397a 4) — consists in order and regularity; even the unexpected changes or catastrophes — indices of the mutability and corruption of the sublunary region — are necessary in order to purify and heal the atmosphere. But not even the worst catastrophes can put at risk the eternal and unbroken permanence of the universe. The supreme laws of harmony and order hold everything together, and all things conspire to preserve this order like in a chorus: God is the chorus leader and the first cause of the elements, and the *primum movens* of the weather (cf. ibid., 399a 15–20, 398b 20–21). In addition to this, *Meteorologica* discusses a large number of weather and atmospheric phenomena, such as winds, storms, hurricanes, whirlwinds, rain (which is, for the first time explained as a result of condensation), mist, snow and blizzards, rainbows, etc. In summary, meteorology deals with natural events which "take

[1] Aristotle describes the Earth also as a mixture of the elements earth and water (ARISTOTLE 1968, 346b 18).

place in the region nearest to the motion of the stars," with the affections which are common to air and water, as well as the "kinds and parts of the earth and the affections of its parts" (ibid., 338b 21–26).

Goethe

While Aristotle is concerned with objectivity, and his descriptions appear to lack any emotional engagement, Goethe observes the cloudscape both as an artist and a scientist. Clouds have always fascinated contemplative temperaments — those that live with their "head in the clouds."[2] In particular, the ever-changing shapes and hues of clouds have been a vivid source of inspiration for painters, and the representations of clouds (one has only to recall the splendor of Baroque skies) serve as anticipation for abstract art. To quote Goethe: "Weder dem Auge des Dichters noch des Malers können atmosphärische Erscheinungen jemals fremd werden, und auf Reisen und Wanderungen sind sie eine bedeutende Beschäftigung" [The atmospheric phenomena can never be foreign either to the poet's or to the painter's eye and they are an important occupation on journeys and walking tours] (GOETHE 1960, p. 778). Already, as a child in the city, Goethe used to spend long hours watching the spectacle of the clouds; later on, his professional duties in Weimar strengthened his interest in weather observation. Goethe began to keep meteorological diaries on his journeys, and even a "diary of the clouds" ("Wolkendiarium"; for example in Karlsbad/Karlovy Vary in 1820). His records combine detailed descriptions of weather conditions and atmospheric phenomena, with measurements along meteorological parameters using the devices of his time (thermometer, hygrometer, barometer).

Like Aristotle, Goethe does not share the Kantian view of a static and apparently empty sky. While Kant's eyes plunge hastily into infinity, Goethe is quite satisfied with the delights of the proximate sky and enjoys observing the play of its qualities. As an artist–traveler, he is definitely a visual type, finding the variations of color, light, and shape and the fine weather in general more interesting than atmospheric disturbances. Also, he seldom takes notes about his being bodily exposed to the weather or about the un/pleasantness of temperature and wind (ibid., pp. 755, 801, 805). His subjective remarks are related only to the beauty of the sky ("Pracht" [splendor], "Herrlichkeit" [magnificence], "Schönheit" [beauty], "Mannigfaltigkeit" [variety]), and the "splendor of the world" that lies at his feet, shrouded in clouds and fog, after he has climbed an Alpine peak (ibid., pp. 758, 767, 754). While clouds used to be regarded in the plains as only something strange and unnatural, as "guests" who visit us for a short while, or "splendid carpets" the gods lay before our eyes in order to cover their own glory, in the mountains one is surrounded by the clouds and wrapped

[2] The hobby "cloudspotters" even founded the CLOUD APPRECIATION SOCIETY, which at present has several thousand members.

in them, thus feeling how the "eternal inner force of nature" moves one's nerves (ibid., p. 758 — my translation). For Goethe, everything is in movement: the sky is conceived as a medium for "aerial phenomena" and "weather stories," as well as the traveling subject who always follows fine weather (ibid., p. 759), and finally, whose eyes watch the "splendid, extremely instructive drama" of the clouds (ibid., p. 797).

In particular, clouds provide the ideal subject for both scientific education and the delectation of the highest sense, vision, being *unterrichtend* and *unterhaltend* at the same time (ibid., p. 767). Goethe does not neglect causal explanations of the weather. However, in contrast to Aristotle, he pays the most attention to morphological aspects which require a sharp sense of observation, and also justify the pleasure found in the play of appearances (in the sense of *utile dulci*). As for his famous theory of clouds, Goethe was influenced by Luke Howard, a British author who published several volumes about the climate of London, and who corresponded with the German artist–scientist (ibid., pp. 817–32); for example, Howard's classification of the clouds (*stratus*, *cumulus*, *cirrus*, and *nimbus*) was set forth by Goethe (ibid., pp. 774–864), and is still used in meteorology. Along with shape, movement is also implicit in the typology of the clouds, since stratus "is rising," cumulus "is clotting/agglomerating" (*sich ballt*), cirrus "disintegrating," and nimbus "is falling" (p. 818). An interesting detail is the praise of the Indian god "Camarupa" — the "wearer of shapes at will," and the principle of the irregular change of shape (p. 817) — at the beginning of Goethe's poem in honor of Howard.

Cioran

The third selected example is also the most subjective: Cioran has no ambitions to offer a scientific explanation of atmospheric conditions, and he even doubts if he could describe them; instead, he confines himself to analyzing the effects of weather on him. And while Goethe often deliberately chooses a vantage point, mostly at a high altitude, for a better observation of the sky (GOETHE 1960, p. 799), Cioran loves to wander for hours amidst the fog on his hiking tours, considering the fog (*brouillard*) "the only thing which has never disappointed me, the most beautiful achievement on the surface of the earth" ["la seule chose qui ne m'a jamais déçu, la plus belle réussite à la surface de la terre"] (CIORAN 1997, p. 970). His enthusiastic praise of the fog is all the more surprising in his case, as Cioran became famous precisely for his skepticism and radical pessimism, gloomy mood, and open misanthropy; known for his nocturnal walks through Paris, his declared love for nature and passionate walking tours in the country passed unremarked. It is obvious that the fog, the mist, and the clouded sky, the rain, and the wind that he prefers to listen in the darkness correspond to Cioran's melancholic temperament; as he confessed, he was fond of bad weather throughout his entire life. Accordingly, instead of causing him *divertissement*, as with Goethe, the clouds inspire confidence in him. He even remarks that he lacks enough light in himself in order to harmonize with sunny weather (ibid., p. 77). And yet, during the cold season, he has to struggle with the winter blues and "this fog which gets down on my brain" ("ce brouillard qui descend sur mon cerveau," ibid., p. 66), and during his holidays in Spain, he recalls with reluctance, the gray monotony of Paris, which he loves and hates at the same time.

But beyond their rather anecdotic character, Cioran's unsystematic reflections on the weather also have implications for a theory on the subject in a causal and an analogous manner. Firstly, his own weather sensitivity proves for Cioran that the subject's autonomy is nothing but a mere illusion: the fact that the slightest variation of the weather makes him change his projects and even beliefs should be regarded as the most humiliating of man's dependences: "What's the point to puff oneself up if one is at the mercy of the Humid and Dry?" ("À quoi bon se rengorger si on est à la merci de l'Humide et du Sec?") (CIORAN 1995, p. 1290), he asks in *De l'inconvénient d'être né*. Also, in another context, the meteorology becomes an epistemic paradigm for the representation of the subject in modern literature. Comparing the "objective" pre-modern authors with the modern "subjective" writers, whose characterization evokes the categories of the "naïve" and the "sentimental," Cioran warns that modern writers — such as Proust and, in a more radical way, the Nouveau Roman — risk dissolving the unity of the self into a "meteorology of feelings" (ibid., p. 1060, my translation). The weather is somewhat synonymous with permanent change — just like feelings are nothing but the "rhythmical convulsions of our flow" (ibid., p. 1061, my translation). Moreover, the subject is a Me rather than an I, a passive screen to be imprinted by stimuli, a sort of Heraclitian subject: the weather plays havoc with the subject's moods, will, and thinking.

One could hardly find another sharper contrast to the Kantian corporeal-rational subject who experiences the sublime. On the contrary, a direct line leads from Cioran to eco-sensitivity and the feeling of being trapped in the weather. Cioran himself condemns unambiguously the environmental destruction caused by modern technology and economy, is fascinated with apocalyptic visions, and caught in the smog of Paris, he dreams of the clear sky of the desert. A few decades later, the climatologist Tim Flannery describes the experience of the unhealthy, humid heat of an August night in New York as an unbearable feeling of being "trapped in a crowded, built-up environment of concrete, hard edges, parched bitumen and sticky human bodies;" the heat itself is "trapped by all the greenhouse gases" and the clouds overhead; the earth cannot breath normally anymore. And the author longs for the "clear desert skies of night" (FLANNERY 2005, p. 24).

It is now time for a short retrospection and preliminary conclusions. The Kantian expansion of the gaze has ended in the feeling of being trapped in the body, which cannot escape the "bubble" (with Peter Sloterdijk, the "sphere") of the atmosphere. We cannot "turn off" the weather like we shut our eyes. The necessity of meteorological phenomena (Aristotle) with their relatively predictable order (Goethe), which has hitherto supported scientific and technological optimism, has been replaced by the belief in contingency, the critique of technology, and a lethargic, almost fatalistic attitude. The sublime of the untouched sky compensated for the tragedy of the human condition in the heyday of humanism; in the ecological age, the anthropological tragic has been converted into the tragedy of the commons. Before looking into this further, let us discuss the sensory effects of atmospheres.

Atmosphere(s)

The scientific and the phenomenological approaches to the weather also diverge in their objects and in their methods: the natural sciences are interested in the objective aspects and causal mechanisms of measured weather parameters, while phenomenological interpretations focus on the sensory and affective experiences of atmospheric phenomena. Nevertheless, they both use the concept of atmosphere.

Climate and weather

A terminological clarification is necessary concerning the words "climate" and "weather," which we have used indistinguishably so far. Upon closer inspection, one may assume that the weather refers to the experiential dimension of atmospheric phenomena, while the climate is only its geographical correspondent; in other words, we feel the weather and research the climate. Climate itself, however, is felt by the body, even if only as the weather (we are leaving aside here metaphorical uses of the "climate" as "medium" or "atmosphere"). This leads us to the criterion of the real geographical distinction between weather and climate: their duration. "Weather is what we experience each day. Climate is the sum of all weathers over a certain period, for a region or for the planet as a whole" (FLANNERY 2005, p. 20). In addition to the weather (German *Wetter*), related to the atmospheric processes during one day, and the climate (*Klima*), which sums the average values of the past 30 years or more in a certain place as well as their long-scale variability, the German word *Witterung* characterizes an intermediate level — the atmospheric conditions during a week or a month (ROTH 2009, p. 14).

Each of these three concepts refer to physical processes which take place in the lower strata of the atmosphere, up to 15 km high, and whose energy source is the sun. The sun is implicitly present even in the etymology of the word "climate," from the Ancient Greek κλίνειν ("to slope," "incline," "bend"), since the climate is related to the incidence angle of sun's radiation on the earth, which varies within a year and according to the geographical latitude. The main weather parameters are the following: air pressure, air temperature, wind, humidity, air density, visibility, cloudiness, and precipitation. The local climate is influenced by air and soil temperature, by precipitation and air humidity, clouds and wind, as well as by the large-scale air circulation in the atmosphere and seas. These factors fall into three categories: 1) the solar energy and the circulation of the energy in the atmosphere (the meteorological factor); 2) the distribution of land and ocean, the composition of the soil, and the height of the land above the sea level (the geographic factor); and 3) the maritime currents and the distribution of the ice over the oceans (the oceanic factor) (ROTH 2009, p. 241). While the weather consists to a large extent of aleatoric processes, climate is built up of long-term regularities. Until the 20th century, the climate was even considered constant, in contrast to the variability of the weather. Specific to climates is their enormous scale in time and space, larger than that of ecological processes which take place on an intermediate scale. This also explains the huge discrepancy between causes and effects — for example, a one-degree decrease in temperature at middle altitude of the atmosphere shortens by one week the warm period which is necessary for cereals to ripen (ibid., p. 34). And humans are placed not only at the end of this causal chain, but they can also interfere with the natural climatic cycles: built environments, artificial lakes, and deforestation create microclimates (such as large urban agglomerations), influence regional climate, and even contribute to climate change.

As has already been remarked, what humans and other living beings perceive is the weather in its dynamics. The major physical process that underlies the weather is convection, by which warm air rises and cold air falls. ARISTOTLE already remarked that "everything hot has a natural tendency upwards" (1968, 369a 21), and he described the circular processes of evaporation (in his terms: moist exhalation) and condensation of vapors as well as rain as a circular process (347a). Later on, GOETHE defined the weather with respect to the same phenomenon using the metaphor of the "contest between the higher and the lower air" (1960, p. 799, my translation). Although the manifestations of convection are rarely observable as such, its importance is crucial for the explanation of the weather. According to Martin Basfeld — who outlined a phenomenology of warmth on the basis of physical data — there is no process of materialization or dematerialization which would not be related to the production and disappearance of warmth (BASFELD 1997, p. 210). Therefore, warmth should be considered as an element, or even as "the most general and originary material being," or the "originary atmosphere" (ibid., pp. 210–11, my translation). However, this *Ur-Atmosphäre* does not coincide with the atmosphere in its geographical meaning anymore — that is, the layer of gases and water vapor that surrounds the Earth; rather, it recalls the concept of element in the ancient philosophy of nature and that of atmosphere in the phenomenology of nature.

Atmospheres, "half-things," and qualities

In 1997, Gernot Böhme and Gregor Schiemann launched the program of a phenomenology of nature with contributions from both philosophers and natural scientists, including the aforementioned Martin Basfeld. Gernot Böhme, who was at that time already well known for his philosophical investigations of nature and his "ecological aesthetics," criticized the "oblivion" of nature in the history of phenomenology and expressed the necessity of grounding a phenomenology of nature mainly on the basis of Hermann Schmitz's "New Phenomenology," but also of Maurice Merleau-Ponty, Helmuth Plessner, and F.J.J. Buytendijk (BÖHME 1997/1997a). The realization of this project, however, would require extending Schmitz's analysis of the body (*Leib*), conceived as the nature in ourselves, to a phenomenology of the corporeal body (*körperlicher Leib*) and of the outer world (Nature). Additionally, transcendental phenomenology should be supplemented by a genetic phenomenology, and the hitherto exclusive interest in "natural," unmediated sensory experience should be enlarged to include the device-mediated experience of nature. In Böhme's opinion, precedents for the intended phenomenology of nature are to be found precisely in Aristotle's theory of the elements and in Goethe's *Farbenlehre*. In spite of the differences of principle between the phenomenological and the scientific approach — given that phenomenology investigates how nature is *for us*, that is, the everyday *experience* of nature — Böhme was optimistic about the possibility of founding a phenomenology of nature in congruence with scientific data. And, in fact, his theory of atmospheres (BÖHME 2001) may be regarded as the realization of this project, in which an important role is played by the weather. As for the concept of atmosphere, Böhme takes it over from Hermann Schmitz, who conceives it as the emotional quality of a place (SCHMITZ 1967, 1969 and 1989). Given the complexity of the subject, the following considerations will be confined to three aspects: the objective or subjective character of atmospheres; their spatial perception; and their multimodal dimension.

Schmitz, Böhme, as well as Hubert TELLENBACH (1968), Michael HAUSKELLER (1995), and other philosophers were particularly interested in the ambivalent, subjective and objective dimension of atmospheres. These refer to emotionally tuned spaces we come across; when we enter them, they induce in us a certain mood, which does not exclude the possibility of standing back and taking a critical stance toward them. In other words, atmospheres have a relational character: as qualities, they have to be felt by a subject; but they have a fundamentum in re (BÖHME 2001, p. 54). Being integral entities, atmospheres are in general difficult to analyze and describe; but they seem to be felt in a similar way by all individuals who enter the same space.

In addition to this, Böhme introduces a further distinction between the atmosphere (*Atmosphäre*) and the atmospheric (phenomenon) (*das Atmosphärische*). Whereas atmospheres are subjective qualities that have reached an almost objective status (for example, the melancholic or the cheerful atmospheres), atmospheric phenomena (such as the voice, the night, or the dusk) manifest an even stronger objective dimension: while atmospheres have to be felt, atmospheric phenomena are found, and their existence registered or recorded. Böhme's *Atmosphärisches* corresponds to what Schmitz calls "half-things" (*Halbdinge*), which mediate between things and qualities (for example, the wind, the gaze, the darkness, the coldness); but it also includes some examples of

Schmitz's atmospheres (cf. BÖHME 2001, pp. 59–71; BÖHME 1997, p. 145). The "half-things" are akin to things insofar as they appear to have an individuality, and are even personified (for example, the winds have specific denominations since antiquity); also they tend to be regarded as objective forces that exist outside us, and have the principle of mobility in themselves. As for atmospheres, Schmitz mentions the "Atmosphäre des Klimas" which comprises the experience of climatic phenomena; these are felt bodily, but as causes which affect the body from outside, and may be embedded in a "klimatisch-optische Atmosphäre" — like the atmosphere of spring storms or of November weather (SCHMITZ 1989, p. 110).

According to Böhme, atmospheric phenomena may be considered a link between the aesthetic and the meteorological concept of atmosphere (cf. BÖHME 2001, p. 64). His examples of *Atmosphärisches* are precisely the seasons, the moments of the day, the wind, and the weather in its multifarious forms (cf. BÖHME 1997, 147). For example, the coldness of an object may be regarded as its quality; but the coldness of a frosty morning develops into an almost autonomous entity, a "free-floating" quality, which can be reproduced and represented aesthetically (ibid., p. 62). Such "half-things" may call for reviving the ancient concept of element, which was also both concrete and abstract — an entity, a force, and a quality.

Finally, a comparison between the scientific and the phenomenological discourses on the weather would remain incomplete without reference to their different concepts of space. On the basis of his theory about the spatiality of the body, SCHMITZ (1967) describes three interdependent structures of lived space. The most complex of them is the three-dimensional "local space" (*Ortsraum*) and consists of places, distances, and directions — like the visual field. This space is built upon "directional space" (*Richtungsraum*), which is structured as a relation between the object and a fixed subject situated in the center of the experienced field. In turn, the directional space itself is constituted on the basis of an "extended space" (*Weiteraum*); the latter is the most primitive of all three types of spaces, since it contains only one dimension — a diffuse amplitude or unstructured field into which sensory stimuli enter. According to Schmitz, an atmosphere is akin to the weather: both are felt in this primitive *Urform* (prototype) of the space called *Weiteraum*, which has neither locality, nor directionality, but only extension or amplitude (SCHMITZ 1969, p. 185). However, this extension is far from being identical with the homogenous and abstract *extensio* of modern science; it consists rather in a sort of pre-dimensional qualitative volume or profundity, called *Voluminosität*, which seemingly manifests a certain analogy to the volume of acoustic and olfactory spaces (SCHMITZ 1967, p. 387). Nevertheless, the most evident example for the *Weiteraum* is the weather, given that the "climatic space" of the air is a boundless and indivisible whole in which the bodily subject is embedded (ibid., p. 48).

It may well seem that Schmitz has in view only the temperature when he speaks about the weather, although he mentions the difficulty of isolating warmth from the complex totality of the climate (cf. ibid., p. 50). And, this calls for a correction, since weather is usually experienced synaesthetically: non-thermal sensory modalities operate not only in the extended space, but also in the directional space (as when one feels the wind and the sunlight on one's skin) and in the local space (for example, seeing a flash of lightning or watching the clouds). Moreover, the sense of temperature itself is able to identify the direction of heat radiation, and to localize on the skin the place that is touched by a source of warmth or coldness (cf. BASFELD 1997, p. 203). In conclusion, what Schmitz calls "climatic sense" may imply *all three levels of space* mentioned by him or, more generally, as many forms of spatiality as the senses that are engaged in the perception of the weather.

This leads to the next question: which are the senses that inform us about the weather? As we know, there is no specific sense for atmospheric phenomena; but their perception may be visual (sunny or cloudy weather, precipitation, northern lights, rainbows, lightning), thermal (air and water temperature), haptic (precipitations, wind), acoustic (the sound of the rain, hail, wind, or thunder), or olfactory (the ineffable odor that announces snowfall). Nevertheless, this distribution of qualities according to the senses corresponds to a rather abstract, analytic approach. In everyday experience, a large number of phenomena address several senses simultaneously or, exceptionally, in slight succession, such as lightning and thunder, which indicated to Aristotle that "sight is quicker than hearing" (ARISTOTLE 1968, 369b 8–9). In summary, atmospheric phenomena demonstrate most clearly that the subject of perception is not the isolated organs of the senses, but the body in its complex unity.

This phenomenological thesis is endorsed by the findings of biometeorology, which emphasize the serious difficulties of an analytical approach to this subject: the weather influences the emotional state, general wellbeing, as also the physical condition in that it can cause various dysfunctions, ranging from blood pressure and vertigo attacks to migraines, rheumatism pains, and biliary colic (cf. ROTH 2009, p. 236). Moreover, the weather may even produce psychological reactions and lead to "seasonal affective disorders," such as the winter blues or summer depression, and recall by that the Hippocratic correspondences between humors, temperaments, and seasons. In conclusion, a full account of the influence of the weather on humans and other animals has to consider not only the "horizontal" unity of the senses, but also the "vertical" interactions between sensitivity and emotional sensibility, and — if we follow Nietzsche or Cioran — even reflection or morality.

Meteorological and aerial aesthetics?

Gernot Böhme elaborated a complex articulated aesthetics of the atmospheres which may be applied to literature and the fine arts, dramatic arts, music, and architecture. In most examples of this kind, the weather plays a role only as a subject of artistic representation. However, the question I would like to raise next is directly related to the aesthetics of nature, and addresses the criteria according to which the weather may be considered an aesthetic phenomenon.

This subject being too vast, I will deliberately put into brackets the entire tradition of aesthetics on this topic, and confine myself to only two recent examples for the sake of a comparison: a popular treatise of meteorology and an aesthetic study on aerial beauty.

Within his scientific explanations of atmospheric phenomena and their perception, Günther Roth occasionally makes remarks about the beauty of the sky. His implicit "aesthetic" is obviously one of pure visibility: a clear, cloudless sky by day or by night is not only "beautiful," but also "healthy," indicating the low level of light pollution. The strongest aesthetic impression seems to have been made on him by a cloudless winter sky on the top of the mountains in calm weather, when the aerial blue reaches the highest intensity and absolute purity (cf. Roth 2009, p. 44). Other comments express the admiration for the chromatic splendor of the dawn, in particular of the alpine glow and during a volcanic eruption (ibid., p. 46). The latter is the only example of the natural sublime in his treatise; for the rest, the aesthetic elements refer exclusively to the beauty of fine weather.[3] Beauty and positive vital values converge, yet without coinciding.

In the second example, David Macauley (2010) recalls R. W. Emerson's diary note from May 25, 1843 that "the sky is the daily bread of the eyes," in order to stimulate our interest in rediscovering its beauty. Macauley's "aerial aesthetic" bears a strong analogy to Roth's meteorological treatise, since both their objects and the emphasized characteristics of beauty indicate a clear primacy of the visual elements. To be more precise, Macauley's "objects" of aesthetic perception are the horizon, the "contents" of the sky (clouds, wind, light, and darkness), the broad range of weather events, the living inhabitants of the sky, exceptional and sublime phenomena (tornados, lunar and solar eclipses, the Aurora Borealis, meteor showers, rainbows), as well as the "perceptual influence of the adjacent or adjoining celestial realm that contains the moon, stars, solar flares, comets, and orbiting planets" (Macauley 2010, pp. 150–51). From all these, only the weather implies non-visual elements. Additionally, according to Macauley, most of the features an aerial aesthetic should consider include the availability and accessibility of the sky; the ephemerality, the permanent change and the play of metamorphoses; the lack of definite frames; "non-anthropogenic qualities" or the "other-than-human" character (the absence of human traces); the "elemental" character, by which the horizon provides "a sense of topographic relief, depth, and location," that is, a visual background or "shelter" for perception, in contrast to the earth; protean colors and the primacy of colors over shapes; and finally, the lack of design. All these are exclusively

[3] On the contrary, the manifesto of the Cloud Appreciation Society says: "We pledge to fight 'blue-sky thinking' wherever we find it. Life would be dull if we had to look up at cloudless monotony day after day. We seek to remind people that clouds are expressions of the atmosphere's moods, and can be read like those of a person's countenance."

based on visual information (ibid., pp. 148, 151–56). A single characteristic, called "ambience and atmospheric," makes reference to our senses ("especially sight, smell, and hearing"), in their connection to the imagination and affective weather dependency. The primacy of the visual recedes only when we are surrounded by clouds, at a high altitude, or when we are caught by a rainfall or snowstorm; then "the sky drops down" and becomes "more palpable, textural, and even tactile" (ibid., p. 155). *Watching* the clouds and being *engulfed* in the snow illustrate the broadness of the spectrum of corporeal interaction between the subject and its environment in weather perception.

At even higher altitudes, on a plane or a spacecraft, the perceptual access to outer space is necessarily confined to vision; correspondingly, the aerial aesthetic is almost purely visual (which does not exclude a tactile look, on the one hand, and occasional vibrations on the other). However, the vehicle's smooth flight and passengers' safety depend on the isolation of the capsule from its environment. Under these circumstances, the unity of the senses is somewhat disrupted: what you see is not what you can grip, and the availability of the open sky is fictitious. The sky is *de facto* no more real than an image: you cannot, are not allowed to, and do not even want to enter it (unless in an emergency). The perceptual "bonus" offered by the extension of visibility is thus achieved at the cost of a sensory deprivation in relation to the natural environment. And yet, it is not merely the Kantian *gaze* which crosses the sky like an arrow, but the *body* itself, sheltered and isolated from the environment.

Finally, when the spacecraft leaves the gravitational field and the eyes pierce through the darkness of cosmic space, when namely Kant's feeling of the sublime would be expected to grow stronger, a surprising reversion occurs: the astronauts look back at the Earth and are overwhelmed by nostalgia, as when the Earthrise seen from the Moon "entrances" Michael Collins:

> Suddenly from behind the rim of the moon, in long-slow motion moments of immense majesty, there emerges a sparkling blue and white jewel, a light, delicate sky-blue sphere laced with slowly swirling veils of white, rising gradually like a small pearl in a thick sea of black mystery. It takes more than a moment to fully realize this is Earth … home (ROLSTON 1994, p. 204).

Hence space travel has made a major contribution to shifting the object of the sublime from the infinity of the sky to the majesty, beauty, and fragility of the Earth. And while humanistic Kantian ethics supported the modern subject's impetus to conquer the world, the new environmental ethics emphasizes the limits to growth and, in its non-anthropocentric, holistic versions, it distances itself from the "arrogance of humanism" (EHRENFELD 1981). A broader, fuller humanity can be reached only after becoming aware of universal interconnectedness, and by enhancing the bonds between humans and their environment. Therefore, environmental philosophy is essentially place-oriented, both on a local and a global scale, since the Earth itself is "a very special place" (ROLSTON 1994, p. 208).

The astronauts' look down at the "tiny" and vulnerable Earth from the Moon[4] was also the crucial episode that inspired Günther Ander's critique of technology. Its complete success has brought about the present discrepancy between what we can produce and what we can imagine, between what we can do and what we can know, understand, and account for (ANDERS 1970, p. 52). Therefore, Anders subscribes to Harold Urey's statement: "The further out he (man) goes, the smaller he seems to become" (ibid., p. 65). The unleashed Prometheus has reached a power (*Können*) which goes far beyond his knowledge; and this calls for assuming responsibility. The aesthetic of looking down at the Earth from cosmic space also marked the outbreak of a new ethic: another astronaut, Edgar Mitchell, felt that the Earth was "something precious that *must* endure" with our support (quoted in ROLSTON 1994, p. 203). In the moment when the Kantian subject may finally be proud of his achievements and openly proclaim his own sublime, the environmental crisis imposes another form of the sublime: the real sublime is the power to relinquish power, the power to refrain from making use of power. And this brings us to the last point of our discussion: the power of influencing the weather.

From weather-makers to climate-makers and from rituals to geoengineering

Let us first discern four types of strategies for coping with strong weather variations and climate change. The first is proper to the higher animal species, and consists of biological adaptation to the changes of temperature in the environment, either through the adaptation of a part of the body or of the entire organism over longer periods of time (acclimatization). Also, in extreme cases, such as natural catastrophes or a swift climate change that affects habitats and sources of nourishment, species may migrate to other regions. For example, a climate change during the Paleolithic Age, which brought an increase in rainfall and the advancement of forests at the cost of the savannahs (as habitat of the *Homo erectus*) in Africa, caused a large-scale migration, and the "first globalization" of the *Homo erectus*, and respectively, of his Acheulean culture (BEHRINGER 2010, p. 28). Later on, it was again a climate change which brought *Homo sapiens sapiens* to the verge of extinction, and forced him to leave Africa and spread all around the world, producing "the globalization of humanity" (ibid., p. 32).

The third strategy of counteracting severe weather conditions is specific to human civilization (in the sense of material culture), and consists of the creation

[4] The image of the Earth still has the same effect, as Lee Jay Hannah's comments on a NASA photograph of the Earth's atmosphere demonstrate: "The atmosphere of the Earth is an amazingly thin layer of gases [...], a thin, vulnerable shroud around the Earth" and a "gossamer protective layer," whose alterations may bring about "major consequences for life" (HANNAH 2011, p. 5).

of successive, protective hulls between the body and the environment, ranging from clothing and habitation to air conditioning and heating technology. These artefacts — along with the climate optimum during the warm and humid "Atlantic period," whose temperatures were two to three degrees higher than today — enabled humans to become sedentary and to replace the semi-nomadic hunter-gatherer culture with the culture of farmers and livestock breeders (ibid., pp. 44–46); in other words, to produce the Neolithic Revolution.[5]

Finally, the fourth strategy refers to cultural reactions *stricto sensu*: representations and practices are the means by which humans attempt to control their feelings of insecurity and fear caused by the weather or unusual atmospheric phenomena. Rituals conjure up the forces of nature and aim to appease the gods, who are supposed to punish humans for their sins by sending natural catastrophes to the earth (for example, the Flood). This was already an attempt to rationalize the unpredictable variations of the weather; later in history — beginning with the first philosopher, Thales of Miletus, who earned a fortune precisely as a result of a correct weather forecast — the fear was expected to be banned through the use of scientific explanations and predictions. Yet, magic rituals of "weather-making" survived till much later: for example, the persecutions of witches are interpreted these days as responses to the negative climate change around 1600, during the so-called "Little Ice Age" (ibid., pp. 128–32). In addition to this, the persecution of witchcraft, to a large extent, is also the expression of the marginalization of previous forms of knowledge by the rise of modern science in Western Europe. The prohibition and repression of magic to influence the weather form a part of this process. In other regions of Europe, pre-Christian practices of "weather-making" have survived even longer, being tacitly tolerated by the Church.[6]

Modern rationality, in the long run, has led to what Max Weber called "the disenchantment of the world." The modern eulogy of the subject's autonomy

---

[5] Nevertheless, Behringer specifies that his cultural history of the climate does not intend to revive obsolete theories of climatic determinism (BEHRINGER 2010, p. 49).

[6] An example is the ritual called "paparuda" in Romania. The word "paparuda," which is these days used only pejoratively, was the name of the goddess of the rain; the word seems to have a Bulgarian origin and to be derived from the name of the Indian god Rudra, which is the divinity of the storms in the *Rigveda*. In scorching and dry summers, a feminine group accompanies the personification of the goddess of the rain through the village, singing and dancing a specific song in order to conjure the rain (cf. GHINOIU 2008, p. 225). The goddess is usually played by a girl or an unmarried young woman (seldom by a boy, an unmarried man, or an expectant mother), who wears a costume made of leaves of *dward elder* or bur. This costume has to be put usually directly on the bare skin in the nearness of a source of water. Occasionally the rainmaker also wears a garland of flowers on her head, and sometimes also bears a cross of wood in her hand. The main moment of the ritual consists in her dance to a rhythmic melody. The audience accompanies the dance by clapping their hands, by sprinkling her and her suit with water, and by offering her gifts.

culminated in the tragic-heroic Kantian conception of the dynamic sublime, according to which humans maintain their ascendency over nature even when natural catastrophes potentially (in imagination) endanger their lives (cf. KANT 2001, § 28, pp. 127–133). The physical distance between the subject and the environment in the dynamical sublime represents a *sine qua non* condition for an authentic (that is, disengaged) aesthetic contemplation. Kant's theory of the sublime may be considered the best illustration of what the historians of the climate call the "apparent uncoupling from the forces of nature" in modernity (BEHRINGER 2010, p. 168). In this respect, we should pay attention to the following significant coincidence: the *Kritik der Urteilskraft* was published for the first time in 1790 — six years after the invention of the steam engine, which marks the beginning of industrialization, and shortly before 1800 — the approximate date of the threshold to a new epoch in the history of the climate change as a result of the intensification of the anthropogenic factors (Paul Crutzen, cf. URRY 2011, p. 39). In other words, there is a deep connection between the Kantian analytics of the sublime, his endorsement of the *Aufklärung* as the ideology that promoted scientific and technological progress, and the stronger effects of industrialization on climate.

As a matter of fact, reconstructions of the evolution of atmospheric composition during the past hundreds of years reached the conclusion that human influences on climate had already begun with the Neolithic Revolution, when economic practices, and agriculture in particular, started to change the landscape (William F. Ruddiman, cf. BEHRINGER 2010, p. 209). However, the mechanization of agriculture and, above all, the massive fossil energy use since the industrial revolution, the large-scale processes of deforestation, and the new means of transportation mark a new step in the history of anthropogenic influences. While premodern weather-making rituals were intended, local, and temporally limited, climate change these days seems to be an inexorable process that takes place on a global and long-term scale. Even Paul Crutzen does not hesitate to proclaim the end of the Holocene and the beginning of the "Anthropocene," the age of the man made climate (cf. BEHRINGER 2010). No matter how the disputes between Ruddiman and Crutzen about the beginning of the Anthropocene with the Neolithic, or around the year 1950, will be settled, the new dimension of the anthropogenic influence on the climate sounds alarming to scientists, and all others as well.

During recent decades, climate change has evolved into a pressing subject of research and global policy. The imminence of global warming is considered crucial evidence. However, and in spite of some isolated greenhouse theories in the 19th century (Jean-Baptiste Joseph, Baron de Fourier; John Tyndall; Svante August Arrhenius), in the 1960s and at the beginning of the 1970s, climatologists were still predicting the end of the present interglacial age known as the "Long Summer," and the rise of a global cooling. Their prognosis was based on measurements which indicated a fall in temperature of 0.3 degrees Celsius between 1940 and 1970 (ibid., pp. 182–205). For the first time, climate change was primarily attributed to anthropogenic causes, such as the filter effect of atmospheric "turbidity" which hinders sunlight in reaching the earth's surface and causes a "global dimming." The Promethean modern subject reacted to this menace (which in its pessimistic prognoses anticipated that the global temperature would reach 0° Celsius by 2015) by elaborating strategies of a technological regulation of the climate and proposing audacious interventions in the environment.[7] The first generation of geoengineers was born. However, the implementation of these gigantic plans turned out to be counterproductive after 1977, when new measurements suggested that global warming and not global cooling was underway. These days, in spite of the irreducible coefficient of uncertainty in the predictions regarding highly complex systems like climates, it is almost unanimously admitted that the main causes of climate change are anthropogenic, and natural processes are only secondary.

The present state of research comprises of extensive literature that deals with the symptoms of global warming, and draws rather optimistic or, on the contrary, apocalyptic scenarios for the next century. The keywords in the predictions for 2035 mentioned in 2009 are the frequency of hurricanes, the melting of glaciers and polar ice, the flows of climate refugees, catastrophic floods, plagues of insects and new epidemics, desertification and mass starvation, the extinction of species, and the depletion of energy resources (HUTTER/GORIS 2009). Some of the pessimistic predictions from climate research seem to be confirmed by the intensification of natural catastrophes and symptoms of global warming during the past few years, whereas skeptics still invoke false prognoses from the past in order to raise doubts about the present ones.

Behind the facts and figures, the reactions to climatic phenomena and to scientific research — from the attempt to build for the first time in history a planetary alliance in order to stop global warming to the strong mediating impact of climate issues — suggest that we are witnessing the transition to a new paradigm in the relationship between humans and their environment. Humans have (or at least should) become aware themselves as being integrated within a highly complex system, and so needing to bear responsibility for its stability. Attributes hitherto ascribed to the body — such as contingency or vulnerability — have been extended to the earth and, recently, to the atmosphere as well. The tragic was converted from an anthropological into an environmental category. The vital character of climatic perception turned out to be congenial with the "sensitivity" of the environment itself: the permanence of life on Earth depends

[7] For example, it was suggested that a dam be built between Russia and Alaska, to cover the polar caps with black foil in order to reduce the albedo effect, to send "giant mirrors into earth's orbit to function as 'extra suns', and creat[e] an artificial 'ring of Saturn' around the earth, made of potassium dust," and even to blow up undersea mountains in order to lead warm ocean currents into the Arctic, to melt the polar ice with hydrogen bombs and heat Greenland by using nuclear reactors, etc. (BEHRINGER 2010, p. 189).

on the "wellbeing" or "health" of the atmosphere that surrounds the planet. The subject–object separation, which is specific to modern rationality, has proved to be not only untenable, but in the context of the environmental crisis, even dangerous. If strategies of geoengineering are still seducing some scientists, they are no longer left unquestioned by environmental philosophy. For example, after analyzing the pros and cons of the injection of sulfate-aerosols into the stratosphere, Konrad Ott opts for the rejection of such intervention based on Hans Jonas's recommendation: in *dubio pro malo* — in case of imprecise predictions concerning the long-range effects of their decisions — human agents have to act as if the most pessimistic prediction were also the most probable (JONAS 1997, p. 175; OTT 2010). Among the arguments against this intervention, Ott mentions the "loss-of-intangible" argument, referring to the possible change of the color of the sky, with more than mere aesthetic implications, as well as the "hubris-argument" which rejects excessive human actions (OTT 2010, p. 42). The ὕβρις was considered in Greek antiquity the primary cause of the tragic, and fear, φόβος, an element of the purifying κάθαρσις (cf. ARISTOTLE 1994, p. 19). At present, we are witnessing not only the revival of the feeling of insecurity towards nature (in its broadest meaning), but also the rehabilitation of the ethical value of fear. For example, Jonas pleaded for a deliberate, "heuristical" cultivation of the fear about the consequences of our actions and the power of technology (JONAS 2003, p. 63). After George Steiner proclaimed the death of tragedy a few decades ago (STEINER 1974), the tragic comes back in a new form — the fear is present, but no signs of *kátharsis* are in sight.

The protagonist of the new, unwritten tragedy is no longer a human individual, but the Earth itself. While modern science banned allegorical figures, such as personified winds or planets, from cartographic worldviews, contemporary scientific findings are interpreted as evidence for the analogy between Earth and a living being. Firstly, the saw-tooth form of the Keeling curve of the CO_2 concentration visualized the *rhythmical* emission of this gas (not to mention the steady rise of CO_2 concentration during the last decades). This diagram filled the climatologist Tim Flannery with admiration: "that is one of the most wonderful things I've ever seen, for in it you can see our planet breathing" (FLANNERY 2005, p. 25). And secondly, the thermoregulation of the Earth and its capacity to maintain a chemical composition that is compatible with the conservation of life, in spite of the variation of its environment, inspired James Lovelock's controversial Gaia hypothesis which emphasizes the analogy between the Earth and a biological system. Put bluntly, the Earth/Gaia "acts" like "a dynamic interactive system," "somehow alive" (LOVELOCK 2009, p. 32), as if it were defending its identity as an end in itself. From this perspective, the atmosphere represents a sort of "biological contrivance, a part and a property of Gaia" — maybe not "a living part of Gaia" but rather a manipulable "non-living component," a sort of "biological construction," like the fur of a mink, the shell of the snail, a cat's fur, or the bird's feathers, "an extension of a living system designed to maintain a chosen environment" (LOVELOCK 1979, quoted in FLANNERY 2005, p. 13; LOVELOCK 2007, p. 212). This radical theory may well enchant artists, poets, or New Age believers (and Lovelock was aware of the fact that the birth of the Gaia concept coincided with the peak of the New Age in 1968 (cf. LOVELOCK 2009, p. 106), but it still causes discomfort to scientists, who find it "mystical" and "teleological." From here, there is only one step left to Gaia's personification as a subject endowed with a will, who is able to take "revenge" and "fight back" against those who have caused damage to her (as in the title of LOVELOCK 2006) — a metaphor which has already found broad acceptance in the media and which supports the "moral" interpretation of the environmental crisis as punishment for the humans' "eco-sins." But, even without going so far, it is still relevant to our topic — the senses and the climate — that the Gaia theory inspired the foundation of the discipline called "geophysiology," which regards the environment not only as a consequence of geological history, but also as the product of the organisms themselves. According to this hypothesis, the oxygen of the atmosphere would be almost completely the product of the processes of photosynthesis, and this would also explain the increase of climatic stability throughout the history of the planet. The systemic thinking about the interdependences within the ecosystems was, thus, extended to the relationship between the biosphere and the atmosphere: living beings are not merely passively exposed to the weather, but in turn condition the climate in long-ranging interactions. It is neither our task, nor the right place to question the scientific correctness of these hypotheses. One can quote Jonas here: "The philosopher has nothing to say about this, but only to listen," (JONAS 2003, p. 330, my translation). These theories are regarded here only as symptoms for a possible emerging epistemic paradigm, which has often been invoked by environmental philosophers (for example, CALLICOTT 2005 and 1999, p. 231). Environmental sensitivity, conceived as dependence on the environment, has been extended to the sensitivity of the environment — of both the ecosystems on Earth and the enveloping atmosphere, confronted with the power of human presence on Earth.

References

ANDERS, G. (1970): Der Blick vom Mond. Reflexionen über Weltraumflüge. – Munich.

ARISTOTLE (1968): Works. Vol. III. Meteorologica. De mundo. De anima. Parva naturalia. De spiritu. – Oxford.

ARISTOTLE (1994): Poetik. – Stuttgart.

BASFELD, M. (1997): Phänomen – Element – Atmosphäre. Zur Phänomenologie der Wärme. In: BÖHME, G. and SCHIEMANN, G. (Eds.): Phänomenologie der Natur. – Frankfurt am Main, pp. 190–212.

BEHRINGER, W. (2010): A Cultural History of Climate. – Cambridge.

BÖHME, G. (1997): Phänomenologie der Natur – ein Projekt. In: BÖHME, G. and SCHIEMANN, G. (Eds.): Phänomenologie der Natur. – Frankfurt /M., pp. 11–43.

BÖHME, G. (1997a): Die Phänomenologie von Hermann Schmitz als Phänomenologie der Natur? In: BÖHME, G. and SCHIEMANN, G. (Eds.): Phänomenologie der Natur. – Frankfurt/M., pp. 133–148.

BÖHME, G. (2001): Aisthetik. Vorlesungen über Ästhetik als allgemeine Wahrnehmungslehre. – Munich.

CALLICOTT, B. J. (1999): Beyond the Land Ethic. – New York.

CALLICOTT, B. J. (2005): The Metaphysical Implications of Ecology. In: CALLICOTT, J.B. and PALMER, C. (Eds.): Environmental Philosophy. Critical Concepts in the Environment. Vol. V: History and Culture. – London, pp. 317–32.

CIORAN, E.M. (1995): Œuvres. – Paris.

CIORAN, E.M. (1997): Cahiers. 1957–1972. – Paris.

CIORAN, E.M. (2008): Werke. – Frankfurt/M.

CLIMACUS, J. (1982): The ladder of divine ascent. – New York.

CLOUD APPRECIATION SOCIETY. http://cloudappreciationsociety.org (accessed December 4, 2011).

EHRENFELD, D.W. (1981): The Arrogance of Humanism. – Oxford.

GHINOIU, I. (2008): Mică enciclopedie de tradiii române'ti. Sărbători, obiceiuri, credine, mitologie. – Bucharest.

GOETHE, J.W. (1960): Gesamtausgabe der Werke und Schriften in zweiundzwanzig Bänden. Zweite Abteilung Schriften. Zwanzigster Band. Schriften zur Geologie und Mineralogie. Schriften zur Meteorologie. – Stuttgart.

HANNAH, L.J. (2011): Climate Change Biology. – Amsterdam.

HAUSKELLER, M. (1995): Atmosphären erleben. Philosophische Untersuchungen zur Sinneswahrnehmung. – Berlin.

HUTTER, C.P. and GORIS, E. (2009): Die Erde schlägt zurück. Wie der Klimawandel unser Leben verändert. Szenario 2035. – Munich.

JONAS, H. (1997): Prinzip Verantwortung – Zur Grundlegung einer Zukunftsethik. In: KREBS, A. (Ed.): Naturethik. – Frankfurt/M., pp. 165–181.

JONAS, H. (2003): Das Prinzip Verantwortung. Versuch einer Ethik für die technologische Zivilisation. – Frankfurt/M.

KANT, I. (2001): Kritik der Urteilskraft. – Hamburg.

KANT, I. (2003): Kritik der praktischen Vernunft. – Hamburg.

LOVELOCK, J. (1979): Gaia. A New Look at Life on Earth. – Oxford.

LOVELOCK, J. (2006): The Revenge of Gaia. Why the Earth Is Fighting Back — and How We Can Still Save Humanity. – London.

LOVELOCK, J. (2009): The Vanishing Face of Gaia. A Final Warning. – London.

MACAULEY, D. (2010): Head in the Clouds: On the Beauty of the Aerial World. In: Environment, Space, Place, Vol. 2, Issue 1 (Spring 2010), pp. 147–84.

OTT, K. (2010): Die letzte Versuchung. In: Politische Ökologie, 28. Jg., Juli 2010, Geo-Engineering. Notwendiger Plan B gegen den Klimawandel? pp. 40–43.

ROLSTON III, H. (1994): Conserving Natural Value. – New York.

ROTH, G.D. (2009): Die BLV Wetterkunde. – Munich.

SCHMITZ, H. (1967): System der Philosophie. III.1. Der leibliche Raum. – Bonn.

SCHMITZ, H. (1969): System der Philosophie. III.2. Der Gefühlsraum. – Bonn.

SCHMITZ, H. (1989): Leib und Gefühl. Materialien zu einer philosophischen Therapeutik. – Paderborn.

STEINER, G. (1974): The Death of Tragedy. – London.

TELLENBACH, H. (1968): Geschmack und Atmosphäre. Medien menschlichen Elementarkontaktes. – Salzburg.

URRY, J. (2011): Climate Change and Society. – Cambridge.

About the Editors

AXEL MICHAELS is Professor of Classical Indology, South Asia Institute, University of Heidelberg. In 2001 he was elected as the Spokesman of the Collaborative Research Centre "Ritual Dynamics." Since November 2007, he has served as Director of the Cluster of Excellence "Asia and Europe in a Global Context." His current fields of interest are social history and the history of Hinduism, theory of rituals, life cycle rites of passage in Nepal as well as the cultural and legal history of South Asia. His major publications include *Hinduism: Past and Present* (2004) and *Śiva in Trouble. Rituals and Festivals at the Paśupatinātha Temple of Deopatan, Nepal* (2008).

CHRISTOPH WULF is Professor of Anthropology and Philosophy of Education, Interdisciplinary Centre for Historical Anthropology, a member of the Collaborative Research Centre (SFB) "Cultures of Performance," Cluster "Languages of Emotion," Graduate school "InterArts" at Freie Universität, Berlin. His research focuses on historical and educational anthropology, mimesis, aesthetics, rituals, and emotions. His recent publications include *Ritual and Identity: The Staging and Performing of Rituals in the Lives of Young People* (co-edited; 2010); *Children, Development and Education: Cultural, Historical, and Anthropological Perspectives* (co-edited with Michalis Kontopodis, 2011); and *Anthropology: A Continental Perspective* (2013).

Notes on Contributors

REMO BODEI was Professor of Philosophy at the University of California, Los Angeles, and is now Professor Emeritus at the University of Pisa. He taught for many years at the Scuola Normale Superiore and at the University of Pisa. He has studied, and taught as Visiting Professor, in various European and American Universities.

GABRIELE BRANDSTETTER is Professor of Theater and Dance Studies at Freie Universität, Berlin. Her research focus is on performance theories; concepts of body and movement in notation, image and performance; dance, theatricality and gender differences. Her selected publications include *Bild-Sprung. TanzTheaterBewegung im Wechsel der Medien* (2005), *Schwarm(E)Motion. Bewegung zwischen Affekt und Masse* (2007, co-edited with B. Brandl-Risi, K. van Eikels), *Tanz als Anthropologie* (2007, co-edited with Christoph Wulf), *Genie — Virtuose — Konfigurationen romantischer Schöpfungsästhetik* (2011, co-edited with G. Neumann), and *Dance [and] Theory* (2013, co-edited with Gabriele Klein).

GÉRARD COLAS is Senior Fellow at the National Centre for Scientific Research (CNRS). He has published on Hindu architectural, religious, and philosophical Sanskrit texts, on Indian paleography, and on 18th century Jesuit writings in Sanskrit and other Indian languages. His major books include *Le Temple selon Marīci* (1986), *Viṣṇu, ses images et ses feux: Les métamorphoses du dieu chez les Vaikhānasa* (1996), *Penser l'icône en Inde ancienne* (2012), and *Manuscrits telugu: Catalogue raisonné* (in collaboration with U. Chauhan, 1995). Her latest publication is *Phänomenologie der Sinne* (2013).

MĂDĂLINA DIACONU studied philosophy in Bucharest (PhD 1996) and Vienna (PhD 1998), and is Dozentin at the Institute of Philosophy of the University of Vienna. She has conducted research and published extensively on the aesthetics of touch, smell, and taste, phenomenology, and urban sensescapes.

MONIKA HORSTMANN (a.k.a. Boehm-Tettelbach) retired as Head of Department, Modern South Asian Languages and Literatures, South Asia Institute, Heidelberg University. Her research focuses on North Indian literatures and religious movements from the early modern period, and on the interface between religion and politics. Her recent publications include: *Der Zusammenhang der Welt* (2009) and *Jaipur 1778: The Making of a King* (2012).

KARSTEN LICHAU studied Education in Berlin and Paris. His doctoral thesis, entitled "Menschengesichte. Max Picards literarische Physiognomik" (forthcoming), was written within the framework of the graduate school "Body Performances" at Freie Universität Berlin. He is currently working as a research associate on a project on "The acoustics of the political body" at the Centre Marc Bloch in Berlin. His primary research interests focus on the body and the senses within historical-anthropological and cultural contexts, and on the role of sound and emotion in staging politics.

ANGELIKA MALINAR is Professor of Indian Studies at the University of Zurich, Switzerland. Her areas of specialization are the history of Hinduism, Indian Philosophy, Sanskrit Epics, and Puranas, Hindi, and Oriya Literature of the 20th century. She has conducted several research projects, for instance on Hindu monastic institutions in Odisha. She is a member of the "University Priority Research Project" on "Asia and Europe" at the University of Zurich. Among her recent publications are *The Bhagavadgita: Doctrines and contexts* (2007), *Time in India* (2007; edited volume), and *Hinduismus* (2009). She is co-editor of *Brill's Encyclopedia of Hinduism* (2009).

ANAND MISHRA has studied Mathematics (at IIT in Kanpur), Sanskrit (in Benares) and Computational Linguistics (in Heidelberg), and is presently working as Assistant in the department of Cultural and Religious History of South Asia, Heidelberg University. His areas of interest include modeling the Aṣṭādhyāyī of Pāṇini on the computer, the grammar of rituals and Vedānta philosophy, especially the Śuddhādvaita of Vallabhācārya. His publications include *Grammars and Morphologies of Rituals* (2010, co-edited with Axel Michaels).

ALAIN MONTANDON is Professor Emeritus of General and Comparative Literature at the University Blaise Pascal, and an Honorary Member of the Institut Universitaire de France, and was a fellow of the Wissenschaftskolleg zu Berlin. He has published about 20 titles, and has also supervised the publishing of a number of others.

JAYACHANDRAN PALAZHY is Artistic Director of Attakkalari Centre for Movement Arts (www.attakkalari.org) and an internationally sought after dancer and choreographer at the forefront of the contemporary Indian movement arts scene. He has trained in India in the dance forms of Bharatanatyam, Kathakali, Indian folk dance and Kalarippayattu (martial art), and in the UK, in contemporary dance at the London Contemporary Dance School. He has participated in many dance festivals, artistic residencies, presented papers, and delivered lecture demonstrations on a range of allied subjects related to movement arts in Asia and the West. He also has piloted an exhaustive research and documentation project "Nagarika" — an interactive information system on Indian physical traditions.

KARIN M. POLIT is an anthropologist and research fellow at the Collaborative Research Centre "Ritual Dynamics" (SFB 619) since 2005. She has worked and published extensively on performance, performativity and heritage. She specialized in North India, has done extensive fieldwork in Uttarakhand and Delhi, and is interested in the intersections of gender, performance theory, medical anthropology, and cognitive anthropology. She is the author of *Women of Honour: Gender and Agency among Dalit Women in the Central Himalayas*, and has co-edited a number of books on ritual, performance, heritage, and gender studies.

SUNDAR SARUKKAI is Director of the Manipal Centre for Philosophy and Humanities, Manipal University, India. He is the author of *Translating the World: Science and Language* (2002); *Philosophy of Symmetry* (2004); *Indian Philosophy and Philosophy of Science* (2005); *What is Science?* (2012), and *The Cracked Mirror: An Indian Debate on Experience and Theory* (2012, co-authored with Gopal Guru). He is an Editorial Advisory Board member of the *Leonardo Book Series* and the Series Editor for *Science and Society*.

WILLIAM S. SAX is Professor and Head of the Department of Ethnology, South Asia Institute, Heidelberg University. He has previously studied and taught in Seattle, Chicago, Banaras, Harvard, and Christchurch, New Zealand. He has published extensively on Hinduism, Pilgrimage, Gender, Ritual, Performance, and Healing. His major publications include *Mountain Goddess: Gender and Politics in a Central Himalayan Pilgrimage* (1991); *The Gods at Play: Lila in South Asia* (1995; edited volume); *Dancing the Self: Personhood and Performance in the Pandav Lilo of Garwhal* (2002); and *God of Justice: Ritual Healing in the Central Himalaya* (2008).

HOLGER SCHULZE is Visiting Professor and principal investigator of the Sound Studies Lab at Humboldt-Universität zu Berlin. His research focuses on the cultural anthropology of the senses, the mediology of audio media, and on sound in popular culture. He is the founder of the international research network *Sound in Media Culture*, and the book series *Sound Studies*. He is also co-editor of the international journal for historical anthropology *Paragrana*. His publications include: *Heuristik* (2005), *Sound Studies* (2008), *Intimität und Medialität* (2012), *Situation and Klang* (2012), *Gespür* (2013), and *Sabotage* (2013).

THEOFANIS TASIS received his PhD in Philosophy (summa cum laude) from the Freie Universität, Berlin. He is a Marie Curie Research Fellow and an invited researcher at the Centre Prospero des Facultes Universitaire Saint-Louis de Bruxelles.

JAN WEINHOLD studied psychology at the Humboldt University, Berlin. Since 2002 he has been working as a research psychologist within the Collaborative

Research Center SFB 619 "Ritual Dynamics" ("Ritualdynamik") at the Institute of Medical Psychology, University of Heidelberg. He has published on the ritualized use of psychoactive drugs and intercultural aspects of ritual healing. His major publications include *The varieties of ritual experience section on Ritual Dynamics and the Science of Ritual, Vol. II — Body, performance, agency and experience* (2010, co-edited with Geoffrey Samuel); *The problem of ritual efficacy* (2010, co-edited with William Sax and Johannes Quack); *Rituale in Bewegung* [Rituals on the move], (2006, co-edited with Henrik Jungaberle).

ANNETTE WILKE has been Professor for the Study of Religion and Department Head (Allgemeine Religionswissenschaft) at the University of Muenster (Germany) since 1998. Her major fields of research are method and theory in the study of religions, Hinduism, intercultural interactions, mysticism, ritual studies, and the aesthetics of religion.

ASTRID ZOTTER is an Indologist who received her PhD from Leipzig University. Currently, she is working on Hindu marriage rituals in Nepal within the framework of the Collaborative Research Project "Ritual Dynamics" (SFB 619) at the University of Heidelberg. Her research focuses on Hindu ritual traditions, as well as on the cultural and religious history of Nepal.